CONFESSIONS OF A RATIONAL MYSTIC

Anselm's
Early Writings

Gregory Schufreider

Purdue University Press
West Lafayette, Indiana

Copyright ©1994 by Purdue University Research Foundation.
All rights reserved.

98   97   96   95   94   5   4   3   2   1

The paper used in this book meets the minimum requirements of
American National Standard for Information Sciences—Permanence of
Paper Printed Library Materials, ANSI Z39.48-1984.

Printed in the United States of America

Interior design by Anita Noble

The Latin text of Anselm's *Proslogion* is reproduced from
F. S. Schmitt's German translation and edition courtesy of the
Frommann-Holzboog Verlag.

Library of Congress Cataloging-in-Publication Data

Schufreider, Gregory
    Confessions of a rational mystic : Anselm's early writings /
by Gregory Schufreider
        p.   cm. — (Purdue University series in the history of
philosophy)
    Includes Anselm's Proslogion, with English translation.
    Includes bibliographical references and index.
    ISBN 1-55753-035-1 (cloth : alk. paper) — ISBN 1-55753-036-X
(paper : alk. paper)
    1. Anselm, Saint, Archbishop of Canterbury, 1033–1109. 2. God—
Proof—History of doctrines—Middle Ages, 600–1500. 3. God—Proof,
Ontological—History of doctrines—Middle Ages, 600–1500. 4.
Mysticism—History—History of doctrines, 600–1500. I. Anselm, Saint,
Archbishop of Canterbury, 1033–1109. Proslogion. English & Latin.
1993. II. Title. III. Series.
B765.A83P872   1993   92-26252
212' .1–dc20   CIP

CONFESSIONS OF A RATIONAL MYSTIC

**Purdue University Series
in the History of Philosophy**

General Editors

Arion Kelkel

Joseph J. Kockelmans

Adriaan Peperzak

Calvin O. Schrag

Thomas Seebohm

In memory of
William Earle and
Paul Wienpahl,
my first and last teachers

A text is not a text unless
it hides from the first glance,
from its first onlookers,
the law of its composition and
the rules of its game.

—J. Derrida

C O N T E N T S

P A R T O N E | Introduction

Anselm and the History of Philosophy

Anselm is a central figure in the history of Western thought. As the pivotal thinker in medieval philosophy, he was both the heir of Augustine and the "father of scholasticism," whose own favorite son is Thomas Aquinas. Unfortunately, so positioned between these two giants, he has in certain respects been dwarfed by the company he keeps. This underestimation of his work results, at least in part, from the contribution to the history of philosophy for which he is normally credited. For however illegitimate a child of his scholasticism may be, the tendency is to regard Anselm's thought primarily in terms of that to which it led. He is remembered as the originator of a strictly rational theology, as is, perhaps, most evident in his traditional identity as the creator of the "ontological proof" for the existence of God. If, however, history is not read in reverse—if a thinker is not viewed solely in terms of what we inherited from him, but in light of that to which he himself was heir—then there can be no doubt that Anselm is first and foremost successor to the legacy of monasticism as well as to a certain mysticism that is characteristic of medieval thought. Put simply, we could say that the difference between the later schoolmen and Anselm is precisely the difference between the university and the monastery.

To complicate matters, however, it must be admitted that something of the movement of Western philosophy that took place in our history between the eleventh and thirteenth centuries, in its migration from the prayer cell to the schoolroom, is already in evidence in Anselm's own writings. Were it not, he could hardly have contributed to the historic transition to scholasticism. On the other hand, to judge Anselm by scholastic standards is to beg the question of *how*

| 1

he could have contributed to this transition and, thus, to fail to appreciate the precise role he may have played in the history of philosophy. It is, no doubt, difficult enough for us to grasp the full scope of the change that took place in this uncloistering of philosophy and the extent of its implications, let alone to understand a thinker who stood on the far side of it. Those who imagine that ideas, especially great ones, are both timeless and spaceless will scarcely be sympathetic to the suggestion that certain thoughts make their best sense in relation not only to the historical situation but also to their topological location. In that case, it might appear irrelevant to stress the monastic environment of and for Anselm's thought. And this may seem all the more the case now that the university, with its modern mission of disinterested research, has come to dominate all approaches to philosophy. But Anselm stands at the threshold of this transition—when the university had not yet emerged as the site of truth—even as he stands at the threshold of that historic point of medieval thought just before the bulk of the works of Aristotle again became available in the West, during the so-called twelfth-century renaissance.

I mention these two developments in our history, which themselves go hand in hand in the movement toward scholasticism, because they have worked together, almost from the start, to obscure the nature of Anselm's thought. In its way, history rather quickly passed him by, as those aspects of his work that were best suited to these historic changes survived in our tradition, while others tended to be left behind. Consequently, those of us now coming to a reading of Anselm's writings will find ourselves historically unprepared for them, even as most of us come to his thought from out of our own scholastic, rather than monastic, training. While these two occupations may not be as unlike one another as we might think insofar as the one was born of the other, there are nonetheless quite decisive differences in the nature of the thought that issues out of each practice, just as there are differences in the nature of the writings of medieval philosophy that have come down to us from each of these approaches. Certainly the style of the scholastics—the stiflingly strict, objective formality of the *quaestio* format, as a method of question and answer befitting a public presentation—suits classroom discussions at the university as surely as Anselm's early works—written in a unique genre of prayerfully introspective, rational meditation—fits the form of monastic life he practiced daily, giving evidence in its very style of his commitment to the intimately private occupation of spiritual elevation. Indeed, as Anselm is himself forced from the cloister into the secular arena, the format of his own written work shows the signs of a similar change.

Needless to say, the development of the various strands at work in Anselm's writings—and the events in his life that moved him away from the prayer cell and toward the schoolroom, only to find himself, finally, competing in the court of kings—cannot be attributed to the later transition from a Platonic to an Aristotelian notion of reason, which no doubt assisted the changes in our tradition.[1] Instead, as history would have it, the diversity of Anselm's writings was, in part at least, a matter of coincidence, determined by the religious offices he held at various times. After finding his way as a wandering scholar to the Benedictine monastery at Bec at the age of twenty-seven, Anselm was, only three years later, made prior. As such, he was essentially charged with the spiritual well-being of his brethren, and the writings from this period (1063–78) reflect that responsibility. These works, which include his *Monologion* (1076) and *Proslogion* (1077–78), are intensely contemplational, as are the prayers and meditations he wrote at this time. We will see that these works trade on what might be called the metaphysics of the monastery, as their philosophical theology is expressly designed to assist the monks in the practice of contemplation. Each has as its format a style of presentation suited to the interests of one who, as the preface to the *Proslogion* puts it, is "striving to elevate his own mind to the contemplation of God."[2] And it is important to note that Anselm would never write anything quite like this again in his lifetime, least of all the kind of philosophical prayer book the *Proslogion* is.

After the completion of the *Proslogion* in 1078, when Anselm became abbot, his writings shift direction, as they begin to take on a schoolbook character. In fact, some are presented in a dialogue form that is later said to be preferable for the "slower in intelligence."[3] These works include the *De grammatico,* a kind of medieval introduction to logic, and the dialogues *On Truth* and *On Free Will* (1080–85), as well as the later *On the Fall of the Devil* (1085–90). Precisely what led to this transition in Anselm's thought is hard to say, and I do not mean to suggest it was merely his new job—a job clearly devoted more to administration than to contemplation. Similarly, it would be too easy to conclude that his late, most clearly apologetic works, such as *The Letter on the Incarnation of the Word* (1092–94), *Why God Became Man* (1094–98), *On the Virgin Birth and Original Sin* (1099–1100), *On the Procession of the Holy Spirit* (1102), *On the Sacraments of the Church* (1106–7), or *On the Harmony of the Foreknowledge, Predestination and the Grace of God with Free Choice* (1107–8), simply reflect his role as archbishop of Canterbury, an office Anselm held from 1093 until his death in 1109. Certainly the titles of the various texts give some indication of the transition that is taking place from the early "monologue," in which the solitary meditator reasons with himself in the quiet of his private contemplation about "the essence of divinity,"[4] to those writings not only addressed to more technically theological, even doctrinal issues, but to the world at large. What we do know is that Anselm was not so much a systematic as an "occasional" thinker, tending to respond in his writings to the concrete events happening around him and to the needs of those with whom he came into direct contact. We know also that he himself regarded his early monastic years as the happiest in his life, perhaps because, as one interpreter suggests, he was better at meditation than at politics.[5] In that case, these early writings may well show Anselm in his truest vocation, at work on the cultivation of what his contemporary biographer called his unparalleled "knowledge of God."[6]

For these and other reasons, I have decided to limit our considerations in the present study to Anselm's early writings, especially to the *Monologion* and *Proslogion,* in part because they are his most philosophical texts, but equally, if not more importantly, because they are, I think, his most historic works. They best show off not only the transitional nature of Anselm's thought but the unique mode of thinking that is most clearly responsible for the distinctive impact he has had on our history. Of course, it could turn out that what allowed Anselm's work to have the historical effect it did required a certain suppression of what is most essential in these early writings, as, to put it plainly, works the later tradition was free to misinterpret. It must be admitted, however, that although Anselm's own later writings were based on his earlier thought, they depart from it in certain respects, and that this may well have contributed to the misinterpretation of his early work. It is equally undeniable that transitional figures in a history will tend to be misunderstood by that to which they give rise. For "precursors" are inevitably adopted by a future tradition in view of its own new standard, even though the pivotal thinker would, in principle, have to have been as obligated to the standards of the past as to those of the future. What this means, in the present case, is that in Anselm's early writings we must look for the traces of the monastic mysticism to which he was heir as well as for the signs of the scholastic rationalism he was to foster through his transformation of tradition. We must watch for the creative combination he was able to achieve, such that we may, through these early works, be put in a position to glimpse the historic dimension of Anselm's thought, to locate that moment when he moves our history; a moment that, as transitional, tends to get lost in the transition, as it is not just overshadowed but obscured by that to which it gives birth.

Not surprisingly, this sort of systematic obscuring of Anselm's thought is nowhere more evident than in what the later tradition has admitted to be his historic contribution: the so-called ontological argument for the existence of God, which appears for the first time in our history in his *Proslogion*. Properly interpreted, this argument must be shown to have its roots in the monastic form of life, whose existential regimen is committed to seeking a vision of God. Needless to say, if we stress the monastery as the site of Anselm's thought, it is because its space, and, for that matter, its time provide the conditions for the possibility of the concrete practice of that specific form of existence that is designed to lead the initiate along the path to such vision. This is not to deny that Anselm's work belongs to a certain rationalistic strain in our history to which he lent authority. Instead, it is to insist that his very rationalism, which was fecund enough to give birth to scholasticism, was itself embedded in the contemplative tradition to which Anselm was heir. If there is any key to understanding Anselm's early work as historically transitional, it is in seeing how his own argumentative clarity can lend legitimacy to a certain rationalistic movement in medieval religious thinking precisely because it was grounded in the visionary forms of thought that were authoritative at his time. Only as such can we appreciate just how the spiritual wealth of Anselm's unique brand of rational contemplation, as its own form of mystical meditation, could give birth to scholasticism.

I would not want to disagree, then, with the received opinion of Anselm, namely, that his moment of greatness lies in the discovery of the ontological argument for the existence of God as set forth in his *Proslogion*. Nor would I deny that there is a sense in which the transition to scholasticism may hinge on this argument—and not only as an original paradigm of the scholastic mission to demonstrate the doctrines of faith by means of reason alone. I will, however, be disagreeing with the way the tradition has interpreted that argument and this transition. In Anselm's argument, we will try to find not just a proof for the existence of God but also the sudden surfacing of the depth and fullness of a mystical insight that is founded upon the practice of rational meditation and which, in turn, served to provide a historic foundation for reason itself. Unfortunately, the preeminence of Thomas Aquinas and the scholastic approach to rationality, not to mention the tendency of our own age to be dominated by an understanding of reason as an instrument of calculation rather than of contemplation, has left Anselm's work suspended in a history that has subjected it to misinterpretation virtually from the start because of the transitional context it created. This is not to deny that certain aspects of Anselm's thought survived this historic change of context, may have even been enhanced by it. Indeed, that is precisely the problem: *certain* elements of his thought, and only certain ones, are inevitably emphasized and thrive in a transformed state in the new world of scholastic thought. Even today, those who uncritically assume the nature of Anselm's argument for the existence of God in the *Proslogion* to be a rational proof, without asking what "rational" and "proof" mean, beg the interpretive question of how Anselm's writings are to be read. For Anselm also stands at that juncture in the history of Western thought when the nature of reason is itself in transition: from a monastic to a scholastic view of rationality.[7]

In speaking of a historical transition in the nature of reason, I do not mean to suggest that the laws of logic change so much as that the history of rationality—the way reasoning is practiced and the way we interpret its results, including our view of the foundations of logic—determines, or at least has a hand in determining, the efficacy we may attribute to it. This is why we will have to be alert to the difference between an essentially intuitive account of reasoning, where the element of direct insight plays a central role (an insight no doubt prepared for by the discursive aspect of argumentation) and a more clearly and unambiguously inferential reasoning, in which conclusions are blindly drawn, as it were, from the sheer forms of inference that would justify them. Such a historic change in the understanding of the nature of reason marks the transition from the visionary rationality of early medieval thought to the formal logic on which scholasticism thrived. The fact that Anselm's thought has an emphatically discursive dimension, that he provides detailed arguments whose logic (as has been demonstrated by others) shows the influence of Aristotle,[8] would seem to leave an aspect of his work intact in the transition to the formalism of the scholastics: it leaves the arguments he gives, at least on the surface, untouched, even if their point, within the context of an intuitive rationality, gets left behind. In that event, the movement of philosophical theology from the monastery to the university could mark a departure that effectively leaves behind the essence of a certain way of thinking while taking along its outward form. This would result in a rather literal dislocation of thought as it is transferred from a site where the process of reasoning remains a contemplative activity directed to elevating the mind to a rational vision of certain preeminent objects of thought to a place where the sheer method of argument can be, in another sense, practiced in the dialectical interchange of the classroom. As such, Anselm's argument for the existence of God is transported from the prayer cell to the logic class, where it has, at least in philosophical circles, remained ever since.[9]

I say this not because I think we should be judging Anselm's early writings on religious rather than rational grounds. Instead, I believe that our judgment of his work must be based not only upon an awareness that philosophical thinking, even in its rational form, is historical through and through but also upon an equally clear understanding of the actual conditions of our own interpretive situation. The historical condition we are in when we open Anselm's works entails a context materially different from the one in which such texts first had their use. Clearly, the original audience for these writings was not composed of scholars seeking justification for their interpretations, but of monks seeking elevation in their contemplation. And while we may rightly feel that we should be able to comprehend the reasoning of Anselm's argument without worrying about our historic distance from it, we should not be so easily convinced that in having followed its logic we will have arrived at the conclusion to which it is designed to lead. For before and behind such arguments stand not only the principles of logic but the historical world that is being formed and transformed by such creative works as the *Monologion* and *Proslogion*.

It is, of course, this "world" that, in some sense, lies in ruin for us, and among which Anselm's work stands as one of the ruins, that will have to be reconstructed in our interpretation. This historical aspect of our account is not, however, primarily motivated by antiquarian interests. On the contrary, I would like to think that the right sort of interpretation, in demonstrating the role Anselm played in the history of philosophy, may be capable of showing off, perhaps precisely at the moment of transition, a dimension of Western thought that not only reaches back virtually to its beginning but that still survives today, and that surfaces in such a way in Anselm's ontological argument that we may be able, finally, both to reveal and to evaluate it.

| Four Ways to Interpret a Text

As complicated and sophisticated as the field of textual interpretation has become, one can hardly begin a reading of work from the history of philosophy without saying something about the methodological approach to be taken. We will attempt in what follows to introduce the reader to the historical world of Anselm's thought, which was in the process of transition thanks to the very texts we will be considering. My suggestion, however, that certain features of Anselm's work survived, perhaps even in an enhanced form, in the history of the changing context for its interpretation, while other features have fallen into a kind of historical oblivion, is not simply an invitation to try to get back to the original Anselm, pure and un-adulterated. Instead, it is an indication that we will need to reenlist those elements that belonged to the world out of which Anselm worked but that have been lost sight of; and we must do so under the assumption that the historical power of his thought can only be appreciated when certain aspects of it are not ignored, let alone systematically suppressed. While, then, in our reading of the *Proslogion,* we are going to be attempting to get back to the original argument for the existence of God by undoing what I regard as the tradition of its misinterpretation, our own account will be unavoidably historical in a number of respects, even as we cannot afford to limit ourselves to the strictly logical approach to this argument to which we have grown accustomed.

In fact, we hope to take advantage of our own historical situation to get at and bring out the nature of Anselm's thought by treating it in a variety of ways, including some that are distinctively twentieth century. Rather than simply approaching Anselm's argument logically or reconstructing it historically, we will also make an attempt to analyze it phenomenologically. As a methodology designed to provide essential descriptions of concrete experience, phenomenology should offer us access to the experiential aspect of ideas and, in so doing, allow us to explicate certain thoughts in terms of the "lived-experience" a thinker would undergo in thinking them through. In so attempting to characterize one's own concrete experience—including one's cognitive experience—in terms of its essential elements, we will be trying to draw attention to the structural features of those inner experiences invoked by ideas as such, attending to the sort of mental phenomena that are at issue in the event of thinking certain thoughts. What this means, in the present case, is not that we will be ignoring the logic of Anselm's argument. It goes without saying that, at least quantitatively speaking, the analysis of its reasoning will inevitably dominate our approach. If we suppose, however, that Anselm's thinking is historically embedded in a contemplative tradition that he is in the process of rendering fully rational, then we may proceed under the assumption that the rational demonstration for the existence of God offered in the *Proslogion* is fundamentally grounded in specific cognitive experiences that can be described and defined, indeed, provoked, as compelling experiences of thought, by the reasoning itself. In this way, once we have reestablished the historical context for Anselm's thought, it should be clear that a phenomenological approach is precisely what is called for insofar as it gives us the best chance of getting at the kind of thinking that would be taking place in an explicitly contemplative tradition, whose profound inner experiences would serve to ground its arguments.

In proposing such a phenomenological reading of the *Proslogion* argument and of the texts that surround it, I do not mean to suggest that the point is to interpret it or them in light of our own era, nor am I inclined to assume any ahistorical experiences we may simply undergo. To be sure, while certain experiences of thought are still made possible by the argument and while the method of phenomenology should allow us some access to those "originary experiences," it may not follow from this that they will hold the same significance for us that they might have had for an eleventh-century thinker. Nevertheless, we will proceed under the assumption, to be justified by this entire study, that Anselm's early thinking was guided by the sorts of concrete cognitive revelations it secured in the practice of rational contemplation. Whether we will be so convinced by those insights cannot be determined until we see for ourselves what is at issue in Anselm's famous argument.

Thus, despite what may seem to be implied by our appeal to experience, we want to keep it clear that, in the end, it will also be important for us to consider the limits of the argument's historical validity. By this I do not mean that it may merely have been true for an earlier age; nor, however, do I think that the argument remains directly available to us thanks to some ahistorical truth, whether one thinks it to reside in the eternal nature of reason or in the immediacy of mystical experience. If the form of phenomenological interpretation we intend to practice allows us to get back to the basic experiences of thought that found, in this case, an argument, then those moments of ecstatic clarity, as we will call them, that the reasoning preserves for us may nonetheless turn out to be essentially historical and, thus, to have their own historic limitations. In fact, as we will find, Anselm himself confesses the limits of his rational insight within the *Proslogion* itself. Consequently, if, as we will also show, a specific vision of God is embedded in Anselm's argument, then we must see how and why he admits the limitations of the vision so accomplished and ask what is implied—signaled, and however unwittingly—by these confessions of a rational mystic.

To do this, we must read the whole of the *Proslogion,* not just excerpt the one short chapter that has traditionally been regarded as Anselm's main contribution to the history of philosophy. And in so doing, we will have to inspect its prayers as closely as we would its arguments, even as our reading of both must be as critical as it is careful, eventually putting sufficient pressure on the text to reveal its breaking point. If we can safely assume that something historic is happening in Anselm's early writings, especially in this first formulation of the ontological argument in our history, and that the format of his work required a unique genre of writing—the philosophical prayer—to accommodate this new brand of rational mysticism, then the problem is to show how the form of the *Proslogion* is relevant to its content. We will insist, in other words, that how we read what the *Proslogion* claims must be determined by the precise way in which it is formulated: by the context and vocabulary in which it is put, including the way its arguments proper are, quite literally, from the beginning to the end of the text surrounded by prayers for a vision of God.

At the same time, however, attention to these formal issues—to the tactics of the text—will, I think, also show that we cannot afford the sort of interpretive innocence that is inclined to take a work at face value. Even if we can get through the logic of the argument to the cognitive experiences that it is designed to provoke, and that alone explain why Anselm feels the need to place his reasoning in the context of his talk of mystical vision, we may not be able to arrive at this phenomenological conclusion without its arousing certain suspicions, especially if it can be shown, through a formal analysis of the structure of the text, that Anselm is trying to conceal specific problems in his confession of the limits of such a vision. If, to put it otherwise, the *Proslogion* can be shown to be most misleading precisely at that point at which it would appear to be most honest, namely, when it is confessing its limitations, then besides the logical, the historical, and the experiential aspects of our account, we will finally, as we find ourselves considering the overall strategy of Anselm's texts, be forced into a somewhat more critical reading of his work. As should eventually become clear, to get at what I regard as the depths of Anselm's argument and, thus, at a deeper critique of it, we will need to undertake a rather more complex approach to the interpretation of his writings than is normally the case.

Briefly put, then, over and above the standard approach to interpreting Anselm, the logical approach, as it were, which includes the assumption of an ahistorical rationality that tends to fuel objective scholarship, we intend to place at our disposal hermeneutical, phenomenological, and deconstructive analyses of his work as well. This is not to say that our own account will not require a dose of scholarship to correct the misinterpretations of Anselm that have been perpetuated in our tradition. On the contrary, our interpretation of the *Proslogion* argument is completely dependent upon such scholarly corrections.[10] It is just that in addition to determining the original intentions of the text, and analyzing the arguments Anselm provides, we will also be engaged in a kind of historical dialogue with his works, one that aims to break through them to their experiential ground. In the end, this will entail not only a certain destruction of the text, in a reading between the lines that aims to see through them, if necessary to pry them apart so as to get at the phenomenological ground beneath them, but will also involve a dismantling of its outer facade that reveals its inner structure.

Such deconstructive exposure of the architecture of a work can hardly help but take notice of the text's self-construction, that is, of the forms of thought it exploits, as well as the figures of speech; of the distinctions it enforces, as well as the ways in which it forces them upon us; of the twists and turns of thought and phrase that may provide the appearance of support in a structure that could well turn out to be self-supporting. Consequently, besides securing some objective knowledge about Anselm's thought, or coming to an understanding, however historical, with it, or, for that matter, gaining phenomenological insight into it, we will also be forced into a certain critical "misunderstanding" of it. This will require us to view Anselm's work in a way in which he would neither have understood himself nor have wanted us to understand him, in an attempt to free ourselves from what the text would like to have us think. Such a reading, to put it simply, neither comes at Anselm's thought from above, as does objective scholarship, nor does it confront the text head on, as a hermeneutical dialogue with it must; nor, however, does it trade on the subversion of the text, as would the phenomenological destruction that aims to get below it to the pretextual ground it is presumably concealing. Instead, this sort of critical approach tries, shall we say, to sneak up on a philosopher from behind, exposing, in a further sense even than phenomenological accounts, what his thought is hiding. Ultimately, we aim to provide such an account of Anselm's early writings, as we seek to show, hidden in his work, what only a perverse reading can reveal, even as the prospect of such an approach should encourage the loss of our own interpretive innocence, cultivating the kind of suspicion that keeps us looking for the wolf beneath the smooth coat of the text.

At the moment, however, we have mentioned these various approaches in part to suggest that our own sketch of Anselm's early work, especially given what we have said of the history to which it has been subject, will be less like mapping the terrain of his thought, as if it were open to view and had merely to be documented, than it is like constructing a composite drawing of someone who is seen while fleeing the scene of a crime. Not only does Anselm do as much hiding in his writings as does any philosopher and not only does he have to do more to conceal his philosophical nature (given the time in which he thought) than we can imagine, but, given our brief allusions to the movement of our tradition, it is not without some warrant that we might assume history has, in certain respects, passed him by without catching a glimpse of him face-to-face. And because our aim is to provide a certain depiction of this lost Anselm, it is important to be clear from the start that the study to follow is, in that case, more like a portrait than a snapshot. It is not designed simply to list a variety of features of, or to provide a general introduction to, Anselm's thought by surveying it as a whole. While the present work would hope to serve to introduce the reader to Anselm, its multidimensional approach paints a picture of him by selectively highlighting those contours that I have come to regard as best revealing the distinctive look of his thought, constructing a view that may reveal the depth of his writings through a particular shading of their surface. Nor do I mean to suggest that the sorts of issues we will be raising and claiming to be essential can be found in everything Anselm wrote. Instead, we are proceeding under the presumption that the essence of a thinker's thought resides in its moment of greatness, which, in Anselm's case, is the *Proslogion.* Not all thinkers have in their work this sort of privileged moment when the depth of their thinking comes so suddenly to the surface as it does in Anselm's argument, even as we may, in the end, be able to show that the ontological argument provides us with a kind of privileged moment in the history of Western thought. We are, then, looking to meet with Anselm not only at the height of his philosophical thinking but also at a critical point in our philosophical history, and this will require not a sudden leap into those depths so much as the building up of an account of his early writings that prepares us for its moment of greatness. Consequently, we will not begin our reading with the *Proslogion* argument but will begin where Anselm did, with his first philosophical writing, the *Monologion,* so as to set up something of the immediate context for, and content of, his second book, which was itself, in ways we will have to demonstrate, formed as a kind of condensation of the earlier work.

Of course, the true context for the *Proslogion* is not simply an earlier book, or even the monastic existence of which both texts give evidence, but the historical world that the monastery, with all the presuppositions that made it possible, served to determine. To emphasize something of the historical difference between Anselm's world and ours and to try to keep in question the nature of his thought, I have introduced the notion of a rational mysticism. I want it to be clear, however, that my point in so doing is not to contend, as some have, that Anselm was "really" a mystic rather than a rationalist or that his arguments are therefore not really arguments. I intend neither to suggest this nor to assume that we all already know how such "proofs" serve as demonstrations, let alone what they demonstrate. In effect, then, I have spoken of Anselm's rational mysticism to discourage the sort of shortsightedness that tends to look at one side or the other of his thought. I have hoped that through this constant reminder we might bring these profiles together in such a way that they would complement one another, such that we might be inclined to regard his rationalism and his mysticism as sides of a single face that would, in each case, require we turn our attention from one to the other if we are to get the full view. In that event, we will not only have to show that Anselm's commitment to rationality modifies whatever mysticism is retained in his work but also that an emphasis on the visionary element of reason alone elevates it to the status Anselm would attribute to it.

While we can, no doubt, safely assume that many, particularly philosophers, will be sympathetic with the claim that the rigor of Anselm's arguments rules out any suggestion of the vagaries of what is too often regarded as a thoughtless mysticism, we cannot be so confident that the explicitly visionary element of his thinking will serve to save it from the emptiness of a mere logical cleverness. With this in mind, I have felt justified in speaking of the mystical not just as a corrective device to keep in view the other extreme from reason, but to maintain our emphasis on the sorts of cognitive experiences that those involved in the practice of rational meditation may undergo in their quest for the vision of God. We intend, then, to moderate our understanding of the possible meaning of mystical experience in view of the acuteness of reason's vision of God, even as we aim to revise our ordinary understanding of human rationality by invoking its visionary capability.

In that case, however, we can no more get at the full force of Anselm's early writings if our logical propensities deafen us to their talk of mystical vision than if our religious enthusiasm leaves us no patience for the details of their arguments. For we want to show not only that rational argument must have a hand in moderating any mystical element to be found in Anselm's work, but also that reason itself comes to be legitimated through the demonstration of its capacity to elevate us to a vision of God—and that this alone constitutes the basis for the creation of a strictly rational theology. According to Anselm, were reason not by nature subject to illumination, were the eye of the mind not an instrument for the vision of God, even if it has lost its full power through the Fall, there would be no point in proceeding rationally; unless, that is, a vestige of vision remained, such that our rationality was capable in this life of enjoying, if not the vision complete, then at least the vision incomplete.

Exactly how this theological scenario sets the stage for the *Proslogion*'s historic redemption of reason is a topic we will address later. Our present point is that Anselm's faith in the power of human rationality to reveal the truth not only directs us to the heart of his thought, and the basis for his dedication to philosophy, but may also direct us to that distinctive moment in our history when the revelatory power of reason begins to hold its own against a strictly religious revelation, upon whose authoritative model it had to be patterned. To begin to see how this happened, to suggest where, when, and why medieval monasticism entered into a phase that would inevitably lead away from it to the university and the scholastic rationality that would forget its own visionary history, we must hope that our talk of a rational mysticism will invite a certain questioning of the distinctions we have grown accustomed to making, or at least keep us from casting Anselm directly into the clearer waters of what came after. By marking the extremes of thought, it should not only force us to raise the specter of mysticism whenever we speak of Anselm's rationalism, just as it forces us to think of reason whenever we speak of the vision of God, but is also designed to name the ambiguous hinge on which medieval philosophy swung, as if from one extreme to the other. Only in so appreciating the range of Anselm's early writings will we be able to reveal this transitional point on which our history turns, and around a thinker of sufficient scope to position Western thought for a change of direction in and through the two companion texts we propose to study.

| Understudying the Tradition

It might be useful to summarize our basic orientation in a final word about the nature of such a study, especially insofar as our all too brief caricature of the multiplicity of approaches that will have to be taken might seem to force the reader into a rather contorted position. We intend to devote ourselves to a close, even sympathetic, reading of Anselm while maintaining a critical suspicion that his texts may not always be the frank and open partner genuine dialogue presumes, just as we will have to assume the necessary objective distance from his work, while nonetheless involving ourselves in its phenomenological element, in an attempt to live through, as it were, the lived-experience of his thought. In interpreting the argument for the existence of God in the *Proslogion,* this means that while we will be attempting to provide a detailed analysis of the logic of its reasoning, we will also be dismantling its rational structure to get, first, to the root of the argument in a certain mystical insight it provides and, then, to the ground from out of which it grows, which will turn out to be the tradition of Western ontology. All of this, however, will have to be based upon a certain amount of objective scholarship that will allow us to correct the official position that the subsequent tradition has taken toward the famous *Proslogion* proof—a tradition that has not only misinterpreted the argument, but done so by failing to locate the whole of it in the text—even as we will have to show why, nonetheless, the fragment of the reasoning that did survive could have the sort of lasting attraction it has in our history. For unlike the remainder of the Anselmian corpus, his ontological argument outlived the medieval world, only to show up repeatedly throughout modern thought, making him, for reasons we will try to indicate, not just the father of scholasticism but a patriarch of modern philosophy.

Of course, stressing the need for an account to come to the text from different directions may simply serve as a reminder of the complex and often ambiguous relationship that obtains between the objective, the historical, the experiential, and the critical element of any interpretation. If, then, our own multidimensional reading of Anselm attempts to make use of all four of these approaches at one point or other (sometimes at the same point), I would like to think that we are taking advantage of them not out of any eclecticism but because they express a certain order of interpretation, an order we will in some sense be following, although not sequentially. In fact, only if we are able to maintain a balance between the various accounts will we be able to show that they are mutually confirming. Just as the objective determination of the location of Anselm's original argument is itself invited by the historical reconstruction of the conditions under which a certain kind of mystical reasoning becomes possible, the replacing of the argument in the tradition of monastic contemplation is what calls for a phenomenological analysis, which alone can provide us with access to those inner experiences that ground the discursive reasoning in intuitive insight. Given this conclusion, however, the problem that our evaluation of such an argument must face, of how it is possible to criticize an insight, will have to be approached by means of the sort of critical reading of the text that can show how these cognitive experiences have been produced, even if in the end we will want to demonstrate that this deconstructive result is confirmed by a logical critique of the argument's reasoning.

The point just now, however, is that in presuming no particular allegiance to any one of the forms of interpretation we have discussed, in attempting to maintain a posture that can keep all these various aspects in view, we do not mean to pretend that our account does not assume its own position. Instead, if we have distinguished the views from above, from below, from the front, and from the rear, all that is left, it would seem, is to propose the possibility of yet another approach, which might be designated as the view from the side, although not any one of the sides we have so far mentioned. What we have in mind here could perhaps be made somewhat clearer were we allowed to imagine philosophers as "in performance." If we assume that philosophy is being performed, indeed, has its opening night in the works of its history, then philosophical texts would have to be treated as the theater of operations for the performance of philosophy. No doubt the appeal to such an image should be of some help later, when we will have to understand how it is that philosophers may be regarded not just as the performing, but as the plastic artists of the mind: creating and manipulating, forming and shaping the experiences of thinking that they are capable of conjuring up, exposing us to, and leading us through. According to this model, Anselm's philosophical writings, in creating a site and scene for thought, would not only address a particular historical audience but would also trade on a specific staging that gets us to think and see in certain ways, even as his thought could be said to have its backstage as well. And the best position to be in to see all that is at work in such a philosophical performance is in the view we would get while watching from the wings: neither as actor nor audience, but the way an understudy might. For like the ambiguous position of the understudy, our attitude toward such historical texts must be invaded by a similar duplicity.

As an understudy, we must attempt not only to see the work from as many different angles as possible but also, rather than simply watch, to develop an understanding of what is to be done: to be prepared should we be called upon to act. To this extent, a certain kind of appraisal of what is presently on stage is always called for, even as our appreciation is enhanced by the anxiety of knowing that, at any time, we, who are less experienced, may have to take over in an emergency. Needless to say, casting ourselves in the role of understudy is not meant to suggest that we will ever be called upon to play a part in the medieval drama in which Anselm costarred. If anything, it is a way of acknowledging that whatever is left of his thought no longer allows us direct admittance to his historical audience. The suggestion, then, that we watch Anselm from the wings may well serve to mark the position we are inevitably forced to stand in with regard to our view of the history of philosophy. This does not mean, however, that we can only glimpse his thought from behind, never catching sight of what the audience sees, or merely from above—really, from nowhere in the theater. Rather, in waiting in the wings, we will allow his work to be invaded by that ambiguity in our viewing and listening that may allow us to see and hear what the audience does, but somehow differently. And in placing us close to the action, such a vantage point may at least keep us thinking about acting ourselves. In this respect, we will not so much be called upon to defend Anselm's performance as to rehearse along with it, to see if we can any longer keep in step. If, at the end, we offer our own critical review, it will not be from the gallery, but with, we hope, a certain behind-the-scenes appreciation of just how intricate the act of philosophizing is.

| N O T E S

1. For the details of Anselm's life and career, see Eadmer's *The Life of St. Anselm* as well as R. W. Southern's *Anselm and His Biographer* or his more recent *St. Anselm: A Portrait in a Landscape.* For a discussion of the nature of the medieval monastery, see David Knowles, *The Monastic Order in England.*

2. *Sancti Anselmi Opera omnia* (ed. F. S. Schmitt), I, 93–94; hereafter referred to as S, followed by volume and page number (e.g. S I, 93–94). All translations are my own.

3. S I, 48.

4. S I, 7.

5. See R. W. Southern's "Anselm at Canterbury."

6. Eadmer, *The Life of St. Anselm,* 51.

7. For a general introduction to the contrast between monastic and scholastic theology, see Jean Leclercq, *The Love of Learning and the Desire for God.* For consideration of another historic transition taking place at this time, from an oral to a literate culture, and with specific reference to Anselm, see Brian Stock, *The Implications of Literacy.*

8. D. P. Henry, *The Logic of St. Anselm.*

9. This is not to deny that a certain Augustinian tradition survived even among the schoolmen—for example, in Thomas's colleague at the University of Paris, St. Bonaventure—or that a more monastic orientation toward Anselm's work cannot be found to the present day in readers such as Anselm Stolz. See his "Anselm's Theology in the *Proslogion,*" available in English in John Hick's *The Many-Faced Argument.* In the latter case, however, the insistence on Anselm's mysticism involves the denial of his rationalism, just as those who emphasize Anselm's rationalism are inclined to deny his mysticism. Our aim will be to show how these two extremes work together in Anselm's thought.

10. I have already attempted such a reading in *An Introduction to Anselm's Argument.*

| Reading for Revelations

Anselm's first attempt at philosophical writing remains among the many unread texts of medieval philosophy, despite, if not because of, the notoriety his work has otherwise received. If Anselm is famous for anything, it is for the "ontological argument," which first makes its appearance in our history in his second book, the *Proslogion*. Consequently, while almost every student of philosophy, whether knowingly or not, has read some portion of the *Proslogion,* few have ever read a word of the *Monologion.* In fact, in what until recently was the standard English translation of Anselm's works, the *Proslogion* is put first in the text.[1] This may not only reflect a certain order of interest but is invited by the fact that the *Proslogion* is by design a simpler, more elegant work, just as its distinctive form is rather more appealing than the arduous contortions often required to follow the route of thinking traced for us in the *Monologion*.

The problems involved in following the complexities of the *Monologion* were apparently no less pressing in 1077. Soon after having completed this "Example of Meditating on the Rationality of Faith"—designed for his fellow monks to make use of in their contemplation—Anselm set out to write a less complicated work that, instead of being made up, as the *Monologion* is, of "a complex sequence of interconnected arguments," could be followed as "a single argument,"[2] no doubt because the brethren found his first book too difficult. The result, as Anselm tells us in its preface, was the *Proslogion*. In that case, it would seem that these two texts, written within a year of one another, stand to some extent as the original to an abridgment: as if Anselm's most famous work were itself a revision of an earlier book. And while there is unquestionably much that is new in the *Proslogion,* it is equally certain that there is much of the *Monologion* in it.

It is not surprising, then, nor altogether inappropriate, that even when the *Monologion* is read it is treated as background for the *Proslogion.* We ourselves shall succumb to this approach, although, in my view, these two texts are best read together, as if they were one continuous work, and in this respect are of equal importance. While the *Proslogion* extends, in its own original way, the consideration of the questions concerning the nature and existence of God raised in the *Monologion,* the *Monologion* fleshes out in its detail the highly condensed form such issues inevitably take on in the *Proslogion.* Indeed, I doubt that most of us would understand the force of much of what is claimed in the *Proslogion* did we not have at our disposal the extensive discussions of the *Monologion,* even as many interpreters have failed to understand the *Proslogion* precisely because of their lack of attention to the earlier work. Be that as it may, while we can look to the *Monologion* for the background against which to read the later *Proslogion,* the *Monologion* itself has its own background, not the least of which includes Anselm's earlier writings. For Anselm's writing career actually began with the composing of prayers and meditations.[3] And just as this more poetic side of his thought finds its way quite explicitly into the *Proslogion,* such a style of writing also infiltrates the *Monologion* insofar as it aims to offer an example of a text designed for the purposes of private contemplation. In fact, while the *Proslogion* is cast in the form of a philosophical prayer, the *Monologion* is composed as a rational meditation.

I mention the form of these texts not only because they are unique in the Anselmian corpus but also because it seems to me that it is critical for us to grasp the context they clearly indicate for his early writings—a context that is the same for the prayers and meditations as for the *Monologion* and *Proslogion.* In order to keep this clear, however, it will be useful to remind ourselves that, besides the earlier devotional writings, there is a further background to Anselm's philosophical texts to which we must remain alert. Certainly Anselm's work has the history of medieval thought behind it, especially the work of Augustine, as he himself insists in his preface to the *Monologion.*[4] But the background to which I am most interested in first drawing our attention, the history that most informs it from out of this tradition, is one we can even more directly sense as in play at the very beginning of the text. The attentive reader should be able to discern something of the character of the historical world from which Anselm's thought arises, the world his work served eventually to transform, perhaps was already transforming, in the opening lines of the *Monologion's* prologue:

> Certain brothers have often and eagerly urged me to put down in writing some thoughts about meditating on the nature of divinity I have proposed in familiar conversations with them, as well as some other matters related to such meditation, by way of an example of that meditation. It is more in accord with their wish than with the ease of the task or my abilities that they have prescribed to me for the writing of this meditation the following form: that nothing whatsoever in it be induced on scriptural authority, but that whatever is claimed from the conclusion of individual investigations, in plain style and by common argument and simple disputation, be concisely connected through the necessity of reason and evidently displayed in the clarity of truth. (S I, 7)

From the very start, we must hear these first words of this first work in which Anselm commits himself to philosophical writing as already saturated with a certain historical form of life. The passage clearly reveals the monastery as the site that calls for such a work, with the brothers appealing to Anselm to get down in writing what has no doubt made them eager in their fleeting conversation—as if, in returning to the solitude of their prayer cells, they would like to be able to take Anselm with them. We must, then, sense here something of the reading situation that would have provided the context for such texts.[5] While we may also hear in this opening passage the echo of that historical moment when rational arguments for religious beliefs become the order of the day, we would not want it to appear as if the brethren were all logicians, looking forward to the publication of Anselm's next proof. At best, they no doubt wanted to have in writing, perhaps so as to be able to follow, the new line of thought that Anselm was assaulting them with in conversation.

It may not be easy for us to appreciate what is so innovative, so revolutionary, about Anselm's early writings and, thus, what is so novel about the new kind of reading they propose; for reading is something quite different for us than it would have been for Anselm's contemporaries. Obviously, Anselm is writing for those involved primarily in the practice of "sacred reading" (*lectio divina*), as it is called in the monastic tradition, just as the paradigm of reading, in that case, comes from the study of, the meditation on, the virtual memorization of, Holy Writ. It is, no doubt, difficult for us to understand the attitude toward texts that was embedded in such a scriptural tradition, where so much power was invested in the word: where language was regarded as enjoying the sort of revelatory force that made it, as the above passage concludes, the bearer of truth.[6]

What should be apparent, however, is how strange it must have sounded—which is perhaps why Anselm puts the demand in the mouths of certain brothers who remain anonymous, as if it were not an idea of his own, indeed, as if this work were itself not of his own choosing—to say that the format of his writing would entail the suspension of Scripture. This placing of the sacred page in brackets, putting its authority and influence out of action, is presumably designed to see whether what it claims can be demonstrated, as it is put in the opening lines of the *Monologion* proper, *sola ratione:* by means of reason alone; or, as the prologue itself puts it, *sola cogitatione:* by, we might say, thinking it through on one's own. In fact, such a demand is what determines the nature of the "monological" structure from which the *Monologion* gets its name, as a monologue in which one essentially argues with oneself. And while Anselm's earlier prayers and meditations were sprinkled with evidence of the sort of referential thinking that issues from a remembrance of Scripture—with the interlacing of the appeal to passages from it, as will certain prayers that appear in the *Proslogion*—they already show the elements of personal devotion, of intimately private meditation, that is not a mere mustering up of traditional passages, but of a deep "introspection." [7]

Of course, in a way, just what Anselm is proposing at the beginning of the *Monologion* is a kind of rational commentary on Scripture, but a commentary that is not allowed to invoke that upon which it is commenting, even as something of the introspective devotion involved in such a task is suggested in the above passage by the repeated emphasis on the form such thinking will take: the form of a meditation. While the format of the text calls for a certain suspension of scriptural authority, its submitting of issues raised in the sacred text to the "necessity of reason" is aimed at displaying those matters in the "clarity of truth" (*veritatis claritas*). Such brilliance sounds dramatic enough to appear to be in conflict with the demand for a "plain" style of writing, for "ordinary," let alone "simple" arguments, and most of all when the object of such meditation is the nature of divinity (*divinitatis essentia*). If, however, the point is to offer an example of a form of meditation on the divine that does not appeal to the influence of Scripture, but instead to the authority of reason, then what the *Monologion* proposes, first and foremost, is to supply us with a way of thinking about divinity. It is designed to provide, as its original title suggests, "An Example of Meditating on the Rationality of Faith" (*Exemplum meditandi de ratione fidei*). And this example is, presumably, to be followed. As much as the *Monologion* supplies us with rational arguments that are to be mulled over, it also proposes a form of meditation that can be undertaken by others, such that the text itself remains merely an example of what is to be done by the monks themselves in their own meditation. In that case, however, its arguments are apparently not so much aimed at supplying rational proofs that will supplant the authority of revelation as they are designed to initiate the brethren into a form of thinking that enjoys its own revelatory structure: in which, by following the necessity of reasoning, the matters under consideration may come to be disclosed in "the light of truth," but as a light whose brilliance is only effective for those undertaking the meditation themselves.

Anselm's announcement of the format for his text—the challenge to make no appeal to Scripture to persuade the reader—must not, then, be allowed to mislead us about the nature of the reading this prior is proposing for his monks at Bec. To suspend Scripture is not to suspend the style of reading that those accustomed to meditating on the sacred page would presume. It is simply to place a different page before their eyes to contemplate. And while I do not mean to say that Anselm thought of his own writings as enjoying sacred status (even if he wrote as if he were one of the Church Fathers, comparing himself to Augustine), I do mean to suggest that this paradigm of reading, the expectation of what a text did to one reading it, infects the nature of Anselm's writing. For meditations on Holy Writ ultimately had one aim: vision; or, to press the image of the light of truth: illumination.

This is especially difficult for us to appreciate insofar as other media have come to embody the visual for us, even as writing has accordingly changed its nature. But the sorts of texts that Anselm's readers would have taken as their paradigm were visionary texts. Such works presumed the power of the revelation of the word, that is, assumed a view of language and writing in which an original, pretextual vision was thought to be embedded in a text, now made available through its reading. This is, of course, why illuminated manuscripts are so much to the point of medieval writing in their explicit visualization of the verbal: in a literal illustration of the vision embedded in the word, often beginning with a depiction of the author receiving the revelation now held in the book before one, to be reopened to the sight of one devoted to its reading. This is also why the discipline of reading may be said to have as its aim the blinding of the outer eye in the hope of the illumination of the inner eye, issuing out in a physiology of reading not only with the eye, ear, and mouth but also in the fatigue that results from the repetitive rereading of Scripture: in a kind of oral-visual chant that, if ultimately effective, was to result in vision, or, if one prefers, in religious insight.[8]

Such reading for revelations would have been as typical in the Middle Ages as reading for information is in the modern world. What this emphasis on illumination, most significantly, on the vision of God, has to do with Anselm's promise to meditate on the divine by means of reason alone we will have to wait to see. We would probably tend to associate any such inner visions with imagination, immediately distinguishing them from the sort of abstract thinking we are no doubt expecting from Anselm. But rational meditation here means something rather more concrete, even as our explication of its aims must await Anselm's own clarification of the nature of reason in M 10.[9] It is sufficient, for present purposes, to repeat that, for Anselm, language is intimately connected to vision, to an inner sight, indeed, to a kind of intuitive insight that occurs on the occasion of its proper usage. For him, true "words" are not tools of speech, as are what he will call "signs." Instead, they are carriers of vision that affect inner sight through the sign that appeals to the outer eye, ear, and mouth. Such a revelation of the word, the illumination or insight that the monk seeks in the diligent reading of sacred writings, is an expectation that Anselm will have to meet if there is to be any point in his readers taking his writings back with them to their prayer cells.

That Anselm is writing for those involved in sacred reading is evident from the fact that he began his career by composing prayers and meditations and that he formally incorporated both elements into his first philosophical texts. Of course, the sort of vision at issue in a philosophical meditation will no doubt be of its own kind, even as the form that such rational revelation takes in the *Monologion* is easy enough to miss. For it is concealed beneath, or really embedded within, the maze of reasoning the text expects us to follow, whose point, like the proverbial forest, can be lost sight of in the attempt to keep the various arguments in view. What the *Monologion* ultimately proposes, in speaking of meditating on the nature of divinity "*sola ratione,*" is to offer something like a rational reconstruction of our vision of God: a kind of reenvisioning or resighting of the "essence of divinity," based not upon faith (that is, not upon the revelation in Scripture, which is to be put aside for the moment) but upon a form of rational investigation that is to bring to us some insight into the nature of God. Such an aim will involve the progressive construction of a rational likeness of God or, to put it otherwise, of an image of the divine that can be seen with the eye of reason. This is why Anselm does not say that he wants to give arguments to justify what he believes, but to give ones that, in their connection, through the necessity of reason, will allow the matter at issue to be evidently displayed in the clear light of truth.

Something of this task, of bringing to view the matter to be thought in the clarity of a rational vision, is indicated in the passage with which the *Monologion* begins:

> If anyone, either because they have not heard or do not believe, is ignorant of the one nature, highest of all that is, alone sufficient unto itself in its eternal blessedness, granting and effecting in all other things, through its omnipotent goodness, that they are something or in any way enjoy well-being, and if he has no knowledge of the many other things which we necessarily believe regarding God and his creatures, I still think that he can at least convince himself of these things in great part, even if his mental powers are very ordinary, by means of reason alone. And although this could be done in a number of ways, I shall adopt the one which I consider to be most available to him. For since all desire to enjoy only those things which they think are good, he can at any time readily turn the eye of the mind to the investigation of that by which these things are good—which he does not desire except as he judges them to be good—such that, with reason leading the way and him following, he may rationally advance to those matters of which he is unreasonably ignorant. (S I, 13–14)

This, we might mention, is the first and last time Anselm will use the term "God" in the text until its final chapter, when all that needs to be shown about this "one nature" has been seen, such that it is clear that the rational reconstruction of the idea of a being which is "the highest of all that is" has accomplished its task: to offer to the eye of the mind a rational vision of what the faithful call "God." Obviously, the very talk here of the eye of the mind suggests the element of vision, even as the rational sighting of what this name signifies involves the progressive elevation of the mind, which requires a certain conversion, a turning of the mind's eye, in its being led by reason in its ascent from the lower goods to the highest Good. And while the reference to one of average intelligence being capable of this may seem a bit pretentious (and all the more so once we see the complexity of the arguments involved), the envisioning of the supreme nature by means of reason is, in the *Monologion,* less the sort of sudden flash of insight resulting from a single virtuoso argument, as is the case in the *Proslogion,* than it is a kind of progressive illumination. Those trying to follow the complex and interconnected chain of arguments are led, a step at a time, to that apex which completes the reconstruction of a rational image of God in a final ontological conversion.

Of course, we would not want to pretend that there is not also a certain pretense in all this talk of the suspending of Scripture or in the way this passage that begins the *Monologion* proper, like its prologue, goes about setting the stage for the work to follow. While its staging of the text is designed to create the impression that we are starting from scratch so as to rethink the issues from the ground up on the basis of reason alone, certain principles of faith remain operative behind the scenes. Thus, while Anselm may put out of action explicit references to what the faithful believe, he nonetheless tends to presuppose the basic principles of a historical world that their faith has already served to inform. Throughout the *Monologion,* we will find him appealing to "self-evident" claims to found his arguments that to us may appear to depend for their own viability on what he is trying to demonstrate. This will be all the more obvious when the principles involved are ones we no longer hold, indeed, when what is at issue are the elements that most distinctively defined the medieval world and that often show up most clearly in the "unquestionable" assumptions upon which such arguments turn. In fact, given the extent of the historical context upon which Anselmian thought depends, we might assume that he is merely invoking, even parroting, rather than transforming, the Christian philosophical tradition that goes back at least to Augustine. This may be true in certain respects of the initial set of arguments in the *Monologion,* which are, by comparison to the *Proslogion* argument, rather traditional.[10] In that case, however, we might take advantage of them to reveal if not an overview, then at least something of the underpinnings of the world in which are embodied the views that Anselm now presumes to be in a position to suspend. In short, we might begin by rehearsing the battery of rather familiar arguments that initiate the rational reconstruction of God in the *Monologion,* if only to remind ourselves of some of the basic principles relevant to the historical nature of the thinking in which Anselm is engaged.

The Initial Battery of Arguments for a Supreme Being

At least two of the arguments for the existence of God that open the *Monologion* trade on a single principle that surfaces in the reasoning designed to begin our ascent from those "lower" goods we all ordinarily desire to the one "highest good" on whose basis we desire them. According to M 1, the rational mind that seeks to become aware of the existence of the one and supreme good need only ask itself:

> . . . although there are goods so innumerable, whose great diversity we experience by bodily senses and discern through the rational mind, are we to believe that there is a single something

through which whatever is good is good or that the various goods are good through various things? But certainly it is clear to anyone who is willing to turn his attention to it that whatever is called anything, such that it may be said to be it in a greater or lesser or equal degree in comparison to another, is called it not in virtue of something that is one thing in the one case and another in the other, but in virtue of something that is understood to be the same in the different things, whether it is considered to be in them equally or unequally. (S I, 14)

Anselm takes it as most certain to anyone who cares to turn his attention to it that if two things can be said to share some specific quality, say, their being white, then there must be something which they share, namely, whiteness. His confidence indicates, I think, the extent to which such a claim remains a fundamental principle that, like others in the text, will not be argued for, but appealed to as the self-evident basis for the arguments that are offered. This is not to deny that there may be some point to the contention that, in relative comparisons, what different things are being compared with respect to, as enjoying to "a greater or lesser or equal degree," must be something that is "the same" in the various cases, even in their difference. What Anselm seems to be suggesting is that we must be considering the same quality, as it were, even if in a different quantity, or else there could be no relevant comparison.

Drawing on the logic of comparison, even in those cases in which two things have the same quality in the same quantity, that is, in which there is no obvious comparative difference in that we simply predicate the same property of two different things, we are asked to treat it as a matter of judging them to enjoy the same feature in an "equal" degree. What this suggests is that, in general, Anselm is not content to leave it at each particular thing having its own completely distinctive features, but that, on the contrary, he tends to think of different things as characterized by the "same" properties. Such a view is bolstered by what may be regarded as the basic Platonic insight that however different, however unique or particular things may be, there is nothing—or for Anselm almost nothing—so unique that it does not share the kinds of features it has with other things. And while that may not as yet justify or even require belief in the existence of universals, it does work from the basic sense that no matter how individual an individual thing may be, it is always also a type of thing; just as, no matter how distinctive a feature may be, it is, in virtually all cases, at least in principle shareable in common with other things and, thus, can be "understood to be one and the same in different cases."

What may bother us in Anselm's exploitation of the logic of comparison is his apparent reading of the claim that there "is" something, some "one," that is one and the same "in" the different things that possess it, whether equally or unequally, and all the more so when we realize that it is not features like whiteness with which he is concerned. In fact, the example with which he follows his general principle is that of justice. If two acts are both said to be just, it must be in virtue of some justness that they have in common: in virtue of the justice that exists in each, to a greater or lesser or equal degree. This is more like the case Anselm is actually concerned with in M 1, namely, goodness. By getting us to attend to this single feature shared by a variety of things, the strategy of the argument is to move our thinking from the diversity of goods in the universe to that which is "understood to be the same in the different cases": to the one "supreme good" in virtue of which whatever is "good" may be so called. That, we will remember, is precisely what the opening paragraph of M 1 goes on to suggest, after its claim to be able to provide demonstrations that will persuade the person who is ignorant of the "one nature, highest of all that is" by means of reason alone:

> For since all desire to enjoy only those things which they think are good, he can at any time readily turn the eye of the mind to the investigation of that by which these things are good—which he does not desire except as he judges them to be good—such that, with reason leading the way and him following, he may rationally advance to those matters of which he is unreasonably ignorant. (S I, 14)

If the principle that draws our attention to the sameness entailed by comparative difference has Platonic overtones, we can here hardly miss the hint of Augustine. Not only do we find the rational mind turning its inner eye toward objects that are only available to reason's gaze, suggesting that the demonstration of these issues *sola ratione* will involve sighting specific objects with the eye of the mind in light of such conversion; but the final reference to what one "judges" to be good suggests that guiding our desire for the diversity of goods we do seek, whether they be perceived by "the body's senses" or the "mind's reason," is a *judgment* that something is good, which must itself be based upon a standard of goodness.

In fact, not only does the very notion of comparison, upon which the fundamental principle mentioned above rests, involve acts of judgment, but we can see it surfacing in the very language of the principle itself. For Anselm claims precisely that we are seeking the good that is *understood* to be the same in the diverse goods. Both times that he uses the phrase *"idem intelligitur in diversis,"* as well as when he says that things "cannot be understood to be just except through justice," he puts it in these terms, that is, both in the general principle and in its application to the examples at hand, including that of goodness.[11] In these cases, "understanding" counts as a reference to judgment, for it means: is discerned by the rational mind. In judging one thing in comparison to another, the mind must pass its judgment based upon something that is discerned to be the same in the things that are being compared, in which case reason must have recourse to a single standard relevant to the comparison, such that we are not just dealing with the unique features of each, but precisely with the consideration of a common characteristic, whether we judge those things to enjoy it to a lesser or greater or equal degree. Presumably, even in those cases where an explicit comparison is not being made, the judgment that any given thing has a particular characteristic would require recourse to a standard that stands behind it, indeed, that rather literally stands behind the rational mind as its standard of judgment. This is why the eye of the mind must turn around, has to be converted, if it is to see what illuminates its judgments from behind.

In this way, while the original principle sounds like a metaphysical claim about a shared good that the various goods have in common and presuppose for their goodness, the argument is, in fact, cast in terms of the mind's discernment of goodness, as it relates to the nature of judgment, and the way in which the eye of the mind determines anything to be good, let alone "better" or "worse" than something else, in light of its knowledge of a standard of judgment upon which its rational insight depends. We must not overplay the element of judgment invoked (admittedly with some subtlety) in the argument of M 1, since Anselm will be drawing ontological conclusions from this epistemological point. There can be no doubt, however, that the talk of the eye of the mind turning its attention to itself and its own judgments tempers the metaphysical claim that there is some one thing, something self-identical "in" the diverse goods under consideration, as it plays off of the mind's inner access to a standard of truth.[12] What seems to be critical in M 1 is that, upon reflection, it becomes clear to the rational mind that its own judgment of relative differences requires recourse to a single standard upon whose basis the judgment is made. This absolute standard is itself not judged in the judgment insofar as it supplies the basis for all judgment. In Anselm's view (what he takes to be the rational view), all other goods may then be said to have "derived" their goodness, that is, are judged to be good, from this paradigm of goodness, which, as the assumed standard, cannot be regarded as understood to be good in virtue of another but only in light of itself. It is, therefore, not judged to be good, but is the goodness on the basis of which any judgment that something is good may be passed. So as to distinguish it from all other goods, which are judged to be good through it, this standard may be said to be good through itself: goodness *per se.*

Consequently, if there is something that can be said to be the same about diverse goods, it is more like a standard of goodness than it is like the goodness of those things that are judged to be good by means of it. This does not stop Anselm, at the conclusion of M 1, from speaking about this supreme good in ontological terms:

> But since nothing can undermine the reasoning we have already seen, it is necessary that whatever things are useful or excellent, if they are truly goods, are good through that very same thing, whatever it may be, that is necessary for all goods to be. But who can doubt that that through which all are good is itself a great good? Therefore, it is good through itself, since all else is good through it. It follows, then, that all others are good through something other than what they themselves are and that it alone is good through itself. But nothing that is good through another is either equal to or greater than that good that is good through itself. Therefore, it alone is supremely good which alone is good through itself. For that is supreme which so surpasses others that it has neither an equal nor a superior. But what is supremely good is also supremely great. There is, therefore, some one which is supremely good and supremely great, that is, the highest of all that is. (S I, 14–15)

We find here one of the deepest principles in the structure of Anselm's thinking: whatever is what it is "through itself" is better or greater than what is what it is "through another." This *per se / per aliud* distinction not only fuels much of Anselm's thinking about the nature of the divine, but so construed, in its axiological implication, will also eventually lead to a tight-knit connection between ontology and axiology—between being and value—which is not uncharacteristic of medieval thought as a whole. No doubt the arguments we have just seen require a fusion, if not a confusion, of the ontological and the axiological, if only insofar as Anselm seems to assume that "goods" are "beings," or at least that goodness is a feature beings possess, even though he himself associates it with a judgment we make about them. Furthermore, Anselm not only thinks that what makes whatever is good good—whatever allows for our judgment that something is good—must itself be good, indeed, a "great good," as he says (to avoid the double talk of a "good good," even a "best good"); he also thinks that what it is to be so good a good, to be best, to be "supreme," is to be better than all other goods by being that good which has no equal, let alone superior, insofar as it is the good that is good "through itself."

We would not want to miss the irony that Anselm has exploited the logic of comparison to arrive at this incomparable good, nor should we want to fail to note, if only in passing, that a certain pattern of thought we will find repeatedly operative in the *Monologion*'s clarification of the nature of divinity is already visible in its first chapter. Certainly, one might imagine that to live by comparison is to die by comparison; that if the notion of some single common feature comes into play based upon the comparison of things to one another, then so might the judgment be passed based upon that comparison, without recourse to an absolute standard. Anselm will himself, in his own way, address this possibility of relative values, so we will postpone discussion of the matter until that point. Meanwhile, we want to note that while the *Monologion* begins its considerations (presumably for the benefit of those ignorant of God) with the goods with which we are all ordinarily familiar, the argument proceeds to draw us in the direction of a good that is essentially unfamiliar and quite extraordinary—indeed, essentially unlike those other goods with which we began. This can be overlooked given the language of degree in which Anselm speaks, especially if we fail to notice the emphasis on the superlative. But what is most striking about this argument is the way it has managed to squeeze an absolute good out of all those relative goods with which we are normally familiar, and precisely by exploiting the logic of relation, even as we begin, through this very reasoning, to be forced in the direction of what looks to be a categorical rather than a relative difference: a difference in kind, not just in degree. The claim that this good is "supremely" good is not simply a matter of its being better than the other goods. Instead, its supremacy consists in its being essentially unlike them: in its alone being good *per se*. This is why Anselm regards this good as incomparably unique. Thus, not only are other goods neither greater than nor equal to it; they are unlike it in a far more radical way.

Such categorical differences will play an important part in the conversion of our thinking that apparently has to take place if we are to see aright. This is why we must appreciate that while we had begun by thinking that the goods with which we are ordinarily familiar were good, a certain reversal has set in along the way of the argument, such that by the time we arrive at its conclusion, we may have changed our minds about the nature of goodness. And what is most critical about the turn of thought involved here is the strategy of reversal embedded within it. This same tactic of conversion is nowhere more essential than in the extended argument for the existence of God in the *Monologion* that runs through M 28. We will ourselves attempt to cover at least that much ground, so it is important for us to be alerted from the start to the strategy at work in the text. For it will eventually draw us into an even more complex and perplexing scenario of comparison as it moves in the direction of an ontological argument—an argument that applies the same tactic to the category of being—and as such will make a similar move, exploiting an even more profound reversal, in trying to make out the ontological difference between the "supreme being" and all other "beings." As we will show later, this longer argument is, in effect, Anselm's original version of the "ontological argument," which is itself condensed, although not without some alterations, in the abridgement that is the famous *Proslogion* proof. For the moment, however, we are only trying to make it clear that the pattern of thought which says: compare ordinary goods to one another so as to discern through them that goodness to which they, in essence, are not comparable, will be repeated not just in M 2, where we are simply asked to substitute "greatness" for "goodness," but also in the longer argument to which we have referred and in which this same strategy is applied to the notion of "being."

In fact, the explicitly ontological reasoning that begins in M 3 is formally more like that of M 1 and M 2 than one might suppose in that it aims to show that just as whatever is good is good through some one good, which we are led to infer is goodness itself (that is, the one good that is good in and through itself), so, too, all the beings that are must be through some one being that is being itself: the one being that "is" in and through itself. And, once again, just as the argument from the variety of goods to the one good began with the goods with which we are ordinarily familiar, the argument from the plurality of beings to the one "supreme being" moves in a similar direction. For rather than straightaway demonstrating the existence of this one being, Anselm begins by trying to show that there is only one such being: that all that is must be through "a single something."

This is shown in M 3 by means of a favorite strategy of Anselm's, namely, by process of elimination. If nothing exists through nothing, to invoke another principle of medieval thought, then whatever exists exists through something, although what it exists through may be either single or multiple, that is, there may be only one such something or many. Now what is perhaps most noteworthy about the procedure involved here is the way in which, during the process of eliminating the undesirable options, Anselm is able to introduce the operative concept. If we assume that that through which the plurality of beings exists is itself multiple, then these multiple "somethings" either are mutually dependent upon one another for their existence, which Anselm assumes to be nonsense, since nothing can provide the ground for that which provides the ground for it, or,

> ... if these multiple things themselves exist through some one,
> then everything does not exist through multiple things, but
> rather through that one through which those multiple things
> exist. If, however, those multiple things each exists indepen-
> dently through itself, then certainly there is a single power or
> nature of existing through itself which they would possess in
> order to be through themselves. There is no doubt, then, that
> they are through the very same one through which they have it
> that they exist through themselves. (S I, 16)

Obviously Anselm's original principle in M 1 is being put to
work once again: if the various presumed multiple "somethings"
through which whatever is exists each existed through itself, then
there would be some one power of "existing through itself" (*existendi
per se*) that is "one and the same" in them all and is actually the operative essence of divinity, that is, the "singular nature" we were
looking to demonstrate as essential to the plurality of beings. This
argument, however, functions not simply to show that there cannot
be plural "somethings" on the basis of which those things are that do
not exist through themselves. For in proposing the possible options,
it serves to introduce the notion of some one nature that exists
through itself and in a context in which such self-existence has a
relevant, even if unthinkable, contrast not simply with what exists
through another, but also with the supposition of multiple causes
that exist through one another.[13]

Anselm knows that this "power or nature of existing through
itself" is a strange one, which may be why he tries to set up a context
for its introduction and is certainly why he attempts to clarify it further in later chapters. Only then, especially in M 6, may we begin to
appreciate why he is not bothered here that, while beginning from
the assumption that nothing exists through nothing, we have apparently arrived at something that at least does not exist through another. This, of course, raises certain questions about the precise
nature of such existence. It would seem that we should at least be
somewhat concerned about whether the notion of the existential
self-dependence of something that "exists through itself" is any
more thinkable than the mutual dependency of beings that exist
through one another. For the moment, however, Anselm is more interested in amplifying the distinctiveness of such a feature, as well
as suggesting how it makes the divine nature the "the highest of all
that is," as he quite literally proceeds to repeat in M 3—as he did in
M 2, and will again in M 4—the conclusion of M 1:

> Therefore, as truth altogether prevents there being a plurality
> through which all things are, there must be some one through
> which is all that is. Since, then, all the things that are are
> through the same one, doubtless this very one is through itself.

Therefore whatever else is, is through another, while it alone is through itself. And whatever is through another is less than that through which all else is and which alone is through itself. Thus, that which is through itself alone is most greatly of all. There is a single something, then, that alone is most greatly and supremely of all. But what is greatest of all and is that through which is whatever is good or great, and whatever is anything at all, this must be supremely good, supremely great and the highest of all that is. There is, then, something which, whether we call it a being, a substance, or a nature, is the best and the greatest and the highest of all that is. (S I, 16)

Here we see the first two arguments, the one for a highest good, the other for a supreme being, beginning to infect one another as being is infused with value. The supreme good (*summum bonum*) and the highest of all that is (*summum omnium quae sunt*) are not just said to be one and the same, but this supreme being is the supreme good, the best of all that is, *because* it is the supreme being; that is, a being inherently and supremely great in that it is through itself alone. In this sense, being itself (*esse per se*) would seem to provide Anselm with an ultimate ground of value; for what could be better—supply a clearer standard of greatness—than that which imparts being to all that is by existing through itself alone? As such, however, being will itself come to be regarded as inherently subject to grades of value difference. Certainly the most fundamental ontological difference, which is also the crowning axiological difference, is between what is supremely great (*summum magnum*), in that it is and is whatever it is through itself, and everything else; such that what is other than this is to a lesser degree precisely because it is and is whatever it is through another. But there will be further value differences inherent to being according to Anselm, different degrees of goodness and greatness expressible in terms of different degrees of being, upon which, in fact, he bases his next argument.

Before turning to the question of the nature of the existence of what "is" *per se,* Anselm concludes his initial arguments for a highest good with one that is, at least to our ears, no doubt the strangest sounding of them all, since it is explicitly based on the medieval doctrine of degrees of reality. The extent to which Anselm merely invokes this doctrine without any argument for it is embarrassingly obvious in the way in which the basic claim being made in M 4 is bracketed by protective clauses that, in effect, argue *ad hominem* that anyone who does not agree is simply not worth arguing with. This sort of cavalier claim to self-evidence is the surest sign that Anselm is standing on shaky ground and that he is staging his presentation based on an appeal to the sort of precarious backdrop a historical world alone can provide.

If one attends to the natures of things, one cannot help but observe that not all enjoy an equal worth, but that certain of them
are distinguished by inequality of rank. He who doubts that by
its very nature a horse is better than wood, and man more excellent than a horse, is surely not to be called a man. And while
we cannot deny that some natures are better than others, reason no less persuades us that among these something is so preeminent that it has no superior. For if this kind of distinction of
rank were infinite, such that there would be no superior degree
than which nothing superior could be found, from this reason
would be led to conclude that the multitude of these natures is
without limit. This, however, no one doubts to be absurd, except someone who is himself absurd. There is, then, of necessity, some nature which is so superior to any other or others
that there is none to which it is ranked as inferior. (S I, 16–17)

If we had any difficulty seeing the point of the claim that a multiplicity of relative goods must lead us to some one good that is good
through itself, we may have even greater difficulty ranking that
multitude of goods in a hierarchy, such that some are essentially
better than others, and from which we would be willing to conclude
that there is a good than which none is better. No doubt, in the rank
and order of existence suggested here, we detect not only the echo of
a distinction between the insentient, the sentient, and the rational
drawn by Augustine (and that will later be drawn in M 31), but we
detect also an appeal to what Anselm took to be common assumptions ordinarily made about the value of things. These views are
simply being formally articulated when it is claimed that while a
piece of wood merely "exists," even if when still a tree it once "lived,"
it is nonetheless insentient, unlike the horse, which is sentient, although, unlike man, not rational, who, while rational, is nonetheless
also sentient, that is, bodily and thus inferior to angels. This neat
hierarchy, reflecting the order of the medieval world, which ascends
from the brute existence of stones through that of plant life to sentient existence, into the various grades of rationality (in short, from
the purely physical to the purely spiritual) is no longer so intact that
we would deny humanity to one who denied it. Perhaps what
Anselm means when he says that a man who thinks otherwise does
not deserve to be called a man is that he is not, in that case, thinking
rationally, that he is not making those discerning distinctions of
judgment that, by nature, make him man. For this, as Augustine
would have put it, is what makes the one who judges superior to
what is judged; just as the human mind is itself not just inferior to
angels but also to the divine reason, which supplies the standards by
means of which all minds judge: that primal truth which the angels
gaze upon without the distraction of bodily phantasms.

The problem, however, is that unless Anselm can show that the highest reality is itself rational, as he will later attempt to do, there is no apparent reason to think that the capacity to reason would make men "by nature" superior to horses. Certainly we might be willing to admit the relative goodness of something, especially when it comes to those goods that Anselm has already in M 1 distinguished as utilitarian. Clearly, a horse is better for riding to town than a piece of wood. But, then, a horse is also better, in this respect, than a man. To avoid this sort of problem, Anselm could appeal to the contrast between inherent "worth" (*dignitas*) and what we might call "use-value" (*utilitas*). In both M 1 and M 2, he had already distinguished in passing between two different types of "good": that which is said to be good because of its utility and that which is desired because of its excellence (*honestum*)—because it is worthy of esteem. As an example of the former, he mentions health; as examples of the latter, beauty and wisdom. In a way, beauty is a more straightforward example, since it may seem more clearly a noninstrumental good; that is, the beautiful would seem to be deserving of a judgment of excellence in and through itself. Whatever value it enjoys is not because it lends to some further good for the sake of which it is appraised, but because it supplies its own standard of excellence.

Anselm's point in M 4, while trading on a somewhat different distinction, nonetheless seems to be that in observing the multitude of things, we discern them to be of different inherent worth: not merely to be better for some particular purpose, but to be better as such; for it to be better for them to be. I mention the distinction between usefulness and natural or essential worth not with the hope of solving any problems so much as to suggest how problematic the topic at issue is for us. We are, I suspect, not only more comfortable passing judgments of use-value than of absolute value, but we may also be inclined to think that such judgments are easier to make when comparing things of the same nature, not when we are comparing the "natures" themselves. Thus it is easier, especially if we have certain purposes in mind, to judge one horse to be better than another than it is for us to determine whether it is better absolutely to be a horse than, say, a piece of wood. In principle, we might, seemingly without end, pass relative judgments of value: that a horse is better than a piece of wood for riding to town, whereas a piece of wood is better for floating across the river, unless the river is not very deep, etc. Such judgments could go on indefinitely, in which case there would seem to be no ultimate determination of the value of anything. In that event, we would have only relative determinations of value that would not entail a linear ascent to some highest good but, instead, would entail a kind of circularity of value, in which things were not measured with regard to some absolute standard but with respect to one another and in relation to the specific context.

Of course, it is precisely because we have use-value in mind that we might think there was an "infinite," or (as Anselm himself says in M 1) an "innumerable" variety of relative values insofar as differences in worth would be based upon our different and differing needs. The point in M 4, however, seems to be that this picture changes radically when we are asked to consider the "natures of things" and thus to determine their "essential" worth. Put otherwise, we might ask under what conditions it would be possible— since these were the conditions that Anselm seems to assume his historical audience to be taking for granted—to pass the absolute judgment that a man is by nature better than a horse. That condition seems to be implied by the claim, which Anselm defends with his talk of absurdity, that if there were no supreme good, the distinction of grades would be infinite. In that case, the multitude of natures or goods would come to no end, would remain unconfined, without limit. We might think of it this way: relative use-value, for example, finds its "limit" in the context and in relation to whatever else is available for use. A stone will be good for hammering if there is no hammer around. Without the limit of the context, however, no such judgment of value would be possible, just as with changing contexts, the determination of something's goodness or usefulness would itself change. But judgments of the absolute or "natural" worth of something, by which we mean the inherent value that ranks one kind of being essentially above another (horses are superior to trees because animals are better than plants) cannot be context bound or made relative to specific conditions or purposes. Therefore, if there are to be such absolute judgments, there must be some limit that defines, as it were, their absolute context. In this sense, the hierarchy cannot go on to infinity, where each thing is simply better than the other, since those judgments of betterness must be based on a context defining "best." This is the absolute context provided by the highest good, against which all that is can be measured with respect to its essential goodness. If, as Anselm assumes, his audience lives in a world in which it is routinely taken for granted that men are better than horses, then to be able to think this, or at least to justify thinking it, there must be a best.

Of course, Anselm may also be exploiting what for a medieval would be the unappealing view that the universe is infinite. In this sense, he may simply be saying that if the degrees of value difference went on indefinitely, if there were no good than which none is better, there would be an infinite number of different goods, which he seems to think would entail an unlimited number of different natures. And this he apparently considers to be a view everyone would regard as foolish, except a fool, even if, as we have inadvertently suggested, it might only mean that all judgments of value are relative and so change with changing needs and contexts. The fact that our judgments could go on indefinitely would not necessarily mean that there was an infinite number of "goods" in the sense of an infinite number of different beings or natures, but simply that there was an illimitable number of possible value judgments. Admittedly, once we allow Anselm to assume that there is such a thing as "essential" value, we find ourselves pushed in the direction of an absolute good. And the way he puts the point—that without a supreme good to which none is superior "the multitude of natures would not be confined by a limit" (*ipsarum multitudo naturarum nullo fine claudatur*), that they would be "endless"—suggests both that there would be an indefinite multitude of beings and that, without an end or limit, the very "grading" that supplies an order of rank would be impossible.

Whatever the case may be, after assuring us that there can be only one such supreme being, the nature of whose supremacy has now been further clarified, Anselm draws together for us the conclusions to be gathered from this initial battery of arguments:

> It follows, then, that there is some one and single nature that is so superior to others that it is inferior to none. But such a thing is the greatest and best of all the things that are. There is, then, a certain nature that is the highest of all the things that are. It cannot be this, however, unless it is what it is through itself and all others that are, are what they are through it. For since, as reason has taught us a little earlier, that which is through itself, and through which all others are, is the highest of all existing things, then either, conversely, that which is highest exists through itself and all others through it, or there is more than one highest. But that there is not more than one highest is obvious. There is, then, a certain nature or substance or essence, which is good and great through itself, and through itself is what it is, and through which is whatever is truly either good or great or something, and which is the supreme good, supreme greatness, supreme being or substance, that is, the highest of all the things that are. (S I, 17–18)

We find reiterated here the radical distinctiveness of what Anselm may as well have called, to maintain the parallelism of options, the supreme something: that on the basis of which anything is something at all. Once again he returns to the emphasis on its "supremacy" consisting in the fact that it is and is whatever it is "through itself," as this "being" or "essence," "nature" or "substance" is not just greater than others but so great that none is greater, and precisely in the sense that with regard to its *"perseity"* nothing else is like it. That the kind of being the supreme something enjoys in its absolute distinctiveness remains to be determined, that, in short, the rational reconstruction of God has only just begun, is highlighted by the fact that we do not as yet know whether to refer to it as a nature or a substance, an essence or, for that matter, a power. The rational image formed thus far of this supreme something would allow us to refer to it as a "nature" or "essence" when thought of in terms of the goodness through which all goods are good; as a "being" or "substance" when thought of as the basis of all that is; or as a "power" when thought in terms of the existence through itself that makes it the very ground of being. The question remains how these various characterizations are connected to one another: not only how the supreme good, as the essence of goodness that supplies the standard for judgments of value, is related to its characterization as the supreme being, but whether we are to think of it as some universal power or as an individual substance. The present indeterminateness that allows for the interchangeability of terms can only be corrected by further determination of this supreme something in the chapters to follow, even as it will first involve a certain culminating clarification of what it is to call it by the name of "being."

Anselm is aware that, in some respects, the very distinctiveness that constitutes the supremacy of the supreme being may create certain problems in thinking it, especially with regard to what may still sound to us to be its most convincing claim to superiority. For if the supremacy of the supreme something consists in its being whatever it is "through itself," then as the supreme "being," its superiority must consist in its "existing" through itself. All other beings remain inferior, enjoy a lesser being than it, precisely to the extent to which they exist through another—indeed, are ultimately unthinkable as existing except through this supreme other and thanks to its existing through itself. The question, however, postponed earlier, that remains to be answered in M 5–6 is just how we are to think this notion of existing through itself (*existendi per se*) as a preeminent power that, in some sense, constitutes the essence (*essentia*) of divinity—the absolute uniqueness of the being (*esse*) of the being (*ens*) in question. If, as the argument in M 3 assumed, nothing exists through nothing, then while it is unproblematic, in a limited sense, to think the existence of those things that exist one through the other, although not through one another, it is not altogether clear how anything could exist through itself. For to do so it must, as Anselm puts it, be both later and less than itself to the extent to which, to invoke two other medieval principles, the cause of anything is greater than the effect, which is always later than its cause. Either that, or it must be thought as coming from nothing. But, then, either such a being provides its own ground, is (to put it in the most contradictory form) the cause of itself—if, that is, it is true that everything exists through something—or it is without ground and, in this respect, arises from nothing. Thus, either the notion of existing through itself is contradictory or the original principle that nothing comes from nothing is violated and therefore no principle at all, in which case there would seem to be no reason to seek a ground for those beings that Anselm wants to contend do arise from nothing but thanks to something: the supreme something.

The key confusion, Anselm seems to be convinced, consists in trying to think this unique form of existence through itself as a superior type of the sort of existence through another with which we are ordinarily familiar; as if the "other" through which the supreme being exists could turn out to be itself. But as M 6 informs us, and in anticipation of a strategy that will become dramatically apparent later in the text, this will not do, since "that which is through itself and that which is through another are not susceptible to the same measure of existence (*existendi rationem*)."[14] The very mode of existence, and thus the account we must give of what exists through itself, is measured by a different standard of being, of what it means for it to be, than are those things that exist through another. The urgency of this point becomes somewhat clearer if we do not forget that what exists through another derives existence from that other, in which case, were Anselm to admit this model, he would be forced to confront the question of how anything can exist through itself in the sense that it derives existence from itself rather than from another. By contrast, of course, he wants to suggest that what is *"per se"* offers a special case of something that does not derive existence from anything in the way that what exists *"per aliud"* must.

Anselm ends up treating this problem with his own brand of linguistic therapy. First, he plays off the difference between "through" (*per*) and "from" (*ex*), suggesting that the supreme being cannot be "through" any other that could have brought it to be, nor can it be "from" itself in the sense that it could have preceded itself so as to bring itself into existence and, thus, derive existence from itself. He then concludes that we can think this appropriately only if we realize that, like goodness, being is not something the supreme being has, but is what it is. Unlike what is through another, which does not enjoy its own being, does not exist simply by being itself, being is not bestowed upon what is *per se,* not even as a self-endowment, but already belongs to it of its very nature. To exemplify the point, M 6 invokes the traditional image of light:

> How, then, in the end, is it to be understood that it exists through itself and from itself if it neither created itself nor arose from its own material nor somehow aided itself to be what it earlier was not? Only, perhaps, if it may be understood in the same way as it is said that light lights or is luminous through itself and from itself. For in that same respect in which light and to light and lighting are mutually related to one another, so being (*essentia*) and to be (*esse*) and being (*ens*), that is, existing or subsisting, are related. Thus, "supreme being" and "to be supremely" and "supremely being," that is, supremely existing or supremely subsisting, are not unlike, in their correlation to one another, "light" (*lux*) and "to light" (*lucere*) and "lighting" (*lucens*). (S I, 20)

Anselm has saved this image for last, perhaps so as to supply his initial arguments for the existence of God with an indelible conclusion. In M 7, he will turn to the question of the manner of existence of what remains besides God, namely, the universe of things. For now, the point is to see—with the help of a certain grammatical clarification—that the being of divinity is distinctive in that being belongs to the supreme being as lighting belongs to light. The event of being (if we can call it that), the verb that asserts being of a being, is to the noun, in the case of being itself, as the subject is to the verb in the assertion that "light lights" or is luminous in and of itself and thus is self-illuminating. To say that light lights is not to predicate an additional feature of it, but to clarify, to amplify, indeed, to reiterate what it is. Similarly, to say that the supreme being is, where its supremacy consists in its *perseity,* is simply to amplify that what it is is to be and, thus, that its being is what it is, and not some further feature bestowed upon it by another or by itself. To be being itself, to be "through" itself and "from" itself, is simply for the supreme being to be itself. And just as light lights insofar as it is light, even as all lighting occurs through its light, so the supreme being is insofar as being is what it is, even as all other beings are thanks to its being.

This is a powerful thought that was no doubt overpoweringly convincing to more than one meditator on it, even if it may depend on a certain word-game Anselm himself is apparently quite willing to play. Whether we find that the term "being," and the tautologizing it inevitably invites, enjoys what a recent thinker has called its own "hidden power," and whether such power is more than merely that of the sort of spell a magic word casts over us, is not exactly to the point just now, although it will be critical to our own conclusion. Instead, we want to stress that the arguments for the existence of a supreme being that begin the *Monologion* inevitably raise the question of the *nature* of the existence of God. We must by now have concluded that rather than imagining that we can understand this *esse per se* as a special brand of the being through another with which we are ordinarily familiar, the reverse will be the case, even as this ontological reversal will eventually have to become explicit in our meditation on the divine. If Anselm next turns to the question of the nature of the existence of beings other than God, this does not mean that his treatment of the "mode of existing" (*existendi rationem*) of divinity is completed, since he does so with an eye to radicalizing the contrast between this supreme being and the beings it is said to create. Thus, as we begin to trace the problems involved in accounting for the mode of existence of created beings, we will be led to an even more extreme understanding of the existence of God. The full power of this thought concerning the "being of divinity" (*divinitatis essentia*) has yet to be unfolded for us, since before returning to it we will have to work our way through a clarification of the existence of creatures, such that the difference between them and what Anselm will soon begin to think of as their creator can be brought out in all its ontological glory.

| Language, Thought, and Reality

The *Monologion*'s treatment of the question of the nature of the existence of everything besides the supreme being revolves around the topic of nothing: the "nothing" which creatures both come from and return to. Of course, the doctrine of the creation of the world "out of nothing" does not itself come from nowhere but is designed to assert the position of the radical creationist against both the classical contention concerning a coeternal matter from which the world of things is formed as well as the emanationist's claim that God created the world not from nothing but out of himself. In contrast to these accounts, the assertion that the supreme being creates the universe of beings "from nothing" may seem to make sense.

On the other hand, Anselm does wonder how such a *creatio ex nihilo* is to be understood. Obviously, if we say that the world was created from nothing, we do not mean that there was something, called nothing, from which it was created, as if nothingness were itself formed into somethingness. On the contrary, as Anselm insists, we mean that it is not the case that there was something from which the world was created: that there was nothing with which the creative being worked to create the universe of beings. In that event, however, if the world was not created from God himself, it does sound as if something came from nothing; not as if we had confused and reified nothing into a something from which the world came, but as if, inherent in the creative act itself, something came to be *ex nihilo*.

Anselm would like to be able to moderate this radical creationism in such a way that it might not seem so blatantly apparent that something came from nothing, even if he does not want to claim that there was something out of which existing things arose. While such creationism may not appear to violate the principle that nothing comes from nothing, insofar as it appeals to the claim that a supreme being creates things, the insistence that this being does not create them from itself may seem to allow a certain violation to loom in the background. In an attempt to avoid this, Anselm turns to the discussion of a form of preexistence that creatures enjoy in the supreme being. Thus, the title announcing what is to be shown in M 9 somewhat paradoxically reads: "That those things that have been made from nothing were not nothing before they were made with respect to the thought of their creator" (S I, 24).

We will pursue more precisely the nature of the thought (*ratio*) of the creator shortly. For now, we are more concerned with what it might have to do with the existence of creatures and how this claim serves to moderate the radicalness of the doctrine concerning their creation from nothing. M 9 goes on to explain Anselm's view of the nature of creation:

> But I seem to see something that compels me to distinguish carefully the respect in which those things that have been made can be said to have been nothing before they were made. For in no way can something reasonably be made by someone unless beforehand in the thought of the maker there is some sort of pattern or, better said, form or likeness or model of the thing to be made. It is evident, then, that before all things were made there was in the supreme nature the thought of what or how or in which way they were going to be. Therefore, while those things that have been made clearly were nothing before they were made in the respect that they were not what they now are, nor was there anything from which they were made, they were, nonetheless, not nothing with respect to the thought of the creator, through which and according to which they were made. (S I, 24)

While the creative being's creation of creatures will turn out to be unique in that it does not take place on the basis of some material substratum nor does it make what is to be made out of itself, it is apparently no different from human creativity in that what is to be created must be envisioned beforehand in the thought of the creator. To this extent, what is created from nothing has a kind of being in the thought of the creative being before its creation. Indeed, this is a truer being than it has "in fact" (that is, after it has been made), because this primal "preexistent" being that creatures enjoy before they are created endures even after they have returned to nothingness. And while one might imagine that the problem of the creation of these divine exemplars simply pushes the question of the *ex nihilo* back one more step, it is not only likely that we will be more inclined to accept the pure creativity of thought, but it is also the case that this divine preconception of creatures does not itself arise from nothing. Instead, it will turn out to be derived from the self-conception or, if one prefers, the reflection of the supreme substance upon itself.

For the moment, however, and with this latter point no doubt in mind, Anselm pursues the analogy already implicitly in operation between divine and human thought in a critical passage that begins M 10:

> But this form of things, which precedes the things created in his thought, what is it other than a certain expression of things in thought itself, just as when an artisan is about to make some work according to his art he first expresses it within himself by means of a conception of the mind. By an expression of the mind or reason, however, I mean here not when the words significative of things are thought, but when the things themselves, which are going to or presently exist, are envisioned in the mind by means of the acute vision of thinking. For it is known from ordinary usage that a single thing can be expressed in three ways. Thus, a thing is expressed either by making perceptible use of sensible signs, that is, those which can be sensed by the bodily senses, or by imperceptibly thinking within us those very signs which on the outside are sensible, or neither perceptibly nor imperceptibly making use of these signs, but by expressing the things themselves inwardly in our mind either through the imagination of bodies or through rational understanding, according to the diversity of the things themselves. For in one way I express a man when I signify him by this name, which is "man"; in another, when I silently think this same name; in another way, when the mind intuits the man himself either though an image of a body or through reason—by means of an image of a body, as when I imagine his sensible figure; by means of reason, however, when his universal essence, which is rational mortal animal, is thought. (S I, 24–25)

Articulated here for the first and, in many respects, most revealing time in Anselm's work is his view of the nature of reason—a view that stands in the background of all his philosophical thought. Of course, the immediate aim of the appeal to our rational understanding is to provide an analogy for the divine preconception of creatures based on human thought. In so doing, however, Anselm makes it clear that his model of thinking, whether human or divine, is founded upon the expressive power of the mind, on its ability to envision the things themselves, to observe them in thought, by means of a kind of mental vision, indeed, in the case of human being, in view of two different forms of mental insight, namely, imagination and understanding.[15] While Anselm is himself more interested, at this point, in the question of the nature of the divine reason, we are, for our purposes, equally concerned with his assumptions about the nature of human thinking, whose features are here presumed to be self-evident.

While all of this may have seemed evident to Anselm, it may no longer be so clear to us. In fact, what may be most problematic for us is precisely what is most at issue in the above passage, namely, what it calls "rational understanding."[16] Even if we get Anselm's point about the sort of inner vision involved in imagination, we might not be so clear about what such rational vision amounts to, about what it is to envision things "by means of reason," especially as it is, like imagining, treated as a matter of entertaining "the things themselves" in thought. Needless to say, it is this aspect of our mental lives with which Anselm must be concerned in the present case, since God does not imagine things in their being prior to their existing but thinks the things themselves, on this model, by means of something more like what M 10 refers to as a "conception" of the mind. Such an "expression of the mind or reason" is aimed, apparently, at giving voice to the things themselves in thought. Or, since the vocabulary is one of vision rather than speech—indeed, since speaking is associated with thinking by means of "signs," in which case it is not a matter of direct insight, but, on the contrary, at best serves an indirect function—the expressive power of reason is better said to aim at bringing into view, catching sight of, observing and discerning with its mental gaze (*conspicio*) the things themselves as they come to be seen, to appear in and to thought, thanks to the acuteness of vision that thinking enjoys.

Consequently, sign-signification, thinking about something by means of signs, is of little interest to Anselm here, except for the sake of its contrast with other forms of human thought. God has no use for a sign-language nor, for that matter, any need, let alone capability, to utter sign-sounds, whether outwardly or inwardly. It will, then, be incumbent upon Anselm to show that the nature of language—and, thus, the "expression" of things in thought—does not depend upon the signifying power of the sensible sign or upon the insensible use of those sounds we ordinarily call words (*voces*) even when they are uttered silently within ourselves. On the contrary, the significance of signs must be shown to depend upon a primal word (*verbum*) that will come to be associated with the "word of the thing" insofar as it is a matter of that expression (*locutio*) of the mind or reason that allows the realities themselves (*res ipsa*) to be directly observed in thought. Meanwhile, the account of such mental

vision is made plausible not only by contrasting it with the signifying (that is, indirect expressing) of things by means of signs but also
by an appeal to that dimension of our mental faculties that is most
clearly engaged in the task of envisioning, namely, imagination.
And while it may not be altogether clear just what is entailed in rational understanding, it is certainly apparent from the way this passage compares it with imagining that for Anselm there is a form of
rational thought that is as different from thinking things by means
of signs as imagining is. Both imagination and reason are regarded
as an articulation of the realities themselves in an expression that
aims not just to signify, but to offer a "likeness" of them, insofar as
the visionary power of the mind aims to catch sight of the thing itself
in thought.

This means that there are at least two elements of human
thinking that Anselm wants to stress in its presumed comparison
with divine thought. First, if the mind is able to think the things
themselves, it is not only capable of entertaining reality by means of
thinking but is, in fact, tied inextricably to it, although, and sec-
ondly, it does this by giving birth to a likeness, an image in thought,
of the reality it is thinking. As we shall see, the first point of comparison is essential to the analogy concerning God's envisioning of
creatures before their creation, although our understanding of the
nature of such divine thought will be clarified through the second
point, as the birth of the word in God, the birth of such divine conceptions, arises as the image and likeness of God in his own self-expression. In any case, when it comes to the characterization of the nature
of thinking upon which this analogy is based, it must be clear that
when we are told that the human mind can think the man himself
"by means of reason" by thinking his essential being (*essentia*) as
rational mortal animal, it obviously cannot be a matter of thinking
the words, that is, signs, "rational mortal animal." Anselm must be
distinguishing thinking about a man by means of these terms from
thinking the essence of man by means of reason. For what is at issue
in thinking about a man rationally is intuiting the man himself in
his essential nature, which, as "universal," might seem not to be a
matter of envisioning the man at all, the way imagining his body
clearly would count as such.

One of the reasons we might be suspicious of the notion of rational insight, especially insofar as "intuition" refers to a direct vision
of the thing itself in thought, is that whereas imagination and perception entertain concrete individuals, reason is said to intuit universal essences. It is important to appreciate, however, that, in
Anselm's view, such an essence nonetheless provides thought with
the distinguishing feature of what is thought. While the designation

"rational mortal animal" may not serve to distinguish one man from another, as imagining his body might, it will, as a defining feature, serve to distinguish "man" from everything else in the landscape of pure thought and so may be said to be the identifying feature of human being, at least as an object of reason. In this respect, rational understanding presumably allows us to think of things, as M 10 puts it, "according to the diversity of the realities themselves": in accord with those essential features that distinguish one thing from another in terms of the kind of thing it is. While imagination may allow the mind to envision bodily realities in accord with their own distinct and distinguishing corporeal characteristics, reason allows thought to entertain the essential reality of things, which is one and the same in a variety of individuals. This common essence supplies the defining character on the basis of which things may be distinguished from one another and sorted, not as individuals, but as natural types in accord with the distinctive and distinguishing nature of each. While talk of a universal essence may give the opposite impression, the point is that such an essential characterization allows reason to isolate the thing itself as an object of thought, to distinguish it essentially from other objects of such thinking and thus to think, for example, of a man in accord with the distinctive differences that characterize such a thing as man. Some differences, then, presumably inessential or accidental ones, are visible to imagination; other, more essential differences are available to a rational vision directed in its discerning gaze to and by those universal natures that allow it to identify the individual in its essential difference from other types of things.

We will have to return to such topics later, and perhaps modify some of what we have said, when we come to apply these issues to the rational vision of God. While it must be clear that God cannot be imagined—in which case, given what we have said, one might think that he enjoys no individuality if the latter is accidental—it will also turn out to be the case that, properly speaking, neither does he have a universal essence. If God is not a type of thing, then, unlike all other cases in which a rational characterization of something's nature distinguishes only a class of things to which, in principle, a number of individuals could belong, there may be ways of rationally characterizing God such that reason may be put in a position to locate the individual in thought through a rational clarification of its "being." For now, however, this is scarcely at issue, since we are at present not discussing our conceiving of God, but his conception or, should we say, preconception of creatures. And it is critical to appreciate that, given this model of rationality, if the things themselves may be said to preexist in God's preview of them, then it is at best in their essential distinctiveness, not in their individual or accidental qualities. They are envisioned in what will soon enough be called the truth of their being—a truth that we most closely approximate not when we are imagining things but when we ourselves think "by means of reason."

While some of what we are saying may be straightforward enough, there are complications that arise as a result of the way in which Anselm has rather quickly created a certain impression of the nature of rational thought by coupling it with imagination. In the first instance, the claims about our mental envisioning of the things themselves within us seem most appealing when we are considering what it is for us to imagine. Thus, we might think that Anselm has not only modeled divine thought on human thinking, but that he has, in turn, modeled the very sort of rational conception at issue in his claims about the divine mind on the nature of human imagination. In that case, we might find all the more ironic his disclaimer, a chapter later, that there is a certain disanalogy with the divine precisely because its form of envisioning things is not like human imagining:

> But while it is evident that the supreme substance first spoke, as it were, within itself all creation, which it then fashioned according to and through its own inmost expression, just as an artisan first conceives in his mind what he later executes in work according to his mental conception, I see in this comparison much dissimilarity. For the supreme substance took absolutely nothing from anywhere else upon which either to construct a model in itself of those things that were to be made or to make them what they are. An artisan, however, is completely unable to conceive in his mind, by imagining, any material body except what he has in some way become acquainted with, whether as a whole all at once or part by part, from other things; nor can he perform the work conceived in his mind if he lacks either the material or something without which the preconceived work cannot be accomplished. For although a man can invent, by thinking or picturing, some such animal as has never existed, in no way could he do this except by putting together in it parts of other things that he has known and taken into his memory. (S I, 26)

It is noteworthy that when Anselm actually discusses the nature of the artisan's mental preview of work to be created, he treats it as a matter of imagination rather than, as he did both at the beginning of M 10 and again in M 11, as a conception of the mind or reason. In that case, we might take "conception" in a more general sense to designate any mode of expressing something in thought: of bringing it to view in the vision of thinking. What should be striking here, however—especially if the nature of reason in its visionary power has been modeled on the more familiar mental envisioning we ordinarily call imagining—is that Anselm has a view of imagination quite different from at least our ordinary one. Indeed, it may appear that what makes our imagination and thus our rationality different from God's is precisely that it is not essentially productive. For the paradigm of imagination seems to be that of imagining something we have already seen, as in the example in M 10 of entertaining a mental image of a man I know, which might just as well be regarded as a case of remembering.

Of course, Anselm is also willing to admit into the discussion of imagining what is no doubt to be excluded from remembering, namely, those cases in which I "picture," as he puts it, something that I have never actually seen "as a whole all at once" but have pieced together, as it were, from "parts" of things I have seen; although even then memory is appealed to as the ultimate source of imagination. Here we might want to distinguish the literal notion of imagination, as the entertaining of a mental image, from free fancy. What these examples suggest, however, is that fancy is not so free for Anselm. Even imagining something I have never seen, perhaps because such a thing does not exist, depends upon what I have actually seen insofar as imagination is free, and apparently only free, to rearrange elements that have been derived from experience. Thus, if I have seen a horn and seen a horse, I can imagine a unicorn by putting a horn on a horse. But this is scarcely a matter of pure creativity in the way in which God's envisioning of creatures apparently must depend upon his taking "absolutely nothing from anywhere else." On the other hand, neither may this latter claim, even in God's case, entail the kind of creativity of which we are apt to think.

To arrive at an understanding of Anselm's account of the nature of rational thought, we must not only avoid the modern view of the creative imagination and its own *creatio ex nihilo,* but we must also be sure that the disanalogy proposed here between human imagination and the rational preconception of creatures in God is not mistaken to be claiming something other than it is. It is not Anselm's view that the divine preconception of creatures is an example of a free creativity, as if it were a rational form of the sort of creative imagination he is denying human being enjoys; an absolute form, in other words, of pure productivity. On the contrary, precisely what we must come to appreciate, if we are to understand Anselm's paradigm of rationality, is that God's thinking has nothing to do with fictive production but is inextricably and perfectly tied to reality. Obviously, God's thinking cannot be constrained by the reality of creatures before they exist. Nonetheless, in God, no less than in human being, thought is unbreakably tied to reality. For the key to the distinctiveness of God's thought does not lie in the fact that he is not thinking of some reality when he previews creatures, as if he thinks them up out of nothing, but that he thinks of no reality *other than himself* in so doing. Nor need God ever think of anything else, even once things have been created, whereas the human mind does most all of its thinking, whether in imagining or in rational understanding, based on realities other than itself. Thus, if the way of generating images in thought can be said to differ in the case of human imagination and divine reason, it nonetheless remains perfectly analogous that both forms of thinking are bound to some reality that is thought, indeed, that, as far as Anselm is concerned, all true thinking, whether imaginative or rational, whether human or divine, is ultimately and directly based upon reality.

In this way, God's own productive thinking is not fictive, but while fully and truly creative, it nonetheless depends entirely upon his thinking about reality, namely, his own reality and, consequently, upon the formation of—or, as Anselm would no doubt prefer to say, his giving birth to—his own self-image. In that case, the freedom of God's thought does not consist in its lack of reality but in the purity of a mind that is and can be thinking about nothing but itself. As we shall see, it is precisely insofar as the divine mind creates the true being of things, what M 10 calls their universal being, by generating an image of himself when he thinks the reality that he himself is, that our rational thinking can be connected to this universal aspect of things in intuition: in their presentation to consciousness not in the bodily image that appears to imagination, but through the rational likeness in thought which is related to their essential reality. At the moment, however, the point we need first to press is that if, in human being, imagination itself remains tied to material reality in its generation of the bodily image of things in its inner vision, then reason is also inextricably related to the things themselves in its formation of the likeness of those realities in their universal essence, which may be as apparent to the mind in the vision of thinking as the image of a body is in the imagination.

For Anselm, then, reason, like imagination, both is and is not a productive feature of human thinking. In effect, rational understanding is an intuitive capacity that the mind has to entertain the things themselves through its own active formation of images. Needless to say, it is Anselm's explicit modeling of reason on imagination that allows him to speak in M 11 of the artisan as picturing what is being thought by means of an image in the mind or in M 10 in terms of there being a likeness of a man's body in our thought. And the precise nature of the model of rationality Anselm is proposing, whether ours or God's, comes out, I am suggesting, only by pursuing the strategy that couples it with a particular account of imagination. Such a comparison, when pressed, yields the result that while the mind's creative element may be said to reside in its formation of images, the truth of those images is a matter of the similarity they enjoy to the reality of which they are presumably a likeness. This should be clear from the fact that Anselm's use of the notion of expression in M 10 is not primarily that of our expressing ourselves, but of a way in which the things themselves are expressed, articulated, or, as it will later be put, "exhibited" by means not simply of signs, but of language. To this extent, Anselm's theory of signs is separable from his philosophy of language insofar as the image of "speaking" or "expressing" or "saying" something is apparently applicable even when signs are not at issue. Consequently, immediately after having distinguished between the sensible use of signs, the silent employment of those same signs, and the expressing of the things themselves in the mind, M 10 proceeds to claim that:

> Each of these three varieties of speaking consists of words of their own kind. But the words of that kind of speaking which I put third and last, when they are not of unknown things, are natural and the same for all peoples. And since all other words have been devised because of these, where they are, no other word is necessary for recognizing a thing; and where they cannot be, no other word is of use for bringing the thing into view. They can, moreover, without absurdity, be called truer to the extent to which they are more similar to, and the more expressly they signify, those things they are the words for. Indeed, with the exception of those things which we use as names for themselves in order to signify them, as is the case with certain sounds, like the vowel "a," except for these, as I say, no other word seems so similar to the thing whose word it is, or so expresses it, as that likeness which is expressed in the acute vision of the mind thinking the thing itself. (S I, 25)

I suppose one could say, if we wanted to ignore the fact that we are in the midst of a discussion of language, that Anselm is here trying to distinguish between thinking by means of signs and thinking by means of images, that is, by means of the likeness (*similitudo*) of the thing itself that may be entertained directly in the mind. In any case, it should be clear that for him both imagination and the thinking by means of reason that he calls understanding involve inner vision. This is not only echoed in his talk at the end of the above passage about the "acuteness" of thinking, but also in the term he uses there for expressing the things themselves in the mind by means of the vision of thinking (*in acie mentis rem ipsam cogitantis exprimitur*), which means, as our term "ex-press" literally does, to press something out, to provide a form or model, and thus to portray or provide a copy or image of it. While this may seem obvious in the case of imagining, where the mind paints, as it were, its own picture of the thing itself in an imaginative vision, Anselm means to suggest that something very much the same is occurring in the case of reason: that the thing itself can be expressed in thought by means of reason, can be depicted in and by the mind, so as to be seen by means of a rational sight that envisions things through a likeness of them formed in the mind's exercising of its own linguistic power, which is not based upon its ability to think in and through a system of signs. On the contrary, sign-systems are themselves assumed to be based on the mind's ability to express the thing itself in the vision of its thinking.

Some of this becomes a bit clearer later in the text. While working from the distinctions drawn in M 10, Anselm puts them to a somewhat different use, although in the service of the same topic, in the *Monologion*'s more detailed consideration of the original birth of the word in God. At that point, M 33 reintroduces the analogy between human and divine thought, once again appealing to what is taken to be self-evident about our own mental experience:

> For whatever things the mind attempts truly to think, whether by means of the imagination of a body or by means of reason, it tries to express in its own thought, to the extent to which it can, their likeness. The more truly it does, the more truly it thinks the thing itself. And this certainly can be clearly seen when it thinks something other than itself, and especially when it thinks of some material thing. For when, in his absence, I think of a man whom I know, an image of him is formed in the vision of my thinking such as I contracted into my memory through the vision of my eyes. That image in thought is the word of that man, whom I express by thinking. (S I, 52)

Again and again Anselm appeals to imagination as the paradigm of thinking the thing itself, although he clearly wants to make use of this appeal to claim that what he says of imagining, in its own way, applies to rational understanding as well. He must think this in the case in point, since the contention in M 33 is that when the mind thinks itself—which, of course, it cannot do except by means of reason, since it is not a body—an image is formed in it of itself. And it is this mental model of a mind thinking itself that will serve to unlock the mystery of the birth of an image of the Father, of the first person of the Trinity, in and as the Son.

At present, however, we are more interested in the active power Anselm attributes to human thought, to its formation of images, indeed, to its "striving to form likenesses" of the things themselves in its attempt to think them. This suggests that "conceptions of the mind" are, like imaginative images, active events of thinking; that

such "expressions of the mind or reason" are to be regarded as mental formations, formulations, we might say, of those things the mind
is attempting to think, and precisely by envisioning likenesses of
them in thought. Here, of course, the talk of "trying" to form such
likenesses suggests that the mind will, in particular cases, be better
or worse in its accomplishment. But we must not be misled by this
possible failure into thinking that Anselm has abandoned the direct
connection between thought and reality or that rational images for
him are mere fabrications of the human mind, for the above passage
also suggests what the standard of success is. While Anselm admits
that the sort of case he presently has in view will be very complicated
and that the begetting of images in the human mind (as the basis for
the analogy concerning the birth of the second person of the Trinity
in God) will itself be clearer when the thing thought is not the mind
itself and clearest in the case of imagining bodies, the principle of
true thought that he wants to derive from all this is itself quite evident. According to Anselm, to think the thing itself truly—that is,
both truly to think and to think something in its truth—amounts to
this: the greater the extent to which the mind can achieve the begetting of a likeness of the thing itself in thought, the greater the extent
to which it can truly be said to think the thing itself. Or: to the degree to which the mind more truly does this, to that extent it more
truly thinks the things themselves (*quanto verius facit, tanto verius
rem ipsam cogitat*).

Obviously, in the case of imagination, the more truly thought
can accomplish, for example, the picturing of a likeness of a man's
body, the more truly it may be said to think the man himself. The
point, however, is that this is apparently no less true of reason,
which is also in the business, when it is doing what it ought to, of
producing in its inner vision a likeness of the thing itself. At the
same time, there is a rather pressing problem that may appear to
follow from Anselm's basing his view of human thinking on the
imagination insofar as the latter is explicitly connected to memory.
If we appeal to memory as the source of imagination, to the image
derived from the bodily eye as the source of our mental vision of the
man, and, more importantly, as if the standard of truth were the man
himself (in that case, his body), then what, one might ask, is the basis for the formation of rational conceptions and what constitutes
their standard of truth: of their being "truer" the truer they are to
the things themselves? What, in other words, is a rational likeness
of things supposed to be like? If the true image of a man in imagination is one that is like the man himself, like his body, what "reality"
is his rational image an image of? If reason is not merely fabricating
its images of things, but involves an intuitive aspect in which there

is a determination of similarity—a "truth" to the images it forms of things—then what is the rational reality of which our conceptions are "likenesses," analogous to the way in which our imagination has grounds for the images it envisions in the vision of its thinking in the bodily realities we originally encounter in perception and recall to mind in memory?

The answer to this question is supplied by the discussion in M 33, in its consideration of the birth of the primal word in God. It should come as no surprise that Anselm's account of our rational understanding is ultimately facilitated by an appeal to those "natural words" in which the human mind may think; not the words of what we would call natural languages, but the words that presumably make those diverse sign-systems possible: the mental expressions or universal words that are common to all languages because they are by nature similar to the things themselves. These alone can assure that the inner expressions of rational thought speak a language that is not of its own making. Instead, it must be the word of God that provides the foundation for truth. In fact, in light of the epistemology suggested above and in view of the conclusion of the initial arguments that began the text, the expression of the Father that is the second person of the Trinity may be regarded as the truth of being itself: the supreme truth, we could say, and precisely because it is a perfect likeness of the supreme being. This would have been evident had we begun the passage we have already cited from M 33 a few lines earlier:

> But certainly that word by means of which the supreme wisdom expresses itself can, according to our earlier reasoning, most fittingly be called its word, because it enjoys perfect likeness to it. For on no account can it be denied that when the rational mind understands itself by thinking of itself, an image of itself is born in its thought, or, rather, its thought of itself is its own image, formed as its likeness, from, as it were, its impression. (S I, 52)

No doubt Anselm is here pushing his epistemological principle—that the greater the extent to which an image is similar to the reality of which it is the image, the greater the extent to which it enjoys truth—to its limit. The second person of the Trinity is not just relatively similar to, but is the absolute truth of the first insofar as the Son is an image born in the mind of a perfect thinker who thinks only of himself and does so in such a way that his self-impression is in perfect accord with the reality of which his self-image is the expression; indeed, whose self-understanding is so perfect that when he thinks about himself his thought generates a "perfect likeness" of what is thought, namely, himself, in his thought. There is also no doubt, however, that Anselm is aware that there may appear to be problems with such a view, even as he senses the promise of catching a glimpse of something profound through, as M 65 would say, this "riddle" of the perfect likeness which is the truth of being.[17] Thus, he pursues the issue in M 33, despite these difficulties, tending to attribute whatever problems we may have in thinking it to the uniqueness of the topic, even if that "uniqueness" is precisely what might make us suspicious in the first place:

> Therefore, when the rational mind understands itself by thinking of itself, it has with it its own image born of it, that is, of its own thinking, formed from its likeness, as if from its own impression; even if it can only distinguish itself from its own image by means of reason. This image of it is its word. Thus, can anyone deny that, in this way, the supreme wisdom, when it understands itself by expressing itself, begets of itself its own consubstantial likeness, that is, its own word? And although nothing can properly or fittingly enough be said about a thing so uniquely outstanding, that word may not unfittingly be called its image, or figure, or imprint, just as it is its likeness. This word, however, by which it expresses what is created, is not, in like manner, the word of creatures, because it is not their likeness but primal being. It follows, then, that [the supreme wisdom] expresses those very creatures not through the word of creatures. By means of what word, then, does it express them, if it does not express them through their own word? For what it says, it says by means of a word, and a word is a word for, that is, a likeness, of something. But if it expresses nothing other than itself or creatures, nothing can be expressed except either by its own or their word. If, then, it expresses nothing by the word of creatures, whatever it expresses, it expresses through its own word. Therefore, it expresses, by means of one and the same word, both itself and whatever it makes. (S I, 52–53)

Anselm would have us think that the word of God, as the primal being (*principalis essentia*) that provides the originary principles on the basis of which all creatures are made, is itself originally formed in the thought of the creator in that "expression of the mind or reason" based not upon the creator's thinking about creation, but on his thinking about himself. Anselm is emphatic about this because he must secure the claim that the primal word is not a likeness of creatures, but, on the contrary, that creatures are a likeness of it. In this reversal, which is critical to the overall argument of the *Monologion* and to which we will return later, what we at first thought was real, namely, the things themselves, assume the ontological status of images; as if what we ordinarily refer to as "reality" (*res ipsas*) were actually a "likeness" (*similitudo*) of something else. Here we may begin to sense the extent of the dependency of Anselm's strategy on the ontology of the image. Not only does it allow him to account for the second person of the Trinity as the perfect likeness of the first—as an impression that God enjoys in and of himself, quite independently of whether or not creatures ever exist—but this word, which originally expresses creatures in the divine wisdom, such that they are not exactly created out of nothing, is, nonetheless, not the word of those creatures but of the supreme being himself, in which case creatures are at best to be regarded as a likeness or image of the supreme truth.

To make out this argument, we have to recall that even God's thinking is constrained by the need to think something; not to think it up, but to give birth to an image in thought by thinking of some reality whose likeness the thought is an expression of. In the above passage, however, talk of the "imprint" (*caracter*)—as if God has made an impression (*impressione*) on his own thinking—is a telling one, as it signals the appeal to memory. Of course, in all cases, the thing itself makes a certain impression on thought, which is what the likeness, the word of the thing, is supposed to express. In that event, however, it must be clear that the truth of the word, the true word, like the memory image, is to be regarded as an expression born of an original impression. To see this clearly, we need only consider imagination. Indeed, the same chapter from which the above citation is taken reverts not only to the discussion of imagination as the clearest example but also to the way in which the image of a man, when not present, can be drawn from memory, that is, to the literal "impression" that has been made on the mind by the reality itself, in that case, contracted by the eye of the body. Such an impression, once made upon thought, can, then, be expressed by the mind as an expression of the impression that the thing itself has left. Consequently, expression, so considered, as "the word of the thing," is the active expression of a passive impression made upon thought by what it is thinking. And this is apparently no less true for God, since the content of his own thought is not itself created out of nothing insofar as he must make an impression on himself so as to have anything to think. God's thought is "self-generated" just in the sense that he is the only possible object of thought before creation.

In that case, however, of a mind thinking itself, in which God's thinking on his own thinking makes a direct impression on itself, we presumably have a perfect self-expression born of his consummate self-impression. That is, we have a perfect likeness of God arising in, and inherent to, the thought of a perfect thinker who is the eternal object of his own thought. In this respect, we might well say that truth belongs to the very structure of God's self-consciousness: that it originates, indeed, has always already happened, in the perfect image that such a reflective spirit would, by nature, have of itself. This "perfect likeness" not only supplies the original model of truth, but is, in turn, the origin of all other truth. As the slightly later dialogue *On Truth* will put it:

Teacher: Do you think that there is anything, at any time or place, which is not in the supreme truth and that has not received from it what it is insofar as it is, or can be other than what it is there?

Student: No, I wouldn't think so.

Teacher: Therefore, whatever is, truly is, insofar as it is what it is there.

Student: You can certainly conclude that all that is, truly is, in that it is not other than what it is there.

Teacher: Then there is truth in the being of all the things that are, because they are what they are in the supreme truth. (S I, 185)

If we have trouble understanding the claim Anselm is making about rational intuition, it may be because we lack the sort of schooling in the nature of truth that the teacher complains about elsewhere in the dialogue: because "while everyone talks about the truth of signification, few think about the truth that is in the being of things."[18] It is not coincidental, then, that the point Anselm tries to drive home in the above passage is addressed to the truth that is a matter not of propositions but of the very being of the things themselves, such that we may say of all things that they "truly are" to the extent to which "they are what they are in the supreme truth." This does not mean that what things in fact are is what they are in the supreme truth, but quite the reverse. Whatever it is for them to be what they "are" is not what they happen to be in having been made, but (as Anselm will express it, just a few lines later) a matter of their being "what they ought to be," namely, what they are in the supreme being before their creation. The truth of things, then, or, as we might call it, the truth of beings, consists in their own imitation— the extent to which they are an image and likeness—of the supreme truth, which, we are told in *De veritate* 10, is the cause of the truth that is in the essence of things, that is, in the true being of beings.

If the truth of thinking involves the formation of likenesses of the things themselves, then in order to undermine, even while exploiting, the "simulative" character of a likeness and, thus, to exclude the possibility that human thought may be a mere fabrication of reality, true thinking must be thought to be *causally* based upon the impression on it made by the thing it is thinking insofar as the thing is itself a likeness of the supreme truth, that is, already has "truth" in it. Just as imagination has the ability to form images of the material realities it has seen with the bodily eye, reason must be claimed to have the capability to form likenesses that are not, according to Anselm, mere simulations, but rational "images" in the literal sense of impressions that the things themselves have made on thought as a result of the truth in their own being. This is what rational understanding is doing when it does what it ought to; that is, the "expression of the mind or reason," when true, is formed from a direct impression of the essence of the thing itself. Thus, for Anselm, the mind can have impressions of rational essences as definitively and as causally as it does of physical objects. This is why, for him, there are not "ideas" or "representations," but likenesses, imprints, images, that is, "effects," all of which suggest the way in which true thought is determined by the things themselves.

Consequently, the chapter on "the supreme truth," *De veritate* 10, extends the claim relevant to our present discussion, for after the teacher has insisted that this truth is the cause of all truth, the student has an insight:

> Teacher: Do you see how this rightness is the cause of all other truth and rightness, while nothing is the cause of it?
>
> Student: I do see, and notice that among these other truths some are only effects, whereas others are both causes and effects. For example, while the truth that is in the existence of things is the effect of the supreme truth, it is the cause of the truth of thought and of the truth in statements, but these two truths are not the cause of any truth. (S I, 190)

The extent of the connection between thought and reality, for Anselm, here becomes clear, as does the extent to which he has found a way to make what would appear to be an indirect presentation of things to thought, in the form of "likenesses" and "images," into the direct effect of reality upon thought. The images in thought that are the true likenesses of things are not simply the expression of the mind's own thinking but the direct result of a truth—that is, a likeness—which is already in the nature of the things themselves. It "causes" the truth of thought and of propositions, and is itself the direct "effect" of that supreme truth, which is, in turn, born as a likeness of the supreme being. In light of the divine paradigm, it must be clear that, like the second person of the Trinity, the greater the extent to which the human mind is able to duplicate the reality being thought in an image of it, the greater the extent to which it truly thinks. Indeed, for Anselm, this is precisely what it means to think, namely, to form likenesses of reality in the mind. And even if this suggests that human thought is twice removed from true being, we are still not altogether separated from it. Our attempt at a mental duplication of reality apparently involves a rather literal verisimilitude insofar as we aim to preserve whatever trace of the supreme truth may remain in the thought-formations of the imperfect thinkers that we are. Thus, whatever remains true in our thought is, for Anselm, to be regarded as a direct remnant of reality: of the chain of likenesses, of cause and effect, moving from the supreme reality to its perfect likeness in the supreme truth, then to its imperfect likeness in the essence of things, and, finally, from the rational nature of things to the rational impressions that our imperfect thought forms of them. In short, whatever truth human thought entertains is ultimately a matter of its preserving the "original" through intervening "likenesses."

If we now place this discussion back into the context of the *Monologion,* it must be obvious that the supreme truth refers to the rational preview of the things that are to be made that the divine reason enjoys prior to creation and that constitutes the truth in the "essence" of things which M 10 calls their "universal being." What may not as yet have struck us is that the result of the ontological reversal that thinks of the things themselves as "likenesses"—and thus of the argument required to make things in essence amenable to the likeness-formations of rational thought—is that Anselm must, in some sense, deny to creatures what he calls "true being." For the things that "in fact" exist, that have been made, inevitably enjoy the ontological status of "imitations," not of "originals"; of "images," not of "reality." This becomes clear in M 31, where we are told that

> . . . if, in some sense, the living man is said to be the true man, whereas in his portrait is the likeness or image of this truth, so the truth of existence is understood to be in the word whose being exists so supremely that, in a way, it alone exists; whereas in those things which, in their way, in comparison to it, do not exist—although they have been made in accord with it, and are made something through it—is considered to be something like an imitation of this supreme being. . . . Thus, it is evident that in the word, through which all things were created, there is no likeness of created things but is, rather, true and simple being; in the things that are created, however, there is not simple and absolute being, but a mere imitation of this true being. (S I, 49–50)

Needless to say, the denial of true being to creatures—indeed, the most radical claim made here, namely, that the "truth of existence," which is in the word, exists so truly that, in some sense, it alone exists—is again dependent upon the ontology of the image: upon the way a likeness has less being than that of which it is an image, even as the things themselves, in becoming a "mere imitation" of the true and sole original, are said, in some sense, not to exist. And while we will have to return to this claim about the supreme being alone enjoying true being, we should have been aware from the *Monologion's* initial arguments for the supreme good that this sort of reversal is inherent to Anselm's thinking about divinity—in this case, a conversion of the meaning of being that has already been effected by this point in the text but that we will have to backtrack, to those chapters between M 11 and M 31, to catch up with. It is this ontological conversion experience, ultimately captured in M 28, that prepares the way for the *Proslogion*. We are thus reserving consideration of it for our concluding treatment of the *Monologion,* with the hope that in so doing it will still be fresh in our minds when we have a look at Anselm's famous ontological argument.

For the moment, we might conclude our discussion of the epistemological implications of this ontological reversal that turns "the things themselves" into "likenesses" by returning to the topic that got us moving in this direction in the first place. If the thought (*ratio*) of the creator provides an order that guarantees the possibility that human reason has access to reality—that reasoning is not a merely human activity, a matter not simply of the human mind's own rational "expressions" of reality, but of the "impressions" of a rational reality upon it—then the conclusion to be drawn from all this is pronounced in M 34, as Anselm himself returns to the image of the artisan:

> But how can such different things, namely, the creating and created being, be expressed by a single word, especially since this word is coeternal with the speaker, whereas the creation is not coeternal therewith? Perhaps because it is itself the supreme wisdom and supreme reason, in which all that is made exists—the way that is made in accord with some art, not only when it is made, but before it is made and after it is destroyed, always exists with respect to the art itself, as nothing other than what the art itself is—in which case, when the supreme spirit expresses himself, he expresses all created beings. For before they were made and now that they have been created and after they are decayed or changed in any way, they are ever in him not what they are in themselves, but what he himself is. For in themselves they are a mutable being created according to immutable reason, while in him they are this primal being and the primal truth of existence, the more like to which created things in any way are, the more truly and excellently they exist. (S I, 53–54)

If creator and creation are "expressed" by a single word, it is nonetheless in different senses. While M 33 speaks of the second person of the Trinity as the "figure" (*figura*) or "image" (*imago*) or "imprint" (*caracter*) of the first, when M 9 thinks of God's relation to creatures, it speaks of their "model" (*exemplum*) or "pattern" (*forma*) or "rule" (*regula*). As it turns out, then, we may have been mislead by the original analogy in M 10, unless we noticed that the artisan is there spoken of as preconceiving his creations "according to his art."

Such a characterization of the nature of creation is not further clarified there, since it is the conception in the artist's mind that is primarily at issue. As the analogy proceeds, however, it becomes significant that God does not exactly envision what he is going to make. Instead, if the origin of the artwork is first and foremost based upon, and regulated by, those rules the craftsman must learn and follow, and that define, even predetermine, the nature of the work, then one can say that the works to be created always already have their primal being, "preexist," in the rules of the art, since they are the originating principles that make the existence of specific works possible. So, too, we are now told, if God is the supremely creative being, then the form or rule for the creation of creatures must already and coeternally be existent in him; not, however, as the pattern for any particular creatures, let alone as individual things, but as the formation rules that determine the grammar of creation in terms of the creator's own inherently linguistic self-conception. The latter is not created out of nothing, but is the very image of the creator himself; as if the model for creation were the likeness of what "he himself is," eternally "begotten," although not made, in his own rational self-image. As such, while the formation rules for creation are formulated in divine thought and are informed by the creator's own supremely rational self-expression, and while such principles predetermine the limits of all creation, it is in this sense alone that creatures may be said to preexist in God. Nonetheless, it is sufficient to provide the assurance that whatever is created will have a rational nature that constitutes its true and primal being and, consequently, that creatures will be subject to rational expression in the human mind thanks to the fact that, like God, human thought is also characterized by an essentially linguistic rationality.

If we now put the discussion of truth and of the primal word as the self-expression of God together with the claims made in M 10 about the nature of language and its treatment of those unspeakable words that Anselm regards as the basis of, and as common to, all spoken sign-systems, it should be clear that the inner vision involved in rational thinking is guided by the truth of the word, as a truth at the root of both the nature of things and of language. Human thought can apparently arrive at this truth by making its way from those signs that merely signify things indirectly to their universal significance, to that truth in the nature of things that can have a direct effect, indeed, a truth-effect upon the mind. The meaning of words is not dependent upon the signifying power of the sign or upon the relation of signs to one another in a system of signs, and not even in God's mind, since there is only one word through which he expresses all that is to be created. On the contrary, we could go so far as to say that, for Anselm, meaning is not even linked to words (*voces*) in the ordinary sense, but that signs enjoy whatever significance they do thanks to the expressive power of the mind. Consequently, "sign-sounds" must be tied to a primal meaning, an original word (*verbum*), which is so called not because it is verbal, a matter of sounds or signs, but because it is an expression (*locutio*) in the mind of the things themselves in the truth of their essential nature. This truth can be shared by all nations—that is, by all language-users—no matter which artificial sign-system they employ, thanks to the natural words that are a likeness of the things themselves. Ultimately, then, signs do not have significance simply by referring to things but with reference to the originally linguistic truth of things, to those ideal significations that are already embedded in the essence of things and can be expressed in human thought and language insofar as the things themselves are an imitation of the primal expression in the mind of God that is the one true word.

In effect, then, the human mind is put in a position to have access to rational essences through the nature of language. It ties divine and human thought together through the mediation of the word—once the reversal has set in on the basis of which what we ordinarily take to be "reality," namely, the things themselves (*res ipsa*), are shown to be the mere imitation of a primal locution that is the expression of a divine reason giving birth to an image of itself in its own thinking about the supreme reality it is. Thus, after its discussion of the natural word that founds all sign-languages, M 10 finally concludes by claiming that

> . . . no other word appears so similar to the reality whose word it is, or so expresses it, as does that likeness which is expressed in the acuteness of the vision of the mind in thinking the things themselves. It, then, is rightly to be called the most proper and primary word of the thing. Therefore, if no expression of any thing approximates the thing so closely as that which consists of words such as these, nor can there be something else so similar to the thing, whether in the future or now existing, in anyone's thought, it can, not inappropriately, be seen that such an expression of things existed with the supreme substance before their creation, that they might be created through it, and exists now that they have been made, so that they might be known through it. (S I, 25)

The concluding remark here is somewhat ambiguous. It certainly refers to God's knowledge in that he knows things, even now that they have been created, through this primal word, that is, not in their actuality, but in their ideality. It might, however, not only be applied to God, since our knowledge of things is also dependent upon this originary word. The expression of things in God's thought (*ratio*) provides the guarantee that reality has an essentially linguistic structure and, thus, that the things themselves are in essence subject to an inner locution in our mind in view of their rational being. The divine and supremely linguistic rationality guarantees that things can be known by us, can be truly envisioned in their expression by rational thinking in "the acute vision of the mind," even as our inner vision provides a model for divine thought. In a sense, then, the concluding remark of M 10 may be taken to refer both to us and to God if it turns out that all knowledge depends upon the part that the primal word plays in Anselm's visionary epistemology.[19]

Of course, the talk of the word existing with (*apud*) the supreme substance before creation, such that things might be created, and now that they have been created, that they might be known through it, is relevant first and foremost to God's thought. On the other hand, the divine mind has, from the start, been modeled on the artisan's "expression of the mind or reason," which allows him to envision a preconception of what is to be created. We would not want to forget that this entire chapter seems to exploit if not the confusion, then at least the intentional fusion of the nature of the human mind with that of the divine, in a kind of interlacing of divine and human thought designed to develop a certain ontological image of creatures as well as a specifically linguistic image of the mechanics of the mind. The sketching of this picture of divine and human thought and language has, in other words, been accomplished on the basis of a rather complex and ambiguous modeling of one on the other. At the same time, such an analogy between the divine and human would not itself be complete unless a certain characteristic reversal were allowed to set in.

As we have suggested, Anselm likes or perhaps needs to use such strategies in his thinking, and not just in the sort of analogical argument that involves, in the end, a kind of mutual modeling—in this case of divine on human thought and, perhaps not so obviously, human on divine thought—but in forms of argument that finally force a conversion that brings everything into a different light. We should not, then, be surprised to find M 32 turning the image, that is, the analogy, around, so as finally to make the image a reality through a tactical reversal in which divine thought turns out not to be "like" human thinking at all. Instead, the human mind will turn out to be an image of the divine:

> But how can it even be thought that the supreme wisdom at any time does not understand itself when the rational mind can not only be aware of itself but also of this supreme wisdom, and understand both it and itself. For if the human mind could have no awareness or understanding of itself or it, it could not

distinguish itself from irrational creatures, or [the supreme wisdom] from all its creatures, by silently debating with itself as my mind is now doing. Therefore, just as this supreme spirit is eternal, so it eternally remembers and understands itself after the likeness of the rational mind; or rather, on the contrary, not in likeness to anything, but principally, and the rational mind after its likeness. (S I, 51)

This reversal, hinged around the "on the contrary" (*immo*), which makes the human mind a likeness of God, not the other way around, and thus turns the analogy into a reality, is a tactical move in the structure of the text as it seeks clarification of the divine Trinity based on its "image" in the human mind, namely, on the tripartite philosophy of mind in which our memory, understanding, and will serve as an image in us of the three persons of the Trinity, as the "mirror" through which this "riddle" can be glimpsed. For our purposes, however, the critical remark here may be the one that is, perhaps, least noticeable, the one that claims that, by means of silent argumentation, as has been going on in the text thus far, the rational mind may be put in a position to discern the difference not only between itself and irrational creatures but also between God and the whole of creation. This distinction—for Anselm, the ontological difference *par excellence*—entails an even more dramatic reversal at work in the *Monologion,* a strategic reversal that has, in fact, just taken place in the text but that we have not yet seen, since, in pursuing God's theological nature, we have gotten a bit ahead of ourselves. Our leap ahead belongs to the structure of the text itself, since once the analogy between divine and human thought is introduced in M 10–11, its further discussion is expressly postponed and only taken up again in M 29. Until we backtrack to the chapters that intervene, namely, M 12–28, which develop the metaphysical nature of the supreme being, it will not be clear why Anselm insists that it is possible for the rational mind to distinguish God from the whole of creation and just how this is made possible by means of the sort of rational meditation the *Monologion* is.

❙ The Time-Spacelessness of God

One of the issues that will be of interest to us is how Anselm goes about producing his rational image of God; how, that is, he is able to bring a likeness of God before the eye of reason, even if our account of this will not always be in accord with what he would like to have us think. In mentioning the strategies of the *Monologion,* we might take note that, in general, there are two basic forms of thought at work in its rational reconstruction of God. The construction of a rational likeness of the supreme being proceeds, on the one hand, through a strategy of accumulation, which adds features a step at a time so as to accumulate the variety of characteristics that are to be associated with this being; and on the other hand, through a strategy of elevation, in which the rational mind is made to experience certain categorical shifts, sometimes based on reversals, sometimes on the violation of the very distinctions that have been drawn. As we will see, the latter tactic is required insofar as the rational vision of God is unlike the vision of anything else, in that as God does not have a "universal essence," since he is not a creature. As such, these two strategies go hand in hand; for as we are accumulating a rational conception of God, all those features must finally be clarified through a certain categorical elevation that brings them into a distinctive light, just as the arguments for the existence of the supreme being will not be complete until that reversal in the meaning of being has set in through which our ontological vision is ultimately corrected.

Effecting this reversal is critical not only to an appreciation of the *Monologion*'s view of the nature and existence of God but also to an understanding of how the argument of the *Proslogion* works, as it will involve getting clearer on just what Anselm thinks this supreme being is, or rather, on how it "is." For the question of the existence of God is more essentially related to the question of the nature of that existence than we might think, and, as we will try to show, to the power of the rational mind to distinguish the creator from all creatures. We have so far only begun to notice the contortions Anselm is willing to go through to achieve his rational vision of God. In fact, the extent of the twists and turns of thought, of the reversals and violations he is willing to make use of in his arguments, is nowhere more apparent than in M 12–28. There we find, especially in the culmination of the discussion in M 28, the clearest, or at least most penetrating, philosophical exposition that Anselm offers of the metaphysical nature of God, before, that is, turning to his theological treatment of the Trinity. And any number of fundamental patterns of argument that determine *Monologion*'s maze of reasoning can be discerned first in the deduction of God's time-spacelessness and second in the discussion it prepares us for of the radical reversal in M 28 that completes the rational reconstruction of Anselm's ontological image of God.

To arrive at the point at which the rational mind will be in a position to distinguish God from all else, we need to pursue the question of the nature of this "supreme being," which Anselm had been discussing before getting diverted into the question of his "word." After all, the latter issue was raised in M 10 to better understand the creation of beings from nothing. To treat the question of the relation between creator and creatures metaphysically rather than theologically will entail thinking through the distinction between being itself and those beings that have been made from nothing: thinking the difference, in other words, between "being" and "beings" by thinking through their relationship to one another. Consequently, to ask about the creator's relation to creation is, in part, to ask about his relation to space and time. Thus, any treatment of the difference between creator and creature, assuming that creation is a time-space event, would have to show how the creator is to be thought in contrast to and as distinct from spatiotemporal beings, as well as the extent to which the supreme being so thought is, nonetheless, to be conceived in relation to creation.

M 13 makes it clear that among the things that must be concluded from the discussion of the creation of creatures *ex nihilo* is not only that creatures are previewed in the thought of the creator but that, insofar as they arise from nothing and have their being through another, they are, and continue to be, only under the preserving and protective presence of that creatively present being (*creatricem praesentem essentiam*). In that case, insofar as the creator must preserve creation with his presence, he must be omnipresent—or, to use Anselm's term, everywhere. If the basic feature of the being of creatures requires that their being be founded upon the being of a being that exists through itself, then Anselm wants to make it clear that the dependency of beings upon the independence of the supreme being is not merely a matter of their having been created, as if at one time they needed this being, but no longer. Instead, if creatures are to "flourish," to survive and thrive in their being, they presently—that is, at all times—require that being's protective and sustaining presence.

Thus, the title of M 14 claims "That this being is in all and throughout all, and all things are from it, and through it, and in it." The chapter that follows this heading is worth citing in its entirety:

> But if this is so—indeed, because it is of necessity so—it follows that where [the supreme being] is not, nothing is. Therefore, it is everywhere, and throughout all, and in all. And since it is as absurd that a creature can in any way exceed the immensity of the creative and sustaining being as that the creative and sustaining being cannot in some way exceed the totality of what is created, it is clear that this being is what supports and surpasses, encompasses and pervades all others. If this is conjoined with what we earlier discovered, then there is some one that is in all and throughout all, and from which and through which and in which all are. (S I, 27)

Where this being is not, nothing is; one might say, if it did not risk its reification, that "nothing" beings came from and would return to were it not for the absolute presence of the supreme being. But just as there could be nothing where this being is not, wherever there is something, this being must be. Thus, the supreme being, whose nature we are still trying to envision, must be everywhere in the sense that it must be present throughout all that is and in all that is. It must be omnipresent in the literal sense that its preserving presence must be present to all that is present, to all that enjoys present existence.

At the same time, however, Anselm wants to insist that the preserving presence which belongs to the being of the supreme being, by means of which all beings enjoy whatever being they do, is not exhausted by its sustaining of them. Just as it is absurd that any creature should exceed that which creates and conserves it, so it would apparently be absurd to think that this omnipresent being was somehow limited to or by the totality of what it had created. In what sense the latter is obviously absurd is not made clear, although what does become clear, if we press Anselm's imagery, is that what he wants to conclude from all this is that we must think of the supreme being as supporting and surpassing, encompassing and pervading, what it has created. The creator somehow provides the foundation for beings, bears (*portat*) them, and yet exceeds them, abounds (*superat*) in the sense that it cannot be limited by them, although in its excessiveness somehow encloses (*claudit*) them, as if it surrounds them to set them in a limit, but in such a way that it penetrates (*penetrat)* them to the very core of their being.

I mention these conflated characterizations—supports, surpasses, encompasses, pervades—because the possibility for some one being (and it will be made clear later that we are talking about an "individual spirit" when we speak of the supreme being) enjoying these features depends upon a clarification of the metaphysical nature of such a being. Perhaps we should say that the illumination of the "essence of divinity" depends upon clarifying the kind of being that can possess the necessary characteristics. Anselm thinks that he can begin to do so by addressing the precise sense in which God may be said to be "everywhere." It must be clear from the start, however, that he will want to have it all ways at once. Anselm is not content to let the supreme being merely be beyond his creation, or, for that matter, in some way to preserve it from a distance with his "power" rather than his "presence." On the contrary, since God's power is nothing but his presence, even while the supreme being is apparently radically distinguishable from its creation, it is not separable from it.[20] The creator must not just create creatures but must permeate and embrace them all, be constantly and everywhere present to, even as it surpasses and exceeds, its creation.

This would not be so perplexing a claim were it not also clear that the supreme being must be utterly simple. Given its indivisible unity, it cannot pervade creation with a portion of its being so as to exceed it in some other respect. Instead, it must be completely and entirely both whatever and wherever it is. Thus, if God exists everywhere, he must be wholly everywhere, and always. Of course, one might think that the point would then have to be that the categories of space and time do not apply to such a being. And yet, I think it is fair to say that matters are not that straightforward; for, as we have suggested, Anselm tends to want to have it all ways at once. In the case in point, he insists upon applying what would appear to be the ultimate, even if somewhat paradoxical, spatiotemporal features to this supreme being that would characterize his distinctive existence in terms of a certain time-spacelessness whose abundance of space and time—we might almost say, excessive spatiotemporality— would nonetheless allow one to claim that God exists "everywhere" (*ubique*) and "always" (*semper*). And with good reason. For if spatiotemporal categories were simply irrelevant to God, it is not clear what his connection could be to creation.

While M 18 raises the question of the eternity (*aeternitas*) of God as the supreme truth, which it argues must be without beginning or end, such arguments are incidental for our present purposes, except perhaps to remind us that the claim to God's beginningless and endless being follows rather obviously from his existence *per se*. Instead, the difficulties concerning the creator's relation to space and time set in at M 20–24. There we find Anselm once again trying to have it both ways at once by claiming that in some sense God exists at all times without being limited by time, just as he is in some sense in every place, while in another sense he is no place. As we would by now have come to expect, Anselm intends to treat these issues by making certain distinctions, reviewing the various options, and drawing the appropriate conclusions. Part of the complication of his discussion in this respect, however, follows from the fact that he compounds the distinctions at issue as he goes along, presumably to make them more precise. But to begin with, Anselm simply distinguishes between what he regards as the three basic options:

> It was concluded above that this creative nature is everywhere, and is both in all and throughout all, and from the fact that it neither began nor will cease to be it follows that it always was and is and will be. Still, I detect a certain murmur of contradiction that compels me to investigate more diligently where and when it is. For the supreme being exists either everywhere and always, or only at some place and some time, or nowhere and never; which is to say: either in every, or in some specific, or in no place or time. (S I, 35)

It might seem to go without saying that Anselm would regard the first option as the obvious choice and the final option as clearly to be rejected. But there are some deep ambiguities that will need to be worked out before any such rejections can take place and the "murmur of contradiction" silenced. The first and last alternatives, as they are expressed here, have not as yet been sufficiently clarified. Indeed, in this passage, Anselm seems to be willing to identify what will later be distinguished as different options. Thus, he speaks here as if he were willing to identify being "everywhere" (*ubique*) with being "in every place" (*omni loco*), just as the passage would seem to imply that being "nowhere" (*nusquam*) is the same as being "in no place" (*nullo loco*). While Anselm does immediately insist that it is absurd to suggest that the supreme being exists nowhere never, he reserves the other option that could be distinguished here, namely, that he exists in no place at no time, for later clarification. Similarly, we must not assume that if Anselm is going to insist that God exists everywhere always that this will amount to the claim that he exists in every place and time, without further distinction or qualification.

What may seem unambiguously clear is that God cannot exist in some specific place and time. If the supreme being must be wherever anything is, so as to preserve whatever is, presumably including space and time, which are themselves "creatures," then if God existed in one place rather than another, there would be a place and time that existed—that is, something would exist—where God did not. And yet, if to be "in every place" is to be in some place, but not some place rather than another, then to be "everywhere" is to be in every "where." The problem this raises comes into view once we realize that the simplicity of God is not, for Anselm, a matter of some homogeneous unity, as if his being provided an underlying or undifferentiated medium of and for beings, and so might be said to be indistinguishably everywhere, but not, in any distinguishable sense, in every place. Anselm thinks that the supreme spirit is a distinct individual—and precisely in the sense that he is not an anonymous principle, not a "universal" common to many[21]—who can nonetheless somehow be wholly in each place, but not in one place rather or any more than in another. If God must be wherever anything is, then if anything is anywhere, or many things are in many wheres, God must be there. And while it would make no sense to think that God could be anywhere but where everything is,[22] we must be clear that for Anselm God is not just generically "everywhere," but specifically "in every place."

There is another way to approach this issue, from the reverse angle, by asking not whether God can be in one part of space (or time) rather than another, but whether part of God can be either in one part of space (or time), with another part of him in another part, or for that matter, whether part of God can be in all of space (or time) while another part of him is outside of space (or time). Here again, Anselm is unambiguously clear that God must be wholly wherever and whenever he is. Thus, if God is in every place and time, then he is *wholly* everywhere and always, that is, the whole of God must be there and then, and nowhere else at no other time. Of course, we could compound our problems by distinguishing the treatment of space from time and asking, for example, whether God can be at the same place at different times, or at different places at the same time, or at different places at different times—although having gone through the various options, it should be clear that we are destined to arrive at the conclusion that God exists wholly at all places at all times. Just as the simplicity of God entails that he cannot be divided by space—as if he existed in one place rather than another, or some part of him here, another part there—so, too, God cannot be "parted" by time, as if part of him existed now, other parts in the past or future. Instead, he must always be whatever he is now and must be it wholly wherever and whenever he may be said to be.

This conclusion, however, clearly creates complications of its own; for, under normal conditions, we hardly know what it would be to think of something that was "always everywhere," let alone something that existed "wholly" in every place and time. Indeed, the very options Anselm rejects seem to be the only ones we can ordinarily conceive of, spatiotemporally speaking. Obviously, we could imagine that something wholly existed in one place at one time and at another place at another time, or that its parts existed at a variety of places at any given time, not wholly at each, and so on. But it is difficult to imagine what it is to exist wholly everywhere and always, and mean by this that something must, as a whole, indeed, as the indivisibly simple whole it is claimed to be, always be in or at every place and time—especially if we are thinking of an individual thing, rather, say, than a collective event. So Anselm must try to avoid this difficulty by insisting that, just as it is appropriate to say that God exists everywhere and always, it is equally true to say that he exists in no place and at no time, which, however, must be distinguished from his existing nowhere never. In fact, Anselm somewhat paradoxically wants to insist that, in a sense, existing everywhere is precisely to exist no place, just as existing always is, in a sense, a matter of existing at no particular time, rather than another.

The key to thinking all of this is supposed to reside in the claim that God is not subject to the laws of space and time. This does not, however, mean that he altogether transcends the categories of space and time, although it certainly is designed to indicate that such a being is not constrained by the limitations that govern beings within the space-time universe. More importantly, Anselm's solution to the problem of the relation between this time-spaceless being and time-space beings requires the introduction of something like a categorical difference between God and everything else, suggesting that the distinction between creator and creature, that is, between the "supreme" being and all other beings, is not a difference merely of degree but of kind. That the distinguishing of God from the totality of creatures is to be achieved through such a category shift—indeed, through a kind of categorical elevation, perhaps even violation—begins to show through in M 22 in a discussion that concludes with the paradoxical talk about God's place being no place and his time no time:

> Perhaps the supreme nature exists in space or time in such a way [*quodam modo*] that it is not prohibited from being wholly at once in separate places or times so that there are not multiple wholes, but only one whole, even as its lifetime, which is nothing but true eternity, is not distributed across past, present, and future. For it appears that things are not bound by the laws of place or time unless they exist in place or time such that [*sic*] they do not transcend spatial extension or temporal duration. Thus, just as of things that are of such a kind [*huiusmodi*] it is said in all truth that one and the same whole cannot simultaneously be wholly in different places or times, this is not necessarily to be concluded concerning what is not of this kind. For it seems fair to say that a thing is some place only if that place contains its magnitude by circumscribing it and circumscribes its magnitude by containing it; and that a thing is only at some time if its duration time limits in some way by measuring and measures by limiting. Thus, that to whose extent or duration no bounds, either of space or time, can be opposed, to it no spatiality or temporality is truly proposed. For since space does not affect it as it does the spatial, or time the temporal, it is not unreasonable to say that no place is its place and no time its time. (S I, 39)

While Anselm may think that the concluding claim is not irrational, more is at issue in it than the mere denial of the limitations of space and time to God. The paradoxical talk of his "place" being "no place" and his "time" being "no time" does not deny the application of categories of space and time to the supreme being so much as it asserts them through a kind of double talk that "places" God no place and makes his "lifetime" timeless. Nor is this simply a matter of some word-play designed to boggle the mind. Instead, we should sense here the complexity, indeed, the perplexity, of the need to maintain something like space-time features as relevant to God, while denying them of him.

The above passage begins by proposing a way of explaining how it is that God exists in space and time, indicating that Anselm assumes that he does so exist, only without the limitations other beings have imposed upon them by the laws of space and time. The explanation is achieved, then, not by trying to render spatiotemporal categories irrelevant, but by claiming that they are anomalously—indeed, anomically—"applicable" in his unique case. Ironically, creatures will eventually end up losing their being—appear, in some sense, not to be, given their limited spatiotemporality—in comparison to God's ubiquitous eternity. At the moment, however, drawing too absolute a distinction between creator and creature might result in the irrelevance of the creator to its creation. While Anselm does, indeed, insist that God is not limited by space and time, this does not mean he can afford to let God simply transcend those categories. On the contrary, he wants to be able to think of the nature of the supreme being in terms of his being everywhere and always, even if he does so by insisting that "everywhere" is no particular place and "always" no specific time. Nonetheless, Anselm also wants to be able to conclude, as a result of this special pleading on behalf of God's categorical distinctiveness, that his relation to space and time must be "of its own sort," in which case—and only in his case—does it presumably make sense to say that while being everywhere and always, and in no place or time, he is also, wholly and simultaneously, in every place and time.

The preferred strategy that is to allow us to envision this entails the assertion of the categorical difference between being itself and all other beings, an assertion that elevates thought beyond the categories of space and time only to reapply those very categories in an elevated sense. This is presumed to offer a certain understanding of the relation between the "supreme being," which is "everywhere and always wholly," and the space-time universe. Of course, we might, at this point, be inclined to conclude that if God is the kind of being that is not subject to the laws of space and time, then, while it may well be true of things that are subject to those laws that "one and the same whole cannot exist simultaneously in different places or times," the fact that God is not of this kind does not mean that he can exist as a whole in different times and places. Instead, it may mean that not just the "laws," but the categories of space and time cannot be applied to him. Thus, for example, the fact that numbers or dreams are not the sort of things that can be limited by space might lead us to conclude not that they are "everywhere" but that they are nowhere—and in a different sense than Anselm wants to give the latter term. That is, we would mean by it that they are not subject to spatial categories.

In contrast to such an approach, Anselm seems to assume that while the "laws" of space and time do not apply to God—do not limit or bound him, as laws otherwise would—in some unique way applicable only to his case, the categories do. This is why he apparently feels free to alter the standard claims that would apply to space-time beings so as to suit a being that is explicitly said not to be of their kind. Thus, when Anselm says that God is "everywhere," it means precisely that he is in every place, even though he is nowhere; that is, it claims that God is limited to no particular place, *even while being wholly in it,* just as his being "always" entails being at all times, while measurable or determinable, let alone terminable, by no time. As M 22 concludes:

> In no place or time, then, is [the supreme being] properly [*proprie*] said to be, since it is not contained by anything else at all; and yet, in its own way [*suo quodam modo*], it can be said to be in every place or time, since whatever else exists is kept by its presence from falling into nothingness. It is in every place and time, because it is absent from none; and it is in none, because it has no place or time. Nor does it take upon itself distinctions of place or time such as here or there or somewhere, now or then or sometime; nor does it exist in this fleeting temporal present which we experience, nor in terms of the past or future did it or will it exist, since these are proper to [*propria*] those things which are finite and mutable, which it is not. And yet, something like these can, in a certain way, be said of it, since it is present to all that is finite and mutable, as if it were circumscribed by the same places and changed by the same times. Consequently, it is sufficiently evident, at least enough to dispel the note of contradiction, how the highest being of all exists everywhere and always, nowhere and never, that is, is in every and in no place or time, according to the harmonious truth of the various meanings. (S I, 41)

If we return now to our original options—that God is in all, some, or no place and time—the conclusion seems to be that all three are true of him, once properly understood. To say that God is everywhere is not to deny that he is in some particular place, wholly and entirely, since this, in his unique case, apparently does not exclude the possibility that he is also elsewhere, in some other, indeed every other place, and just as wholly and entirely. To the extent, however, to which he is not limited to any single place, he may be said to be in no place. But this is not to say that he is nowhere. Instead, it is precisely to claim that he is "everywhere," which is, according to the next chapter, more properly said of God than that he is "in every

place," although it is more the "in" than the "every" with which Anselm would take issue. Similarly, it is not so properly said that God
is "at every time" as that he is "always"—that is, at all times—insofar as, according to M 24, his perfect eternity entails his being all at
once as a whole (*totum simil*). And all this is not to say that God is
without place or time; or, it is to say this, but in an ambiguous fashion that still allows God to exist in some relation to the space-time
universe. By violating the very categories that would appear to be
at issue, by, in the name of the unique, sufficiently distorting those
categories, in applying them to a kind of being to which the laws
that define them are expressly said to be inapplicable, we arrive at a
"proper" conception of the supreme being that presumably accords
with its own distinctive way of being (*suo quodam modo*).

We have seen Anselm violate distinctions before and will see it
again; indeed, we have noticed it frequently enough to suggest that
there may be something like a strategy of violation at work in his
thought. In this regard, Anselm reveals his own awareness that he
is toying with a contradiction that is apparently necessary to make
his point about God's relation to the world. Strangely enough, he
also seems to be admitting that this dispelling of the threat of irra-
tionality has been achieved only to a degree, although sufficiently
for the purposes of showing that the paradoxical claim that God is
everywhere and nowhere, always and never, makes sense. Of course,
the contradiction would not seem so threatening were Anselm simply willing to disassociate God from the universe, leaving it at the
claim that God is not subject to categories of space and time. But he
does not. In fact, Anselm wants to connect his supreme being so intimately to the beings it creates that he goes so far as to say that while
the highest of all beings transcends space and time, it is, nonetheless, so closely associated with the time-space universe that it is as if
it were itself "circumscribed by the same places" and "changed by
the same times"—presumably in being present to, if not in them—as
are those creatures that are subject to the laws of space and time.
And while this may seem to be a bizarre claim (may even be written
off as the overstatement of a passing comment formulated explicitly
in terms of an "as if"), it shows the extremes to which Anselm must
go to keep a space-timeless God relevant to the universe of spatiotemporal beings, so as not to disjoin creator and creature. Consequently, rather than simply disassociating God from space and time,
Anselm insists, even as he denies that the supreme being is "in" either, that God may be said to be "with" space and time.[23] This is supposed to capture the intimate sense in which the supreme being,
even in its time-spacelessness, somehow remains in conjunction
with space and time. While not subject to the laws of space and time,

God must nonetheless remain in close contact with all that is by nature spatiotemporal. For it is critical that Anselm not create an absolute disjunction between creator and creature, at least not yet.

As we have suggested, Anselm is able to achieve all this through the crucial claim that in fact dominates and orients both passages we have cited from M 22: that God has whatever features he does "in a certain way of his own" and can enjoy what would appear to be at best paradoxical characteristics precisely because he is his own "kind" of being. Of course, this turns out to mean that the supreme being may be said to enjoy, albeit in his own way, features that apparently do not properly pertain to the kind of being it is. In the case in point, for example, we are asked to apply something like a spatial feature—or at least what is hard to think as anything but a sort of pseudo-spatial characterization, that is, "everywhere"—to a being that is claimed by its very nature to transcend space, that is, to be such that spatial features do not apply to it. And while this claim to the unique and proper implicitly acknowledges that such characterizations would appear to be inappropriate, even improper, if applied to anything else, it forms the basis for the contention that the absolutely distinctive kind of being God is not only allows for these sorts of paradoxical predications, but may even require them. This seems evident from Anselm's admission, in M 26, that no creature-feature, as it were, can be directly applied to God in that the difference between that which is whatever it is through itself and what is whatever it is through another is so vast that whatever God is is absolutely unique to him—although such a strategy may seem even more paradoxical later, when it will behoove Anselm to claim, somewhat at odds with the needs of the special pleading presently at issue, that we cannot know God "properly."

In any case, this will turn out to be why, to return to our earlier distinction, the strategy of accumulating features that apply to God must be complemented by a strategy of elevation, that transforms our understanding of how those features apply to him. For rational thought must ultimately transcend the categories it has made use of to clarify the supreme being, even if not always in the same way it has here "transcended" the categories of space and time. Still, we have now been alerted to the possibility that such elevation may be accomplished through a strategy of violation, that a kind of cognitive transcendence may occur through the categorical reversal of the distinctions that allow us to think about this "supreme being" as we both deny *and* apply creature-features to the creator. While we know that there must be some similarity between creator and creatures, since the latter are a likeness of that supreme truth, we also know that it is essential for Anselm that creatures be thought of as a likeness of God, not the other way around.

One way to achieve this inversion of our rather natural tendency to begin from that with which we are most familiar is to insist upon the categorical distinctiveness of God. While we may begin by considering the nature of creatures, as we did from the start of the *Monologion,* its constant clarification through talk of the "supreme" good or being, truth or life or wisdom, etc., will turn out not simply to be a matter of taking the relevant feature to the highest degree but of transforming our orientation so as to arrive at a clarity of insight that can only be achieved through a kind of mental conversion. And such an approach is well exemplified in the rather tortuous route Anselm must take to produce an account of God's relation to space and time. This is why we have tried to follow it so closely, although what may be most important about it is our deciphering of the strategies that allow him to arrive at the (so he insists, not irrational) conclusion he does. The employment of spatiotemporal notions with respect to the supreme being get pushed to the limit, such that while Anselm does not speak of "supreme" time or "supreme" space, as he does of the supreme good or the supreme being, talk of God's being "everywhere" and "always" is designed to have the same effect. Our familiar notions of space and time are pressed so far that, under such pressure, they are made to reverse themselves and, as such, are elevated, pushed to a higher order, that would appear, in certain respects, to serve to violate the very conceptions at issue.

Be that as it may, the application of the seemingly conflicting features we encountered earlier in thinking of God's relationship to his creation—that he surpasses yet permeates, encompasses yet penetrates the universe—is supposed to be rendered more intelligible by this attempt to elevate our thinking to a higher category in a kind of shifting of mental gears. This is not just a matter of pushing our understanding to the extreme but, in so doing, of enforcing the notion that what was first thought of as a difference in degree must ultimately become a difference in kind. As we try to conceive of a being of a different order than the beings it nonetheless stands in relation to, it may appear to make sense that such a being could be everywhere and yet nowhere, permeating the universe, and yet transcending it, somehow in every place, so intimately that it penetrates each and every being to the core of its being with its sustaining presence, and yet remains distinct from this universe of beings, distinct from everything else by being *categorically* different from it. And just as we arrive at this conception of what is "proper" to God by undergoing a kind of conversion of our normal understanding of beings, so, too, will we find that the clarification of the extraordinary being of the supreme being will result in a similar, even more radical reversal.

Whether, then, Anselm has satisfactorily resolved all the contradictions is less critical at this point than our awareness that we have seen certain strategies at work before in the *Monologion,* and that we will see them again, in all their power, at the moment of thought we must regard as the high point of this "meditation on the being of divinity." Our present discussion offers only a sample of the extremes to which Anselm is willing to go in his attempt to envision the unique and distinctive mode of being of a being that is categorically unlike all other beings. For the rational reconstruction of God at work in the text will come to turn upon even more fundamental categorical reversals and violations. If the only way to allow for the conflated characterizations of God's relation to the world is by assuming that he is of a different order of being than are beings, then the ultimate metaphysical vision of the supreme being will require an elevation of thought that allows it to sight the ontological difference between creator and creature at an even more radical extreme. In effect, the apparently and inherently paradoxical relation between God and his creation will eventually have to be resolved on the basis of a strategy through which all other beings begin to disappear in light of their ontological difference from the supreme being, and not just as a difference of degree or of kind, but insofar as God can be absolutely distinguished from everything else that is.

The Ontological Difference between Creator and Creature

The title of M 28 reads like a hallmark of the extremes to which Anselm must go in making out the rational reconstruction of our vision of God in the *Monologion* and of the way in which the mind's clarity in these matters requires a certain categorical elevation at whose dizzying heights the claims to contradiction can no longer be heard. The problems about the creator's relation to creation all tend to disappear along with those beings whose very being comes finally to be seen in a new light in view of the reversal in the meaning of being we have been reaching towards since M 1 began the battery of arguments leading to a supreme being. Indeed, the title of M 28 records the result of the maze of arguments and clarifications we have worked our way through as the ultimate conclusion we are to be drawing from them concerning the existence of God. After having insisted in M 27 that the absolute uniqueness of the supreme substance—that he is neither a "universal" common to many nor shares anything in common at all with anything else—justifies our regarding him as an individual substance, and better as spirit than as body, the chapter heading of M 28 proclaims: "That this spirit exists simply (*simpliciter sit*), and created beings, compared to it, do not exist." The chapter itself begins by elaborating this claim as the conclusion of the considerations developed thus far:

> It is seen to follow, then, from the foregoing, that this spirit, which exists in so wonderfully unique and uniquely wonderful a way of its own, in a certain sense alone exists, while others, howsoever they may appear to be, compared to it, do not exist. (S I, 45–46)

The radicalness of the ontological reversal at the heart of the *Monologion*'s rational vision of God could not be made any plainer than it is in this announcement of his absolutely unique existence. Put simply: God alone exists. This is, presumably, because he exists in so singularly marvelous and marvelously singular a way of his own that, compared to this measure of true being, nothing else can properly be said to be. Of course, it is not surprising to find that the sort of being that is and is whatever it is in a "way of its own"—a being that can exist everywhere and always as a single whole, who transcends all creatures and yet pervades them, surrounds the universe and yet permeates every being to the core of its being, whose simplicity is not parted by its existing in every place and time, nor is subject to change insofar as it is beyond space and time—would have to exist in a manner remarkably unlike other beings. Either that, or it could not be conceived to exist at all insofar as it would seem to violate the conditions set for the existence of those beings with which we are ordinarily familiar and from which we otherwise draw our measure of being. As such, the very possibility of such an extraordinary being must be secured through the ontological conversion on the basis of which it is claimed that it alone supplies the standard for what it means to be and, thus, is not subject to the conditions of existence to which other beings are. On the contrary, since apparently all other beings are subject to such conditions, they "in some sense," namely, in light of the meaning of being supplied by this supreme being, do not exist.

Obviously, Anselm thinks that he has justifiably arrived at this extreme conclusion, indeed, that it follows from what he has been arguing all along. As its opening line suggests, M 28 offers the consummation of the *Monologion*'s reasoning about the nature of the existence of God, condensing the result of all that Anselm has been claiming into a final flurry of metaphysical thinking, before taking up at the outset of the next chapter the theological question of the Trinity. The latter topic was, we will recall, first introduced in M 9–11 in view of the question of how beings are created from nothing, but its discussion is postponed in M 12 precisely because it requires further clarification of the nature of the supreme being. In fact, it requires the reversal in the meaning of being at work in M 28.

With that discussion in mind, however, and because Anselm never wants to appear unreasonable, he immediately moderates the radical claim that begins M 28 while continuing to insist upon it. Thus, he proceeds to repair the damage that may be done by this extreme to which the chapter has taken us, appearing to take back, to some extent, what it has just claimed, so as not to leave matters hanging in the lurch of this ontological reversal in which beings cease to be regarded as being in view of the strong measure of being that the supreme being imposes. This does not mean that he has abandoned the radical posture that claims that God alone exists, but that he would seem to be concealing its extremity by admitting that, in some sense, beings do exist, even if, in another sense, only God truly is. Consequently, M 28 continues, after the shock and beauty of its initial claim, to clarify both what it means to say that God exists and the sense in which beings other than God may be said to be:

> For, if one attends intently [to the matter], it will be seen that this spirit alone exists simply, and perfectly, and absolutely, while all others will appear almost nonexistent and scarcely to exist at all. For since, on account of its immutable eternity, it can in no way be said of this spirit that, according to some alteration, it was or will be, but simply that it is, neither is it, by changing, anything which at any time it either was not or will not be, nor is it not at any time what it was or will be, but is whatever it is once and for all, and interminably—since, I say, its being is of this kind, it is fairly said that it exists simply and absolutely and perfectly.
>
> Since, however, all others, in some respect and at some time and by changing, either were or will be what they now are not, or are now what at some time they were not or will not be, and since what they were is not now, just as what they will be is not yet, and what they are in this fleeting and most brief and barely existing present barely exists—since, therefore, they exist so mutably, it is not unfitting to deny that they exist simply, and perfectly, and absolutely, and to insist that they are almost nonexistent and scarcely exist at all. (S I, 46)

Apparently the concentrated effort required to glimpse the nature of the existence of God is not unconnected to the diligent attention necessary to follow the arguments for his timeless ubiquity. Not only are those arguments what started us on the path to this extreme, but their conclusion is being put to use here to distinguish the "immutable eternity" of God's absolute presence from the "fleeting" temporality of those beings that "barely exist" precisely because they exist in the "brief and barely existing present" of time, rather than in the eternal and "interminable" present that characterizes the lifetime of a being that simply "is," and so is what it is, once and for all (*semel et simul*).

Of course, the difference between these two types of being has been with us, in some form or other, ever since Anselm announced in M 6 that what exists through itself and what exists through another are not susceptible to the same standard of existence. To appreciate, however, just what is at issue in the attempt in M 28 to think our way around beings in order to get a glimpse of God, we will have to follow out the traces of that strategic conversion we have seen at work from the beginning of the text, so as to specify in somewhat greater detail how it works in the critical case of Anselm's drawing of the classical distinction between "being itself" and "beings," or, as it would be put in his account of the ontological difference, between "creator" and "creature." Most importantly, we must not allow the reinstatement of beings to distract us from the moment of the reversal itself, since the ontological disappearance of beings, as we might call it, must precede their reappearance as existing, but "barely." We must first concentrate, in other words, not on the results of the reversal, but upon the achievement of that moment of conversion during which God alone exists.

To do so, we must attend to how Anselm has gone about, despite the long preparation, rather suddenly distinguishing God from all else, so as to set the ontological standard in terms of which beings may be reinstated in their being, but as "hardly existing at all." Needless to say, in thinking of beings as not being, one might assume that they are simply returning in thought to the nothingness from which, according to M 7–11, they came, just as a certain elevation of the mind, which positions us for this view of them, has already taken place in the category shift, at issue in M 13–24, that is supposed to allow us to conceive of something as everywhere and always wholly. Such a characterization, which eventually forces us to think of God as his own kind of being, indeed, as M 26–27 would have it, as a kind of his own, sets the stage for the ontological conversion that reverses the meaning of being and, in so doing, radically distinguishes the supreme being from all other beings. To a certain extent, then, these categorical clarifications have been at work throughout the whole of the *Monologion,* including in its discussion of the various degrees of being, which were always essentially differences in kind. But something even more stunning is going on in M 28, quite different from a mere continuation of the scale of beings or goods that earlier aimed to arrive at the supreme being and highest good. Nor is this scaling of the wall of beings, presumably to have a look at what is on the other side, ultimately achieved by simply making a further categorical distinction, since M 28 instead takes us to what might be called the ultimate difference. And like Anselm's approach to dealing with God's relation to space and time, namely, through the violation of those categories, this ultimate ontological difference turns out to be a difference that ends all differences: a difference so different that, in drawing it, the difference itself would seem to disappear.

It may not be easy to appreciate the peculiarity of the distinction that is being made out here, especially insofar as Anselm would appear to be moderating its extremity even while it is being drawn. What we must try to impress upon ourselves, however, is that Anselm clearly does not think that he can express the claim he needs to make simply by insisting that God exists to a greater degree than do other beings nor, for that matter, by merely claiming that he has a different kind of being. Instead, the being of the supreme being must be so extremely different that it can only be adequately articulated by asserting that God alone exists, and exists in so absolutely unique and uniquely absolute a manner of his own that, compared to him, other beings do not exist. Only this claim is strong enough both to capture what Anselm has been arguing all along about the ontological distinctiveness of God and to put him in a position in M 29 to pursue his account of the Trinity.

In this respect, the argument of the *Monologion* as a whole may be said to pivot around the ontological insight of M 28. It alone allows the text to shift from metaphysical to theological concerns insofar as Anselm's rationalization of trinitarian doctrine depends upon the reversal that turns beings into a mere "imitation" of being, and precisely because their "true being" can be shown to be located not in their actual existence, but in their eternal essence, in which resides their greatest "likeness" to the supreme being. To arrive at such an understanding of the truth of the being of beings, however, we must go by way of the ontological conversion of the meaning of being at work in M 28. The *Monologion*'s insistence that creatures are an imperfect likeness of that perfect likeness which is the thought the creator has of itself first requires the drawing of a distinction on the basis of which the concrete existence of things turns out to be nothing, in which case, we must seek their "being" elsewhere, namely in their universal essence (*essentia*), which is more like the thought a mind would have of them than is their factual existence. Consequently, a certain nullification of the existence of beings is required before it can be argued that the "truth of existence" (*veritas existendi*) lies in the word of God, that is, in the primal being that beings enjoy prior to their existence in the thought of their maker and that now resides in their essence.

As elegant as this overall argument may appear to be, precisely what is so awkward about it is the way in which it requires Anselm to treat the ontological difference between the supreme being and all other beings as if it were an absolute rather than a relative difference. While he cannot afford to deny the relationship between "being itself" and the beings it creates, since this is where he must start, and while he cannot altogether avoid the relative nature of any relation, including a relation of difference, insofar as difference is itself a relation between what differs, he does the next best thing and reverses the relation, but in a reversal that must incorporate into it the element of denial, of negation, of nihilation, as it forces one aspect of the relation to disappear in its difference from the other. This appears to absolutize the other aspect, as well as the difference itself, precisely by defeating it as a difference. Not only, then, is the difference between creator and creature to be regarded as absolutely distinctive insofar as it is the most different difference that can be thought, but this ultimate difference is to be thought through the obliteration of the difference on the basis of which it presumably has been thought. Through a kind of self-violation, the difference is taken to such an extreme that it recoils back upon itself, so that one of its two elements effectively disappears into the difference between them.

In that event, however, the ontological difference has become so extreme—the difference, to put it simply, between being and beings has become so vast—that there may no longer appear to be any difference at all insofar as beings cease to be thought of as being, that is, they cease, at least in thought, to be. To this extent, we may seem to be left with only one side of the difference, absolutely distinguished not so much from the other but in itself, when this has all been achieved through the other, albeit in a strange kind of defeating of its difference. The conversion of thought at issue here does not simply serve to distinguish being from beings so as to attribute true being to the former. In simultaneously denying true being to the latter, this reversal allows being to form a whole of its own out of a difference of which it is, in fact, originally a part. And all of this comes as a result of the disappearance of beings into the abysmal difference that has opened up between them and the supreme being— through, we might say, the ontological departure of beings into the original parting of being and beings. In short, "being" first appears as part of a difference through which, however, it eventually becomes "itself" only insofar as its counterpart, namely, beings, vanishes.[24]

While Anselm may appear to be moderating the extremity of his claim in conceding some measure of being to beings, he is simply using beings, as he must, to make out the difference into which they are to disappear. If being must be thought in its difference from beings, then for beings to disappear into this difference, they must nonetheless be maintained in their difference from being if the distinction is to be drawn into which they vanish. In order to stabilize this movement of thought that would attempt to think God on the basis of a disappearing difference—for when beings disappear, so does the difference between being and beings, that is, so construed, the ontological difference ultimately disappears into itself—beings must be reinstated in some form of being, if only to establish the difference on the basis of which they remain subject to obliteration. While Anselm may go on to reinstate beings after the insistence upon their nothingness, this restoration of the being of beings can only take place after the reversal that denies them being. When beings reappear as "hardly existing at all," they are appearing under the conditions of the conversion of the meaning of being. As we have said, they are now subject to a second conversion in which their "being" is regarded as residing in their eternal essence, not in their temporal existence.

In this ultimate application of the strategy of conversion, a difference is established that, when pursued intently enough, overcomes itself by pushing its elements to such an extreme that the one is obliterated while the other is left to stand alone. The latter element is now distinguished, but without difference, from the former element, which has been extinguished in light of the very difference one would have supposed both elements would be required to make out. In so overcoming their difference, being becomes "supreme" in its now strangely nonrelative supremacy over beings. In that event, however, the sovereignty of being would appear to be founded upon a logic of suppression, insofar as one side of the ontological difference must somehow be both included and excluded. Beings must appear in contrast to the supreme being not only so as to distinguish being from beings, but so that, at the extreme, beings will disappear against the authoritative measure supplied by being itself, only to reappear again out of the reversal in the meaning of being in order to stabilize a difference that itself would otherwise disappear were it not maintained in this ontological interpretation of the nothingness of beings.

We cannot afford to pause here, although we will later, to raise the question of whether, in fact, this ultimate ontological difference does not have behind it, or perhaps hidden within it, an even more ultimate and even more obviously disappearing difference upon which it depends, a "preontological" difference in which being is thought, as it has been virtually from the beginning of the Western philosophical tradition, on the basis of its unthinkable difference from "nothing." That the distinction between being itself and all other beings in Anselm's creationist metaphysics hinges on the nothingness from which creatures presumably were created and to which such temporal beings inevitably will return, might well suggest this, as would the basic strategy that, as we will try to show, ultimately conceives of the being of the creator through the nothingness of creation. Suffice it to say, for now, that Anselm has designed the ontological difference so that in drawing the distinction between the supreme being and all other beings, beings do not just enjoy less being but cease to be thinkable as being at all. The aim is to produce an absolute difference in which all relativity has been obliterated by projecting a rather literal vanishing point, not where the two elements of the difference meet, but where, as they approach one another in infinity, one element is projected to diminish to such an extent that by the time we reach the point of comparison, it will no longer be there.

The question remains just what we are to make—and what Anselm has made—of this strange kind of disappearing difference and of the cognitive vanishing act in which God is distinguished from the whole of creation insofar as the latter is extinguished in thought by presenting the rational mind with a distinction that, when rigorously clarified, disappears into itself. Put more generally, we will eventually have to ask how far reason can get by taking away with one hand what it has given with the other, or whether the incessant employment of such a tactic does not threaten us with a certain unintelligibility—and one of a deeper sort than Anselm is admitting in his repeated defense of the apparent inconsistencies. Nor can we exclude the possibility that Anselm may be operating not so much out of the fear that he might not be making sense as out of the conviction that what he is trying to think ultimately requires that he undercut or "overload" whatever sense he has made. And if, soon enough, the text explicitly enters into the domain of the incomprehensible in its treatment of the Trinity, where Anselm will announce in M 65 that we can only see through "mirrors" and "riddles," there is no reason to believe that he will elsewhere shy away from the incomprehensibility to which he seems to be attracted and which he has a tendency to defuse by admitting. For it is critical to the strategy of both the *Monologion* and the *Proslogion* that the logic of Anselm's overall procedure requires a confession of the limitation of whatever vision is accomplished based upon this element of divine incomprehensibility, in an argument to the effect that God cannot exactly be seen in the rational image the texts have produced of him, indeed, that he is "both seen and not seen" by the rational mind that seeks a vision of God.

Our present point, however, is that a certain vision does, indeed, accompany these riddles and paradoxes with which we have been assaulted. The rational mind is not only being put to work in the oddest sorts of ways but also is being manipulated in a rather specific manner through the drawing of an ultimately self-defeating difference. Of course, one might wonder in what better way rational thought could catch sight of God than by means of the ontological obliteration of those creatures that stand in the way of our view of their creator, by contemplating the creator in the absence of creation, and thanks to the most radical distinction reason can make out between the supreme being and the whole of beings. While it remains to be seen whether rational thinking can afford to proceed by defeating the differences it has drawn, it is not impossible that the final resting place of reason resides in this strange obliteration of all differences, or at least that reason would find itself in a rather unusual position when forced to draw such "ultimate" distinctions. Certainly the form of mental elevation at work here is not entirely unlike the way in which negative theology achieves its mystical elations through a paradoxical strategy that must both invoke and deny, express and suppress, a difference at one and the same time. Just as the *via negativa* needs the "divine name" that does not apply—so that it can rise above it by means of negation in its elevation to that which is beyond all names and the distinctions upon which they depend—Anselm works from distinctions that he ultimately aims to defeat, depends upon differences he violates, and works off of contrasts he will finally want to repress. In both cases, the strategic misapplication or violation of terms produces certain cognitive contortions, not to say distortions, that must be taking place in the rational mind undergoing these profound reversals, which are effected by pushing a distinction to such an extreme that it recoils back to destroy itself, without, however, appearing to be altogether self-defeating.

In what it would seem fair to call Anselm's negative ontology, in the tactical maneuvers involved in his attempt to think being without beings—and that means to think the supreme being by means of the ontological annulment of beings—a certain alteration of our inner vision is accomplished through the rational violence of these cognitive violations. In the mental event not just of disrupting or even interrupting the normal train of thought, but of rupturing rational thought at its very seams, the banks for the flow of thought that distinctions provide are allowed to overflow, but in an elevation of thought that is nonetheless kept in close control. Such an expansion of the mind occurs in the radical reversal at work in M 28, when reason is called upon to try to envision the ontological absence of beings and is forced into the sort of empty vision that would ultimately be incited by a self-defeating difference. Moreover, it is no coincidence that a certain dispersion of thought has already taken place in preparation for this conclusion in our thinking about the omnipresence of God. The attempt to envision something that is everywhere but nowhere, "whose place is no-place and time no-time," does not just involve the categorical elevation achieved through paradoxical negations but invites a rather literal expansion of thought. As we will develop in some detail in our discussion of the vision of God in the *Proslogion,* a kind of "defocusing" of our mental vision, a "dilation" of the eye of the mind in an extension of our normal focus of attention, is called for in the attempt to sight what is everywhere and always wholly insofar as it is not subject to the specificity of definable space-time limits. As the rational mind strives to entertain in the vision of its thinking a mental image of what is "everywhere," it loses a focal center, which is why it must simultaneously think of it as "nowhere," that is, as without determinable limits. In that case, however, as well as in the not so apparent employment of contradiction, as in speaking of a "perfect likeness" or of an "absolute being," the rupture is so controlled, the disruption or breaching of the distinction so subdued, that we may not even notice the dislocations of thought. And this is certainly no less true of the violence of the disruptive reversal in M 28, whose disturbing result—that God alone exists—is immediately moderated through the restitution of beings after their ontological disappearance.[25]

While we may still not be clear just how we can make out a difference once it has been obliterated, such a strategy for thinking God should come as no surprise. As M 26 begins to suggest, to think such an extreme being on the basis of the "names" derived from other beings, human rationality would have to exceed its normal categories of thought as surely as the creator exceeds his creation, even while inevitably needing to think in terms of these categories. Consequently, such a moment of rational excess is, in multiple senses, a moment of the most excessive rationality: the moment when the train of reasoning that has lead us to this point culminates in a thought that demands we exceed our ordinary categories of thinking. The chain of interconnected arguments that lays the track of thought to be followed by the rational meditator is destined for a thought that can only be thought by effectively disrupting our normal distinctions, but as the most rational conclusion that can be drawn in a moment of rational excess. In this way, the perspicuous gaze of the eye of the mind is both converted—redirected toward its proper object—and opened or extended in its vision through a strategic interruption of thought that occurs at the moment of the reversal in the meaning of being.

At this critical point, we are asked to think being in and through the ontological vacancy left by the departure of beings, which is itself incited by a kind of interruption of thought, indeed, by a rather literal "inter-ruption," insofar as the distinction we thought we were drawing ultimately ruptures itself. At the same time, this specific procedure for securing a vision of the supreme being is not simply a matter of directing the eye of reason to its proper object by distinguishing God from the whole of creation. For, in a strange way, God does not exactly appear in this vision. At best, we catch a glimpse of him out of the corner of the eye of the mind, while we are "turning," in the dizzying reversal which is itself moderated as quickly as we are assaulted by it and is stabilized through a vision of the creator in his reverse image: in the negative image that creatures alone can provide. And the point is to put us in a position to effect yet another mental conversion that aims to convert this negative vision of beings into a positive vision of God in an attempt to project a rational likeness of the supreme being through a converted image of creatures.

There can be no doubt that Anselm's aim is not just to glimpse the creator in the vanishing of creation but to secure his vision of the supreme being in the nothingness of creatures. In this sense, he is quite literally attempting to contemplate the creator in the absence of creation, albeit as a kind of ontological absence: in view of the lack of being that creatures may be seen to possess. The imbalance this creates, especially at the height to which Anselm has taken it, is clearly—or, tellingly enough, not so clearly—articulated in the awkward claim that creatures "hardly exist and are almost non-existent." Indeed, the inelegance of such a characterization of beings stands in stark contrast to the elegant talk of what "exists in so wonderfully unique and uniquely wonderful a way of its own" that begins M 28. The chapter concludes by reasserting the position that would have it both ways at once:

> Again, since all beings which are other than this [spirit] have come from nonbeing to being not through themselves, but through another, and since they would return from being to nonbeing, as far as their own power is concerned, unless they were sustained through another, how would it be fitting for them to exist simply, or perfectly, or absolutely rather than scarcely existing or almost not existing? And if the existence of this sole ineffable spirit can in no way be understood either to have begun from nonbeing or to be subject to any faltering from what it is into nonbeing, and if whatever it is it is not through another but through itself (that is, through that which it itself

is), is not such an existence rightly alone understood to be simple and complete and absolute? Surely what so unconditionally and alone, in every way, exists perfectly, simply, and absolutely, can, in a certain way, fairly be said alone to exist. By contrast, whatever, according to the above reasoning, is known to exist neither simply nor perfectly nor absolutely, but scarcely to exist at all, or almost not to exist, is, in a certain respect, rightly said not to exist. According to this reasoning, then, the creator-spirit alone exists, and all creatures do not exist. Still, they are not altogether nonexistent, since through that which alone exists absolutely, they have, from nothing, been made [into] something. (S I, 46)

M 29 will return to the question, postponed in M 12, of just how beings were made "from nothing," that is, through the "expression" of the supreme being, which is here designated as the "creator-spirit" to prepare us for the upcoming considerations. As we already know, the text will now indulge in a long and detailed discussion of the way in which the divine mind begets its own image of what it will create not in relation to an other, but in its own absolute self-relation, as Anselm's negative ontology quickly covers its tracks with a more positive theology. We, of course, have tried to reorder the priorities and have paused where Anselm wants to proceed, so as to show how his later discussion of beings as a kind of imitation of being must have embedded into it the strange reversal in the meaning of being of M 28. This inversion of our thinking about being may seem reasonable enough so long as we do not watch for the moment in which it first occurs—the moment when God alone exists—but are distracted by the reinstatement of beings, not to mention the explication of their creation in light of trinitarian doctrine. For beings continue to appear, however invisibly, in light of the repressive difference we have seen at work in Anselm's conversion of the meaning of being in that their reappearance as creatures reinstates them precisely under the conditions of their ontological suppression.

All of this should now be quite clear in the above passage, which incorporates into it the reversal that denies being to beings, only to reinstate them in their "almost not existing." What may not be so obvious, however, is the way the elevation of the supreme being to the status of its wondrous supremacy has come at a cost that, at some point, will have to be paid. The excessiveness of Anselm's negative ontology shows up most evidently in the barely detectable conclusion that will, eventually, have to be drawn from the *Monologion:* that, properly speaking, "being" applies to nothing at all.

To see how we are forced in the direction of this at present scarcely imaginable conclusion, we must recall that, from the beginning of the text, we have taken the being of those beings whose being is here put into question for granted; and now, it would seem, in the reversal, we have no right to do so. This is a kind of kicking out from under us of the ladder that allowed us to climb to this height. What we must notice here, however, is that we have achieved this scaling of the wall of being by standing still. While the ascent to the supreme being begins from those beings that we ordinarily take for granted, it creates a scale of being on which those very beings later weigh in as not being. In a sense, then, we have not ascended so much as beings have declined right before our rational eyes, as we have arrived at the supremacy of being through a demeaning of beings that allows us to get them out of the way of reason's sight, and not just by grading them as lower on the scale of being but by degrading them in an ultimate ontological degradation, in which they disappear altogether—or almost.

Of course, after this reversal that diminishes the ontological claim that beings make on us to nothing so as to clear the way for a vision of being, they must be reinstated and regraded so as to reestablish some support, however weak, based on what Anselm regards as the true grading. In that case, however, beings are graded and scaled in their being on the basis of that moment of ontological degradation which has always preceded their reappearance as "hardly existing at all." M 28 makes clear that this ontological failure of beings to make the grade is not ultimately a matter of their merely being degraded to a level of lesser being, but of their slipping away altogether insofar as they can supply us with no true standard of being, or at least none that belongs to them as their own. Instead, all rightful claims to being are placed outside of them, even to the point of locating whatever being they may be said to enjoy in that truth of being which properly belongs not to their concrete existence, but to their universal essence. In that case, it would appear, at least as far as reason's eye can see, that creatures may best reveal their creator by fading from sight.

While it has become clear that beings lack true being, the claim—always most essential for Anselm—about the absolutely unique nature and existence of God leaves us in an equally awkward position when it comes to thinking of the supreme being, and all the more so now that the existence of creatures has proven to be so incomparable to it. The being of God is apparently so distinctive that it is beyond comparison with any other being; that is, God enjoys such an extreme being that, ultimately, even the term "being" does not properly apply to him. Of course, Anselm has warned us about the obvious cases of relative predication (of those features that are applied to God only relative to creatures) although, in a less visible way, the fear of relativity is beginning to seep in at all levels. The *Monologion* must eventually try to secure the absoluteness of the

absolute being by questioning whether any features that beings
have, including the feature of being, can properly be applied to a god
who is so incomparable to them. This is perhaps the most extreme
indication of the way the category shifts—which achieve a sense of
elevation, of rupture, and (as will become clearer in the *Proslogion*)
of rapture—are effected so as never exactly to arrive at any conception of God, or, at best, to arrive at the conception of a god to whom
none of the features attributed to him properly apply. And the tactical duplicity involved in this need to take back with one hand what
has just been offered with the other is nowhere more apparent than
in the conclusion that would presumably have to be drawn from the
Monologion as a whole: that being neither "truly" applies to creatures nor "properly" applies to God.

M 65 underscores our point in raising the question of how we
can know anything about this "ineffable" spirit, as M 28 called it,
that exceeds all human understanding:

> What then? Have we, in a certain way, discovered something
> about this incomprehensible object, while, in another, seen
> nothing of it? For we often speak of many things that we do not
> properly (*proprie*) express as they are, but signify through an-
> other (*per aliud*) that which we either will not or cannot prop-
> erly express, as when we speak in riddles. And often as we see
> something not properly, in the way the thing itself is, but
> through some likeness or image, as when we look upon
> someone's face in a mirror. In this way we often express and do
> not express, see and do not see, one and the same thing. We see
> and express it through another, but do not see and do not ex-
> press it through its own proper character. For this reason,
> nothing precludes the truth of our discussion thus far concern-
> ing the supreme nature, and yet it itself remains no less inef-
> fable if we consider not that it has been expressed according to
> the peculiar nature of its own being, but somehow designated
> through another. For whatever names seem as if they can be
> said of this nature do not reveal it to me in its own proper char-
> acter, but hint at it through some likeness. For when I think
> the meaning of these terms, I more readily conceive in my mind
> of that which I see in created things than of that which I under-
> stand to transcend all human understanding. For it is some-
> thing much less, indeed, something far different that is formed
> in my mind through these meanings than that toward which
> my mind, by means of these tenuous significations, is striving
> to advance in order to understand. For neither the name "wis-
> dom" is sufficient to reveal to me that through which all things
> are made from nothing and are preserved from nothingness,
> nor is the term "being" able to express to me that which
> through its unique loftiness is far above all others and through
> its peculiar character is beyond all. In such a way, then, is this
> nature ineffable, since words can in no manner express it as it
> is, and yet it is not false if, by leading reason to it through an-

other, as in a riddle, something can be approximated concerning it. (S I, 76–77)

All of this is claimed in the name of the proper, of the unique distinctiveness and distinctive uniqueness of God, which, apparently, despite the fact that language is itself grounded in his primal word, leaves us without a proper name for him, that is, a name that can designate him "as he is." Of course, the immediate occasion for the discussion of our not expressing something "properly" (*proprie*)— envisioning it in terms of its own peculiar character (*proprium*)— arises as a result of the way in which Anselm has had to articulate the mysterious riddle of the tri-unity of God through another (*per aliud*), namely, in its mirror image in human being. The birth of the word in God has been modeled on a mind thinking of itself, even as the unity of the three persons of God find their image in the unity of memory, understanding, and will in our own mental lives. But Anselm mixes the talk about the mystery of the supreme "wisdom" with, one must now suppose, the equally enigmatic talk of the supreme "being." Neither term apparently applies to God properly, even if it may be less obvious that the enigma of being has itself been clarified in and through the dark mirror of beings: in a vanishing act whose technical maneuvers may not be as analogous to the way in which the supreme wisdom is reflected though the mirror image of God in the mental life of human beings as Anselm here pretends.

It is no little irony that Anselm admits that he has had to revert to mirrors to show us a rationally reconstructed image of his god. Needless to say, he does not mean by this that it has all been a trick, that he has done it all with mirrors, but that God has only been seen through a looking glass (*in speculo*), and darkly (*in aenigmate*). For Anselm, these dark images presumably have some natural connection with the reality at issue such that, through another, we may catch an enigmatic, although nonetheless true, glimpse of God, in a vision of him in the dark, or at least in the shadows. It is also ironic that Anselm would now prefer to stress the extent to which such images are simulacra rather than a direct impression of the reality itself. He seems once again to be intent upon exploiting the peculiar ontology of the image in its essentially ambiguous character as both like and unlike that of which it is a likeness. Admittedly, one may claim that he is, by his own account, justified in having it both ways, since even if our mental images are, for him, the direct "impression" of reality, the reality of which we have an impression is the reality of creatures, which is itself an "imitation" whose "likeness" in thought, consequently, is the likeness of a likeness of God and thus twice removed from the supreme reality. More interesting to us, however, is the way in which Anselm's own exploitation of the image of seeing the face of someone in a mirror inadvertently characterizes his basic ontological tactic of glimpsing the being of the creator not only in the mirror of creatures but, in that case, through a reverse image that is admittedly obscure.

Anselm's convoluted strategy is nowhere more apparent than in its insistence upon these two extreme claims: that when it comes to "true being" only God has it, in which case beings enjoy whatever being they do only thanks to God; and, yet, when it comes to speaking "properly" of something, no name, not even "being," applies to God. But where does this leave us, for whom apparently the term "being" truly and properly applies to nothing? Where are we to get our understanding of being? The answer is: in the moment of conversion, as a reversal that occurs "between" being and beings, that is, in the withdrawal of the being of beings, without the appearance of what is apparently beyond being or, rather, of what can only appear in its negative image in the distortion of being in beings. As such, our vision of being must be corrected through the negation of the ontological negativity of beings, not as a double negation that returns us to their positive being, but in a turn of thought that depends upon maintaining the nullity of beings. To catch a glimpse of God, the negative image of being in beings must itself be reversed at the moment of thinking in which beings are negated, even as they are reinstated. In this rational conversion—which reverses the meaning of being but is not obliged to show its warrant for doing so, since what warrants the reversal does not itself appear except in the reversal—the supreme being is both seen and not seen in the moment of categorical contortion. In the twist and turn about of the reversal, indeed, in the doubly distorted vision that ultimately aims to catch a glimpse of the creator not so much in the mirror of creatures, as in the reversal of their ontological vacancy, Anselm attempts to project a positive image of God by reversing this negative image of creatures on the basis of a rather literal conversion process.

In the distortion of this double vision, the establishing of the creator's presence in the ambiguous house of mirrors and shadow images of the human mind occurs through a mental operation that tries to correct our ontological vision by viewing the mirror image in yet another mirror. For the rational mind produces its ontological image of God by reversing the reverse image of being in creatures. As complicated as this may sound, the point is that the stabilizing of the omnipresence of what does not exactly appear is effectively achieved through the ontological manipulation of the appearance of beings, by establishing their presence as creatures, through whose negative image the creator can be obscurely "mirrored" without actually showing up to declare rights to his domain. Instead, the creator can secure his sovereignty without "showing his face" inso-far as it is legislated in the process of the ontological disappearance and reappearance of beings. In this cosmological vanishing act, we at best catch a glimpse of the supreme being, not as "he himself is" but in a converted image of the nothingness of creatures.

In a rather strange way, then, we do ultimately see the creator in the dark mirror of creation, and have been from the start of the *Monologion,* even if Anselm will go on to show another sense in which, once reinstated, creatures are a mirror image, a "likeness," of the truth of the creator's being—a move that is itself entirely depen-dent upon the radical claims of M 28. Needless to say, all of this is part and parcel of the *Monologion's* essentially cosmological ap-proach of beginning from the beings with which we are most famil-iar, only to find our way to that conversion in our thinking that reverses the meaning of being, leaving us in the rather awkward, or at best ironic, position that such a way of making out the ontological difference results in the claim that, properly speaking, "being" ap-plies to nothing at all, at least as far as human thought is concerned. In the end, such a cosmological strategy seems bound to lead not only to a double vision of being but to a kind of cross-eyed vision, whose unfocused insight may well result from a complex crisscross-ing of the ontological difference that ultimately crosses it out by re-doubling the already double image of being as both applying and not applying to both creator and creature.

Perhaps the inevitable obscurity of such an approach is one of the reasons why Anselm, in the *Proslogion,* does not attempt to scale the wall of beings to get to the supreme being. Instead, he leaps right to the top, to the incomparable "something than which nothing greater can be thought," and aims, in so doing, to get at the *proprium dei:* to offer a clear vision of what is distinctive about God's being, such that we might find our way directly to him, or at least not so obviously through the distorted mirror of creatures. This is not to say that the *Proslogion* may not be trading in its own brand of converted images, or that the very name "something than which nothing greater can be thought" may not itself be a negative image operating on the basis of a complicated conversion of our ordinary understanding of greatness. Nor do we mean to deny that there is a certain ontological argument at the heart of the *Monologion,* or that the *Proslogion* argument should not be so called precisely because it also incorporates this reversal in the meaning of being into it. On the contrary, it is our contention that the prototype of Anselm's famous ontological argument originally occurs in the *Monologion.* It is just that in the *Proslogion* the sort of ontological conversion at work in M 28, as well as its cosmological foundation, is harder to detect. This means that if the ontological proof of the existence of God has the virtue of operating, in some sense, a priori, the *Proslogion* argument must nonetheless be made to reveal the metaphysical groundwork that has had to be laid in order to secure an experience of beings in terms of a certain understanding of their being. For it too works off of a conversion of the meaning of being, but with a conciseness that even more covertly moderates its extremity, since beings scarcely come up at all and, when they do, appear under conditions that have been set so severely that their suppression is far more quietly accomplished.[26]

In any event, there can be little doubt that the *Monologion*'s philosophical vision of God is ultimately unlocked through the ontological reversal that takes place in M 28. It constitutes the metaphysical high point—whether one thinks of it as a breaking point or a breakthrough—as well as the theological turning point of this rational meditation on the being of God. As such, it alone completes the promised clarification of the existence of God begun in M 1, while setting the stage for the discussion of trinitarian doctrine that takes up most of the remainder of the work. For our philosophical purposes, then, the rational reconstruction of at least the metaphysical element of divinity has come to a close in this ultimate ontological conversion. Having made our way up the ladder of being to the supreme being, when we look back at those beings we scaled to get there, they must disappear, so that a new measure of being may impose itself upon us. In this reversal, after having been exposed in their nothingness, beings must be reinstated in some degree of being. Consequently, while Anselm starts out strong in M 28, boldly insisting that all other beings, compared to the supreme being, do not exist, he moderates this claim in speaking of their existing "hardly at all." The latter contention, however, is not exactly a model of ontological precision. What it tries to make evident is that, in a certain sense, only God exists, even if other beings do as well. No doubt, this rather perplexing conclusion is one on which the contemplative is to meditate, and as hard and as long as the convoluted path is that has brought us to this extraordinary height from the presumably ordinary beginnings of the *Monologion* and that will eventually lead us to the *Proslogion*. For if the rational clarity concerning the existence of God sought in the *Monologion* finally shows up in all its glory in M 28, then it is this radical understanding of what it is for God to exist that Anselm will carry with him to the *Proslogion,* where, in fact, it will be brought to greater precision.

| N O T E S

1. *The Basic Writings of St. Anselm,* translated by S. N. Deane.

2. S I, 93.

3. See Benedicta Ward's translation of *The Prayers and Meditations of Saint Anselm with the Prosologion.*

4. S I, 8.

5. On the assumption concerning the relation between orality and writing in the suggestion, in the above passage, that the written word is a matter of "putting down in writing" the spoken word, see Brian Stock, *The Implications of Literacy.* As some indication of the inappropriateness of this assumption, one might simply ask whether the chain of arguments that constitutes the *Monologion* could be followed orally.

6. For assistance in imagining this, see Jesse Gellrich, *The Idea of the Book in the Middle Ages.*

7. For a discussion of the revolutionary nature of Anselm's prayers and meditations and their contribution to the development of a new form of private devotion, see, besides Ward's commentary in her translation, R. W. Southern's remarks in both *St. Anselm and His Biographer,* 34ff., and *The Making of the Middle Ages,* 224ff., as well as in his introduction to Ward's translation.

8. On the mantric character of monastic reading, see Leclercq's *The Love of Learning and the Desire for God.* Anselm's own comments in the preface to his prayers and meditations (S III, 3) make it clear that they are designed to "excite the mind of the reader," as the *Proslogion* will suggest at its beginning, and thus are not to be read quickly or cursorily, but are to be mulled over in a "deep and intense meditation." For a discussion of examples of illustrated versions of Anselm's own writings, see Otto Pacht, "The Illustrations of St. Anselm's Prayers and Meditations." In one manuscript (Pacht, 15a), Anselm is depicted with his eyes looking up to heaven, while in a number of others (16 b, c, and d—16c being an illustration of the first page of the *Monologion*), he is shown surrounded by monks, to whom he is presumably offering his vision of God.

9. For convenience, references to chapters from the *Monologion* and *Proslogion* will make use of the abbreviations M and P respectively.

10. See, however, F. S. Schmitt's "Anselm und der (Neu-) Platonismus" for a somewhat different view.

11. Jasper Hopkins has noticed the shift from *dicunter* ("is said") to *intelligitur* ("is understood") in the argument and is right that Anselm is using the former to appeal to ordinary thought, although he fails to note why this must become *intelligitur* in the principle at issue. See his analysis of M 1–4 in vol. 4 of *Anselm of Canterbury.*

12. See, in this connection, the similar line of argument developed by Augustine in, for example, his *De vera religione.*

13. We might just note that the initial appeal of the claim that the beings with which we are ordinarily familiar all "exist through another" is, in fact, based upon their existing through one another, although not mutually; that is, the "other" that any such being may be said to depend upon for its being is, at least in the first instance, not some self-sufficient being but simply another being that itself "exists though another."

14. S I, 18.

15. For a discussion of the visual imagery at play in Anselm's thought, as well as in the tradition from which it grows, see the article by Helmut Kohlenberger "Zur Metaphorik des Visuellen bei Anselm von Canterbury," as well as his book-length study of Anselm's epistemology, *Similitudo und Ratio.*

16. There has not only been some disagreement about what this phrase means but about how it should be translated. In the Hopkins/Richardson translation, for example, the reference to *rationis intellectu* in M 10 is mistranslated as "by understanding their respective definitions" (*Anselm of Canterbury,* 19). We need not repeat here the grammatical technicalities of this error, in part because Hopkins has conceded the mistake and corrected it in his more recent translation, now rendering the phrase as "through rational discernment" (*A New, Interpretive Translation of St. Anselm's Monologion and Proslogion,* 87). I would, however, refer the interested reader to my discussion of the problem in "Reunderstanding Anselm's Argument."

17. Even if we accept Anselm's rather odd view of self-awareness—that when the human mind thinks about itself an image of it appears to it that is born in it as a direct impression of it—it does not render any less perplexing the birth, in the case of a perfect thinker's thought, of what Anselm is apparently not reluctant to call a "perfect" likeness. While one can press the notion of likeness, as Anselm's doctrine of truth would have it, more and more toward the perfection of an image, once we arrive at its perfect fulfillment, when a likeness is in no way unlike that of which it is the likeness, have we not pressed the notion too far? Could we have arrived at this at best paradoxical notion of a "perfect likeness" had we not begun by modeling these topics on the nature of human thinking, where likeness is the most we can expect, in fact, where likenesses are required precisely because our imperfect thought cannot think the thing itself? That is, were the nature of thought not modeled from the outset on a mind in which the complete coincidence between thinking and what is thought can never come to pass, would there have been any need to speak of "likenesses" in the first place?

18. S I, 188.

19. See also M 63: "Just as it belongs to the supreme wisdom to know and understand, so it is clearly of the nature of such eternal and immutable knowledge and understanding always to behold as present [*praesens intueri*] what it knows and understands. For the supreme spirit to speak in this sense is nothing other than for it, as it were, to behold by thinking [*cogitando intueri*], just as the expression of our mind is nothing other than a mental vision [*cogitantis inspectio*]" (S I, 73).

20. As M 20 insists, God's "power" is nothing but what he himself is (S I, 36), which, as M 22 claims, means it is his very essence (S I, 39–40), in which case his conserving power cannot be where he is not. In this respect, attempts to account for the omnipresence of such a "creative" and "sustaining" nature epistemologically, as if its knowledge were what is all-pervasive, not only obscure the ontological role of God's "presence" but are misleading if they suggest that his knowledge "extends" to where, in some sense, he is not. For an innovative discussion of these issues, see Brian Leftow, "Anselm on Omnipresence."

21. See M 27 (S I, 45).

22. We will avoid, as Anselm does, raising the question of whether omnipresence is a feature God enjoys only relative to creation.

23. S I, 41.

24. It took a mind no less subtly and powerfully dialectical than Hegel's to discern this way of construing the ontological difference as at the root of arguments for the existence of God—although, by his time, of what would have been distinguished as the "cosmological" argument. As one might imagine, he approved of such mental maneuvers. See his *Lectures on the Philosophy of Religion,* especially the section of his 1827 lecture appropriately entitled "Religious Knowledge as Elevation to God" (1:414ff., especially 424–25). At the same time, the event of the vanishing or diminishing of creation in the face of the creator is part of the founding mythology of the Benedictine tradition. It plays a central role in Gregory's interpretation of Benedict's "vision" at Monte Cassino, which we will have occasion to cite at a later point.

   25. We will attempt to confirm the relevance of the elevation involved in the dilating of the eye of the mind to Anselm's thought in our reading of the *Proslogion,* for which the present discussion is designed to prepare us. We would like to take note here, however, that the expansion of the mind in its vision of God, and the contraction of creatures in the face of their creator, are embedded in the original mythology of the Benedictine tradition. In his account of Benedict's vision—in which, while standing at a window one night, a brilliant light illuminated the dark such that he glimpsed the whole of creation in a single spectacle (not to mention the soul of the bishop of Capua being carried off to heaven in a fiery ball)—Gregory the Great explains:

> To a soul that is seeing the creator, every creature is contracted. For however little of the light of the creator it beholds, all that is created becomes small, since by the light of this innermost vision the bosom of the mind is expanded, and so extended into God that it is above the world. Indeed, the soul that is seeing even comes to be above itself, when in the light of God it is rapt beyond itself, is amplified interiorly, and, while elevated, looks down and comprehends how small is that which, in its lowly state, it could not comprehend. The man of God, then, who, beholding the fiery globe, also watched the angels returning to heaven, doubtless could not discern these things except in the light of God. What wonder, then, if he saw the whole world gathered before him, he who was raised up in the light of the mind and came to be outside the world? For to say that the world was gathered before his eyes is not [to say] that heaven and earth were drawn together, but that the soul that sees is dilated; he who, rapt in God, could see without difficulty what is beneath God. In that light, then, that brightened his outer eye, came a light to his inner mind, which, since it enrapt the seeing soul to what is above, showed how contracted is all that is below. (*Dial.* 2.35)

   26. It has, of course, often been claimed that the cosmological argument depends upon the ontological argument. We will, to some extent, suggest the opposite, or at least that a certain cosmological strategy paves the way for the ontological argument, however covertly. At the very least, this will be shown to be, as a matter of historical fact, the case in Anselm's corpus. While the ontological argument would, no doubt, like to have us think that it starts from scratch, it implicitly begins from the understanding of being provided by beings, which must then be converted to arrive at God's being in contrast to them. Thus, we might speak, as we have with respect to the *Monologion,* of a cosmological strategy, if not of a cosmological argument. Needless to say, at least one aspect of our response to the question of the basis of the ontological argument will depend upon a demonstration of the extent to which the *Monologion* invades the *Proslogion.*

| Praying for Insight

As we mentioned at the outset, Anselm did not begin his writing career with a philosophical treatise but with a set of prayers and meditations of a rather more spiritual variety. In a strange way, the uniqueness of the *Monologion* resides, at least in part, in its lack of religious fervor or of any obvious devotional character. If anything, its dispassionate rationality displays a philosophical devotion that is to provide an example of a new sort of meditation on the ground of faith. Consequently, after our account of the *Monologion*, one may wonder what warrants our speaking of mysticism at all, given its apparently—indeed, all but unprecedentedly—thoroughgoing rationalism; even as one might imagine that the brethren may have been disappointed, if not confused, by the work for similar reasons. In the *Proslogion*, however, these two dimensions of Anselm's thought come together in one text in a way they had not before and never would again in his corpus—perhaps never would again in the history of Western thought. For the *Proslogion* is a distinctive kind of work, is, we might say, a kind of philosophical prayer book, and thus it offers a form of writing better suited to the rational mysticism that is intent upon securing a vision of God than any of the other works Anselm would write.

The format of the *Proslogion* itself indicates the extent to which Anselm stands between traditions; for its alternation between prayer and proof shows the signs of the monasticism to which he was heir moving hand in hand with the scholasticism to which his thought would eventually lead. It is this ability to incorporate the impassioned excesses of spiritual devotion with the cool and calculating moderation of a philosophical rationality—and in such a way that they work together to achieve a single result—that allowed the

| 97

Proslogion to initiate a form of thought that has, at least implicitly, kept it alive in the minds of Western thinkers quite beyond, we would argue, the explicit interest in the reasoning of Anselm's argument. For within the *Proslogion* itself, the ontological argument appears as something other than an exercise in rational cleverness insofar as we encounter in it a consummate unity of logical precision and mystical insight, in which each extreme moderates and enhances the other. And we would eventually like to show why these seemingly opposed elements must work together to legitimate Anselm's historic founding of rational theology.

It is not surprising, then, that the *Proslogion,* unlike the *Monologion,* would begin with a prayer: "An excitation of the mind to the contemplation of God."[1] In this initial chapter, we find the first indication of the blending of the rational considerations of the *Monologion* with the expressly devotional character of Anselm's earlier prayers, and in an explicitly mystical context. The leitmotif of P 1 is the blindness of humankind in its fallenness from the vision of God. This evocative prayer precedes the rational arguments and serves a specific rhetorical function in setting the mood for them. The anxiety of its passionate lament will finally reach a crescendo that yields to petitionary tones of humble desire, pleading that the vision which is the point of human existence be supplied to whatever degree is fitting, as it calls upon God to cleanse the eye of the mind for, as the subtitle of the *Proslogion* suggests, this "faith seeking understanding." It should perhaps be mentioned, however, before pursuing the images of the prayer of P 1 itself, that the overall form of the work has its roots in Anselm's own experience in the writing of the text. In view of his biographer's description of the origin of the *Proslogion* and as Anselm himself reports in its preface, it is not far-fetched to suppose that some breakthrough to a certain vision of God he had been seeking led him to write "in the person of one striving to elevate his own mind to the contemplation of God."[2] Indeed, he claims to have arrived at a joy he hopes the book might bring to its readers—a joy, in other words, that he would try to embed within the work itself.

Exactly why the strategy of the *Proslogion*'s overall argument requires recourse to joy will have to be shown later. For now we only want to take note that a certain experience apparently accompanied the discovery of whatever lies at the heart of the text. Here is how one of Anselm's companions described the inception of the work:

> After [having composed the *Monologion*] it came into his mind to seek a single and short argument that could prove that which is believed and preached about God, namely, that he is eternal, unchangeable, omnipotent, wholly everywhere, incomprehensible, just, righteous, merciful, true, truth, goodness,

justice and several other things, and how these all are one in him. And this matter, as he himself would say, caused him great difficulty, partly because the thought took away his desire for food, drink and sleep, and partly because—and this weighed more upon him—it disturbed the attention he ought to have directed, at matins and at other times, to divine service. When he became aware of this, and still could not altogether lay hold of that which he sought, he supposed that such a thought was a temptation of the devil, and he tried to banish it from his mind. But the more vehemently he tried to do this, the more this thought molested him. Then suddenly one night, during the night vigil, the grace of God illuminated his heart and the matter became clear to his understanding, and immense joy and jubilation filled his whole inner being. Thinking, therefore, that others would be gladdened along with him if they knew of this, he immediately and ungrudgingly wrote it on writing tablets and gave it to one of the brethren of the monastery for safe keeping.[3]

We know from other reports by Eadmer that Anselm was in the habit of fasting, and the description here confirms that the condition he must have been in was one of a dedication that distracted him from both eating and sleeping.[4] Perhaps the most notable aspect of this characterization, however, is the implication that Anselm did not merely condense the arguments of the *Monologion* into a shorter version in the *Proslogion* but sought to achieve something that apparently had not been accomplished in the earlier work—and sought it with no little difficulty. Certainly the *Monologion* provided the basic views from which the *Proslogion* was conceived, and yet there was something newly arrived at in the later work. In this way, the *Monologion* supplies an indispensable background for the *Proslogion,* the first ground, philosophically speaking, Anselm had to stand on. But once he had gained his footing—on a ground in large part prepared by others—he took off on his own.

There are, of course, any number of different ways of reading what it might have been that came to Anselm that night at matins, just as there are a number of ways of taking his desire to find a "single" argument, which Anselm also mentions in his preface to the *Proslogion.*[5] What is clear, even from the vocabulary in which the text itself speaks, is that whatever Anselm so suddenly discovered was regarded, not only by him, as a kind of revelation, as an illumination that fulfilled his seeking and filled his heart with joy. Perhaps this discovery should not be identified with any single argument in the *Proslogion* but with some fundamental insight, or even with the form of argument that apparently allowed Anselm to reconstruct the text as a whole even after the original tablets upon which it was written were stolen.[6] Still, we cannot ignore the fact that the most prominent expression of gratitude in the *Proslogion* itself, explicitly thanking God for the "illumination," comes at the end of P 4, which we will regard as the conclusion of its argument for the existence of God.[7]

In any event, while the occasion for the writing of the *Monologion* was the request of certain brothers for a recipe for their meditations, the immediate occasion for the writing of the *Proslogion* was a specific experience Anselm himself had had, such that the claim of the joy it provided becomes the aim of a text which is itself presumably designed to incite in the reader a similar revelation. This, of course, would account for the form of the *Proslogion,* which begins by arousing the mind to the contemplation of God, so as to prepare those thinking along with it for the kind of clarity that came to Anselm as if in a revelation—indeed, to put it in a language that will be repeated both in P 1 and in P 4, as if "the grace of God illuminated his mind." And while other interpreters of Anselm might agree that Anselm's text aimed to present an argument that would serve as a kind of expression of his insight such that it might be incited in his readers,[8] the task we have set for ourselves is the detailing of the precise sense in which this is true and the precise ways in which his reasoning meets this demand.

This will require us to consider the overall form of the text, which operates in terms of a specific relation between prayer and proof. We cannot assume that the fact that Anselm's argument is preceded and followed by prayers is irrelevant to it as a proof, nor can we assume that reason is simply defending Christian faith, as if it does not itself have a vested interest in its own theological grounding through the narrative that the prayers provide. Neither can the connection between Anselm's argument and the inner joy whose immensity completely filled his heart and mind—when the "thing" about which he was thinking was "revealed" or "exposed" (*patuit*) to his understanding—be ignored or dismissed, the way the prayers themselves usually are, as a merely rhetorical element. For while these prayers may be irrelevant to the rules of inference that govern the logic of any reasoning Anselm may offer, they are not irrelevant to the manner in which his arguments are supposed to function as "proofs." It is Anselm himself who sets the stage for the reading of his text, quite differently from his staging of the *Monologion,* by appealing to the joy that was the occasion for its writing. In fact, much of Eadmer's characterization of the inception of the *Proslogion* reads like a citation from Anselm's own preface. Here is what Anselm says about the origin of the work:

> After having written at the urging of several of my brethren a short work, as an example of meditation on the rationality of faith, in the person of one who seeks by silently reasoning with

himself that of which he is ignorant, considering that it was composed of a complex sequence of interconnected arguments, I began to ask myself whether it might be possible to discover a single argument that required nothing for its proof but itself alone and would alone be sufficient to demonstrate that God truly is, and that he is the supreme good, needing no other, but which all need for their being and well-being, and whatever else we believe concerning the divine substance.

But as often and as eagerly as I turned my thought to this, it sometimes appeared to me that what I was seeking might be almost in my grasp, while at other times it altogether eluded the keenest vision of my mind, so that finally in desperation I was about to give up, as if I were looking for something that was impossible to find. When, however, I had resolved to shut this thought out altogether, so as not to keep my mind, in being occupied by the pointless, from other thought with which I might make progress, it then began in my unwillingness and resistance to force itself upon me more and more insistently. And then one day, when I was totally exhausted from resisting its troubling persistence, what I had despaired of finding appeared in the midst of the very conflict of my thinking, so that I eagerly embraced the thought that, in my anxiety, I had repelled.

Considering, then, that what had given me joy to discover, if it were written down, would afford pleasure to those who might read it, I have written the following short work, on this and various other topics, in the person of one striving to elevate his own mind to the contemplation of God and seeking to understand what he believes. (S I, 93–94)

What is here made clear, and is not in the citation from Eadmer, is that Anselm was seeking to find a single and shorter argument because of the complexity of the *Monologion*. This work, as we have seen, involves an intricate chain of reasoning, in which one argument leads to the next and is presupposed by it. It is fair to infer from what is said here that, insofar as the book was composed of such an extended series of interconnected arguments, the brethren for whom it was written must have found its overall argument too elaborate to follow. At the same time, if we take Anselm at his word, the aim in writing the *Proslogion* was to demonstrate what had been shown in the earlier book, but by means of a single argument, or at least a single form of argument that, instead of developing sequentially, could simply be repeated.

What is also indicated here, as it was by Eadmer, is that, if the *Monologion* was conceived in the calm of rational disputation, the *Proslogion* was born of conflict and anxiety, from the darkness of desperation to the sudden illumination that brought calm in the joyous clarity of an unexpected vision of what was sought. Is it any wonder that, bred in this atmosphere, the *Proslogion* would take on the cast of a work seeking elevation to the illumination that is neither a matter of some manic mysticism nor of the dispassionate rationalism of mere argumentation? What we find here an indication of the kind of rational revelation that would have alone fulfilled what Anselm was seeking and, as such, had to be presented in a form that begins with a prayer lamenting our human blindness even as it asks for whatever degree of illumination is appropriate to reason given its fallen condition. That reason should be involved in more than just silent disputation with itself, that it should be able to reveal its consummate object so as to allow for a joy that overcomes the conflicts inherent in thought and resolves the anxiety that had beset Anselm, is not just worked into the story of the writing of the *Proslogion* but into the text as whole, just as the story of its genesis is offered in the preface precisely as an interpretative guide to its reading.

In this way, the above citation clarifies the difference in the "persona" under which Anselm's first two philosophical works were written. The *Monologion* was to be an example of pure ratiocination, of a reasoning in which one discourses silently with oneself about what the Christian faithful believe. This is why it is a "monologue" in which reason talks to itself. The *Proslogion,* on the other hand, addresses God and is written under the guise of one seeking not just rationalization but elevation. This uplifting of human being out of the condition into which it has fallen, according to the rhetoric of the *Proslogion,* requires the illumination of the mind by God—as Anselm apparently experienced that night at matins. In that case, however, it is not surprising that the *Proslogion* begins with a petitionary prayer designed to recreate the sense within the text itself that Anselm's own revelation was a gift from God. Indeed, the citing of this "pretextual" experience in the preface is obviously aimed at creating just such an aura around the written text. And if, as P 1 finally puts it, all of this requires God to "reveal himself," then it should be clear why the text proper begins with an appeal to God that, while urging human beings to undertake the quest for God, also makes it clear that human thought cannot simply operate, as the *Monologion* seemed to suggest, *sola ratione.* As such, the prayer of P 1 formally works off of a dual exhortation, appealing first to us and then to God.

The claim that human being cannot succeed by itself in its seeking of God is not only implicitly confirmed in Anselm's own pretextual experience and embedded in the very form of his prayer. The helplessness of his personal desperation also invites a parallel with the depths of the Fall of Adam, to which human beings are by nature subject, just as Anselm's subsequent illumination finds its historical parallel in our redemption by Christ. As the theme will be pursued in the imagery of the *Proslogion,* it is a matter of trying to set oneself upright after the Fall, which involves our rising up from out of the dross of existence in order to extend our thinking beyond the mundane concerns in which we are engrossed, so that, through the grace of God, our hearts and minds may be illuminated. Thus, the text proper begins by calling upon us to enter into the inner chamber of the soul, into the inner "cubicle" where the dialogue of thinking takes place, but not just in talking to itself. Instead, if the seeking of an inner vision of God is to become the order of the day, it will require both an arousing and arising of the human mind to the contemplation of God as well as the invocation of God to reveal himself to those involved in such seeking. As was, in fact, the case with Anselm's epistemology in the *Monologion*—although even more extremely—it will require an active undertaking on the part of the human mind, which depends for its ultimate truth upon the passive determination of thought by that which it is thinking.

Consequently, the incantation that opens the text begins by exclaiming:

> Come now, O insignificant man,
> > flee a while from your busy tasks,
> > put aside for a moment the confusion of your thoughts,
> > discard now your distracting cares and
> > postpone your busy labors.
> Free yourself a little for God, and
> > rest a while in him.
> *Enter into the inner chamber* of your mind,
> > exclude everything, besides God and what can be of help in
> > seeking him, and
> > *close the door* to seek him.
> Speak now, *my* whole *heart,*
> Say now to God:
> > *I seek your face,*
> > *For your face, O lord, I search.* (S I, 97)[9]

The litany of imperatives marshaled to begin each line repeatedly make their point clear: the contemplative is ordered to flee, put aside, discard, postpone, empty—that is, free himself from the everyday world, indeed, from the world as such, so as to open himself to God. This return to one's cubicle is not simply a matter of going to the prayer cell, but of finding that designated place of rest in the mind itself (*cubiculum mentis*). Thus, the image of "closing the door" behind one, of closing out, "excluding" everything but God, implicitly invokes the radical distinction between the supreme being and all other beings we saw appear in all its metaphysical glory in the *Monologion,* even if it here shows up in a rather more familiar garb. Whether, by the end of the *Proslogion,* we will have succeeded in excluding everything from our thought but God and gained anything like an inward vision of him remains to be seen.

What is apparent here, however, is that this is precisely what does remain to be seen; that is, whatever is to be seen, is to be seen with the eye of a mind that has as its aim the refrain: "I seek your face, for your face, O lord, I search." Of course, one may insist that these are not Anselm's words, that he is merely citing Scripture (Psalm 26). But then the question becomes why Anselm decided to begin the *Proslogion* with a prayer that interposes even as it transposes fragmentary passages from Scripture, and one in which he has chosen, as his biblical motif, the quest for the vision of God. One would hardly question the sincerity of Anselm's citation of Psalm 13 in P 2, where he casts his argument for the existence of God as an answer to the fool who "said in his heart that there is no God." In either and all such cases, the point will be to see how Anselm has appropriated these pious intonations to his own philosophical purposes, although we will reserve for later discussion the relevance of the obvious fact that, unlike in the *Monologion,* from which such appeals are explicitly excluded, quotations from Scripture are interlaced throughout the *Proslogion.* In the opening lines of P 1, such references are undoubtedly designed to set the mood for the work as a whole.

The plea that the mind's vision be elevated from out of its state of loss, that it be repaired and reformed, constitutes the other side of this prayer. Its exhortation operates not simply as an order to humankind to give up its own self-serving labors and to seek God but also as a supplication begging God to aid in that search. Thus, the prayer continues by calling upon God in exactly the same terms in which it first called upon man:

> Come now then, you, O my lord God, teach my heart
>> where and how to seek you,
>> where and how to find you.
> Lord, if you are not here,
>> where should I seek you in your absence?
> And if you are everywhere,
>> why do I not see you in your presence?
> Surely *you dwell in inaccessible light!*
>> But where is the inaccessible light,
>> and how can I approach such unapproachable light?
> Who will lead me to and bring me into it,
>> so that I may see you there? (S I, 98)

The paradoxical theme of the inaccessible presence of a ubiquitous God will be treated later, although it is clear here, given the reference to the "inaccessible light," that it remains a question of vision, of how we can be so blind as not to see what is everywhere. The apparent answer is: not so much because God is in the dark, hidden from us, but because he dwells in an overabundance of light; as if he were so absolutely present, so excessively in being, that the light of being which he is, is too blinding. Of course, this image of the *lux inaccessible* is standard fare in mystical theology. It is cited from Paul's letter to Timothy, to whom the Pseudo-Dionysius addressed his negative theology, while the image of a hidden god, who has turned his face away from us, is an essential element of the original psalms, especially Psalm 12, fragments of which will also be cited in P 1.

As one might expect, the question of human blindness is a matter of our own "natural" darkness, which is the result of original sin. Consequently, the primary image for traditional mysticism plays off of the theme of the original paradise that Adam lost.[10] Before we watch Anselm himself turn to these images of a mystical paradise in which we dwell in the direct vision of God, we need to be clear that the question of who will lead us to this "unapproachable light" has, in its own way, already been answered with a rhetorical question that effectively assumes that God alone can serve as the guide and teacher. We will see this characterization repeated in the first line of P 2, where the transition is made from prayer to proof under the guise of an appeal to the "lord, who grants understanding to faith." Presumably, this is a reference to the grace and guidance of divine understanding. Philosophically speaking, however, it amounts to an appeal to the divine reason, which will be called upon to illuminate the eye of the mind with the very light of truth, such that we might catch sight of God despite our own blindness. To do this, however, human thought will need a "sign"—perhaps in a rather more literal sense than Anselm thinks—no doubt sent from the one who "dwells in accessible light":

> By what signs,
> > in what profile, should I seek thee?
>
> Never have I seen you, lord my God,
> > I have not known your face.
> What shall he do, O lord most high,
> > what shall this far-flung exile do?
> What shall your servant do,
> > anxious for your love,
> > > but *cast far from your face?*
> Breathless from the struggle to see you,
> > your face is too far off.
> He desires to come close to you,
> > but your dwelling place is inaccessible.
> He longs to find you,
> > but does not know where you are.
> He aspires to seek you,
> > but does not know your face.

O lord, you are my God,
    and you are my lord,
    yet never have I seen you.
You have made and remade me
    and have given me whatever goods I have,
    and still I do not know you.
I was made to see you
and have still not accomplished that for which I was created. (S I, 98)

We are never informed just what the nature of the sign is that Anselm requests, although we can surmise from the remainder of the text that it is probably the key phrase that serves to name God in the *Proslogion* and fuels the unique form of argument that will, so we shall try to show, unlock a certain vision of God. And while it may seem strange that we insist upon speaking of such vision even while Anselm is announcing that he has never seen God "face-to-face," we can no more doubt that this is part of the staging of the text than we could know, at this point, that the reference to "profiles" under which the face of God may be seen will be critical to an explication of how God is both seen and not seen by those seeking him. What must certainly be clear is that Anselm thinks that the very meaning of human being, that for which it was created in the first place, is to enjoy the vision of God. This is not only our original condition in paradise but also marks the direction back toward which human life is moving in its exile after the Fall.

As we have already mentioned, the topic of mankind's fallen condition provides a historical parallel to Anselm's personal darkness, which he experienced in his helpless desperation to find his single argument. The breakthrough he experienced during the night prayer will be associated with the revelation of grace and will eventually find its own historical parallel in the continuing revelation of God through rational theology. In either case, the image is pursued in P 1, first by means of a lament for the fallen children of Adam and Eve, followed by a request for assistance. First the lament:

O miserable lot of mankind
    when he lost that for which he was made!
O that hard and hapless fall!
    What was lost and what was gained,
    what departed and what remained?
He lost the beatitude for which he was made,
    and found the misery for which he was not made.
He lost that without which nothing is happy,
    and gained what is itself nothing but misery.
Then *man feasted on the bread of angels,* for which we now hunger,
    now we eat *the bread of pain,* which he knew not.

O the common affliction of mankind,
  the universal lament of the sons of Adam!
He tasted fullness;
  we sigh with hunger.
He abounded;
  we beg.
He happily had and miserably deserted;
  we unhappily lack and long in our misery.
Alas, we remain empty!
Why could he not have kept for us what would have been so easy
                                                        then,
  but now so hard to lose?
Why did he deprive us of the light
  and shroud us all in darkness?
Why did he take away our life,
  inflicting death upon us?

O wretched ones,
  from where are we expelled,
  to where are we impelled?
  from where have we been cast down,
  to where are we sinking?
From the homeland into exile,
  from the vision of God into our blindness. (S I, 98–99)

The mystical mood of what will eventually turn into a prayer of promise is unmistakable in the lament over a paradise lost, where humankind originally dwelled in the vision of God as its "homeland." I have, consequently, allowed myself a certain freedom in translating Anselm's rhapsodic modulations in the hope of capturing not just the sense but the passion of the passage. Some of its formal characteristics may seem a bit emotional for the presumably clearheaded logician Anselm has been thought to be. But I do not think it betrays a false pathos so much as the deep feeling that most properly expresses Anselm's ultimate commitments and interests. Doubtless, for him, the excitation and exhortation to struggle against the Fall and to elevate our mind against the now natural (although not original) drift downward requires just the sort of poetic inspiration that a mystical song is designed to evoke.

Obviously, a certain spatial imagery is at work in the conflict between elevation and fallenness, between rising up out of the morass of the world and sinking down into a kind of pit of spiritual darkness. That imagery is echoed in the expulsion from the garden as an original turning away, being literally impelled to walk the path that leads away from God, which accounts for our paradoxical separation from an omnipresent being who remains nonetheless "unapproachable." Interestingly enough, these spatial images are amplified by the temporal imagery that is invoked to form yet another distance and difference: between then and now, between our earlier condition and our present situation. This historical separation from God will, in Anselm's view, inevitably be overcome, as no doubt will the spatial separation when we finally "enter into the joy of the lord," as the *Proslogion* puts it at its conclusion.[11] For now, however, we stand between this original nearness to God in paradise, when "the bread of angels"—those pure spirits who do nothing but rejoice in their constant nourishment on the vision of God—was our daily bread, and now, when "the bread of pain," fruit of the crucifixion, brings us into an occasional communion with God through Christ's body and blood, which heals the distance between ourselves and him even as it promises eternal communion in the final redemption of a life to come. Between the original vision, for which, as P 1 puts it, we were made, and the final vision that we are still awaiting lies our present existential condition: in exile from the vision of God, wandering in the dark along the path that Adam began to forge when expelled from the garden, sinking into the darkness of a blindness that carries us ever further, both temporally and spatially, from our original home as the native land of that for which we were made, namely, a dwelling in the uninterrupted vision of God.

Our plight, however, is not hopeless. This historical exile has its own historical solution, including the promise of vision, and not just in a life to come. Between the blindness of faith and the full experience of God stands the insight of rational thought. Spurred on by its longing for the sight of God, if not face-to-face, then at least from the depths, true faith, for the *Proslogion,* as its subtitle would suggest, seeks "understanding."[12] Thus, the transition begins from the lament to the invocation in terms that sound not inapplicable to Anselm's own condition before his revelation at matins:

> O my misery!
> One more miserable son of Eve,
>> far removed from God.
> What have I undertaken,
>> what have I accomplished?
> For what was I striving,
>> to what have I come?
> To what did I aspire,
>> for what do I sigh?
>
> *I sought goods,*
>> *and, behold, confusion.*
> I reached for God,
>> and tripped over myself.
> I sought rest in my solitude,
>> and *tribulation and pain have invaded* my inwardness.

I wanted to laugh in the joy of my mind,
and am forced *to cry out with the groan of my heart.*
I hoped for gladness,
and, behold, these sighs oppress me.

And *you, O lord,*
how long?
How long will you forget us?
How long will you turn your face away from us?
When *will you look upon us and hear* us?
When *will you illuminate our eyes* and *show* to us *your face?*
When will you restore yourself to us?
Look upon us, O lord,
hear us,
illuminate us,
show to us yourself. (S I, 99)

In the end, Anselm seems to be commanding—and before that virtually reprimanding—God in a paradoxical form of invocational prayer in which the plea finally appears as an order: show yourself. No doubt the question of "how long" the lord will "forget us" is an allusion to the failure of Christ to appear at the millennium, as Anselm's generation is among the first to have to deal with this event that did not happen. Nonetheless, in his view, the historical location of his generation is still timed by its placement between revelations: between the first and second coming of Christ. This historical reference, however, quickly turns to the personal, to the question of one's own illumination. Of course, Anselm seeks not the sort of absolute revelation that will occur at the end of the world, but the vision in the dark that remains a possibility even in our desperate condition, if only the God of Truth will "hear us," "look upon us," turn his "face" toward us, so as to "illuminate our eyes." The moment of restoration cannot come without God's revelation, although Anselm will make it clear that he does not expect to see God face-to-face in this life. Still, he prays not to be left in the darkness of a blind faith:

Let me look upward to your light,
if only from afar,
if only from the depths.
Teach me to seek you and
show yourself in my seeking;
for neither can I seek you unless you lead the way
nor find you unless you show yourself. (S I, 100)

Anselm neither wants his vision of God to result in his being blinded by a light that, he will argue, is too bright to be viewed directly in our current condition, nor is he content to be left in the blindness of faith, awaiting the restoration of our original experience of God in the paradise of a life to come. Instead, he wants God to show himself, but under the guidance that might allow for a certain distant vision. No doubt human reason, with the aid of the second person of the Trinity, may perform the role of mediator and, in a way, protector insofar as the vision by means of a "likeness" is the safest, as it may glimpse God's "truth," albeit partially, and thus without danger. Our present rationality may well allow for what might be regarded as a partial vision—a vision from afar, from the depth (*vel de longe vel de profundo*), indeed, in the shadows, if not ultimately in the dark—should it turn out that the *Proslogion*'s consummate vision offers us insight precisely into God's "inaccessibility." Be that as it may, our ability for vision while still in the darkness of our fallen state, as Anselm himself saw in the dark of his own desperation, nonetheless requires the lightening flash that illuminates, if only momentarily, that which we long to see. The joy this brings, although it may not be complete, presumably allows for a taste of that absolute and unconditional delight promised in the life to come, when "our joy will be full."[13]

As we will find, the *Proslogion* must attempt to offer some sign of that fulfillment if it is to argue, as it does, that a life to come is indicated by the very partiality of our present understanding and is confirmed by this taste of joy as a foretaste of an experience that can only be enjoyed in its unqualified completion in a future life. In our present life, a certain restraint is required, in which case Anselm does not seek to understand God in his impenetrable heights, but only to elevate his mind to the extent to which it is deemed appropriate. Neither, however, can he be content with faith alone. And if, as we are often told, Anselm does not presume to seek to understand so that he may believe, this may at least in part be because, logically speaking, faith is only necessary where knowledge—not to mention experience—is lacking. In Anselm's view, belief is not the original condition of human being, nor will it be necessary in the life to come, when our vision will be complete. Instead, faith is the condition of fallen mankind and holds only a promise of the fulfillment for which we were made, in the realization, consummation, and restoration of our original nature in the vision of God. It is with this in mind that we must read the famous conclusion of the prayer of P 1:

> I acknowledge, lord, and give thanks,
>> that you created in me *your image*,
>> so that I may remember you, think of you, and love you.
> But it has been so effaced and worn away by my faults,
>> is so clouded by the smoke of sin,
> that it cannot do what it is made to
>> unless you renew and reform it.

I do not strive, lord, to penetrate your heights,
     for my understanding is in no way equal to it;
but I do desire to understand to some extent your truth,
     which my heart believes and loves.
And neither do I seek to understand so that I may believe,
     but believe so that I may understand.
For this also I believe:
     that *unless I believe,*
     I will not understand. (S I, 100)

As much as this concluding passage may appear to stress the importance of Christian belief, there should be no doubt that concealed in it, as in P 1 as a whole, is a plea for reason as much as a plea to the God of faith for assistance. This will show up most explicitly in Anselm's later reversal of the biblical dictum that "unless I believe, I will not understand." After the argument that follows this Augustinian dictum, P 4 will offer up a prayer of thanks which claims that "even if I did not want to believe, I would nonetheless be unable not to understand."[14] In the midst of all the praying, we will eventually have to discern the nature of the rational apology that the text is designed to provide: not just the standard theological apologetic, in which reason presumably defends the beliefs of the faithful but, on the contrary, an apology in which the articles of faith are used to defend the practice of reason for a faith seeking rational understanding. Anselm must undertake this defense in his attempt to found a rational theology, which must not only convince us that faith may be defended by means of reason but also must convince the faithful that there is a theological justification for the religious application of their rationality, even if this defense is made out not on the basis of reason but through the poetic narrative provided by the prayers.

Such an attempt to establish a certain relation between faith and reason marks the entire approach of the *Proslogion* in its need to defend the practice of argumentation and disputation in its spiritual relevance. This is worked out rhetorically in terms of the formal relation between prayer and proof to which we will return much later. For the moment, however, let us just note that the assurance that one does not seek to understand in order to believe is an anticipatory defense against exactly what the text is doing, namely, substituting reason for faith, albeit on the basis of certain theological doctrines. While this famous dictum suggests that understanding is not required for faith, but faith for understanding, it fails to mention that faith is no longer required once understanding has been achieved. In that case, however, if reason is empowered to deem faith unnecessary, at least with respect to those issues it can understand, it is critical that faith accept its obsolescence, indeed, that it insist upon it. Thus, Anselm must work out a theology of reason that complements and confirms his rationalization of theology. The prayers and proofs must appear to be mutually consistent and mutually enhancing, as reason is to be regarded not only as relevant to biblical theology but also as an essential element of that for which man was made—which is not faith. Instead, faith is only necessary as a result of mankind's loss of its original estate: its dwelling in the vision of God.

As in the above passage, it is the divine reason, whose image is in us, to which Anselm will ultimately appeal to defend the new procedures he is importing into theological discussions, while, biblically speaking, it is the Son of God who redeems mankind from its fallen condition. When Anselm, later in his career, attempts to defend himself and his intrusion of rational practices into religious thought, he will preface a letter to one of his works that goes so far as to suggest the possibility of an ongoing historical revelation of God through and to reason, a kind of continuing revelation of divine "truth" through the second person of the Trinity, now that the revelation of faith has come to pass—indeed, is past. Not surprisingly, in a tradition that thinks of truth as a matter of revelation, rationality must be shown to have its own revelatory power if it is to legitimate its relevance. Reason must be shown, in other words, to be relevant to the vision of God for which we were made, or else its practice is essentially irrelevant to what is alone essentially relevant to humankind. And while reason is never mentioned by name in P 1, the unmistakable appeal to the "eye of the mind" and to the "illumination" that would allow for an inner vision of God serves to place the practice of rational contemplation—which no doubt met with displeasure in some, given its fate in the *Monologion*—into a context in which it makes some spiritual sense.

In its own historic way, then, the *Proslogion* is as much a demonstration of the efficacy of reason in relation to the God of faith—that is, it is as much a defense of philosophy—as it is a demonstration of the rationality of the faith of those who believe in God. This is why what we will be regarding as the vision of God that lies at the basis of Anselm's famous ontological argument for his existence must be counted among the great moments of rational theology. For the circularity of the relation Anselm attempts to establish between faith and reason, or, perhaps better put, between God and rational insight, has served to place a kind of hermetic seal on the practice of philosophical theology that has, to this day, scarcely been broken.

▌ Anselm's Famous Argument

If we were not altogether inspired by at least the initial arguments for the existence of a highest good and a supreme being offered in the *Monologion,* we may be all the more impressed by the *Proslogion* proof. In a way, the difference in their arguments for the existence of God constitutes the difference between the two books. On the one hand, the *Monologion* begins from, even if it does not conclude with, a consideration of common features, whether goodness or being, shared by ordinary things so as to argue to a highest good or supreme being, thus emphasizing the likeness of God to creatures, or rather, of creatures to God, even if it will later radicalize his difference from them. The *Proslogion,* on the other hand, begins by invoking the absolute distinctiveness of God. It jumps right to the heart of the matter, without at least the same concession to those who are "ignorant" of God, which presumably led Anselm in the earlier work to begin from things with which we are all familiar. Instead, the argument of P 2 gets started by characterizing God in terms of a complex title that forms the basis for the reasoning of the text as a whole. After the mystical preparations supplied by its initial prayer, in the throes of its excitation of the mind to the contemplation of God, it leaps right into its famous argument—a leap that springs from the "name" of God with which it begins.

It is, no doubt, best to cite this most famous passage in Anselm's writings in its entirety:

> Therefore, lord, you who give understanding to faith, grant me that I might understand, to the extent you know to be beneficial, that you are as we believe and that you are that which we believe. And we believe that you are something than which nothing greater can be thought.
>
> Or is there, then, not something of such a nature, since *the fool said in his heart that there is no God?* But certainly this same fool, when he hears what I say, namely, something than which nothing greater can be thought, understands what he hears; and what is understood is in his understanding, even if he does not understand it to be.
>
> For it is different for a thing to be in the understanding than for that thing to be understood to be. When, for example, a painter preconceives of what he is to make, he indeed has in his understanding what he has not yet made, but he does not yet understand it to be. Once he has painted it, however, he both has in his understanding and understands to be that which he has now made.
>
> Even the fool, then, is convinced that something than which nothing greater can be thought at least is in his understanding, since he understands this when he hears it, and whatever is understood is in the understanding.

> But certainly that than which a greater cannot be thought cannot be in the understanding alone. For if it is in the understanding alone even, it can be thought to be in reality also—which is greater. If, therefore, that than which a greater cannot be thought is in the understanding alone, that than which a greater cannot be thought is itself that than which a greater can be thought. But certainly this cannot be. Therefore, without doubt, something than which a greater cannot be thought exists both in the understanding and in reality. (S I, 101–2)

The "therefore" (*ergo*) that begins this chapter—and it will be as important later as it is here to note that the *Proslogion* was originally not divided into chapters, but written as one long prayer[15]—serves to announce that it follows on the heels of, and follows from, the elevation of the mind to the contemplation of God begun in P 1. P 2 is clearly to be regarded as part and parcel of the petition for a vision of the God who grants such understanding to the faithful. In this way, the proof is presented from the start as the first step in putting into action the project proposed in the *Proslogion*'s initial prayer. And this reminder, at the outset, of the basic invocation of the lord to grant "understanding" must, as we will show, whether we reach back to *Monologion*'s treatment of the term or to the language in which the request is made in P 1, be a reference to some form of rational insight.

Anselm petitions the lord to allow him to understand that the God whom the faithful believe in exists as they believe him to and is what they believe him to be. Some have taken this proposal as an indication of a dual purpose in the *Proslogion*. On the one hand, so it has been claimed, Anselm wants to prove *that* God exists, and, on the other, he wants to show *what* God is. According to this account of the basic design of the *Proslogion,* Anselm will first demonstrate the existence of God in P 2–4 and then turn to the demonstration of his "essence"—of the various characteristics that determine what God is, e.g., justice, goodness, etc.—in P 5–26.[16] Apparently, in the preface Anselm had already expressed something of this duality:

> After having written at the urging of several of my brethren a short work, as an example of meditation on the rationality of faith, in the person of one who seeks by silently reasoning with himself that of which he is ignorant, considering that it was composed of a complex sequence of interconnected arguments, I began to ask myself whether it might be possible to discover a single argument that required nothing for its proof but itself alone and would alone be sufficient to demonstrate that God truly is, and that he is the supreme good, needing no other, but which all need for their being and well-being, and whatever else we believe concerning the divine substance. (S I, 93)

Whether what is claimed at the conclusion of the above passage should be read into this first line of P 2 remains an open question, although it is clear from the title of P 2, "That God truly is," that this chapter begins to address the tasks set in the preface. However, if we look at the beginning of P 2, it would seem that within the immediate context of that chapter, if what Anselm wants to show is that God is that which the faithful believe, this may not involve a multiplicity of characteristics, but one single designation. The claim of the line that follows the opening one is simply that God is something than which nothing greater can be thought. What it might mean to show this, to gain the understanding that God is "that which we believe" in the sense that he is something than which nothing greater can be thought, remains to be seen. As should be evident, however, whichever way one takes this particular petition, Anselm must somehow demonstrate that his designation of God is something other than an article of faith. Thus, even if we imagine that he is first going to demonstrate that God exists and then demonstrate what God is, it would seem that Anselm will have to show, first and foremost, that God is something than which nothing greater can be thought, or else it will be clear, as some have claimed, that the *Proslogion*'s arguments remain based upon faith, that is, on the *belief* that God is something than which nothing greater can be thought.

Not only our own previous discussion of the conclusions about the nature of the existence of God to which the *Monologion* finally comes, but also the first petition in P 2, which asks to understand that God exists "just as" (*sicut*) the faithful believe, should make us suspicious of the neat distinction between demonstrating "that" God is and demonstrating "what" he is.[17] It could be said that the "true existence" of God is not demonstrated in the *Monologion* until M 28, when he is seen to exist absolutely, simply, perfectly, and, as M 31 says, truly. Clearly, Anselm seems to feel obliged in the *Monologion* to complete his analysis of that supreme being argued for early in the text with a clarification of the nature of the existence of God that allows the eye of the mind to distinguish him from everything else that is. This, however, would presumably make it possible for us to determine what God is, or at least which one he is, by clarifying the distinctive way in which he exists. And if we take Anselm at his word, the *Proslogion* must come to a similar conclusion, although by means of a different route; that is, according to the above passage, it aims to arrive at the same conclusions as the *Monologion,* but by means of a single argument that avoids the complexity of its intricate chain of reasoning.

In any event, it should already be clear from Anselm's earlier work that if he is going to demonstrate the existence of God—given that God exists in a "wonderfully unique and uniquely wonderful way of his own"—he will have to demonstrate that distinctive way of existing before he has demonstrated the existence *of God*. And it would not be surprising if something of this found its way into the initial petition in P 2. Anselm knows better than anyone that he will have to show what it is for God to exist and that he exists in the specific way the faithful believe him to before he has demonstrated the existence of God. The question remains not only if but when, that is, where this is demonstrated in the text and when he will have a right to claim to have shown this. And the same holds true for the second petition.

Whether one interprets this further request—to understand that God is that which the faithful believe him to be—as a petition to understand all of the features that determine what God is or as a request to understand that God is something than which nothing greater can be thought, it would not hurt to mull over this key phrase, since it is the beginning, the origin, as it were, of Anselm's argument. The claim that God is "something than which nothing greater can be thought" is, properly speaking, the first step in the overall argument of the *Proslogion,* whether for the existence or the essence of such a being. This is, apparently, the "sign" sought in P 1, that aspect or profile under which a vision of God may be pursued by those who have not seen him face-to-face.[18] And at first sight, it might appear to be a rather enigmatic sign, as it may be difficult to see just what it is supposed to be signaling.

We do, however, have some clues from the *Monologion* not just as to what the phrase could mean, but also as to why it is so constructed. In M 15, Anselm speaks of God in somewhat similar terms. In a discussion of relative predication, of the way in which terms such as "greatest" or "supreme" cannot serve to characterize God essentially, since they are applied to him only relative to other things, Anselm concludes:

> . . . for just as it is nefarious to think that the substance of the supreme nature might be something which in some respect it would be better not to be, so it is necessary that this substance be whatever is, in every respect, better to be than not to be. For it alone is that than which nothing at all is better, and that is better than all things that are not what it is. (S I, 29)

This characterization of God as "that than which nothing is better" may look similar to the *Proslogion*'s designation of him as "something than which nothing greater can be thought," even if it is, in essence, quite different. The difference, however, may not be altogether obvious, to some extent because of the complexity of the phrases at issue, to a larger extent as a result of the extraordinary precision involved in the *Proslogion*'s careful phrasing of its designation of God. A monk who responded to Anselm's reasoning made the mistake of thinking he could substitute for "something than which nothing greater can be thought" his own simplified formula, "that which is greater than everything,"[19] resulting in a fatal misconception of the argument in question. Perhaps we can get at something of the subtlety of the *Proslogion*'s key phrase by contrasting it both with Gaunilo's rephrasing and with the terminology Anselm had himself made use of in his earlier work.

The *Monologion* had claimed that any relative designations, such as the "greatest" or the "highest"—or, as Anselm's first critic would say, "that which is greater than everything"—are not properly predictable of God insofar as they are applicable to him only relative to that "everything" he is, in that case, claimed to be greater than. In a way, Anselm is trying to correct for this in the *Monologion* itself with his more careful characterization of "that than which nothing is better," which falls somewhere between the extremes of "something than which nothing greater can be thought" and "that which is greater than everything." Unlike the latter phrase, "that than which nothing is better" seems, perhaps in its negativity, not to involve recourse to such clear relativity. It attempts to exorcise the appearance of relative predication by avoiding any reference to something being "better than" everything else. Instead, it is put in reverse: nothing else is better than it. Still, if this is preferable in certain respects to Gaunilo's phrase, both nonetheless suffer not only from the possibility that something could be better than either of the two "somethings" so designated, but also from the possibility that something greater could be thought. For the other two characterizations take their measure of greatness from what is, in fact, the case, whereas the designation in the *Proslogion* apparently takes its measure from what is thinkable or conceivable as such. And this is no small matter when it comes to the argument for the existence of the "something" at issue. As we will find, for example, when we follow Anselm's response to Gaunilo's interpretation of his argument, there is no contradiction involved in denying that "that which is greater than everything" does not exist in reality, just so long as nothing else does.

Admittedly, having made out these distinctions, it is hard to tell just what to think about the demonstration of the existence of God in the *Monologion*. One could say, if one looked only at its initial arguments, that the difference between Anselm's first two books consists in the fact that in his first work the "greatest" good or the "supreme" being, like Gaunilo's "that which is greater than everything," is being conceived relative to that "everything"—those goods or beings— it is claimed to be greater than. In that case, what we have called Anselm's cosmological strategy may well be thought to infect his thinking about God in the *Monologion,* given its tendency to start at the bottom and work its way up. This is in contrast to the *Proslogion,* where "something than which nothing greater can be thought"— which is not being conceived relative to anything else, but is simply that than which no greater is thinkable—requires us to start at the top and perhaps end there as well. The *Proslogion* never leaves this elevated plane at which it arrives through its key phrase, indeed, to which it leaps, and as suddenly, no doubt, as the revelation that came to Anselm that night at matins.[20]

At the same time, we would not want to ignore the fact that the *Monologion* is itself quite sensitive to the subtleties that are involved in these "names" of God, and that it would have well prepared Anselm for an expression such as "something than which nothing greater can be thought." After having undertaken the ascent up the ladder of being from lower to higher goods, the *Monologion* itself saw the need to go on to radically clarify not simply God's existence but all of his characteristics so that they were not considered relative to those creatures he is conceived of as absolutely different than. And something of this ultimacy, of the absolute difference between creator and creature, is captured from the start in the phrase "something than which nothing greater can be thought." In fact, the whole of the argument of P 2–4, as Anselm also tells Gaunilo, depends upon the absolute uniqueness of the matter so designated. As we will try to show, the reversal in the meaning of being in M 28 lies at the basis of the argument of P 2–4 (however deeply beneath its surface), just as there can be no doubt that Anselm extracts his notion of "greatness" in the key phrase of the *Proslogion* from certain doctrines we considered in the *Monologion.* At best, this means that we should let our own earlier discussions help to clarify the various conceptions at play in the *Proslogion.* At worst, however, this may itself suggest that a certain view of reality covertly stands behind P 2–4 that may surreptitiously require that we presuppose precisely what its argument aims to conclude. In either case, the question remains how we are to characterize Anselm's strategy in the *Proslogion,* if it is not, like the *Monologion,* obviously cosmological.

We would be inclined to say that the *Proslogion's* approach is semiological. Rather than beginning from those beings or goods with which we are ordinarily familiar, it begins from this "sign" of God, that is, from the words "something than which nothing greater can be thought." It is, as we shall see, the phrase itself that unlocks the

Proslogion argument. Of course, we would not want to deny that when Anselm wrote the *Proslogion* he had something quite specific in mind in speaking of something than which nothing greater can be thought. He had in mind the absolute being whose existence and nature he had clarified in the *Monologion* by developing the incomparable difference between creator and creature, thus securing the uncontestable candidate for the title of greatest conceivable being in the inconceivably surpassable greatness of "being itself" in contrast to any other imaginable being. In this respect, the phrase "something than which nothing greater can be thought" is, at least for Anselm, no empty string of terms; rather, it is an attempt at an extraordinarily concise naming—perhaps tries to provide a verbal or nominal revelation—of that wonderfully unique and uniquely wonderful being he had discerned in his earlier meditations. This, however, does not mean that we all share this understanding with Anselm or are immediately able to see just what this sign of God is designed to signify. And that may be truest of the fool with whom or against whom the *Proslogion* is apparently arguing.

There can scarcely be any doubt that Anselm assumed his readers would know what he was talking about, even if their understanding, at the start, lacked the precision that the *Proslogion* argument itself aims to provide. His reply to Gaunilo makes obvious not only the extent to which the argument depends upon others sharing his conception of God but also the degree to which the *Monologion* infiltrates the claims made in the *Proslogion*. When pressed to explain himself, Anselm repeatedly reverts to topics discussed in the earlier book.[21] One of the things we want to show is that and how the extremity of the *Monologion*'s position is built into the *Proslogion* argument, even if it is more carefully concealed, indeed, more cautiously monitored, by its rational precision. No doubt we have already noticed that the very issues that get the argument of P 2 moving from its starting point in the key phrase are reminiscent of the earlier work, first, in raising the question of the nature of the "understanding" enjoyed by those of us for whom the phrase "something than which nothing greater can be thought" may just be a string of words, and, second, in the clarification of this matter not just in light of the *Monologion*'s theory of signs but through its much-used example of an artist.

Perhaps in an attempt to conceal how much is packed into this key phrase while, at the same time, establishing what we have called his semiological starting point, Anselm formulates the argument in terms of the "fool" of the Psalms who "said in his heart" that God does not exist. This staging allows him to frame the question in terms of the claim that God is "something than which nothing greater can be thought," while beginning from an understanding of the words alone. Once having established this nominal foothold, the argument of P 2 will take off in a rapid-fire fashion that not only betrays the suggestion that it is addressing a fool, but that we will have to slow down in order to follow more closely. After the initial invocation, which secures the smooth transition from prayer to proof, and after having set the stage by introducing its distinctive name of God, the argument proper begins:

> Or is there, then, not something of such a nature, since *the fool said in his heart that there is no God?* But certainly this same fool, when he hears what I say, namely, something than which nothing greater can be thought, understands what he hears; and what is understood is in his understanding, even if he does not understand it to be.
>
> For it is different for a thing to be in the understanding than for that thing to be understood to be. When, for example, a painter preconceives of what he is to make, he indeed has in his understanding what he has not yet made, but he does not yet understand it to be. Once he has painted it, however, he both has in his understanding and understands to be that which he has now made.
>
> Even the fool, then, is convinced that something than which nothing greater can be thought at least is in his understanding, since he understands this when he hears it, and whatever is understood is in the understanding.

In a way, Anselm may be forced to give away the key to his kingdom in this first line. While it is critical for him to translate the question of the existence of God into the question of whether "something of such a nature" (*aliqua talis natura*) exists, namely, of the nature of something than which nothing greater can be thought, at least one critic thinks that there being such a nature depends upon there being a God.[22] In one sense, of course, Anselm knows this, for in speaking of a being "of such a nature," what he means to do is tie up the question of the existence of God with the nature of God as something than which nothing greater can be thought, in which case, the denial that God exists amounts to the denial that such a being exists. On the other hand, this way of putting matters, asking whether there is "something of such a nature," is somewhat ambiguous. It may mean that some such thing exists or that such a "nature" exists, where the latter would raise the question of whether there can be a nature such as "something than which nothing greater can be thought," that is, whether there can be something such that nothing greater than it can be thought.

In so articulating the issue, Anselm in effect, and however inadvertently, invites the question of whether something of such a nature is even thinkable: not whether there happens to be some such thing, but whether there is such a nature. Clearly, Anselm thinks that his key phrase, as well as what it names, is conceivable, although his reason for supposing that there is no problem about the very nature of something than which nothing greater can be thought, at first, and perhaps in the end, may seem rather weak. He assumes the intelligibility of the conception by insisting that the fool "understands what he hears," that he understands the words "something than which nothing greater can be thought." Perhaps Anselm is assuming that if one can entertain, as he has in the *Monologion,* a vision of the thing itself in thought, there is scarcely any question of whether the conception of such a thing makes sense; although, admittedly, this specific conception, of something than which nothing greater can be thought, was not at issue there, nor, for that matter, is the *Monologion's* vision of God, especially given the cognitive contortions in M 28, altogether clear.

At the same time, the critical claim in P 2 that the fool at least "understands what he hears" undoubtedly draws us back to M 10 and its theory of signs, where a thing may be said to be thought when the signs that signify it are "heard," whether sensibly or silently, that is, outwardly or inwardly. At that point in the *Monologion,* such thinking is not called understanding, as the latter term is reserved for the insight into the thing itself that the eye of reason may enjoy. Apparently, then, Anselm must have a weaker sense of "understanding" in operation in P 2, even if that fact may cast some suspicion on the inference he aims to draw in his attempt to avoid the host of issues that seem to come charging in on him from the very mention of the name "something than which nothing greater can be thought." While we might, in some elementary sense, feel we understand a string of words, perhaps because we understand its elements, this by itself would not seem to guarantee that, by understanding those words when we hear them spoken, the total conception becomes intelligible, nor would it follow from this that there is something "in our understanding" other than the words themselves.

Now one might well insist that the intelligibility of his key phrase was never an issue for Anselm. His point is that assuming some nominal understanding of such a conception as "something than which nothing greater can be thought," the sort of minimal verbal understanding even the fool is expected to enjoy, we must admit that one who denies God's existence must understand what it is he is denying and at least concede that whatever is understood is in his understanding. This concession, so we are assured, does not commit the fool to the claim that he understands anything to exist, that is, understands it to be anywhere but in his understanding. Of course, one could say the same thing about contradictory conceptions, as opposed, for example, to babble, since they, too, must be sufficiently intelligible to determine that they are nonsense. Be that as it may, the assumption that "whatever is understood is in the understanding" raises complications of its own. Not only would it not be the case if we were dealing with a self-contradictory concept, such as square-circle, that we would have to concede that there was something "in our understanding" we were denying existed (even though we would have to "understand" the conception sufficiently to discern its self-contradictory nature); but, as Anselm himself has elsewhere seen, even in a case in which a concept is fully intelligible, it does not necessarily follow that because it is understood we have anything in our understanding corresponding to it.

In standard cases, when we conceive of something by hearing the words for it—or, as M 10 would put it, when we think about something by means of the signs that signify it—if that something is understood by means of those signs, then, according to Anselm, we have something in our understanding, ultimately, what we would normally call the conception, or what Anselm would, no doubt, prefer to call the "likeness" of the thing. But Anselm was also clear that this was not the case with certain negative expressions. In explicating various uses of the word "something" (*aliquid*)—the term upon which the formation of his key phrase turns—Anselm himself notes that

> ... we properly call "something" that which is expressed by a name of its own, and is conceived by the mind, and exists in reality, as does a stone or wood. For these are designated by their own names, and may be conceived by the mind, and exist in reality (*in re*).
> We also call "something" that which has a name, and is conceived by the mind, but does not exist in truth, like a chimera. For a certain mental conception of the likeness of an animal, which does not, however, exist in reality (*in rerum natura*), is signified by this name.
> It is also customary to call "something" that which only has a name, without any conception coming to mind through the name, and which altogether lacks being, as is the case with injustice and nothing. For we call injustice something when we say that one who is punished on account of injustice is punished on account of something. And we speak of nothing as something if we say that something is nothing or that something is not nothing, since whether a statement is true or false, we say that something is affirmed of something or that something is denied of something. Nevertheless, there is, in the mind, no conception of injustice or of nothing, even though we have an understanding of them, as we do of indeterminate names. Indeed, to have an understanding and to have something in the understanding

are not the same. For we have an understanding of "not-man" because it causes the hearer to understand that "man" is not contained in the signification of the word but is to be removed from it. Nevertheless, it does not determine something in the understanding that is the signification of the word, the way "man" does determine a certain conception which is signified by this name. Thus, "injustice" removes the requisite justice but does not posit anything else, while "nothing" removes something and does not posit something in the understanding.[23]

Anselm encounters a problem here that is inherent to his philosophy of language, which refuses to see meaning as generated through the sign-system itself and instead insists upon its being derived from words referring to reality. Thus, he must try to account for the significance of those signs that do not seem to be signifying anything, that is, that do not seem to refer to anything, under the assumption that they function through the negation of terms that presumably do have their meaning on the basis of some reality to which they refer. His claim, then, is that negative names signify by means of a kind of mental "remotion," by naming a reality that is withdrawn from thought—as if, in thinking of injustice, the mind negates the positive conception of justice it supposedly has. Or, to take the more problematic point, in thinking of "nothing," the positive conception of "something" that is in the mind is negated. This, of course, would seem to be as ironic as it is false, for it is doubtful that, in Anselm's terms, we have a positive conception of "something." Indeed, an abstract pronoun is perhaps the worst example Anselm could have chosen, although there is no doubt that this is why he must try to "clarify" its use, for such terms rather more obviously enjoy whatever significance they do in view of the function they serve as placeholders in the sign-system and require no positive conception, in the sense that Anselm means it, to be attached to them. Consequently, Anselm avoids explicating the actual workings of the term "something" by distracting our attention to the nouns (stone, chimera, justice) for which the pronoun can itself stand in. But this listing of various types of nouns, including those that apparently refer to nothing, scarcely shows that "something" has its proper use only in the first case, when it serves to designate what has a name of its own, is a conception in the mind, and exists in reality. If anything, it suggests that terms need not refer to any reality or bring anything to mind to have "significance," that is, to play a role in a system of signs.

Our point, however, is that the distinctions Anselm draws in the above passage include an option that is not mentioned in the *Proslogion*. P 2 distinguishes between what exists in the understanding and what exists in reality, but it omits the possibility of what "only has a name." In fact, thought in terms of the above clas-sifications, it would seem (even conceding Anselm's philosophy of language) that "something than which nothing greater can be thought" is more like "not-man" than like "man," and thus would appear to fall into the third category rather than into either of the first two.[24] As we shall argue later, it is not altogether clear that we are here dealing with anything but a name. That is, it is not clear that we have a "conception" of, let alone any access to, the "reality" at issue.

At the very least, the above citation casts direct suspicion on the general principle that "whatever is understood exists in the under-standing," just as it may eventually serve to block the move to an-other principle which P 2 covertly assumes: that whatever exists in the understanding either exists in the understanding alone or exists both in the understanding and in reality. This becomes all the more pronounced when Anselm himself announces that the fool need only "understand what he hears," namely, the words "something than which nothing greater can be thought." "Having an understanding" of the verbal formula, in the case, for example, of "not-man," would not entail that we "have something in the understanding" corre-sponding to this name. And while "something than which nothing greater can be thought" may not so obviously appear to be nega-tively conceived based upon the negation of some particular concep-tion, we might think that whatever understanding we may be said to have of it is formed on the basis of the negation of all those things than which a greater can be thought. Either that, or we might be thought to have no conception of it at all, but only, shall we say, a certain nominal understanding.

Of course, given the stronger and weaker notion of "under-standing" that we have already suggested may be in operation in Anselm's argument, it could turn out that demonstrating that God is something than which nothing greater can be thought and that the phrase is intelligible will require showing that one can generate an understanding through the name itself that may eventually lead from the signs to the reality they signify. Such issues, however, and the questions they will raise, can only be addressed once we have gotten through the argument and have seen what Anselm's key phrase is supposed to designate. For now, it may still not be alto-gether clear, even assuming the intelligibility of this complex ex-pression, just how minimal our understanding of it can afford to be. In amplifying the claim that something than which nothing greater can be thought must be regarded as in our understanding, Anselm appeals to a case with which we are already familiar from the *Monologion:*

When, for example, a painter preconceives of what he is to make, he indeed has in his understanding what he has not yet made, but he does not yet understand it to be. Once he has painted it, however, he both has in his understanding, and understands to be, that which he has now made.

It is not unambiguously evident just what this example is supposed to exemplify. We know that the *Monologion* gets quite a bit of mileage out of its model of artistic preconception with respect to God's preconception of creatures. Here it is put to somewhat different use to show that something may "exist in the understanding" without it "existing in reality," as the distinction will soon be put. Apparently, the example is designed to make plausible this distinction and not to confirm or propose the precise sense in which we have anything "in the understanding" when we think the words "something than which nothing greater can be thought," although it may be suggestive in this regard.[25] For reasons we have indicated, however, if it were so taken, it could be quite misleading. That the artisan can picture something in thought without understanding it to exist seems uncontroversial. On the other hand, the fool does not as yet enjoy in his thought any such "likeness" of something than which nothing greater can be thought, as the painter presumably does of his future painting but, so one would assume, has at best a merely verbal understanding of it; just as the painter, to make Anselm's point in the *Monologion,* cannot entertain such a preconception by means of signs.

Nonetheless, while there may be nothing literally called to mind in hearing this string of terms, our own considerations in distinguishing it from other, similar characterizations (such as Gaunilo's "that which is greater than everything" or the *Monologion's* "that than which nothing is better") have indicated that we can come to some understanding of the basic, even if essentially linguistic, conception of something than which nothing greater can be thought— and of what may be entailed by it. Such a verbal understanding is presumably sufficient to draw conclusions about what is consistent and what is inconsistent with the linguistic expression, on the basis of which, however, Anselm may be able to direct our understanding to the appropriate object of thought. In fact, the key to Anselm's key phrase lies in the strange connection between the sign and the conception in this particular case. What is most remarkable about "something than which nothing greater can be thought" is the way it functions as a self-clarifying expression insofar as this complex linguistic sign itself includes a built-in criterion that will allow us, working from the verbal formula alone, to determine what pertains to and what does not pertain to its conception. Thus, it is uniquely suited as a name for making the transition from the linguistic expression to the "expression of the mind" that involves beholding a likeness of the thing itself in thought.

In this respect, Anselm's argument begins from, and hinges entirely upon, a certain "name" of God. The generation of an image of the thing itself in thought through which the reality itself may become visible to the eye of the mind results from the clarity of a self-clarifying expression that can lead reason to the matter at issue simply by following a criterion built into the verbal formula itself. All the rational mind needs to do is run through a list of possible features, asking whether the possession of each is consistent or inconsistent with something's being that than which a greater cannot be thought, rejecting those that are inconsistent and including those that are consistent. What could be more obvious? Its point, however, is easy to miss. The seemingly formulaic procedure that we will follow throughout the *Proslogion,* with its incessant application of the built-in criterion to one feature after another, is designed to allow the mind to formulate, as the *Monologion* did, its own rational image of God. If the phrase "something than which nothing greater can be thought" is uniquely suited for getting through the signs to the likeness in thought of the thing so signified, it is because it has been precisely designed as a formula for thinking the thing itself.

In any case, whether we are considering the verbal expression or the expression of the thing itself in our thought, both of which Anselm seems to want to regard, at least in P 2, as a matter of something's "being in our understanding," the latter category is clearly aimed at getting around the problem of whether we do indeed have to concede that something of such a nature exists or that there is something than which nothing greater can be thought before we can begin to draw conclusions about it. Instead, Anselm wants to claim that we can entertain something of such a nature in thought, if only based upon the understanding of the words when we hear them. These words, however, are so constructed as to allow us to proceed with a clarification of the matter thanks to the self-clarifying nature of the expression itself, in the first instance by applying a built-in criterion to the question of the existence or nonexistence of such a nature. Once this has been established, Anselm is free to take up what has traditionally been regarded as his argument for the existence of God:

> Even the fool, then, is convinced that something than which nothing greater can be thought at least is in his understanding, since he understands this when he hears it, and whatever is understood is in the understanding.

> But certainly that than which a greater cannot be thought cannot be in the understanding alone. For if it is in the understanding alone even, it can be thought to be in reality also—which is greater. If, therefore, that than which a greater cannot be thought is in the understanding alone, that than which a greater cannot be thought is itself that than which a greater can be thought. But certainly this cannot be. Therefore, without doubt, something than which a greater cannot be thought exists both in the understanding and in reality.

To make this argument go though, we would have to include an implied and seemingly innocuous premise to the effect that whatever exists in the understanding either exists in the understanding alone or exists both in the understanding and in reality. With that inclusion, we can formulate the reasoning of P 2 as follows:

1. God is something than which nothing greater can be thought.
2. "Something than which nothing greater can be thought" is understood when it is heard.
3. Whatever is understood exists in the understanding.
4. Whatever exists in the understanding either exists in the understanding alone or exists both in the understanding and in reality.
5. That than which a greater cannot be thought cannot exist in the understanding alone.
   a. Assume it exists in the understanding alone.
   b. Then it can be thought to exist in reality also, which is greater.
   c. Thus, if it exists in the understanding alone, it is that than which a greater can be thought.
   d. But then, that than which a greater cannot be thought is that than which a greater can be thought; which is absurd.
   e. So premise 5 is shown.
6. Therefore, without doubt, something than which a greater cannot be thought exists both in the understanding and in reality.

I am inclined to schematize the argument as I have, and to include the suppressed premise (premise 4), to avoid confusion.[27] It is critical to see that the famous *reductio ad absurdum* portion of the argument—the part I have subsumed under steps 5 a–e, which operates under the argumentative strategy of assuming the opposite of what is to be shown and demonstrating it to lead us into contradiction—is designed to justify a single, albeit critical premise, but that the existence of God is not directly concluded from it. Otherwise, there is tendency to overemphasize this aspect of the argument, especially if one gets the feeling that it is here that existence in reality is being imported into the discussion. But if existence in reality is brought into play at any point that is directly relevant to the conclusion of P

2, it is in premise 4. The existence "both in the understanding and in reality" that is invoked in the conclusion at 6 follows from 4, not from the subargument under premise 5. In fact, the conclusion that something than which a greater cannot be thought—which we might simply abbreviate as "S"—exists both in the understanding and in reality only indirectly follows from the *reductio* argument insofar as it follows from a demonstration that employs the premise which this *reductio* shows. The conclusion that S exists both in the understanding and in reality is not and cannot be shown by the *reductio* proper. Instead, it follows from a direct demonstration that makes use of premise 5, together with a claim that can be derived from its first four premises, namely, that S either exists in the understanding alone or both in the understanding and in reality. If there are only two alternatives and one is shown to be impossible, namely, that S exists in the understanding alone, the other is doubtless the case, namely, that it exists both in the understanding and in reality. This conclusion, however, follows from the direct demonstration (1–6), not from the famous *reductio* portion of the argument (5 a–e).

This may seem an unimportant difference, since the somewhat negative approach—of backing into the conclusion that S exists in reality by first limiting the options to its existing either in the understanding alone or both in the understanding and in reality and then showing it cannot exist in the understanding alone—depends upon the demonstration of the critical premise 5. Consequently, one might still think this to be the heart of the argument. And so, in a sense, it is. But regarding the *reductio* as a subargument not only makes it clear that it is not at this point or from this point that existence in reality enters into the argument, but it also allows one to raise the question of the dispensability of this *reductio,* or rather, certain of its claims, if they prove to be unacceptable. In that case, if we should find problems with the argument of 5 a–e, all we need to do is provide not another argument for the existence of God but another argument that would be sufficient to demonstrate premise 5.

What I have in mind here can be put rather simply. While there is a tendency to assume that Anselm's argument depends upon the claim that it is greater to exist in reality than in the understanding alone, and while Anselm does, indeed, believe the latter claim and appeals to it in the argument as it stands, the more essential claim in P 2 is that whatever exists in the understanding alone is something than which a greater can be thought. That is, for any X, if X exists in the understanding alone, something greater than it can be thought.[28] And there are any number of different ways to try to defend this latter claim or at least more ways to defend the claim that it is greater to exist than not to exist. Anselm himself suggests some alternatives in his first reply to Gaunilo and, in so doing, clearly indicates that the critical principle in P 2 may not be that it is greater to exist than not to exist, but that something greater can be thought than what exists in the understanding alone.[29]

Before turning to that self-interpretation on Anselm's part, we must nonetheless address the controversial claim—whether as blatantly appealed to in P 2 as it stands or as perhaps covertly assumed in the revised versions of P 2 offered in his replies—that it is greater to exist than not to exist. That his first critic does not question this principle suggests that Anselm was right to regard it as a self-evident or accepted dimension of the world of his historical audience. Clearly, the basic doctrine of the hierarchy of being stands behind the view that there is a certain inherent greatness, a different degree of reality, relevant to various levels of existence. In M 31, for example, Anselm attempts, albeit negatively, to whet our intuitions in this respect about the nature of being:

> If we think of some substance that is alive and sentient and rational to be deprived of its reason, then of its sentience, then of its life, and finally of the bare existence that remains, who would not understand that the substance that is thus destroyed, little by little, is gradually brought to less and less existence, and ultimately to nonexistence? If what is removed, however, respectively reduces a being to lesser and lesser existence, when added to it, in the relevant order, it leads to greater and greater existence. (S I, 49–50)

Here, I suppose, one could say that we were dealing with matters of essence, not of existence. And yet, since the issue of the degree of being is inseparable, for Anselm, from the kind of being at issue, it is not surprising that some have tried to find the justification for the claims made in P 2 in the doctrine of degrees of reality. Certainly Anselm is here suggesting that it is greater to exist than not to exist; although if we were to say why, given this passage, it would seem to be because, in failing to exist, a thing does not just lack some one feature it would have if it did exist but would appear to fail to have any feature at all. Of course, one can still think about the features which things that do not exist might have if they existed; but this does not mean that they enjoy the reality of such a set of features, even though, while the conceptions we would then be entertaining are mind-dependent, the features themselves are not. According to the *Monologion*'s philosophy of mind, we can think up and rearrange sets of features—for example, in imagination—dependent upon and only based upon those realities which the mind has access to not in thought but in experience.

To this extent, Anselm himself insists a few chapters later in the *Monologion* that things are less real in our thinking than they are in themselves, while they are less real in themselves than they are in God's knowledge of them. This is because in our thinking, we do not entertain the things themselves but their likenesses, just as those things ultimately come to be regarded as likenesses of the true reality which is the expression of the thing in God's thought. It is this whole set of issues surrounding the discussion of thinking in the *Monologion* and the human mind's formation of likenesses that is most relevant to the issue before us. For the difference in P 2 is not between existence and nonexistence, as it is portrayed in the passage from M 31, but between what exists in the understanding alone and what exists also in reality.

To appreciate what it is to exist "in the understanding alone" and why, as such, it is not as great as existing in reality, we must appeal to Anselm's epistemology as much as to his metaphysics. Indeed, we must recall how they fit together. Anselm himself explicates the relevant difference in M 36, although in a rather different context than in P 2:

> For no one doubts that created substances are much differently in themselves than in our knowledge. For in themselves they are through their own being; in our knowledge, however, is not their being, but their likeness. It follows, then, that they are more truly in themselves than in our knowledge to the extent to which they are more truly anywhere through their own being than through their likenesses. (S I, 54–55)

Given the *Monologion*'s account of the nature of human reason and the generation or formation of "likenesses" of things in thought, it is clear that something's existing in the understanding alone does not so much involve a different degree of being—like the difference between a man and a horse—as it plays off of the difference between a "reality" and a "likeness" by invoking the issue of the ontological status of images. In this respect, Anselm is more emphatic here than we might expect, for he is not just saying that the likeness is less real than that of which it is a likeness, but he is implying that, as dependent upon the human mind, the likeness in a sense enjoys no "being" at all. That is, it is only "in themselves" (*in seipsis*) that things can properly be said to have being, whereas in our minds they do not exist in virtue of their own being (*per ipsam suam essentiam*) but rather in terms of their likeness (*per suam similitudinem*). Working from the same general principle—that the original is more real than its imitation, if only because the latter depends upon the former— Anselm wants eventually to conclude, even though he admits that it is incomprehensible, that the things themselves enjoy less being,

exist less truly, in themselves than they do in God's original knowledge of them in the supreme truth.[30] Fortunately, for our purposes,
we can stick with the claim that operates at the more mundane
level, namely, that a likeness is not just less real than the original,
but that it enjoys an ontological status of a completely different order that is not nearly so much a matter of degree as a difference in
ontological kind.

In that case, Anselm's contention is that "the things themselves" are more real than the likenesses of those things generated
in and by thought, indeed, are more real in whichever degree of being they have, whether that of a stone or of a man, to the extent to
which they have the status of "being," whereas what exists in the
understanding alone has the dubious ontological status of a "likeness." Once we appreciate that what is at work in P 2 in the difference between what "exists in the understanding" and what "exists
in reality" is the difference between a dependent likeness and the
thing itself (which enjoys its own relatively independent reality), it
should be easier to see why Anselm thought it was greater to exist *in
re* than *in intellectu* based on the traditional assumptions about the
ontological inferiority of images. Construing this difference, however, as an ontological one suggests that, for Anselm, existing in reality was not a matter of something's having one more feature,
namely, existence, which it would be lacking if it existed only in the
understanding, such that, in making a list of the properties of a nonexistent S and the properties of an existent S, the existent S would
be greater because its list of features would be longer by one. On the
contrary, judging from what we have seen—and because even in P 2
Anselm speaks of something's "being" in the understanding—being
as such would appear to be the condition for having any features; in
which case, it seems fitting to claim that existence is not to be regarded as one feature among others. Perhaps, since what is at issue
in P 2 is not exactly the distinction, as it is construed in M 31, between existence and nonexistence, we should put it this way: the difference between existing in the understanding and existing in
reality is not a difference in one feature but rather a difference in the
ontological status of a set of features. Thus, for Anselm, any existing
thing has an enhanced ontological status, is greater than any likeness of any thing in thought, no matter what features it is presumed
to have; or, more revealingly put: any likeness has a reduced ontological status as a mere dependent image of reality. Consequently,
we need not compare the same set of features—the same being, as it
were, existing in reality and existing in the understanding—to make out
this contrast, although the relevant difference, as a strictly ontological one, may be clearer when we do.

In claiming this, we may appear to be playing into the hands of the standard criticism of the argument of P 2, namely, that insofar as "existence is not a property," that is, is not among the features that pertain to the content of the concept of something, it cannot alter the concept, whether for the better or the worse. In that case, all the wrangling about whether it is greater to exist in reality than in the understanding alone may be regarded as quite beside the point, if we agree that existing in reality does not add a further feature to the list of properties that a being is claimed to have but, instead, involves a difference in the ontological status of a set of features. We will postpone dealing with that criticism just now so as to address it when it may serve a number of purposes, although we might note that, in our account, both in P 2 or P 3, the question is essentially that of the ontological status of something than which nothing greater can be thought. For present purposes, it is enough to suggest why Anselm would have thought that it is greater to exist in reality than in the understanding alone and to suggest that this is, in his mind at least, based on the ontological difference between an original and a likeness.

We mention the standard criticism of the *reductio* portion of P 2 not only because it suggests that we must compare the same being existing in reality and existing in the understanding alone to draw the conclusion that the latter would be less great than the former, since it would lack the feature of existence, but also because it is assumed in those criticisms that it is a matter of simple existence. Premise 5, however, as stated, appears to claim something stronger than this; for its aim is not to show that S does not exist in the understanding alone but that it *cannot*. Ironically, certain philosophers, hoping to avoid what they regard as a devastating criticism of P 2, have recently looked to P 3 to find an argument for the necessary existence of God, under the assumption that "necessary" existence adds to the concept of something, even if "simple" existence does not; and they have defended, or tried to defend, the claim that something's necessarily existing makes it greater than what contingently exists. In so doing, they have not only misread, as we will argue later, the meaning of the distinction in P 3 and, thus, the point of its claim, but they have systematically, for the sake of contrast, underrated the force of P 2.[31] If there is any hint of a "modal" argument for the existence of God in the *Proslogion,* any argument that trades on questions of possible and necessary being, not simply on factual matters of existence, that argument must be in P 2. And there is some indication of this, I think, in its insistence that S cannot exist in the understanding alone, just as there is a similar suggestion of impossibility expressed not simply, as one would expect, in the conclusion of the *reductio* at premise 5 but in the claim that the conclusion of the demonstration as a whole in step 6 can be drawn "without doubt." To appreciate what might be at issue here, however, we must look more carefully at the heart of the argument.

On Various Readings and Misreadings of *Proslogion* 2

At least two basic aspects of the strategy of P 2 suggest the strength of the contention made there. First, one way of thinking is barred as inconceivable, that is, S existing in the understanding alone is not just claimed to be factually false but to be conceptually impossible. Second, this is shown by constructing an argument that has avoided making use of any factual premises, that is, premises that could conceivably be otherwise.[32] In both respects, the force of Anselm's argument in P 2 comes into relief quite concisely in contrasting its logic with Gaunilo's misunderstanding of it.

We said earlier that Gaunilo's misinterpretation is the result of his altering the key phrase from "something than which nothing greater can be thought" to "that which is greater than everything," apparently not realizing that in so doing, he must also change the form of the argument. At the critical point in the *reductio* where Anselm says, "But if it exists in the understanding alone, it can be thought to exist in reality also, which is greater"—from which it can only be concluded that something greater can be thought than S if it exists in the understanding alone—Gaunilo must import a further premise into the argument. It is simply not the case that because something greater can be thought than what exists in the understanding alone, there would be something greater than that which is greater than everything. In a world in which, as a matter of fact, everything else failed to exist, that which is greater than everything could itself, and without contradiction, fail to exist. Nor can we claim that if that which is greater than everything existed in the understanding alone, it would be less than itself if it existed, since its existence is precisely what is in question. Thus, if it failed to exist in reality, there would still be nothing greater than it, just so long as nothing else existed.

Consequently, Gaunilo must not only alter the form of the argument, but his version must also include a premise that actually defeats the main virtue of Anselm's original strategy. According to Gaunilo's reading, the reasoning of P 2 can be characterized as follows:

... and this is proved on the basis of the fact that it is greater to exist also in reality than in the understanding alone, and that if it exists in the understanding alone, whatever existed also in reality would be greater than it, and thus that that which is greater than everything would be less than something and would not be greater than everything, which is obviously contradictory. Therefore, it is necessary that that which is greater than everything, which has already been proved to exist in the understanding, exist not in the understanding alone, but in reality as well, since otherwise it would not be greater than everything. (S I, 125)

It is not surprising that Anselm would insist in his reply that "nowhere in all that I have said will you find such an argument." [33] The critical difference, however, is not simply a nominal one, that Anselm does not speak of "that which is greater than everything" but of "something than which nothing greater can be thought." Certainly he strenuously objects to this substitution, but because, I would suggest, for the argument to go through in Gaunilo's version it must include a factual premise—that something exists in reality— so that that which is greater than everything will have to exist if "whatever existed also in reality," as Gaunilo puts it, is not to be greater than it.[34] Thus, Gaunilo's argument runs: If anything exists, then that which is greater than everything must exist, or else it would not be greater than everything. And however innocuous the assumption of the antecedent—that something exists—may seem to be, the moment it is included in the argument, the demonstration of the existence of that which is greater than everything becomes a factual matter, not a conceptual one, in which case, its nonexistence is possible; that is, it has not been shown (even were we to be convinced by the argument) that it "cannot" exist in the understanding alone but rather that, as a matter of fact, it does not, given that something besides it exists.

By contrast, of course, all Anselm's argument requires is that, whether anything else actually exists or not, something greater can be thought than what exists in the understanding alone. Presumably, something greater than S existing in the understanding alone is thought when S is thought to exist in reality. Needless to say, this does not as yet show that S exists in reality. It is only supposed to demonstrate that something greater can be thought than S existing in the understanding alone. According to Gaunilo, however, the "something" which "that which is greater than everything" must exist to be greater than would not only have to exist, but would have to be something other than it, since, as we have said, we cannot assume that that which is greater than everything would be less than itself if it did not exist, since whether it exists or not is precisely what is in question. In any event, what is most striking in this attack and counterattack is that while Gaunilo moves in the direction of a factual demonstration, Anselm launches his response by highlighting the modal dimension of his argument, emphasizing that it is clearly a matter of necessity that S exist both in the understanding and in reality.

In his first reply, Anselm himself reformulates his argument as follows:

> From the fact that something than which a greater cannot be thought is understood, it does not follow, you claim, that it is in the understanding, nor if it is in the understanding, that it therefore exists in reality. But I say with certainty that if it even can be thought to exist, it is necessary that it exist. For that than which a greater cannot be thought cannot be thought to exist except without beginning. But whatever can be thought to exist and does not exist can be thought to exist through a beginning. Therefore, that than which a greater cannot be thought cannot be thought to exist and yet not exist. If, therefore, it can be thought to exist, it exists of necessity.
>
> Furthermore: if, indeed, it even can be thought, it is necessary that it exist. For no one who denies or doubts that something than which a greater cannot be thought exists denies or doubts that, if it existed, it could neither actually nor conceivably not exist. For otherwise, it would not be that than which a greater cannot be thought. But whatever can be thought and does not exist, if it existed, could either actually or conceivably not exist. Therefore, if that than which a greater cannot be thought can even be thought, it cannot not exist. But let us suppose that it does not exist, even if it can be thought. Now whatever can be thought and does not exist, if it existed, would not be that than which a greater cannot be thought. In that case, even if that than which a greater cannot be thought were to exist, it would not be that than which a greater cannot be thought, which is utterly absurd. It is false, therefore, that something than which a greater cannot be thought does not exist, if it even can be thought, and all the more so if it can be understood and be in the understanding. (S I, 130–31)

Certain interpreters have found here what they take to be a modal argument for the existence of God, an argument for his necessary existence, or at least for the claim not just that he does, as a matter of fact, happen to exist, but that he cannot fail to exist.[35] Oddly enough, when these same interpreters have looked to the *Proslogion* itself, they have sought such an argument in P 3, which aims to show that S cannot be thought not to exist, whereas the above reply would appear to be offering an alternative rendering of the argument of P 2. This is indicated not only by the fact that the reply goes on to address the issues raised in P 3 but, even more to the point, by the fact that its claim that S cannot not exist (*non potest non esse*) is not equivalent to the contention in P 3 that S cannot be thought not to exist, but rather to the claim in P 2 that S cannot exist in the understanding alone. In that case, it would appear that Anselm thought more was entailed by his argument in P 2 than the mere demonstration of the factual existence of something. He thought he had shown, as the conclusion of P 2 puts it, that something exists "without doubt." And for questions of existence to be beyond doubt requires that the matter cannot be otherwise.

Now, admittedly, there is, in the above passage, a certain mixing of the arguments of P 2 and 3, as Anselm refers to what can "neither actually nor conceivably" (*nec actu nec intellectu*) not exist, although I think it is fair to say that the claim that S cannot actually not exist is what is at issue, not the claim that it cannot be thought not to exist. As the concluding argument here emphasizes, in echoing the arguments that have come before, Anselm's point is that S cannot not exist because whatever can not exist, even if it existed, would not be something than which a greater cannot be thought. And this point is, indeed, quite suggestive—if, as we have said, the claim that S cannot not exist is equivalent to the claim that S cannot exist in the understanding alone—for a clarification of the argument of P 2.

Rather than arguing about whether it is greater to exist than not to exist, one might take what we earlier labeled as premise 5 to suggest that the very characteristic introduced there, namely, that S cannot exist in the understanding alone, should be regarded as the kind of feature that would make something than which nothing greater can be thought greater than those somethings than which a greater can be thought. In fact, since we already know from our reading of the *Monologion* (to which reply 1 is appealing in its claims about a being without a beginning) that Anselm has a conception of the supreme being as something that exists *per se*, it must be clear that, for him, anything that does not, that exists "through another," is less than what can be thought. Thus, the argument of 5 a–e might be recast to run something more like: Assume S exists in the understanding alone; but then, it does not exist *per se*, that is, if it does not exist, its nature cannot be such that it exists through itself, in which case, even if it existed, it would have to be thought of as existing through another. But if it is greater to exist *per se* than to exist through another, something greater can be thought than S, etc. Or, even more simply: If S exists in the understanding alone, then it can exist in the understanding alone; but something can be thought that cannot exist in the understanding alone, and this is greater, etc. These approaches at least have the virtue of appearing to be more directly relevant to the presumed point, namely, to show that S cannot exist in the understanding alone, and of keeping it clear that it is not simply the factual existence of something that is at issue in P 2, but the nature of a being—namely, S—that would fail to be itself if it could exist in the understanding alone. And the basic assumption, the basic insight, here would, then, not simply be that existence is greater than nonexistence, but that being the sort of thing that cannot fail to exist is greater than being the sort of thing that can.

One way to justify my tendency to read around the *reductio* as it stands—and not just because it is subject to criticism, for I do not think the richer reading Anselm proposes is any less assailable—is to question the extent to which that argument is sufficient to demonstrate what is clearly a modal premise; for whatever is shown in 5 a–e must be sufficient to establish the strong claim of premise 5 that S cannot exist in the understanding alone. Indeed, the emphasis on this "cannot" (*non potest*) is even more pronounced in the Latin, as Anselm alters the way he expresses the "cannot" (*nequit*) of his key phrase so as not to distract from it. And whatever analysis we provide of this portion of his argument must preserve the force of this emphatic "cannot," just as whatever criticisms of the argument we might want to level must be directed at its strongest claim. Somehow, the *reductio* must be sufficient to show this modal claim, and in a sense it is, once we see how it works, even as Anselm proposes it. But it does not so clearly and unambiguously achieve this as one might like, as it obscures its own aim as well as a number of other, finer points as it stands. I would like to amplify a few of them in the hope of giving some indication of why I think there is good reason to admit that there is a modal element to the argument for the existence of God in P 2, even if the basis for it cannot be fully exposed until our conclusion.[36]

First and foremost is the problem that suggests that Anselm is importing existence into the argument at the controversial juncture where he says that if S exists in the understanding alone, it can be thought to exist in reality also, which is greater. All he needs to show at this point is that something greater *can be thought* than what exists in the understanding alone. In that case, we are in effect considering the ontological status of what exists in reality, not the fact of existence. In other words, we are reading this line to claim that if something is such that it is thought of as existing in the understanding alone, then something that is thought of as existing in reality provides thought with something greater to think. This is confirmed in reply 2, where Anselm says: "For if it exists in the understanding alone even, can it not be thought to exist in reality also? And if it can, does not one who thinks this think of something greater than it if it exists in the understanding alone?" (S I, 132). Presumably, all

Anselm means to conclude at this point is not that S exists, but that something greater than it can be thought if it is thought of as existing in the understanding alone. At this stage of the *reductio,* and again in contrast to Gaunilo's misunderstanding, it is strictly a matter of thought, not of actuality; of what is conceivable, not of what is in fact the case.

Notice that according to the substitute reading suggested above, the claim that S exists in the understanding alone together with the claim that something can be thought that cannot fail to exist would appear to justify the conclusion that S cannot exist in the understanding alone without directly entailing that S is the being we thought of as unfailingly existing. The relevant conclusion of the *reductio* (premise 5) would only require that something greater can be thought than what exists in the understanding alone. This is why Anselm can reformulate the basis for that claim in any number of ways in his reply. If we are not sure whether we want to admit that whatever exists in reality is greater than whatever exists in the understanding alone, all we need to concede is that something greater can be thought than what exists in the understanding alone—for example, a being that cannot fail to exist, or one that is without beginning or end, or one that exists *per se,* etc.—to show that whatever exists in the understanding alone is something than which a greater can be thought, without, of course, needing to assume, at this point, that S is this being without beginning or end, etc. At this stage at least, we would be committed to thinking only that if S existed in the understanding alone, something greater than it could be thought, and thus that it would be something than which a greater can be thought; from which, needless to say, we might try to conclude, given further premises, that it must exist in reality, since it cannot exist in the understanding alone if something is conceivably greater than what exists in the understanding alone. But in that case, we have concluded that S exists in reality because something greater can be thought than what exists in the understanding alone, and not because what was conceivably greater happened to be something that necessarily existed, and S happened to be this something.

This is a hard point to keep straight, especially given the first way Anselm reformulates the argument in reply 1. And this is why I want to insist that the issue of existence in reality has two distinct dimensions in P 2, and why I have cast the argument with the *reductio* as a subargument. One aspect of the issue of existence, introduced at premise 4, is relevant to the direct demonstration that concludes with step 6, while quite another is relevant to the *reductio* itself. If we conclude that S cannot fail to exist both in the understanding and in reality, it is not because we have introduced the issue of existence, whether contingent or necessary, into steps 5 a–e. The fact that the conclusion of the argument as a whole does not directly trade on the *reductio*'s consideration of the "greatness" of reality can best be seen by attending to how the form of the argument avoids what would be a sleight-of-hand importation of existence into it. Notice that in Anselm's original version he contends that if S exists in the understanding alone, then "it can be thought to exist in reality," which is, presumably, greater. Obviously, Anselm does not mean that what makes it greater is that it "can be thought" to exist in reality. Instead, the "can be thought" here belongs to the form of the argument, not to the content of the phrase; that is, what is greater is that it "exists in reality," not that it is able to be thought to exist. This becomes evident once we realize that much of what exists in the understanding alone can be thought to exist in reality, in which case, if Anselm means this by his claim, there would be no relevant contrast. Rather, what he means, as he confirms in his reply to Gaunilo, is that one can think of something that exists in reality, and thinking this is to think something greater.

Anselm is clearly not assuming that just because we can think something to exist that it would directly follow that it exists. This is what is so clever, not just about the strategy of his argument but about the way the key phrase makes such a strategy possible. As a result of the contradiction that can be generated thanks to the key phrase, it will follow that if we can think that S, or anything, exists, and existing is greater than not existing, then something greater can be thought than what exists in the understanding alone. But it does not follow from this that S exists, but rather that S, existing in the understanding alone, would then fail to be "something than which nothing greater can be thought" insofar as, given what has just been said, its existing in the understanding alone would allow us to think something greater than it, which is presumably impossible. Similarly, if what cannot fail to exist is greater than what can, then if S existed in the understanding alone, it would be the sort of being that can fail to exist, in which case, one can think of something greater. It would not immediately follow from this, however, that S cannot fail to exist, but only that something greater can be thought than S; from which, again, one might try to show, given further premises, that S cannot exist in the understanding alone, i.e., that S cannot not exist. But this conclusion could be reached whether we assume that it is greater to exist than not to exist, or that it is greater for something to be such that it cannot fail to exist, or such that it is without a beginning or end, etc. Consequently, it should be clear that these principles are not directly responsible for the relevant conclusion. Still, the apparent coincidence between the conclusion and the principle that supports it in P 2 as it stands is precisely what can mislead us in our understanding of the logic of the argument and the strategy of its procedure.

This confusion arises because the conclusion we want to draw from the direct demonstration and the conclusion to be drawn from the *reductio* each, but in its own way and with a different purpose, speaks to the topic of existence: the one to show that something exists, the other to show that something greater can be thought. Perhaps we can bring out this difference more clearly, as well as what hinges on it, by considering the traditional criticism of the argument, whose discussion we earlier postponed. That criticism, which has been regarded as the classic refutation of the ontological argument, does not question, in a certain rather important sense, whether it is greater to exist than not to exist. It, instead, operates at an even more fundamental level, questioning whether existence can in any way alter the content of the concept of something. Obviously, if existence does not alter the concept, it can hardly alter it for the better. And whether or not this criticism is properly applied to Anselm—since it was not directed at his argument but at the later Cartesian version, which does work from the "concept" of God—it has been so applied, such that, if we assume Anselm is asking us to compare the concept of a nonexistent S with the concept of an existent S to see which is greater, so this argument goes, there will be no difference. For assuming that something exists can add nothing to the determination of its concept, or else what existed would not be the same thing we conceived of. In the standard example of a hundred dollars, the contention is that there is no difference, "not a penny more," in the concept of a hundred real dollars and a hundred imaginary dollars; not, in other words, any conceptual difference, but only a factual difference in whether or not those dollars actually exist.

It would seem that there is something misleading going on here, perhaps as a kind of tactical distraction. For the example draws our attention to an irrelevant dimension of the contrast, to the concept of "dollars" rather than to the real/imaginary difference, which is what is at issue. Even if we admit that the concept of "one hundred dollars" remains the same—that both a real and an imaginary one hundred dollars contain an equal number of dollars, whether existent or nonexistent—we may not be willing to admit that "real dollars" and "imaginary dollars" amount to the same concept. It may be that this example shows that existence and nonexistence are irrelevant to the concept of "one hundred dollars," but it does not show that the notion of existence is conceptually irrelevant to all concepts, as it would not seem to be irrelevant to the concept "imaginary dollars." All such an argument would demonstrate, then, is that dollars are not the sort of things that are conceived of as by nature existing or not existing and that, to the extent to which we do think of them as existing or not existing, it is a factual matter. But this only shows that, in the case of dollars, the concept is indifferent to or neutral with respect to questions of existence. In that event, however, it is a bit like saying that there is no difference between red and blue because whether you add red twos or blue twos, it all amounts to four. Of course, it does; but all this shows is that the concept of two is indifferent to color concepts, not that there is never a case in which being red or blue alters the concept of something.

In this same way, even if we can count up one hundred dollars, imaginary or real, that does not answer the question of whether this is because of the concept we have chosen or because there is no case in which existence is relevant to the determination of the concept of something. Apparently, it is not irrelevant to the concept "imaginary dollars" or to the concept "real dollars," since we have just been entertaining that difference conceptually. Nor, as Anselm thinks, is existence irrelevant to the concept "accomplished artwork," if we take the painter example in P 2 seriously. But let us take more obvious examples. Is it irrelevant to the concept "fictional character" that what it designates does not exist? Or is it irrelevant to the concept "hallucination" or "mirage" that what one is seeing is not real? Or to the concept "imaginary," as we were suggesting a moment ago? Certainly, when we speak of a child's "imaginary friend," we mean the concept—not of "friend" but of "imaginary friend"—to be determined by the nonexistence of what it designates. This is not to deny that, in most cases, existence may well not be an element in the determination of a concept. It is, however, to insist that, given a broader set of examples, there may be a need to distinguish between what might be called factual and conceptual uses of "exist." What I am suggesting is that, in certain cases, existence may well be completely irrelevant to the concept of something—is simply a matter of fact—as in the case of existence-neutral concepts, such as "dollars." But it is not clear that this is the sort of concept with which Anselm is dealing, if he can properly be said to be dealing with a "concept" of "something than which nothing greater can be thought." The question, in that event, is whether existence is ever relevant to the concept of anything and whether the latter is one of those cases.

One of the ways to see that there are conceptually relevant uses of "existence" is to appreciate—and precisely in accord with what is claimed as a basis for this criticism—that in the case of those concepts to which existence is relevant, in the negative cases, it is never the same thing that exists and of which we have the concept, or in the positive cases, if it exists, of which we have only a concept. For example, if nonexistence were relevant to the concept of something, it could not be the same thing that existed and of which we had a concept. If what we were claiming, say, to be a hallucination turned out to exist, we would not be willing to apply the concept "hallucination" to it. In that case, it is right to say that it is not the same thing we were thinking and which existed, in the same way that if one hundred imaginary dollars existed, they would not be imaginary dollars but real ones. It is not the concept of dollars, of course, which is in that event altered but the concept of "imaginary"; or rather, in the face of the existence of the dollars, the concept "imaginary dollars" simply no longer applies.

Notice, also, in this connection, that one can admit—as Anselm no doubt would insist—that existence is not simply one property among others but may, for example, be a matter of what we earlier called the ontological status of a set of features, without denying that there can be conceptually relevant existential determinations of certain concepts. Whatever analysis I may be inclined to give of existence, including that it is not a property, I might still insist that in claiming that hallucinations do not exist in reality but in the understanding alone, I am trying to make a conceptually relevant point—and a point rather different from my claiming that, as a matter of fact, a hundred dollars do not at this moment exist in my pocket but only in my mind. Clearly not all concepts are like the examples we have suggested, such that they may allow for a certain existential analysis at the conceptual level. But then, we are not here concerned with all concepts. Instead, we are interested in the notion of something than which nothing greater can be thought and with the apparent contention that somehow existence is relevant to its very nature, in which case, we would need to consider further appropriate cases of conceptually relevant uses of "exist"—of concepts in which existence plays a role in their determination—and not allow ourselves to be distracted by irrelevant examples.

When we do, however, we will find that while this claim about conceptually relevant cases of existence would seem to solve one problem, it leads to another. Of course, it can to some degree serve to allay, at least momentarily, the inclination to think that the sort of conceptual analysis in P 2 is irrelevant to matters of existence. For this may now appear to be a result of our being overly familiar with a certain set of examples, surrounded, as we are, by things whose existence is apparently irrelevant to their conception. Obviously, those who would defend such an approach as Anselm's would insist that there is no *prima facie* basis for the tendency to think that logic cannot decide such matters, but that our assumptions in this regard depend upon which "face" of existence we take to be "first." Indeed, if the argument offered is to the point, it provides the paradigmatic counterexample, showing this ordinary propensity to be the result of a rather literal shortsightedness. And there are, admittedly, some less extraordinary cases in which existence, or the lack thereof, could be said to pertain to the "essence" of what is being thought. Negative cases are frequently suggested as the type of example on which the positive case of God is to be modeled. Thus, it is sometimes said that just as logic is in a position to determine that, by nature, self-contradictory things do not exist—that, for instance, there are no square circles—so, too, in the case of God, logic is in a position to determine that something does exist, and by its very nature. Perhaps even more to the point, we have found that there are positive cases in which existence is essentially relevant to the concept of something. In that event, we must ask whether these examples would serve to whet our intuitions about what it is for something not merely in fact, but in essence, to exist, or would bode poorly for Anselm's argument if they turn out to be the sort of cases that, despite our admitting the validity of the claim that existence could be shown to pertain to the concept of something, nonetheless left us unconvinced that something existed.

Needless to say, despite any of these other examples, one can always take refuge, as Anselm frequently does, in the claim that the case of God is unique and so must be kept distinct from all others. Still, we should think it would have to be more like the conceptually relevant cases of existence than like those concepts that are existence neutral. And while the discovery of positive cases of existence-relevant concepts may appear to allay our fear that logic is irrelevant when it comes to questions of existence, which are matters of fact rather than of concepts, it can only do so momentarily insofar as we may have already noticed that such cases also show that conceptual existence (if we can call it that) does not entail factual existence. We can imagine, for example, someone explaining to a child the difference between the concept of a "fictional" and a "nonfictional" character by insisting that fictional characters do not exist in reality but only in works of fiction, or, perhaps one could say, only in our understanding. Then, by contrast, one might note that nonfictional characters do not exist in the understanding alone but in reality as well. This claim that "nonfictional characters exist both in the understanding and in reality," would, in that case, not be a claim to the actual, factual existence of anything. It would, instead, be a conceptual reminder that serves to clarify the concept "nonfictional character." To put it otherwise, here we seem to have a case in which existence could be said to pertain to the nature of something, indeed, not only alters but determines the concept, without it being the case, however, that something exists. For it is quite possible that there actually be no nonfictional characters, that is, it is a matter of fact if there happen to be any, even though, in a certain sense, conceptually speaking, existence is of their essence.

In the case suggested, this is, of course, because "nonfictional character" is being considered as a type of thing, not as if it referred to some particular thing. Thus, the necessary invocation of existence in the conceptual clarification of the type would not entail that there exist any particular examples of that type. Consequently, while the nonfictional character case may indicate that there are positive cases in which existence pertains to the nature of something, it also suggests that, at least in this case, showing that a type of thing requires the concept of existence to define the type does not show that anything of that type exists. In fact, we might, as others have, see something of the exploitation of this ambiguity hinted at in P 2 in its transformation from talk of "something" than which nothing greater can be thought (*aliquid quo . . .*) or of "something of such a nature" (*aliqua talis natura*), which sounds more like a type of thing, to the phrase "that" than which a greater cannot be thought (*id quo . . .*), which sounds like a particular thing.[37]

One could, no doubt, insist that Anselm simply turns to this phraseology in premise 5, which speaks of "it" (*id*), or "that [thing]," instead of "something," so that the contradiction—that "it itself" (*id ipsum*) or "the very same [thing]" than which a greater cannot be thought is that than which a greater can be thought—more clearly shows through. Still, we might ask whether this is not precisely because the force of the contradiction depends upon our thinking not of a type of thing but of some specific thing. For instance, in the case of the class of nonfictional characters, it makes sense to say that, conceptually speaking, nonfictional characters exist, by which we mean to clarify the concept in contrast to the concept of a fictional character, while it is nonetheless always possible to claim without contradiction that, as a matter of fact, nonfictional characters do not exist, just in case there turned out to be, in fact, no such thing as a nonfictional character, that is, nothing "of such a nature." In that case, while we might be forced to admit that a nonfictional character "cannot exist in the understanding alone" or that it "exists both in the understanding and in reality," we might also insist that it can exist in the understanding alone; but this would not entail a contradiction if we meant by it that there might be no nonfictional characters. As Anselm himself often does, we would clarify our way out of the seemingly conflicting claims by noticing that the sense in which nonfictional characters cannot exist in the understanding alone is a different sense than the one in which they can. Conceptually speaking, in terms of the determination of the class, nothing can be a nonfictional character and exist in the understanding alone, while, factually speaking, it may be that no such thing as a nonfictional character exists; or, perhaps better put, it may turn out that nothing is a non-fictional character.[38]

If, in general, being committed to asserting a conceptual claim to existence to clarify a type of thing does not commit us to asserting the factual claim that there are any things of that type, then one might similarly argue that Anselm has provided us with a conceptual clarification of "something than which nothing greater can be thought" that shows that existence pertains to "something of such a nature" without having shown that there is anything that has this nature. As in the case of a nonfictional character, while, conceptually speaking, anything that is something than which nothing greater can be thought might have to be conceived of as existing, it could still turn out, as a matter of fact, that there was no such thing. Unfortunately, the issues are not quite this clear-cut, since, we will recall, these topics arise at the level of the *reductio*. The question would seem to remain whether the conclusion in step 6 suffers from them as well. Is its contention that something than which nothing greater can be thought exists both in the understanding and in reality "without doubt" precisely because it is a conceptual claim that commits us to no more than would the assertion that a nonfictional character exists both in the understanding and in reality, which is also "indubitable" when we mean by it not that some specific character as a matter of fact exists, but that any such character must be so conceived if it is to be conceptually distinguished from a fictional character? Of course, one might argue that while we do not know, and least of all at the level of the *reductio,* whether or not S is like the case of a nonfictional character, that issue may, in either event, be irrelevant to the argument as a whole if the claim to conceptual existence is sufficient for the *reductio.* For, as we have insisted, the existence concluded in step 6 enters the argument at premise 4, not at 5 a–e, which is why we have wanted to keep these two dimensions of the discussion of existence in P 2 separate.

The point should be clear if we appreciate that the *reductio* explicitly operates at the level of conceivable greatness, as a matter of what "can be thought," not on the basis of any claim to factual existence. The contradiction is generated based on the conceivability of something greater than S if it exists in the understanding alone, and, so one might say, on the conceptual existence relevant to this conceivability, not on the basis of any claim to actual existence. Our treatment of conceptually relevant uses of "exist" not only shows that there can be cases in which existence is relevant to the determination of the concept of something, but it also shows that it would make sense to say that in, for example, comparing a fictional with a nonfictional character, if we believe it is greater to exist in reality than in the understanding alone, something greater is being thought when we think of a nonfictional character, even if no nonfictional characters actually exist. And that is all Anselm may appear to need for the *reductio* to go through. This is not to deny that there might not still be a problem concealed in the transformation from the generic term "something" to the individuating "it," but only to insist that the contradiction generated for the *reductio* is a matter of something greater being thought or being thinkable, whether or not anything of such a nature actually exists. As to the issue of the transformation from *"aliquid"* to *"id,"* it could turn out that the argument somehow depends upon seeing that, in this unique case, the type and the individual are one and the same, that there is only one possible individual that meets the relevant description: in short, that God is his own type of thing. In that event, the argument may only work, if it works at all, based upon a certain insight into the thing itself.

At the moment, however, we are interested in the possibility that, in some important sense, factual existence is never at issue in the *reductio* but only the absurdity of something greater being thinkable than something than which nothing greater can be thought, even if one might suspect that this deepest virtue of Anselm's argument, which distinguishes it so clearly from Gaunilo's, could also, in the end, be its greatest weakness. It may turn out that the very possibility of avoiding the issue of factual existence within the *reductio,* thanks to the form of argument the key phrase makes possible, does, indeed, leave the argument at the level of the conceptual rather than the factual. And even if we can get around this by distinguishing the issue of existence as it arises within the *reductio* from the issue of existence at work in the conclusion of the direct demonstration, there can be no doubt that having discovered certain conceptually relevant uses of "exist," we know that we can speak of something's existing, it even being necessarily the case that it exists both in the understanding and in reality, without, however, meaning anything more than that it must be thought or conceived of as existing. This raises certain suspicions that are not allayed but enhanced when we are told that the contradiction for the *reductio* is not based upon the actual existence of that which would be greater than S if it existed in the understanding alone, but simply upon the claim that something greater can be thought. Our discussion has alerted us to certain ambiguities that would allow us, in some cases at least, to concede that existence must be admitted as necessarily pertaining to the nature of something, without being forced to admit that anything of such a nature existed. The question would remain, then, whether the existence shown to be relevant to S is of the conceptual sort or whether the demonstration of its presumably factual existence in P 2 has convinced us otherwise.

Either way, the point remains that the existence in reality that Anselm would no doubt like to think follows from his overall argument is concluded from premise 4, not from the introduction of the question of existential greatness into the *reductio,* even if that conclusion, in step 6, itself may now appear to be riddled with ambiguity. Still, one might suppose that Anselm has avoided these problems through a direct demonstration that essentially backs into its conclusion by excluding all other options. If premise 4 introduces the claim that anything that exists in the understanding either exists in the understanding alone or exists both in the understanding and in reality, then the exclusion of the former option through the *reductio* would seem to leave us no choice but to admit the actual, factual existence of S. And yet, somehow, the virtue of Anselm's argument in contrast to Gaunilo's—that it can get away with an appeal to conceptual existence at the level of the *reductio*—cannot escape the suspicions it raises with respect to the conclusion in step 6. While the direct demonstration presumably shows the indispensability of existence in reality to "something of such a nature," this could appear to amount precisely to showing the relevance of existence to the concept of something than which nothing greater can be thought—its conceptual relevance—but perhaps no more. And if one now insists that it is clearly factual existence at issue in premise 4, we might note that, in all cases of conceptually relevant uses of "exists," it is factual existence we conceive of as relevant to the concept. In that case, we are left with the ambiguity that may be at work in the conclusion of P 2: whether its insistence that S exists both in the understanding and in reality is itself to be regarded as a factual or a conceptual claim.

Of course, as we have said, Anselm can always insist that the case of God is unique, even as one might also argue that conceptual existence, or a conceptual conclusion, is all that Anselm needs in P 2 to continue his argument to its next phase. The one thing that is clear is that the argument begun in P 2 is not completed there. This should be obvious if we simply look at the title of this second chapter, "That God truly is." The conclusion of P 2, however, speaks neither of "God" nor of "true being." What's more, both reappear in P 3. Perhaps, then, a number of these issues will be addressed if, unlike the traditional approach, we postpone our criticism of Anselm's argument until we have read beyond the *Proslogion*'s second chapter.

▍ *Proslogion* 3

There is, I think it is fair to say, no argument in the history of philosophy that means more but says less than the argument of P 3. For there may be no single distinction that condenses as much into it as the one drawn in P 3 and yet leaves so much in silence. It is as if the sharpness of its precision is capable of cutting a rift between God and everything else without a sound. Similarly, the argument that shows this distinction to be necessary to an understanding of something than which nothing greater can be thought runs its course in a flash, following a format with which we are familiar from P 2:

> And surely it so truly is that it cannot be thought not to be. For something can be thought to be that cannot be thought not to be, and this is greater than what can be thought not to be. If, then, that than which a greater cannot be thought can be thought not to be, that than which a greater cannot be thought is itself not that than which a greater cannot be thought— which is contradictory. Therefore, something than which a greater cannot be thought so truly is that it cannot be thought not to be. (S I, 102–3)

The conciseness of the distinction drawn here, which slices being in two, is so cleanly cut that we may not immediately feel its effect, just as the directness with which Anselm is able to show how it is necessarily applicable to something than which nothing greater can be thought may seem to leave us with little to think about. And, in a strange way, it does—and not just insofar as it is designed to leave thought with nothing to think about but God. At this point, however, it might be helpful to take note of a couple of issues that we must consider before making this final cut, which directs our thought to what we have already called the ultimate difference.

The first thing we need to notice to appreciate the full import of the distinction between what "can be thought not to be" and what "cannot be thought not to be" is that its introduction in P 3 clearly follows on the heels of P 2. As we have mentioned before, the original text was not divided into chapters, and the use of a relative pronoun (*quod*) to begin its discussion makes it clear that P 3 is a continuation or extension of the conclusion of the argument immediately preceding it. This is important because, to feel the full force of the distinction between what can be thought not to exist and what cannot be thought not to exist, we must realize that, in each case, we are speaking about what does in fact exist. While, logically speaking, what does not exist can be thought not to exist, the significance of P 3 centers around the claim that certain things that exist also can be thought not to exist. In that case, the possibility arises, thanks to the conclusion of P 2, of drawing a distinction between two different ways of existing "both in the understanding and in reality." That this is the point Anselm has in mind here is clearly indicated by the fact that the use of "exist" in P 3 remains unmodified; he no longer speaks of what exists "in the understanding alone" or "in reality," but simply of what "exists." This can only be because, in P 3, Anselm takes the argument to be operating under the restricted scope of "exist" demonstrated in P 2. Thus, the reasoning of P 3 begins from the conclusion of P 2 and assumes that "exist" now means "exists both in the understanding and in reality." In that case, however, what P 3 is arguing is that, *of the things that exist in reality* (as S has been shown to by the argument of P 2), some so exist that they can be thought not to exist, whereas something can be thought that exists so truly that it cannot even be thought not to exist, and this is greater than those things that can be thought not to exist, even while existing.

The fact that the scope of "exist" has been limited to what exists in reality is emphasized in the first line of P 3 with its reference to what "so truly exists" or, as we could say, "truly exists in such a way" that it cannot be thought not to exist. For to exist "in truth" means to exist in reality, as opposed to the unreal things Anselm would call *"falsa."* We will, however, have to return to the problem of true existence momentarily, when we will see that certain ambiguities are built into the notion, and based upon the very distinction in P 3. At that point, we will then have reason to note that the title of P 3, "That [it] cannot be thought not to exist," does not itself include any mention of something truly existing, which, however, the conclusion of the argument of P 3 does. For the moment, we can make our point by looking carefully at the line that captures the essence of the argument of P 3. It says: "For something can be thought to exist that cannot be thought not to exist, and this is greater than what can be thought not to exist."

Apparently, there are three distinct phrases involving "thinking" and "existence" that make up this line: can be thought to exist, cannot be thought not to exist, and can be thought not to exist. They are so formally similar that they are distinguished only by the inclusion of "not." This apparent similarity, however, can be misleading. Now that we are acquainted with the strategy of Anselm's reasoning about "something than which nothing greater can be thought" in P 2, it should be clear that only in the latter two cases does the reference to what "can be thought" actually belong to the content of the phrase. In the first case, it belongs instead to the form of the argument. That is, in the first phrase, speaking of what "can be thought to exist" is designed to accommodate what is being claimed to the logic of the argument about something than which nothing greater can be thought, whereas in the latter two cases the "can be thought" belongs to the content of the distinction being made. Thus, Anselm is not claiming here that there is something that can be thought to exist and cannot be thought not to exist; rather, he is claiming that it can be thought that something exists that cannot be thought not to exist, and that to think this is to think something greater than something else that can be thought, namely, what exists such that it can be thought not to exist. Obviously, if something that exists in such a way that it cannot be thought not to exist can be thought, and is greater than what exists in such a way that it can be thought not to exist, then something than which nothing greater can be thought cannot exist such that it can be thought not to exist, or else something greater than it could be thought.

In that case, however, to maintain the parallelism of the distinctions, the parallel in what "can be thought," the scope of the phrase that begins the above line, which speaks of what "can be thought to exist," whether it can or cannot be thought not to exist, must extend to both phrases distinguished after it. That is, if in speaking of what "cannot be thought not to exist" we are speaking of what exists in reality in this way, then, to maintain the relevant contrast, in speaking of our ability to think of what "can be thought not to exist," we must also be thinking of what exists and yet can be thought not to exist. Needless to say, it is not contradictory to claim that something exists and can be thought not to exist, for we are not contending that it can be thought to exist and cannot be thought to exist, but simply that it both can be thought that it exists and nonetheless can be thought not to exist. And while we would not want to deny that what does not exist also can be thought not to exist, we would not want this to distract us from the more relevant point that the claim that something can be thought not to exist also applies to what in fact exists. In P 3, the full force of the distinction requires that we appreciate that what is at issue is a difference between two ways of existing in reality, in which case, what "can be thought not to exist" must also be taken to refer to what exists, albeit in this specific way.

That this is how Anselm intends for us to take the force of his distinction is made clear in reply 4:

For even if none of the things that are can be understood not to be, all, nonetheless, can be thought not to be, except that which supremely is. For all and only those things can be thought not to be that have a beginning or end or are composed of parts, as well, as I have already said, as whatever at any time or anywhere does not exist as a whole. But that alone cannot be thought not to be in which [there is] neither beginning nor end nor composition of parts and that thought finds [to be] everywhere and always wholly. (S I, 133–34)

We will return to the difference at issue at the beginning of this passage, between "understanding" and "thinking," in P 4. For now we might take advantage of Anselm's claims about the nature of what "cannot be thought not to exist" to suggest that, in drawing the distinction of P 3, he has a quite specific content in mind; indeed, that what is at issue, as we know from our reading of the *Monologion,* is at the heart of his ontology. As we shall see, Anselm attempts in P 3 to capture not only the essence of his earlier thinking about the existence of God but also the very heart of medieval metaphysics—its greatest and most sublime thought—in a single distinction, once it is understood as something more than a string of terms. Only when it is actually put to work in and on our own thinking will it allow our thought to discern "that which is without beginning or end, or conjunction of parts, and is everywhere and always wholly." And we will see how the distinction of P 3 works, and works to do so, in our discussion of P 4.

If we wanted to pursue the claim that when Anselm speaks of what "can be thought not to exist" in P 3 he is speaking of what exists, we would only need to continue the text of the above reply, where he deals with the issue in further detail. More of interest, for present as well as future purposes, is the way in which this reply proceeds to claim that it is a "distinguishing feature" of God (*proprium dei*) that he cannot be thought not to be. Apparently, while there may be other senses in which other things cannot be thought not to exist, there is a distinctive sense in which this applies only to God. Anselm's comments here are meant in part as a response to Gaunilo's questioning whether I can think of myself as not existing, and, if so, why I cannot also think of God as nonexistent, even if I am as certain that he exists as that I exist.[39] And Anselm's answer seems to be that anyone who thinks that the indubitability of one's own existence offers an example of something that cannot be thought not to exist needs to see that the certainty of my own existence is a strictly factual matter, in which case, even if, in some sense, I cannot doubt that I exist, that does not mean I cannot *think* of myself as not existing. On the contrary, all I need do is imagine that I had never been born.

But if such factual certainties about existence leave open the possibility that things could conceivably have been otherwise, we might wonder about the status of those conceptual uses of "exist" we discussed earlier, of which Anselm was apparently not aware and which would seem to allow for no conceivable alternative. For example, one might think it true to say that, in some sense, nonfictional characters cannot be thought not to exist. For if they could be thought not to exist, they would be fictional characters. Here, however, we would seem to be encountering the flip side of the argument concerning one's own existence, indeed, of the difference between factual and conceptual uses of "exist." As we saw earlier, conceptually relevant uses of "exist" do not necessarily guarantee the factual existence of what is so thought, any more than factual certainties entail conceptual necessities. Consequently, while we might concede the conceptual truth that nonfictional characters necessarily exist both in the understanding and in reality, we are also clear that, as a matter of fact, there may be no nonfictional characters. This is even clearer, of course, when we are not considering the type but some individual nonfictional character, who obviously can be thought not to exist in the sense that he or she may no longer exist. In any case, if the knowledge of my own existence seems to secure factual indubitability but no conceptual certainty—if, even knowing for certain that I exist, I can still be thought not to exist—the nonfictional character example seems to supply the conceptual impossibility of nonexistence without securing factual actuality, for what is at issue can, at some factual level, always be thought not to exist.

Clearly, then, Anselm would have to think that the sense in which God exists such that he cannot be thought not to exist, and thus the sense in which it is unthinkable that God not exist, differs both from the factual certainty of my own existence as well as from the merely conceptual necessity of the "existence" of nonfictional characters. Anselm no doubt thinks that he has discovered a unique case if the sense in which God cannot be thought not to be distinguishes him from everything else that is. Indeed, we might say that if the intuition of my own existence, however certain, remains a merely factual matter, while the existence of nonfictional characters is strictly a conceptual issue, then the sense in which God alone and distinctively cannot be thought not to exist would have to be an odd kind of conceptual-factual matter. As we shall see, part of what this means for Anselm is that the thing itself, in its distinctive nature, must be such that it constrains thought to think of it as existing, or at least as unthinkable as not existing. In effect, Anselm thinks that he has discovered a thought that cannot be thought otherwise. What this may be taken to suggest, at least at present, is that the very nature of the existence of such a thing would have to be such that it would allow for no conceivable alternative, even as its inconceivability as nonexistent would have to leave no factual loopholes. If one can avoid the factual certainty of one's own existence conceptually and avoid the conceptual certainty of the existence of nonfictional characters factually, then the sense in which God cannot be thought not to exist must be different from either of these: it must allow for neither factual nor conceptual moderation of the claim to the impossibility of its nonexistence (*nec actu nec intellectu posset non esse*).[40] It requires, in other words, the absolute inconceivability of any possible alternative, and perhaps most importantly, it requires that it be based upon the nature of the thing itself, that is, on the distinctiveness of what it is we are thinking.

This latter point seems clear in the above passage insofar as Anselm appeals to the nature of what exists everywhere and always wholly, without beginning or end or multiplicity of parts, to secure his claim to the uniqueness of God's inconceivable nonexistence, so as to close those loopholes through which God may be thought not to exist and to distinguish him from all other possible examples. In this respect, one could argue that the case of God is as different from that of a nonfictional character as it is from one's own existence insofar as the inconceivability of God's nonexistence is not simply based on the single feature of existence being built into the thought itself, whether as a matter of fact or of concept. Instead, it is based upon God's collective features, upon the nature of the thing itself, that it exists everywhere and always wholly, without beginning or end or composition of parts, and through itself alone. Thus, in Anselm's view, it is not as if we have simply included existence in the concept, as we have in the case of nonfictional characters, but rather as if existence has grown out of it. The claim that S cannot be thought not to exist follows from the set of features that characterizes the kind of being it is, and one whose inconceivable nonexistence is also quite different from the factual indubitability of the *cogito*.[41]

This is why it will be particularly important for Anselm to insist in P 4 that he has not simply concocted a conception of God from which his existence follows, but that the reality itself, when properly thought, exercises a kind of conceptual compulsion upon our thinking insofar as the impression it makes on our thought forces us to think in a certain way about it, such that we are unable to think otherwise, given the nature of the thing itself. In fact, this is why Anselm must attempt to bring before the sight of the eye of the mind, through the distinction being drawn here, a certain object of thought, so that, in accord with his epistemology, the "truth" of the thing itself may compel—or, as *De veritate* would say, "cause"—our thought to think as it does. And it is equally striking that when Anselm attempts to explain the distinction drawn in P 3 to Gaunilo, he reverts to the discussion of the nature of God in the *Monologion*.

According to the claim that concludes the above passage, "that alone cannot be thought not to be in which [there is] neither beginning nor end nor composition of parts and that thought finds [to be] everywhere and always wholly." Obviously, this is a sudden and powerful condensation of a long string of arguments offered in Anselm's earlier work to clarify a supreme being that exists "through itself," is utterly simple, and yet exists everywhere and always wholly. The unique features of such a being—and for Anselm there could be only one such being—suggest how it is that it cannot be thought not to exist; for if it had a beginning or end, one could think of a time before or after which it existed. Were it not everywhere, one could think of a place where it was not. Were it not utterly simple, it could be thought not to exist by decomposing it in thought into its constituent parts, etc.[42] And yet, this set of logical issues hardly gets to the point of the passage, which is that one must have the right being in mind if what Anselm has to say is to make proper sense. For the key to his claim seems to involve appreciating that there is a unique case of a being whose nature is such that it must be thought of as existing through itself alone, and thus as without beginning or end, which is not subject to the limits of space or time, is not composed of parts, and which thus must be contemplated as everywhere and always wholly. And Anselm seems to be suggesting that only when this is thought, this which Anselm thinks is something than which nothing greater can be thought, does the claim that something can be thought to exist that cannot be thought not to exist take on a meaning it has in no other imaginable case.

All that we have claimed about P 3 (including our insistence that the distinction it is drawing is between things that exist) is designed to give some indication of what Anselm must be thinking here, just as our suggestion about how the claim that something "so exists that it cannot be thought not to exist" properly fits neither Gaunilo's case of his own existence nor our case of nonfictional characters is directed to this end, as is our taking note that the response in reply 4 condenses into it much of the rather complex argumentation we made our way through in our reading of the *Monologion*. Of course, it would not be surprising if the more extensive elaborations in the earlier work gave us the best clue as to what Anselm is thinking, even if we might assume that however much the *Monologion* stands as the background, what remains unprecedented in the *Proslogion* is its ontological argument, especially when we consider the rather traditional arguments for the existence of God that are rehearsed at the opening of the *Monologion*. On the other hand, if we take Anselm at his word that, as its preface claims, he set out in the *Proslogion* to simplify the intricate argumentation of the *Monologion,* then, while we would not expect to find the exact arguments, we would expect to find him attempting to draw the same conclusions. We should then not be surprised to find in the *Monologion* a certain prototype of what was destined to become the ontological argument in the *Proslogion*.

Such a recovery of what might well be thought of as the origin of the ontological argument would not only require us to take seriously the full extent of the *Monologion*'s reasoning about the existence of God and the way in which it develops across a complex series of interconnected arguments that culminates, at least for all ontological purposes, in M 28; it would also require an understanding of just what the *Proslogion* argument originally amounted to. With this in mind, what we have tried to make evident is that the distinction at issue in P 3, between what can and what cannot be thought not to exist, works to distinguish between different types of existence, and that as such, the distinction is designed to show how what the *Monologion* called the supreme being "is." It tells us, in other words, what it is for "that which supremely is," as reply 4 refers to it, to be. To this extent, we want to insist that this single distinction in P 3 must involve, indeed, must condense into it, the ontological reversal we encountered in M 28 in its thinking away of the being of beings other than God. In its own concise way, P 3 must supply a standard of being sufficient to show that all the things that exist, but nonetheless can be thought not to exist, lack a certain kind of being. The demonstration of the radical existence of God requires thought to arrive at a being so supreme that, compared to it, nothing else exists; or, perhaps more appropriately put with regard to P 3, an existence so extreme that, in contrast to it, even those things that are known to exist pale, at least in thought, into nonexistence insofar as they "can be thought not to exist."

As the *Monologion* finally suggests, the beings with which we are ordinarily familiar in our thinking about being—those beings the *Proslogion* will designate as what can be thought not to exist— tend to get in the way of our thinking about what alone so exists that it cannot be thought not to exist. In effect, the invocation of the distinction of P 3 must attempt to get those beings out of thought's way so as to bring what cannot be thought not to exist into view, that is, to bring it before the eye of the rational mind. Thus, the appeal to this difference, between what can and cannot be thought not to exist, must be designed to achieve the same result we saw at work in the long argument of the *Monologion,* that runs from M 1–28, and to achieve it even more concisely, perhaps in a suddenness that may leave us stunned or simply cause us to bypass what is at issue here, or to read our way through what, in that event, is in danger of becoming a merely verbal argument. Anselm will expressly warn against this danger in P 4, where the nature of our thinking about such issues will be called into question. There we will see how Anselm's argument must work if it is to work at all. For now, what must be clear is that nothing less is at issue in P 3 than the conversion in our thinking about the meaning of being we encountered in M 28. In that case, however, a good deal of the reunderstanding of Anselm's argument I want to propose hinges on an appreciation of the relation between the *Monologion* and the *Proslogion,* especially insofar as it may serve to clarify the relationship between P 2 and P 3. This, in turn, alone should allow us to understand the nature and extent of Anselm's *Proslogion* argument and thus the point of the conclusion to be drawn from it.

Appreciating the force of the conclusion of Anselm's argument depends upon a rereading of the relationship between P 2 and P 3 that is aided immeasurably by an understanding of the nature of the existence of God that Anselm had already proposed in the *Monologion.* If we understand what it is for God to exist and what Anselm thought was involved in demonstrating the existence of God, it will become clear that his great innovation in the *Proslogion* involved not just the discovery of the argument of P 2 or of the use to which he could put the key name "something than which nothing greater can be thought." Instead, it is a matter of the way he found to condense the long process of argumentation in the *Monologion* (the one that led to the radical conclusion that God alone exists) into a single argument, indeed, into a single distinction, which, while drawn in P 3, cannot be made out until the argument of P 2 has been set forth. Consequently, we must be able to appreciate what Anselm came to see was at issue in showing the existence of God in the *Monologion* and how extreme a demonstration this finally requires while acknowledging that the originality of the *Proslogion* consists in its finding a way to reframe that long and complicated chain of reasoning by condensing it into a single argument that spans P 2–3 and is sufficient in its conciseness to demonstrate the distinctively unique and uniquely distinctive existence of God.

On the Relation between *Proslogion* 2 and *Proslogion* 3

The account of the *Proslogion* argument I want to provide depends entirely upon my claim about its location across P 2–3. Unfortunately, there is a long tradition that would take issue with this. Until quite recently, it was assumed that Anselm's argument for the existence of God was contained exclusively in P 2. A more recent tradition, which is responsible for reviving interest in Anselm's argument in the twentieth century, would also dispute the account I want to offer, as it distinguishes P 2 from P 3 as if each contained its own separate and independent argument for the existence of God.[43] In this case, we are told, P 2 argues for the simple existence of God, and P 3 for his necessary existence. And since this view regards the reasoning of P 2 as invalid and that of P 3 as valid, it depends upon a reading of P 3 as a self-contained argument, although these interpreters do not think Anselm intended the separation they suggest. To complicate matters even further, there is yet a third, still more recent approach that contends that while P 2 and P 3 develop a series of existential claims about a being characterized as something than which a greater cannot be thought, they are together insufficient to show that this is God.[44] Proponents of such a view argue that only the whole of the *Proslogion* is sufficient to show the existence of God; for, from P 5 through to its conclusion, Anselm must go on to show that the being shown to exist in P 2–3 has all the features normally attributed to God. According to this view, while Anselm has a right to claim that he has shown that something exists and cannot be thought not to exist in P 2–3, he does not have any rational right to claim he has shown this to be God until the conclusion of the entire *Proslogion*.

I do not want to enter the maze of disagreements over these various readings of the *Proslogion,* detailing what is right and what is wrong with each of the accounts, in part because I have done so elsewhere.[45] For our present purposes, what must strike us about each of the three views mentioned is that none of them systematically raises the question of the relation between P 2 and P 3. The first one either ignores P 3 as if it were not there, as the tradition tended to, or—as at least one recent commentator has done in defending that tradition—claims the distinction at issue in P 3 is not relevant to the existence but rather to the nature of God.[46] The second approach also treats the two chapters as if they were irrelevant to one another, even though its proponents admit that Anselm never intended any distinction between the two arguments. The third account, while arguing that the whole of the *Proslogion* contains Anselm's argument for the existence of God, is not interested in how specific chapters are related to one another but simply regards the text as having a cumulative effect. And while each of these accounts has its own problems—the first in failing to appreciate the relevance of the distinction in P 3 to the existence of God; the second in ignoring the possibility that P 3, as it stands, is insufficient to demonstrate the existence of anything; and the third in that it must avoid the fact that Anselm does conclude that "God" exists in P 4—they all tend to mistake the relevance and role of the distinction drawn in P 3; indeed, we might say that they mistake the radicalness of this distinction and what it is designed to achieve.

This is not surprising, since most of these interpreters read the *Proslogion* exclusively, that is, they do not look to the *Monologion* for any assistance. And even if the argument of the *Proslogion* must, to the degree to which any argument can, be sufficient unto itself, our understanding of it may not be. To some extent, our prospects for appreciating the full force of the highly condensed distinction drawn in P 3—and thus the key insight that allows for a proper rendering of the relation between P 2 and P 3—hinges on a clarification of the point of this distinction in part with the help of Anselm's earlier work. No doubt this claim may seem rather ironic, since the key distinction—between what can and what cannot be thought not to exist—is not drawn in the *Monologion*. In fact, it is about the only distinction relevant to these issues that shows up in the *Proslogion* but does not appear in the earlier text. And yet, when Anselm is called upon by Gaunilo to clarify the difference at issue in P 3, he reverts to the detailed topics raised in the *Monologion*. Not, however, to the point I want to concentrate on; for I am less interested in questions about the time-spacelessness of God or his beginningless or endless existence, as in the way such issues contribute to our understanding, later in the *Monologion,* of the claims about his radical ontological distinctiveness. It is there, I think, that we will find the direct link to the argument of P 3, and in a form of clarification that goes beyond the awkwardness of its formulation in M 28.

Of course, there is a certain elegance about M 28 as well. Its beginning must be numbered among the few poetic moments in the *Monologion.* Following, I suppose, the adage that when you find the poetry, you have found the poet, we have taken it that this one moment, as concise as it is, reveals the essence of the *Monologion*'s ontological insight into the existence of God. But if this critical passage at the start of M 28 begins beautifully, it ends awkwardly; and its very awkwardness in speaking about the being of beings other than God is amplified by the beauty of its characterization of the being of the supreme being. We will recall that M 28 begins—after its title has informed us that the supreme spirit exists simply, while other beings, compared to it, do not exist—by insisting:

> It is seen to follow, then, from the foregoing [considerations] that this spirit, which exists in so wonderfully unique and uniquely wonderful a way of its own, in a certain sense alone

exists, while others, howsoever they may appear to be, compared to it, do not exist. For if one attends intently [to the mat-
ter], it will be seen that this spirit alone exists simply and
perfectly and absolutely, while all others will appear almost
nonexistent and scarcely to exist at all. (S I, 45–46)

Here, it seems to me, we see on display both the elegance and
the awkwardness of Anselm's position in the *Monologion*. For the
passage shows both the brilliance of his vision of God and the cloudi-
ness of his view of all other beings as they remain in the ontological
shadow cast by this "supreme spirit." The supreme being has its being in a "wonderfully unique and uniquely wonderful" way of its
own; so wondrous, in fact, so extraordinary, that compared to this
amazingly and absolutely unique way of existing, it seems most appropriate to Anselm to say that other beings do not exist. This is, as
we have argued, not merely a matter of degree but of a categorical
difference in the kind of being each may be said to possess, of the
ontological difference between creator and creature, between what
exists simply, perfectly, absolutely, everywhere and always wholly,
without beginning or end, or multiplicity of parts, etc., and whatever
is other than this. If such supreme being supplies the measure of
true being, then creatures can categorically be said not to be, even as
the clarification of the being of the creator is achieved in a reversal in
the meaning of being ultimately based on a certain degradation of
those beings we normally take as the standard of what it means to
be. This is why the ultimate position assumed in the *Monologion* is
that there can be no comparisons drawn between the supreme being
and created beings; or, more precisely put, that when such a comparison is attempted, beings do not appear as lesser or lacking but
as nonexistent.

We have taken this to indicate that, strategically speaking, the
drawing of the ultimate distinction between creator and creature is
accomplished by one side of the comparison disappearing in the
making out of its difference from the other, such that in the vanishing of the difference, the creator is left to stand seemingly without
otherness, in his absolute difference from that which has disap-
peared in the drawing of the distinction. To appreciate how this can
be tactically achieved, it is critical that, in the comparative ascen-
sion of the ladder of beings, we arrive at a superlative degree of being that enjoys supremacy over beings not merely in the sense that it
has more being than they do, but in that it possesses a being all its
own, in which case, what is in order is not a comparison, but an ontological reversal in which beings pale from sight, in effect relinquish-
ing their claim to being. At the same time, however, this reversal must
be set in motion based on the being of those beings we eventually

find to be lacking true being. Consequently, after having made his proclamation about the singular existence of the supreme being, Anselm must immediately moderate it, but so as to embed the reversal in the meaning of being into the less than true being of the things that are, that "almost do not exist and barely exist." The passage just cited from M 28 proceeds to clarify this "scarce" existence of creatures by contrasting it with the absolute, simple, and perfect being of God:

> For since, on account of its immutable eternity, it can in no way be said of this spirit that, according to some alteration, it was or will be, but simply that it is, neither is it, by changing, anything which at any time it either was not or will not be, nor is it not at any time what it was or will be, but is whatever it is once and for all, and interminably—since, I say, its being is of this kind, it is fairly said that it exists simply and absolutely and perfectly.
>
> Since, however, all others, in some respect and at some time and by changing, either were or will be what they now are not, or are now what at some time they were not or will not be, and since what they were is not now, just as what they will be is not yet, and what they are in this fleeting and most brief and barely existing present barely exists—since, therefore, they exist so mutably, it is not unfitting to deny that they exist simply and perfectly and absolutely, and to insist that they are almost nonexistent and scarcely exist at all.
>
> Again, since all beings other than this [spirit] have come from nonexistence to existence not through themselves, but through another, and since they would return from existence to nonexistence, as far as their own power is concerned, unless they are sustained through another, how would it be fitting for them to exist simply or perfectly or absolutely rather than scarcely existing or almost not existing? (S I, 46)

This long passage, as well as the contrast at work in it, bears comparison with a similar one in the *Proslogion:*

> You alone, then, lord, are what you are and you are who you are. For what is one thing as a whole and another in its parts, and in which there is something mutable, is not altogether what it is. And what began from nonexistence and can be thought not to be and returns to not being unless it subsists through some other; and what has a past which is no longer and a future which is not yet—it does not exist properly and absolutely. But you are what you are, since whatever you are at any time or in any way, this you are wholly and always.
>
> And you are the one who is, properly and simply; for you have neither past nor future but only present existence, nor can you be thought not to be at any time. (S I, 116)

For all practical purposes, the claims made in both citations are identical, except for one. Each speaks of what exists simply, absolutely, and immutably, what exists everywhere and always wholly, without past, present, or future, and what always exists not just fully but purely insofar as its being is not blended with nonbeing. P 22, however, proceeds to characterize all of this in terms of what "cannot be thought not to be," just as, instead of speaking of creatures as barely existing, it characterizes them as what "can be thought not to be." And what I want to suggest is that this contrast, indeed, this final designation of God as what cannot be thought not to exist, is not merely one more feature added to the list in the *Proslogion*. Instead, it is the crowning characterization. It is what Anselm, as we have seen, can refer to in his replies as a distinguishing feature (*proprium*) of God with respect to his existence in that it sums up the ontological difference between God and all else. In effect, all the features of God's uniquely wonderful and wondrously unique existence can be inferred from the claim that he so exists that he cannot be thought not to exist. In that case, this addition in the *Proslogion* is not simply a further designation but a way Anselm had discovered to condense all that he had claimed about the existence of God in the *Monologion* into a single distinction.

Of course, one may insist that these issues only arise later in the text, in fact, as late as P 22. But it is clear, if we look carefully, that the critical issue of the distinctive, radical existence of God is in play from the very beginning of P 2, that is, from its title: "That God truly exists." To see this, we need to recall how Anselm goes on in the *Monologion* to deal with the existence of creatures after the stunning claims of M 28. As we have indicated, Anselm does not altogether deny that beings exist, but only that they enjoy the incomparable kind of being that the supreme being does. Thus M 29 begins the treatment of the being of beings not just in light of their creation from nothing but in terms of the truth of being that resides in the primal word whose likeness they are, and on the basis of which created beings enjoy whatever "being" they can be said to enjoy in their eternal essence, not in their temporal existence. For the true being of creatures must be shown to reside in their essential preexistence in God, in which respect they have not been altogether created out of nothing—as is apparently the case with their factual existence—so much as on the basis of God's own eternal self-conception. To accomplish this, however, Anselm has to insist upon the reversal that pivots around this ambiguous "truth of being," which, while a "perfect likeness" of "being itself," is not a likeness of beings, but they a likeness of it. So M 31 claims that

> . . . the truth of existence is understood to be in the word whose being is so supremely that, in a way, it alone exists; whereas in those things which, in their way, in comparison to it, do not

exist—although they have been made in accord with it, and are
made something through it—is considered to be something like
an imitation of this supreme being. Thus, the word of the supreme truth, which is itself also the supreme truth, does not
become greater or lesser to the extent to which it is more or less
similar to creatures, but it would have to be the case that all
that is created more greatly exists and is more excellent to the
extent to which it is similar to that which supremely is and is
supremely great. . . .

Thus, it is evident that in the word, through which all things
were created, there is no likeness of created things but is, rather,
true and simple being; in the things that are created, however,
there is not simple and absolute being, but a mere imitation of
this true being. (S I, 49–50)

Omitting all the moderating riders, this would appear to be, at best,
a paradoxical way of putting Anselm's point: a mere likeness of being, of the true being of the supreme being, which so exists that it
alone exists, exists in those beings that do not exist.

Be that as it may, the unmistakable result is the contention
that the existence of creatures does not unambiguously constitute
"true being." This point could scarcely be any plainer than it is in the
concluding line of the above passage, where, as is suggested by our
earlier citation from P 22, true being is correlated with "simple" being because of the immutability that the latter implies—which is, no
doubt, why it must be denied of the "mutable" existence of creatures.
In fact, if we look at the list of modifiers used to characterize the "singularly unique and uniquely singular" being God is claimed to have
across the various passages we have cited, we will see that they include "supreme," "absolute," "simple," "primal," "proper," "perfect,"
and "true" being, as well as the basic contention that a number of
these modifiers are designed to capture: that God enjoys an eternal
being that remains "pure" or unmixed with nonbeing, unlike the being of creatures. In short, any reference to existence invoked in relation to God must have a sense all its own, and one of the ways to
articulate that unique existence, as the passages we have cited from
the *Monologion* show, is in terms of a certain "true being" that God
alone may be said to enjoy.

Needless to say, the most radical form of the determination of
God's incomparable existence is expressed in the claim that he "so
exists . . . that he alone exists" (*sic . . . ut*), whether in M 28 or in M
31. The point we are trying to make, however, is that it is no coincidence that the very grammatical form in which the lead distinction
of P 3 is expressed reproduces, even as it modifies, this radical claim
to the nature of the existence of God. In P 3, rather than claiming
that God so exists that compared to him other things do not exist,
Anselm contrasts what truly exists in such a way that it cannot be

thought not to exist (*sic vere est ut nec cogitari possit non esse*) with what so exists that it can be thought not to exist. This formulation of God's distinctive being ultimately serves to achieve the same effect as the distinctions drawn in the *Monologion,* but in its own more precise way. The awkwardness of speaking of creatures in M 28 as "almost not existing and scarcely existing at all" has been replaced by the elegant distinction of P 3, which would allow us instead to characterize them as existing in such a way that they "can be thought not to exist." While Anselm technically avoids speaking in a manner that would attribute "true being" to creatures in P 3, he makes it clear nonetheless that their actual, factual existence must be modified to include the disclaimer that if they may be said in any sense to exist or, for that matter, to "truly exist," it is in such a way that they can be thought not to exist. The distinction of P 3 thus enforces the ultimate ontological contrast between the conceivably nonexistent existence of creatures and the true, simple, absolute, proper, pure, and immutable being attributable only to that which "so truly exists that it cannot even be thought not to exist." And we contend that, from the start of P 2, Anselm intends to demonstrate the true being that is said in the *Monologion* to pertain to God alone and that he has found a way to capture in the *Proslogion* in terms of the ontological difference between what can and what cannot be thought not to exist.

If we return to the argument of P 2–3 with the *Monologion* in mind, we should be able to see more clearly how the two relevant chapters are related to one another. The title of P 2 announces what Anselm's argument is designed to show: "That God truly is." It is obvious that this is not claimed to have been shown in P 2 itself, since neither "God" nor his "true being" (*vere est*) is mentioned in its conclusion, but only "something than which nothing greater can be thought" and its "existence" (*existit*) both in the understanding and in reality. If showing that God truly is requires the demonstration of his distinctive form of being, then Anselm simply has not demonstrated that in P 2. That is, he has not shown the existence *of God.* Nor do I think it makes sense to suggest that the argument first shows the "general" existence of God in P 2 and then goes on to show his "special" existence in P 3. God does not enjoy any such general existence, nor can his distinctive existence be adequately determined by simply adding certain features to an otherwise generic being, as if his ontological distinctiveness were merely a specialized version of some more general existence. On the contrary, it is critical to Anselm's whole account that God exist not just in a way in which nothing else can but that he exist in a manner so categorically distinct, so ontologically different, that no comparisons can properly be

made between the distinctive existence of God and the generic existence of anything else. Indeed, when such comparisons are made,
other beings cease to be thought as being. And it is this absolutely
incomparable existence that must be demonstrated before one can
claim to have shown the existence of God. No one knew this better
than Anselm, as his strategy clearly indicates. For he does not conclude that he has shown the existence of God until after the argument of P 3, which claims to demonstrate that something so exists
that it cannot be thought not to exist and which, P 3 itself goes on to
argue, constitutes the true and proper, that is, the unique being of
God.

What I am suggesting, then, is that Anselm found a way in the
Proslogion to condense into a remarkably concise distinction the
"wonderfully unique and uniquely wonderful" being of God and that
this allowed him to advance beyond the maze of argumentation in
the *Monologion* by capturing much of its complex chain of reasoning
in the single claim that God so exists that he cannot be thought not
to exist. In demonstrating this, he would not only have shown the
distinctive nature of the existence of God but that what has been
shown to have such existence is God.[47] I do not, however, want to
place too much emphasis on the mention of "true being" in the title
of P 2 as a basis for my reading of the relation between P 2 and P 3,
for, as is undeniable, it is possible to speak of ordinary things as
"truly existing"—as undeniable as the fact that reserving the phrase
vere esse for application to the being of God goes back at least as far
as Augustine.[48] Of course, even if talk of something truly existing
can be employed with respect to creatures, that in itself would not
resolve the question of its meaning when applied to God, of what it is
for God to "truly exist." Not only does the begging of this latter question ignore the complications involved in the attribution of true being to creatures, it also fails to take into account the fact that
nowhere in P 2 or P 3 does Anselm explicitly speak of anything but
God as truly existing. Given the way the new distinction is gram-
matically formulated in P 3, in the form of the "so . . . that . . ." (*sic
. . . ut*) clause, it would be awkward to speak of creatures as truly existing in these terms, since it would result in the claim that they "so
truly exist that they can be thought not to exist," in which case it
would appear that their being able to be thought not to exist followed from their truly existing, rather than, as is clearly the case for
Anselm, from their lack of it. Thus, the only proper claim using this
form of expression is to say of God that he so truly exists that he cannot be thought not to exist, which is what is claimed as the conclusion of P 3.

Now even if one regarded all of this as a matter of superficial textual details—that "God" is not brought up in the conclusion of P 2, nor is the "truly exists" that is mentioned in its title; that the original text had no chapter divisions, and when Anselm did place numbers in the margin corresponding to a separate list of chapter headings, here, as elsewhere in the text, what is shown within a chapter may not correspond to what that chapter announces as its title; that "God" is brought back into the discussion in P 3 but only after the "so truly exists that it cannot be thought not to exist" is shown—what cannot escape our notice is that the conclusion drawn in P 3 does not follow from the argument offered there. In this sense, the title of P 3 is no more correlated with its conclusion than is the title of P 2, although it is correlated with the *reductio* argument that is offered in P 3. In fact, the title of P 3 is neither in complete correlation with its conclusion nor with its opening line. Its title claims to want to show "That [it] cannot be thought not to exist," whereas the conclusion drawn after the *reductio* and mentioned in the opening line claims that something than which a greater cannot be thought "so truly exists that it cannot be thought not to exist." Thus, the question arises: From what argument is this conclusion supposed to follow?

On the account I am proposing, the opening line of P 3 is to be regarded as announcing not what is to be shown in P 3 itself, in its argument proper, which is what the title of the chapter proclaims, but notifies us of a conclusion to be drawn from the conclusion of its *reductio:* a conclusion that follows from an argument that begins in P 2, even as P 3 itself follows not just after, but under the influence of, and therefore from the reasoning of, P 2. In that case, P 3 would contain a conclusion drawn from the single argument that spans these two chapters, as our earlier account of the line following this initial one would suggest. In fact, the first two lines of P 3, which both speak of what "exists such that it cannot be thought not to exist," stand in contrast to what is shown within the limits of its argument proper, as they differ not only with the chapter heading, which simply claims that something "cannot be thought not to exist," but consequently with the assumption for the *reductio* itself. If it leads to a contradiction to assume that S can be thought not to exist, it would have been shown that S cannot be thought not to exist, but it would not follow from this that S exists, let alone that it so truly exists that it cannot be thought not to exist. And yet, this is clearly announced as the conclusion of the argument, both before and after the *reductio* proper; not, I contend, as the conclusion of the argument of P 3 alone but of an argument that began in P 2 and spans the two chapters to find its conclusion drawn after the *reductio* of P 3 has been completed.

This does not mean, however, that Anselm has merely conjoined the conclusion of P 2 with the conclusion of P 3 to draw the complex conclusion that S exists and cannot be thought not to exist, as if the issues might be argued separately and then put together as a summation of what has been shown. In fact, thinking of P 3 as a second stage in a single argument that spans chapters 2 and 3 can be a bit misleading, since the argument of P 3 does not so much move beyond the conclusion of P 2 as it moves within it; for it focuses on the kind of existence by which the being shown to exist in P 2 must be characterized. This is not an additional feature of the existence shown in P 2 but the necessary clarification of its ontological status, given the different kinds of existence in reality that there are for Anselm. Thus, the conclusion of P 2 remains incomplete and underdetermined with respect to the question of existence and, in any case, has clearly not yet shown the existence *of God.*

At the same time, however, the argument of P 3 alone is not designed to show the existence of anything. On the contrary, in P 3 the existence of S, we have suggested, has been assumed from P 2, although it is not, at that point in P 2, yet the existence of God that is claimed, nor is it yet clear that S is God. This is why it is critical to see just when Anselm is willing to reidentify S with God, and to appreciate that he can avoid misattributing a general and as yet underdefined conception of existence to "that which supremely is" precisely by withholding the claim that it is "God" that has been shown to exist both in the understanding and in reality in P 2. Instead, working from the conclusion of P 2, that whatever we are talking about in P 3 exists, it must be shown that it exists in such a way that it cannot be thought not to exist, such that Anselm is willing, then and only then, to conclude that S so truly exists that it exists in the way God alone does or can, thus not only clarifying the existence of S but, as such, showing that it enjoys the existence of God: possesses the kind of being only God can. In that case, however, once having shown this, we are justified in identifying S with God on rational grounds, can claim that the being than which nothing greater can be thought, insofar as it enjoys the unique existence reserved for God, is, indeed, God, in which event, it is not surprising that Anselm proclaims this immediately after he has drawn the conclusion of the argument that spans P 2 and P 3.

If I am right that the conclusion stated in P 3 cannot be the conclusion of the *reductio* of 3 alone but follows from an argument that began in P 2, and that this argument justifies the claim that S is God based upon this distinctive and distinguishing form of existence demonstrated by the single argument that spans P 2 and P 3, then it should be clear what is wrong with the other three accounts of the relation between these chapters I have mentioned. If Anselm thinks that demonstrating the true being of God, announced as what is to be shown according to the title of P 2, requires an argument showing his distinctive form of existence, such a conclusion could not follow either from the argument of P 2 or P 3 alone, since neither can stand alone to demonstrate the existence of God. In that case, the traditional account of the *Proslogion* proof, which assumes it to begin and end in P 2, only touches on a fragment of the argument at its initial stage and thus takes the conclusion of the argument to be claiming simply that God exists both in the understanding and in reality. In point of fact, however, "God" is not mentioned in the conclusion of P 2, and, as we now know, with good reason. The second, more recent account, which claims Anselm offered two different arguments for the existence of God in the *Proslogion,* one in P 2 and the other in P 3, does not, at least, ignore P 3, where it looks for a modal proof for the existence of God but, on the contrary, puts too much weight upon it, and instead tends to ignore P 2, which it regards as offering an invalid proof. This account is misled, when it tries to isolate P 3, by the fact that while this chapter does contain the proper conclusion concerning the existence of God, it is not a conclusion that follows from the argument contained in that chapter. For if the reasoning of P 3 depends upon the conclusion drawn in P 2, then P 3 does not itself contain an independent argument for the existence of anything, any more than P 2 is sufficient to demonstrate the existence of "God." Finally, the third account, which seeks to show that the entire *Proslogion* alone suffices to demonstrate that God exists, simply conjoins the conclusion of P 2 to P 3 as it puts all the chapters of the *Proslogion* together to form a "single" argument for the existence of God, thus failing to appreciate the precise relation between P 2 and P 3. More importantly, this account fails to see that Anselm is rationally justified in claiming to have shown the existence of God in P 3. He does not have to wait to claim that S is God until he has shown that it has all the attributes attributable to God; rather, he can do so once he has shown that S has the distinctive existence—that singularly wonderful and wonderfully singular kind of being—that God alone can enjoy. Evidently, as his procedure clearly indicates, Anselm does not think the existence of God can be claimed before the argument of P 3 is concluded, although he is neither reluctant to reinvoke the name of God at that point, as he was in P 2, nor to answer the fool who claimed that "God" does not exist in P 4.

By contrast, my contention is that there is a single argument that spans P 2–3 and presumes to demonstrate the existence of God.

As to the justification of the latter aspect of this claim, namely, the insistence that Anselm thinks he has a right to conclude that it is "God" he has shown to exist, we need only turn to the remainder of P 3 to clarify what its conclusion is and how it exploits what we have been regarding as the ultimate ontological difference.

The Ontological Element of the Ontological Argument

Most accounts of Anselm's argument, even if they are willing to follow it this far, assume that it is over at this stage. In fact, however, the drawing of the conclusion that something than which nothing greater can be thought so exists that it cannot be thought not to exist really places us at about the midpoint of the argument. Not only are we presently in the middle of P 3, but, without chapter divisions, there is—not unlike its relation to P 2—a kind of seamless connection between P 3 and P 4, at whose conclusion the argument is formally brought to a close. Indeed, it was chapters 2–4 that during Anselm's own lifetime were extracted from the text and circulated, along with Gaunilo's responses and the author's replies, as the *Ratio Anselmi.* Consequently, if we are to interpret the whole of Anselm's argument, not to mention the whole of the *Proslogion,* we must look as carefully at the remainder of the argument as we have at the argument thus far. Not only must we show that the identification of God with something than which nothing greater can be thought is part and parcel of its reasoning, but also that it is based on a certain "insight" that will work itself out in rather strange ways later in the text.

If our detailed discussion of the relation between the *Monologion* and the *Proslogion* has provided any key to the relation between P 2 and P 3, it has done so by showing what is at stake in the distinction drawn in P 3 and how much may be concealed within it. We will wait to develop the full implications of the conclusion of what we regard as Anselm's argument until he does, namely, in P 4, although we do need, at this point, to address the more immediate implications of our account, which may help to prepare us for that later discussion. After drawing the conclusion of the single argument that spans P 2 and P 3, Anselm turns his attention to the question of the identity of God and something than which nothing greater can be thought by appealing once again to a condensed version of those topics from the *Monologion* that we have claimed are at work at the depths of the *Proslogion* argument:

> And this is you, lord our God. You so truly are, then, lord my God, that you cannot even be thought not to be. And this is fit-

ting. For if some mind could think of something better than you, the creature would rise above the creator and judge of the creator, which is completely absurd. Indeed, whatever else is, other than you alone, can be thought not to be. You alone, then, most truly of all, and thus most greatly of all, possess being—for whatever else is does not so truly possess being and thus is to a lesser degree. (S I, 103)

Now one might think, at first glance, that Anselm's point is rather the opposite of the one we want to make. We are contending that, given the conclusion drawn in P 3, there is reason to claim that something than which nothing greater can be thought is God, whereas in the initial lines here the direction of the inference may appear to be the opposite. They seem to be saying that insofar as God is S, the conclusion just drawn in P 3 pertains to him as well. That is, after Anselm exclaims: "And this is you, lord our God," he goes on to say: "You so truly exist, then, that you cannot even be thought not to exist." In that case, it may seem that he is simply reinvoking the identification made on the basis of faith at the beginning of P 2, that Anselm is saying: If S so exists, and God is S, then God so exists. At this point, then, it may appear that talk of "God" reenters the discussion based upon the original assumption that begins the reasoning of P 2, that "we believe that you are something than which nothing greater can be thought," not based upon any rational argument that would justify the identification.

And that is how it might appear if we looked only at the opening lines of the above passage. Undoubtedly, the first line does serve to reintroduce the original identification, to remind us that while for the past two chapters we have been talking about something than which nothing greater can be thought, from the beginning we have identified it with God. But the direction of the inferences begins to shift at the precise point where Anselm says: "And this is fitting." For the argument that follows this claim is not simply assuming the identification of God with S but is aimed at providing an elaboration of, and justification for, the identification, as if Anselm's initial exclamation that "this is you, lord our God" is based upon an assumption that the faithful have been making which now has to be shown as "fitting." In effect, then, we understand this first line as announcing the assumption we have been operating under all along, only to proceed, as is Anselm's fashion, after this pronouncement, to justify it.[49]

Admittedly, the justification of the claim that God is something than which nothing greater can be thought is itself initially concealed in what would appear to be a religious appeal to the impropriety of the creature "judging" the creator, as if this would involve presuming one might be able to think of something "better" than God. It may well be, however—as is Anselm's fashion as a rational theologian—that the invocation of this religious ban is his way of reporting something philosophically fitting that he has discovered about the nature of our thinking about God, and is only a first indication of the force of his conclusion, which ultimately claims that thought neither is in a position to, nor need, pass any judgment on the nature of the creator, including on his existence. As P 4 will insist, the human mind is compelled to think as it does about the existence of God without any room for decision or doubt. Indeed, it is precisely the power of such a conclusion that leads to a problem Anselm feels he must address. But before we follow his discussion into that next chapter, we will have to complete our consideration of the argument still going on in P 3.

It seems evident that the pivotal point in the above passage is the contention that, in contrast to God, everything else that is can be thought not to be. Given our account of the *Monologion* and its relation to the *Proslogion,* it should be clear that this claim is itself an expression of the ontological difference between creator and creature, which should presumably allow the rational mind to distinguish God from all else based upon the distinctive nature of his existence. After this, Anselm will turn to the doctrine of degrees of reality, whose details we need not pause to rehearse, since we have already been introduced to them in the *Monologion.* So as not to be misled, however, we will have to attend rather carefully to the order of the argument, since the direction of the inference at issue here is the reverse of that of the earlier work. While both texts may lead to the same conclusion, the *Monologion* begins from the beings with which we are ordinarily familiar, scaling them by degrees so as to reach their creator, even if it results in the denial of any ultimate ontological comparability between being itself and the beings it creates. By contrast, the *Proslogion* argument works exclusively on the basis of the distinctive nature of something than which nothing greater can be thought, only to arrive in its conclusion at an existence so distinct that it distinguishes God from all else.

Still, in the above passage, a certain comparability between creator and creature might be thought to arise, not only in speaking of God as existing "most truly of all" (*verissime omnium*) or in speaking of beings as existing to a "lesser degree" (*minus habet esse*), but insofar as the talk of creatures existing "not so truly" (*non sic vere*) may itself be regarded as a comparison. In fact, the grammatical construction used throughout P 3, in speaking of what "so truly exists that it cannot be thought not to exist" (*sic vere esse ut . . .*), may appear to be a comparative claim insofar as it can be taken to mean that God exists to such an extent that he exists to a higher degree than everything else. No doubt, the "so" (*sic*) is ambiguous with respect to manner or degree; for saying that something "so exists that . . ." could mean that it exists to such a degree or that it exists in such a way that it cannot be thought not to exist. Clearly, Anselm is prepared to exploit this ambiguity to suggest that both are the case, namely, that God exists to such a degree that he exists in a distinctive way. But the point is that in the passage we have just cited from P 3, the direction of the inference is not from degree to manner, is not designed to emphasize that God exists to such an extent that he exists in a specific way, but quite the opposite: it is inferring degree *from* manner. Thus, immediately after reminding us of the impropriety of the creature judging its creator, Anselm begins the argument by proclaiming that "everything else that exists, except you alone, can be thought not to exist." It is from this way of existing, the manner in which creatures exist, that it may be inferred that they do not exist "so truly" as does something than which nothing greater can be thought. Because God is the sole exception to what so exists that it can be thought not to exist, it follows from the fact that he alone exists in such a way that he cannot be thought not to exist, that he exists "most truly of all" and thus "maximally" possesses being. And this is not just because all other beings possess less being insofar as they exist to a lesser degree, but because they have a categorically different type of being: they so exist that they can be thought not to exist.

It must be clear, then, that the concluding appeal in P 3 to the doctrine of degrees of reality is itself designed to reinforce the claim to God's distinctive form of existence, not to make any claim to comparison between creator and creature. Even the insistence that God exists to the "highest" degree (*maxime omnium habes esse*) is, for Anselm, not a relative claim, as if God merely has "more" being than do creatures, as creatures do compared to one another. In asserting the superlative, it is designed to express unsurpassability rather than comparability and entails that the "supreme" being, in enjoying the "most," indeed, the utmost being, exists in a way utterly unlike and categorically incomparable to all other beings.[50] When we developed this point in our discussion of the *Monologion,* we saw not only that God "so supremely is (*sic summe est*) that, in a certain sense, he alone exists,"[51] but, consequently, how strangely wrought is what we there called the ultimate difference. It was precisely the nature of the supremacy of God's being that led us to insist that Anselm's understanding of the ontological difference between being and beings, while not just a difference in degree but in kind, requires it be treated in an even more radical form. We know, in other words, from the earlier work that when we finally scale the wall of beings to arrive at the top, at "maximal being," a categorical transformation takes place in light of which the manner of existence of what exists supremely is revealed to be such that, compared to it, everything else is not just viewed as at a lower level of being but ceases to be regarded as being at all.

In that case, however, there is a philosophical point at issue here that we do not want to lose sight of in arguing about the philological question of the relation between the two relevant chapters in the *Proslogion*. In fact, we first want to try to sight this point by insisting that the conclusion drawn in P 3 condenses into it a whole series of issues that led, in Anselm's earlier work, to the radical result of M 28. Obviously, our detailed treatment of the relation of the two texts would entail that the ontological reversal at issue in the categorical elevation of thought designed to change our thinking about the nature of being in the *Monologion* must somehow be replicated in the *Proslogion*. This ontological conversion, even given the reinstatement of creatures after they are shown to be thinkable as nonexistent, should be sufficient to suggest that it would be an optical illusion to imagine that there is ultimately a consistent ascent in this movement instead of a sudden shift of thought. Unless beings disappear at the moment of truth, they cannot be reinstated based upon the new understanding of their "scarce" being. In view of the strategy in M 28—which must find a way to withdraw being from those beings it nonetheless must maintain in some form of being so as to distinguish the supreme being from them—we might well suspect that in the new distinction of P 3, beings would have to be granted a "degree" of being that, however, their "manner" of being would in some sense rescind. To claim that beings exist such that they can be thought not to exist is, in effect, to take back in thought the very existence they are thought to have. As such, a certain standard of being may well impose itself upon us in the moment of conversion during which beings are thought not to be, appear, as it were, in their nothingness, in their ultimate ontological difference from God. And however moderated and masked that difference may come to be in the *Proslogion,* ordinary beings must there also disappear as what can be thought not to exist if they are to reveal, in their withdrawal, something that so exists that it cannot be thought not to exist.

The point, then, is that only a proper appreciation of the radicalness and precision of the distinction at issue in P 3 will put us in a position to raise the question of just how this difference has been made out and whether it is not also the case there that God is distinguished from all else not so much through a positive determination of his being as by means of a certain ontological conversion of our understanding of beings reminiscent of the *Monologion*. If we stressed, in our reading of the earlier work, the epistemological conditions under which such a change of mind is effected, we have done so in order to show how the identification of S as God in the *Proslogion* is itself based upon a specific ontological insight. The visionary epistemology that the *Monologion* espouses requires that "the thing itself" be brought before the eye of reason. If we now aim to stress that the distinction in P 3 between what can and what cannot be thought not to exist is supposed to offer us an identifying mark of God, it is because it serves to distinguish God from everything else by providing the rational mind with an odd kind of formula for bringing such an object of thought before the eye of the mind, not only to justify the identification of S with God but so that the nature of the thing itself may determine our thinking about it. It is this "psycho-logical" strategy, as we will call it, that is most critical to the inner workings of Anselm's argument and requires that what is at issue in its conclusion be more than a merely nominal identification of "God" as "something than which nothing greater can be thought." Instead, as P 4 will make clear, it must involve an insight into the thing itself that determines our rational understanding of it. Indeed, it is precisely the contention being made at this stage of the argument in P 3 that leads to and legitimates its ultimate claim—and eventual demand—to have secured a vision of God.

The point, therefore, of rereading the relation between P 2 and P 3 is not only to suggest that Anselm's argument has never been properly understood, nor simply to claim that an understanding of it is dependent upon an understanding of the relation between the *Proslogion* and the *Monologion,* nor merely to show that his infamous argument has been underrated in its interpretation in terms of the so-called ontological proof. It is, rather, aimed at showing the full extent of the *Proslogion* argument and for the first time asking what its conclusion entails. The argument is apparently sufficiently forceful to provide reason with a distinction powerful enough to distinguish God from the whole of creation. This allows the rational mind to distinguish the supreme being from everything else that is and, as such, to offer to our rational understanding an insight into God's being. That what is at issue, in that event, is an "ontological" argument seems clear, but precisely in the sense that the distinction of P 3 condenses into it and thus offers to rational thought Anselm's ultimate ontological vision, even as it trades off of the "logic" of "being" no less than does the conversion experience in M 28. Indeed, Anselm's argument clarifies even further the ontological difference between what the *Monologion* called "being itself" and all other beings, in which case the *Proslogion* argument must afford an even more rigorous rational insight into the meaning of being.

In what follows, we will concentrate in some detail on this "onto-logical" element of the argument and on the nature of the rational vision of being it is designed to produce. In preparation for that discussion, we have taken this opportunity to remind ourselves that asserting the existence of God is not, for Anselm, simply a matter of claiming that one more being is to be included in the domain of factual existence. In this respect, one might well say that he proposes not so much an ontical as an ontological argument; that is, his strategy is not merely to get us to admit that a particular being exists but to do so by getting us to think differently about the nature of being. This is why I have insisted that, in accord with Anselm's ultimate insight, God's existence is to be construed as so unlike the existence of creatures that they must be nullified to reveal it. The point just now, however, is that a sensitivity to such tactics forces us to raise the question of just what we are doing when we assert the existence of God. And it is not easy to say. One thing, however, is clear: the clarification of the being of God entails an uncanny transformation in, virtually a denial of, our normal ways of thinking about being, such that we are not to attribute to God the existence familiar to us from our experience of those beings that can be thought not to be. Rather, we are to admit to a kind of being that cannot be conceived on the model of creatures and whose revelation ultimately requires that those beings pale to nothingness in view of what we have earlier called Anselm's negative ontology.

While, then, the distinction of P 3 may appear to imply a certain comparability between being and beings, it is, in fact, designed to assert their radical difference. While both creator and creature must be said to enjoy some degree of being, the point of P 3's way of making out the ontological difference is to distinguish two categorically different types of existence, such that God alone may be said to exist in such manner that he cannot be thought not to exist. If this distinctive way of being serves to justify the identification of God with S, then it requires something more than a nominal understanding either of something than which nothing greater can be thought or of this distinction that defines its unique being. Instead, it depends upon a certain rational insight into the thing itself. In that event, however, this final stage of P 3 is actually announcing what might well be thought of as the turning point of Anselm's argument, as it turns on the conversion of thought on which the *Proslogion* trades, namely, on the movement from a nominal to an essential understanding of something than which nothing greater can be thought, and based upon the conversion in the meaning of being contained in the distinction of P 3. What will need to be shown, then, is all that is entailed by this way of construing the ontological difference, and what it is to understand this distinction, not simply as a string of terms but instead, as P 4 will insist, in "taking it to heart." As such, it will be necessary for us to make the transition in our own interpretation from an analysis of the logical aspect of Anselm's argument to what we are claiming is its phenomenological basis, or from a more scholastic to a more monastic approach to its reasoning.

In anticipation of that account, I do not think it is unfair to insist that Anselm's ontological argument in the *Proslogion* also proceeds *sola ratione,* or *sola cogitatione,* that is, by means of thinking alone. It does so, however, by impressing upon the rational mind a distinction that can bring to its inner vision a certain object of thought that, in turn, will determine its thinking about the meaning of being. The demand for this rational vision of being, which we claim lies at the heart of Anselm's argument, is what has led us to stress the fact that the *Proslogion* proof is to be regarded—and regards itself—as a matter of meditation, of elevating one's mind to the contemplation of God by means of a specific image of the divine. Perhaps we could, for the moment, put it this way. If a response to the question of the existence of God requires a cognitive transformation in our understanding of what it means to be, then it should not be surprising that one would claim that the question can be addressed at the level of thought, that one should be able to think his or her way to the existence of God through rational contemplation. In this regard, we may well find that there is ultimately no need to leap from the logical to the real if what is at issue is a matter of how we are to think at a fundamental level about the nature of being. This is not to deny, as we know from our earlier treatment of Anselm's epistemology, that for him our thinking would not be in a position to determine such matters unless something presented itself to our thought that compelled the conclusion we are suggesting he reached: unless something appeared in the vision of thinking that demanded the conversion in our understanding of what it means to be. It is this vision of God, which we claim is embedded in the argument of P 2–3, to which I want to draw attention, as the compulsion it entails will alone show how the religious ban on the creature judging the creator mentioned in P 3 can be translated into a philosophical claim in P 4. In effect, a certain insight into God that rational thought can have within the "inner chamber" of the mind lies at the root of Anselm's ontological argument. We will later have to show how this specific cognitive experience produces the conviction that God exists.

Of course, the pressure of a certain troubling ambiguity—not to say confusion—between the ontical and the ontological, between beings and being itself, may be felt most strongly at precisely this point. Anselm clearly had something ontical in mind when he claimed to have shown the existence of God. He thought that he had shown something to exist, indeed, something than which nothing greater can be thought, not just that he had gotten us to think differently about the nature of existence. In short, Anselm certainly thought that "being itself" was, or resided in, a particular being. And while this must be admitted, we will have to deal with the fact that, later in the *Proslogion,* Anselm himself admits, whatever we think he would like to have thought, that no such being, no ontical reality, unequivocally presents itself to thought in this rational vision of God. The mode of presentation to consciousness of the supreme being, in the insight that rational thought has into it, enjoys a logic of its own. In fact, it will turn out to be essential to the revelation of the god who "dwells in inaccessible light" that he does not unambiguously appear as an object of human thought—at least not in this life. Thus, once having followed the reasoning of the argument, we will not only have to ask where it has led, but if, as we are assuming, it has led to a vision of God, we will also have to ask what appears to thought in this ontological argument; that is, just how such a supreme being presents itself to human cognition. As we will show, the answer to this phenomenological question is expressly, even if unintentionally, revealed in a confession Anselm will make later in the *Proslogion.*

We first have to verify that Anselm's argument itself calls for a certain understanding of "the thing itself." With that in mind, the point we have been making is that the claim underscored in P 3 by its concluding appeal to the doctrine of degrees of being is not one to comparison but to the distinctive existence of God. As such, it reinforces the contention that the conclusion of the single argument that spans P 2 and P 3 is sufficiently forceful to justify the rational identification of God. Such a powerful conclusion, however, is not without problems of its own, nor is the distinction that Anselm has employed to capture the essence of the existence of God. For if God so truly exists that he cannot be thought not to exist, how could the fool think that God does not exist in the first place, indeed, how can any of us think this when it is unthinkable? "Why then did *the fool say in his heart that there is no God,* when it is so evident to a rational mind that you of all things are to the highest degree? Why, indeed, unless because he was stupid and a fool? (S I, 103)."

We will not feel the force of Anselm's question if we do not appreciate that for something to exist "to the highest degree" means, for him, that it exists such that it cannot be thought not to exist. And if we think the problem this raises may be solved simply by reminding us that the fool is a fool, this will remain a mere *ad hominem* unless Anselm can show what is involved in the stupidity to which we are all apparently subject. Were this answer sufficient, it would not have been left in the form of a question, designed to lead, as it does, to P 4. A clue heading us in this direction is hinted at, as is Anselm's actual response to the fool, in the above passage when it suggests that such things should be "evident to a rational mind." For so formulating the issue invites the question: What is it for the existence of God to be evident to the rational mind, and in what, precisely, does such rational evidence consist?

| *Proslogion* 4

One of the issues that should strike us in working our way through the various accounts of Anselm's argument for the existence of God in the *Proslogion* is not only that conflicting readings have been given of the relation between P 2 and P 3, and that what has for the most part survived in our history as the "ontological proof" is a mere fragment of the argument as a whole, but that insofar as interpreters have located different arguments, they have also come to different conclusions and thus have differed in their view of what the argument claims to show. As I have suggested from the outset, part of the fragmentation in our tradition of Anselm's argument is the result of its being ripped out of its original context. That context is formed by monastic practices, especially the practice of contemplation, which defines the task set for the *Proslogion* in its preface as a text designed for one "striving to elevate his own mind to the contemplation of God." And I would like to think that such "elevation" can be shown to be embedded in the argument itself, indeed, that it is far more revelatory of how the argument works as an argument than any tracing of its reasoning. Of course, the reasoning proper is not irrelevant to the argument. It is just that to understand the original context for that reasoning is to understand the nature of rationality as Anselm thought it and to apply that understanding to our understanding of the argument of P 2–3.

Fortunately, in P 4 Anselm himself provides us with a certain clarification of how we are to understand his argument. There he is forced to confront a problem that would seem to follow from his reasoning, and in a chapter whose very existence in the text serves to confirm our claim that he thought the conclusion of his argument was the one drawn in P 3. That conclusion alone can be regarded as so forceful as to cause the problem Anselm addresses in P 4, clearly indicating that, for him, what is at stake in the question of the existence of God is the conclusion of P 3, not of P 2. But if the argument has shown that God so exists that he cannot be thought not to exist, the problem remains how the question of God's existence can arise in the first place. If thought is powerless to think God not to exist, if reason lacks the power to pass judgment in such matters insofar as the matter itself is uniquely characterized by the inconceivability of its nonexistence, how can the fool have even thought that God does not exist, indeed, how can any of us? And the answer to this problem leads to the central topic of P 4: the question of the nature of thinking.

The critical point in Anselm's response to this question is that he never retreats from the claim that, in a certain sense, rational thought is not in a position to doubt the existence of God. He consistently asserts that the matter itself compels the mind to think as it does, that it is so binding upon thought that our thinking remains unfree to think otherwise. Of course—and this is Anselm's way out of the problem, although a way we must also understand quite precisely—the rational mind must be thinking, and thinking properly, to be so compelled. Here we might begin by recalling that, according to the *Monologion,* the proper role of the mind's visionary nature, including the aim of its reasoning power, is to form true likenesses of the things themselves: to envision in thought the reality itself, whether by means of an imaginative image or a rational impression of what is being thought. And while M 10 also makes it clear that there are other inner activities that may be called "thinking," it should, in that case, be apparent that in P 4 Anselm formulates the way out of his difficulty in a manner that is clearly reminiscent, as are so many other claims that are defended in the *Proslogion,* of his earlier work.

> But how has he said in his heart what he could not think, or how could he not think what he said in his heart, when to say in the heart and to think are one and the same?
>
> For if he truly—or rather, because he truly—both thought, because he said it in his heart, and did not say it in his heart, because he could not think it, something is not said in the heart or thought in only one way. For in one sense, a thing is thought when the word signifying it is thought; in another sense, when that which the thing itself is is understood. In the first sense, then, God can be thought not to exist; but, in the second sense, not at all. For no one understanding what God is can think that God does not exist, even though he may say these words in his heart either without any or with some foreign signification. (S I, 103–4)

While Anselm may be citing Scripture when he speaks of the fool "saying in his heart" that there is no God, we know that this way of putting the matter will play directly into the hands of both his view of the expressive power of the mind and his theory of signs. M 10 claims that thinking is a form of inner locution, an expression of the mind or reason, a kind of "saying" in the heart, although it also explains that, in accord with common usage and thus with the manner in which people ordinarily speak and think, there are a number of ways in which such inner expression can take place. A thing can be claimed to be thought, that is, expressed in the mind, not when the thing itself is envisioned by forming a likeness of it in the vision of our thinking but by silently thinking within us the signs that signify a thing: by inwardly employing those sign-sounds that when outwardly employed serve in the public language of a people and, we might say, the purposes of ordinary thought. On the other hand, and apparently by contrast, a thing may more properly be said to be thought when the thing itself is inwardly expressed in the mind, either by means of imagination or by rational understanding, that is, when "that which the thing itself is" is understood.

Anselm does not, then, regard the fundamental form of the expression of things in thought, thinking by means of that primal word which is the likeness of the thing itself, to be the only form of thinking or "saying in the heart," or perhaps even the most often practiced. Instead, we are no doubt more likely to think, especially about such "things" as God, as the fool does, not by intuiting the things themselves, conceiving of and observing them directly in thought, but by thinking indirectly of them by means of signs, even if we do so inwardly by silently employing (*tacens cogito*), as M 10 says, those significative sounds that when outwardly expressed are audible. And this latter is, in its own way, not only a kind of thinking but is also to be regarded, as is all thinking, as a way of thinking some "reality." This is why Anselm does not distinguish between thinking and not thinking, or between saying in the heart and babbling, or even between thinking a thing and thinking a sign, but between two different ways in which one and the same thing can be thought: between thinking about a thing by means of the signs that signify it and thinking the thing itself. Thus, the fool is not a fool because he merely utters sounds but because, rather than thinking essentially, he is only thinking the matter indirectly, via, shall we say, the indirection of signs. In that case, his "saying in the heart," his inner expressing of the matter at issue, is not by means of the visionary word that involves the formation of a likeness or expression in the mind. Instead of this direct impression of the thing upon thought that allows us to envision the reality itself in the inner vision of our thinking, the fool thinks solely by making use of those signs that are merely indicators, signifiers, tools used by thought, and have, even as their ultimate aim, their own way of getting at the things they signify.

It is not, therefore, just *what* the fool thinks that constitutes his foolishness but *how* he thinks; indeed, it is how he thinks that alone

apparently makes it possible for him to think what he does. Nor is
this to claim that the fool is not thinking about these issues at all, for
such an explanation would be of no assistance to the brethren, who
know from their own experience that doubt is a real possibility. Instead, Anselm must show that there is a form of thinking in which
the existence of God cannot be doubted and yet suggest that this is a
level of thought as difficult to achieve as it is to maintain. For it is
riddled with the possibility of slipping back into derivative forms of
thought that, in some sense, allow us to "think" about the matter at
issue, but not essentially, even as, in trying to think in the proper
way, we may miss the mark and envision some "foreign signification." In either case, the question that needs to be addressed is just
what it is to think "the thing itself" and just how we are to behold
the appropriate "reality" (*res ipsa*) that is God in thought, if not by
means of the silent, inward "saying in the heart" of the signs that
only signify but do not show the thing to our inner vision. For this
talk of saying in the heart, and the implication that we must be taking the reasoning of P 2–3 to heart, are connected to a form of rational intuition that is clarified in M 10 not simply by contrasting it
with the merely verbal but by comparing it with the inner vision
that imagination allows for: when we observe the thing itself in the
vision of the mind. In the present case, of course, it is not a matter of
an imaginative image but of a rational expression, which, if true, is
not a mental concoction but a direct impression made upon rational
thought by the truth of the thing itself.

To explicate the precise nature of the rational vision of God that
Anselm's argument must afford, we will also have to consider, in comparing the rather abrupt claims about the nature of thinking in P 4
with the more detailed analysis in M 10, a certain difference in their
accounts. In the *Monologion,* given the topics at issue, Anselm treats
rational understanding as a matter of entertaining the thing itself
in thought in light of the "universal essence" that is "the truth in the
nature of things," against which our likenesses can be measured and
which, *De veritate* 7 claims, is the cause of true conceptions. Just as
I entertain an impression of a man's body, not his body itself, in
imagination—although my image, if true to the man (true to life, as
Anselm puts it) is determined by the nature of the thing itself,
whether he is present to me or I draw his image from memory—so, too,
when I think that man rationally, I entertain a likeness of him as
well, and one equally determined by the nature of the thing itself.
The rational likeness of the man is not an image of his corporeal existence but of his essential being. It is this truth in the being of
things that makes an impression on the mind and supplies the standard against which rationality can measure its likenesses. Indeed, it

causally determines the rational image that the mind formulates of reality. Consequently, even if the human mind is in some sense active in the formation of its conceptions of things, it is nonetheless passive with respect to, as it is determined in its thinking by, the truth of what is being thought.

In the case of creatures, this truth is based on the form or model of things in God's thought (*ratio*) thanks to which whatever has been made will have a common nature that it shares with other beings, since each was created in accord with an original form of which they are examples. Insight into this rational form is supposed to provide us with access to the thing itself in its true being, even if a certain conversion of the meaning of "being" that turns on an ambiguity in the term *"essentia"* is what allows Anselm to regard the essence of a thing as showing us more truly and originally what it "is" than its mere factual existence. Admittedly, it might still not be altogether clear just what is at issue in such rational intuition, or how reason can be said to have access to the thing itself in thought, in part because its inner vision may not be as much like imagination as the *Monologion* pretends. On the other hand, if one assumes that this is because rational insight entertains abstract objects of thought, "universals" that can be observed in themselves "pure and simple" (*sola et pura*),[52] although in their relevant application to the things that exemplify them, it is noteworthy that in speaking of thinking the thing itself in the case of God, P 4 does not talk, as M 10 did, of envisioning a universal essence but of understanding "that which the thing itself is" (*id ipsum quod res est*). The question in P 4, then, no longer revolves around the notion of rational understanding in general but of what it is to envision something "by means of reason" in this particular case.[53]

To see what is at stake here, we must appreciate that in the case of God, talk of understanding his universal essence would be inappropriate, not only because we cannot know his essence but also because that essence is in no sense universal. Since, as M 27 insists, God has nothing in common with anything else—this being that "neither divides itself among many substances" as a universal must do, "nor unites with any other by virtue of a common essence" as all other individual things do—it is not surprising that M 65 would claim that the term "essence" no more applies to him than do those other common categories that characterize creatures. In short, the *Monologion*'s insistence that God is an individual rather than a universal is, first and foremost, a way of expressing the fact that he is completely unique, that "there cannot be more than one of this kind."[54] Through this somewhat paradoxical contention, Anselm means to suggest not simply that God happens to be "one of a kind," but that he is an absolute individual, more individual than any of those individuals with which we are ordinarily familiar can be, as he shares nothing in common with anything else. We might say, then, that if the "universal being" of created substances is determined by the essential nature they share with other individuals of their kind, then God is not a kind of thing; or that if the basic Platonic insight may be said to consist in the claim that no individual is so unique that it does not share some features, including its essential ones, with other members of its kind, then for Anselm, the "singularly unique and uniquely singular" being that supplies the basis for all being is the absolute exception to this rule. Not only are all the features of the creative being essential to him, but God is the only individual that is so different from all else that he in no way shares his nature with, has nothing in common with, other individuals in that he does not just possess features of his own kind, but is himself a kind of his own.

In Anselm's view, then, when, in the case of all other individuals, we consider their essential nature, we will always be thinking of something for which there could, at least in principle, be a number of examples. Given his account of the nature of creation, the essential designation of any creature will not pick out a unique individual but a class of possible individuals. This is, no doubt, what leads us to think that reason, in understanding the essence of something, is not entertaining a concrete individual but an abstract universal. In the case of God, however, rational thought is in a position to sight the individual designated by its essential description insofar as it is capable of providing a characterization that could not be common to a number of possible individuals. In effect, reason can, in this case alone, supply thought with the rational description of an absolute individual.

In this way, the rational mind is given the possibility of envisioning what we might refer to not as the universal, but as the individual essence of God, by which we mean his uniquely singular being. This is, of course, not an essence in any ordinary sense, that is, it is not a matter of the defining features shared by a number of individuals that nonetheless make each what it is, but a matter of the "true being" proper to God alone. In the case of God, a rational clarification of his distinctive being should allow the eye of the mind to pick out of its field of inner vision one and only one possible individual that meets the description. Nor does such a vision require that we have insight into the essence of God "as he is in himself." For the distinguishing characterization that allows rational thought to sight God can take place at the level not of what we think in other cases as a matter of essence, but at the level of existence. God is the only being the nature of whose existence distinguishes him essentially from everything else, in whom essence and existence are indistinguishably one in his uniquely singular being, unlike the case of a creature, whose existence is even more "common" than its essence. If the eye of the mind is in a position to entertain objects of thought, whether we think of them as universals or—as in imagination—as individuals, then in the case of God, a concise rational characterization of his distinctive existence should allow reason to locate the being at issue quite precisely in the landscape of pure thought and to identify it as the absolute individual that Anselm takes God to be.

We eventually want to show how the reasoning of P 2–3 is designed to allow rational thought to do just this and consequently that there is a specific vision of God embedded in the argument itself, which in fact lies at its basis. This would only require that the conclusion drawn in P 3 be sufficient to distinguish God from everything else based upon the unique existence proper to him alone, namely, that he exists in such a way that he cannot be thought not to exist. Our present point, however, is not just that such an absolutely distinguishing form of existence, this *proprium dei,* as it is called in the replies, would allow reason to identify "something than which nothing greater can be thought" as "God." Instead, it is that this very identification is based upon a rational intuition of the thing itself, an essential insight into "it itself which the thing is" (*id ipsum quod res est*) that allows us to isolate and identify the being at issue in the vision of our thinking. Such an identification of God would, however, require a certain movement of thought from the merely logical considerations at issue in the single argument of P 2–3 to what we have referred to as its phenomenological basis. If reason always stands in danger of the superficiality of nominal understanding—of the possibility of following an argument at what we might call the level of blind inference, which lacks the visionary element that is essential to Anselm's notion of true conceptions of the mind—then there would have to be a moment of truth embedded in his argument, a moment of vision, as it were, if it is to succeed in its aim. It is this moment of intuitive insight, to which the discursive reasoning is designed to lead, that is implicitly demanded in the distinction between two ways of thinking drawn in P 4.

If we required any further proof of this, we need only notice that the sort of nominal understanding criticized in P 4 as that of a fool is where the argument itself began. The kind of "understanding" that was necessary to set the argument in motion and supplied virtually the first step in the reasoning of P 2 required only that the fool understand "what he hears," that is, that he understand the words "something than which nothing greater can be thought." At that

stage in our discussion, we referred to this strictly nominal conception of S as the argument's semiological starting point—a starting
point that, thanks to Anselm's philosophy of language, leads to a
quite different kind of conclusion. Clearly, P 4 is announcing that
the argument of P 2–3 must have brought us further than the
merely verbal understanding with which we began. It must have
taken us from this nominal beginning to some essential intuition
into the thing itself, from a semiological to an ontological understanding of "something than which nothing greater can be thought."
Otherwise, there is no compelling denial of the fool's claim that God
does not exist, for P 4 admits that at the level of signs, God can be
thought not to be. The moment of truth, then, that resides at the
heart of the argument must occur where and when reason breaks
through the words to the thing itself in a moment of vision, or, as M
10 would say, in the "acuteness" of a certain "rational understanding." If the argument begins from mere words, its aim must be to
develop our understanding such that, in the end, it offers the consummation that P 1 prays for in leading our thinking from those
signs to a rational sighting of God.

What we are suggesting, then, is that there must be certain experiences of thinking—certain thought-formations or inner visions,
in short, a specific rational vision of God—embedded in Anselm's
argument that supply its epistemological basis. Needless to say, the
cognitive experiences at issue, while not a matter of imaginative intuition, nonetheless involve the eye of the mind and its inner sight in
the sighting of a matter to be located in thought by means of the
stunning precision of the rational distinction between what exists
such that it cannot be thought not to exist and what exists such that
it can be thought not to exist. Like imagination, however, and unlike
thinking by means of signs, this rational insight is determined by
the nature of the matter being thought and thus is subject to a certain truth-determination to the extent to which genuine thinking,
for Anselm, is not concocting its inner visions but expressing the
things themselves in thought by means of mental images that are
causally determined by the impression those realities make and
leave upon the rational mind. In fact, if we still sought further confirmation of this in P 4 itself, we would find it in the concluding lines
of its discussion, which capture the essence of the argument. They
show this to be the point not just of P 4 but of the argument as a
whole, as they review the argument from beginning to end, emphasizing our thinking in an appropriate manner about such issues and
the way in which the proper object of thought will determine what is
to be thought. P 4 concludes its response to the fool by insisting:

For no one understanding what God is can think that God does not exist, even though he may say these words in his heart without any or with some foreign signification. For God is that than which a greater cannot be thought. Whoever really understands this clearly understands that it itself so exists that not even for thought can it not exist. Therefore, whoever understands that God is such, cannot think him not to exist. (S I, 103–4)

The opening line expresses the heart of Anselm's insight: no one understanding what God is can think that he does not exist. Its point, however, will be missed if we do not notice that Anselm speaks solely and repeatedly of "understanding" and that this is designed to stress the kind of thinking at issue with respect to the claim that God cannot be "thought" not to exist—the thinking of one who "really understands." And we will understand what that means only if we appreciate how the appeal to true understanding in these lines is ruled by the distinction already drawn in P 4.

The classic point, which will later in the tradition be characterized in terms of God's existence pertaining to his essence, is itself in danger of being misconstrued here if we do not appreciate that when Anselm speaks of our understanding what God is, he is not talking about God's essence in some generic sense. Instead, he is referring to our understanding "that which God is": which one God is, we might say. What this means, however, only becomes clear if we realize that the point of the above passage is determined by the fact that Anselm is applying the general distinction—between thinking by means of signs and understanding the thing itself—to God. Thus, it begins by insisting that no one who understands that which God is (*id quod deus est*)—not just thinking the signs that signify the matter to be thought but thinking the thing itself (*id ipsum quod res est*)—can think that he does not exist. And we are immediately told why: because God is something than which nothing greater can be thought. But to appreciate how it is that in understanding this we will be unable to think that God does not exist, it is critical to hear the line following this one as echoing that same basic distinction between the two ways of thinking, for it says that anyone understanding the thing itself understands that it itself (*id ipsum*) so exists that not even for thought can it not exist. In that case, as the final line concludes, anyone who truly understands that God is such a thing cannot think that he does not exist.[55]

This is not, however, simply because God is something than which nothing greater can be thought and something than nothing greater can be thought has been shown to exist such that it cannot be thought not to exist. Instead, it is because, as the concluding line suggests, in having thought our way through to the thing itself—whether we call it "God" or "something than which nothing greater can be thought"—our thinking has come to be determined by the reality being thought. This claim about the effect the thing itself is supposed to have upon our thinking is in fact highlighted throughout these final lines by certain grammatical transformations of the term "thought." That an understanding of the reality itself impels us to think in a specific way about it, that the impression made upon thought by something than which nothing greater can be thought is such that it cannot be thought not to exist, should be evident once we notice that Anselm does not put it exactly in these terms. For he is here trying to draw a further conclusion from the conclusion of P 3 by drawing on the grammar of the distinction at issue there thanks to the discussion in P 4.

What Anselm says is not simply that whoever really understands that God is something than which nothing greater can be thought understands that the very thing itself so exists that it cannot be thought (*cogitari*) not to exist, as it has been put thus far in the argument of P 3, but that it itself so exists that not even for thought (*cogitatione*) can it not exist. This in turn sets the stage for the final conclusion Anselm wants to draw, his answer to the fool as it is given in P 4, with a second transformation of "thought" in the final line, which claims that one who understands that God is such cannot think (*cogitare*) that he does not exist. This grammatical transition from the passive to the active—from the feature of God's existence that he cannot *be thought* not to exist to the active voice in which, when God is the subject (or rather, when the subject is one who really understands) thought cannot *think* nonexistence—formally reflects the force of the conclusion Anselm means to assert: that the nature of the thing itself, once sighted, is so compelling that it actively determines our thought such that we cannot think otherwise. When "that which it itself is" is entertained in thought, our thinking is impelled to think as it does by the reality itself and is not free to conceive it as not existing. In intuiting the thing itself in the vision of our thinking, its conception in the mind is determined by the direct impression on thought of the truth of what appears, or at least is glimpsed in and through the radical distinction of P 3. In that case, rational thought operates under a certain truth-determination and can think in no other way, thanks to the nature of the thing it is thinking, that is, thanks to which thing it is that reason is thinking.

Admittedly, there is a certain ambiguity in the reference here to what one is to understand. When Anselm speaks of "whoever really understands this," the "this" could refer to "something than which nothing greater can be thought" or to the entire claim of the preceding line, namely, that God is something than which nothing greater can be thought. Obviously, these two options go together. For "really understanding" S, that is, coming to some essential insight into the matter itself, is what allows us to see that S is God. This becomes clear when it is claimed in this very line, in application of the general distinction between two ways of thinking a thing in that case in which the reality (*res*) being thought is God, that one who so understands will understand that the very thing itself so exists that it cannot be thought not to exist. In either case, what is critical for both the clarification of the nature of the existence of something than which nothing greater can be thought and the subsequent justification of its identification with God is not simply the initial and apparently nominal designation of God as "something than which nothing greater can be thought" but the way the development of our understanding has supposedly allowed us to glimpse the thing itself in thought, to distinguish it from all else, and to justify the identification of God with S based upon its being shown to enjoy the absolutely unique existence proper to God alone. It is, of course, this distinctive brand of being that allows the mind to entertain the thing in thought by sighting what exists in such a way that it cannot be thought not to exist and, in so doing, to see the one God is. What we must notice, however, is that this very characterization of what exists such that it cannot be thought not to exist is put to use in these final lines to express the conclusion of Anselm's argument not only in a way that lays stress on the nature of the thing itself but also, as the *Monologion* would have, on the effect that the reality itself has on the thinking of one who "really understands."

The point, then, is to bind our rational vision to reality in its causal truth-determination through an insight into the thing itself. This is designed, in part, to show how (at that moment of elevation, when the mind has arrived through its contemplation at the appropriate inner vision of the proper object of thought) one so understanding God cannot think that he does not exist, and why (as soon as we lose sight of the reality itself in thought, can no longer hold our thought to it, as it were, and retreat to nominal forms of thinking) God can be thought not to exist, as the fool has thought all along, since, in that case, the "truth" of the thing itself cannot determine our thinking. For Anselm, once reason is clear about what is being thought, and in that form of thought in which the thing itself is entertained in the vision of its thinking, it no longer needs to determine whether what it is thinking exists or not. And not because it has now seen the reality itself and so knows that it exists, but because of the distinctive nature of the being at issue. It is no coincidence, then, that the claim is expressed in P 3 in terms of the creature not being in a position to pass any judgment on its creator immediately after the conclusion of the argument for the existence of God and in anticipation of the discussion in P 4.

The possibility of our appreciating the epistemological nature of Anselm's rational vision of God as an indubitable insight grounded in our inability to think otherwise revolves around a clarification of the single argument that spans P 2–3. It draws as its conclusion the claim that something than which nothing greater can be thought exists in such a way that it cannot be thought not to exist, which serves to condense the ontological intuition into what exists properly, simply, absolutely, immutably, perfectly, and truly, without beginning or end or multiplicity of parts, and everywhere and always wholly. It is this "conception of the mind," the inner vision of the likeness of such a reality, that presumably thwarts our thinking otherwise once we understand what God is. Such psychological compulsion depends upon the unique position in which reason is put in its opportunity, as a result of P 3's highly refined characterization of which one God is, to sight an absolute individual and thus to demonstrate its own privileged access to reality.[56] And none of this will cease to be true, despite appearances, when the *Proslogion* later admits that what alone would be the proper object of the eye of the rational mind is, in some sense, beyond the scope of its vision. On the contrary, it will remain critical to a strategy that attempts to ground rationality on a preeminent object of thought that never actually appears.

Anselm's Argument and the Vision of God

In order to appreciate how Anselm ultimately redeems reason by confessing the limitations of its vision, in an attempt to read the *Proslogion* argument in light of its place in the work as a whole, we must first try to make out more precisely just what the vision of God in P 2–4 is like, even if some of what we will be claiming can be confirmed only later in the text. Such confirmation, however, will require that we put sufficient pressure on the text to force to the surface what is going on beneath it. Our pursuit of the phenomenological element of the ontological argument, as well as of the remainder of the *Proslogion,* may, in some respects, appear to be doing violence to the text, as we will not only have to indulge in a kind of "reading between the lines," but may also have to pry them open to see what is at their root. This is, of course, why we have tried to begin by documenting that Anselm's own self-interpretation of his argument in P 4 calls for a certain insight into the thing itself. And while there is ample evidence, as we have seen since the beginning of P 1, that the *Proslogion* aims to supply a vision of God, we will at various points in our phenomenological destruction of the text have to articulate the formations of thought that we think are at issue in terms other than the ones with which Anselm might feel most comfortable. This will be all the more true as we attempt to reveal not just what lies beneath the text but also what it is hiding; although, for obvious reasons, we will try to keep our vocabulary as consistent with Anselm's way of thinking as we can.

The critical question is just how the ontological distinction in the conclusion of Anselm's argument in P 3 works to direct the eye of the mind to the proper object of thought. Needless to say, given the ground we have covered and the way in which we have covered it, I am of the view that the new way of putting matters in the *Proslogion* not only captures the essence of the existence of God but is quite explicitly recasting the radical distinction of M 28. In that case, the insight into God that the *Proslogion* argument provides should not be altogether unlike the vision of the supreme being arrived at in the *Monologion*. Of course, the more refined distinction introduced in the *Proslogion* is designed to designate God more rigidly, to provide not just a more precise but a more positive characterization, a more definite description, of what the eye of the mind seeks to get within its sights, in contrast to the vaguer, less concise, rather negative result that the *Monologion* achieves. The *Proslogion*'s discovery of this *proprium dei* directs the eye of the mind not only away from creatures but far more directly to, or at least toward, the sole and single object that can meet the precise description. Still, the critical difference at issue in P 3 may serve to force thought in the appropriate direction by enforcing the reversal in the meaning of being that we have shown to be at issue in M 28. Clearly, P 3's characterization of beings other than God operates at the level of what we earlier referred to as their "reinstatement" after their ontological disappearance. Indeed, if we are correct, the claim that creatures "exist such that they can be thought not to exist" is a way of rendering more exact the *Monologion*'s contention that beings "barely exist and almost do not exist," in contrast to God, who alone "so truly exists that he cannot be thought not to exist." Consequently, while the dramatic reversal announced in M 28, where God alone is seen to exist, might appear to be moderated by the precision of P 3, in which creatures are unquestionably afforded a certain degree of being, their nullification may nonetheless be quietly secured if it is covertly contained within the very manner of being attributed to them in the *Proslogion*'s revision of the ontological difference.

On this account, the elegant simplicity of the distinction of P 3 provides a more sudden and strikingly condensed prescription for thinking God than the complex chain of interconnected arguments leading to the rather awkward negation of the being of beings in M 28. Not only does the *Proslogion*'s version of the ontological difference allow rational thought to distinguish God from all else, but it does so by holding the key to the conversion that, for the *Monologion* at least, is apparently among the main points of the practice of rational contemplation. What remains to be seen, however, is just what, as P 4 would put it, it is to take this distinction "to heart," or, as the *Monologion* would say, just how the rational mind is supposed to formulate a likeness of the thing itself in thought, to enjoy an inner vision of it. If it cannot simply be a matter of words, then what we need to know is how rational thought goes about isolating the thing itself, distinguishing it from everything else that is, so as to entertain the reality itself in the vision of its thinking. And I would like to suggest that, not unlike M 28, the contemplative does so by effectively performing the ontological annulment of existing creatures in the proposed conceivability of what exists in terms of its nonexistence.

The basic strategy—we might even say, the cognitive act—that allows thought to think something that cannot be thought not to exist involves the negation of the being of those beings that can be thought not to exist precisely insofar as rational thought may conceive of them in view of their nonexistence. In that case, the double negation that aims to think what cannot be thought not to exist must begin from the thought of the nonbeing of creatures, even if it presumes to proceed by converting their ontological negativity, that is, by categorically transcending them through the negation of their conceivable nonexistence, so as to arrive at what cannot be so thought. Such an approach is designed not simply to clear those beings that can be thought not to exist out of the way of reason's sight but also to redirect its attention to what cannot be thought not to exist by invoking a standard of being against which beings appear in absolute contrast in their ontological nothingness. In either event, the rational mind is left with nothing to think but God insofar as creatures disappear from sight as they withdraw in thought into nonbeing. To this extent, the radicalness of the ontological difference finally made out in the *Monologion* is not only captured from the start in the distinction of P 3 but is waiting to be unleashed in the actual practice of rational meditation. The contemplative is put in a position to think God through the prescription contained in the distinction itself; not just to distinguish him from everything else, but to show, and in a similar way to M 28, that God alone so truly exists that he cannot be thought not to exist by appealing to the claim that all other beings can be thought not to exist, and by exercising that cognitive possibility in so thinking them.

The thought formation at work here may become clearer once we realize that the designation of God as what cannot be thought not to exist is actually providing a formula for thinking the thing itself. Not altogether unlike the way the characterization of God as something than which nothing greater can be thought supplies us with a certain procedural access to God, as it contains within it the key to the rational procedure by means of which a reconstruction of a likeness of God becomes possible, the claim that God cannot be thought not to exist serves to supply a conception of God that determines the appropriate matter for thought by characterizing it in terms of the cognitive procedures one must go through to proceed to the reality itself. In the case in point, a specific object of thought is delimited by drawing attention to the cognitive peculiarity involved in thinking it, as God is determined precisely as that which the rational mind cannot think not to exist. If we refer to this as a psychological determination of God, it is meant strictly in terms of Anselm's philosophy of mind, of his philosophical psychology, or, as I would prefer to say, in view of the phenomenological character of those cognitive events that Anselm claims have a certain logical compulsion attached to them.[57] A noetic analysis, invited by Anselm's own account of the nature of thinking, will eventually have to be directed to the clarification of what we will have occasion to refer to as the psychodynamics of the thought of God, to the question of how the thought of God presents itself to the rational mind and to the "psycho-logical" constraints that may occur to rational thinking in entertaining such thoughts, especially those that may be delimited by the manner in which they are thinkable, or, as we shall see, ultimately unthinkable. Such an account will be indispensable for clarifying my earlier contention that the ontological argument is essentially a matter of certain cognitive experiences that logical thought may undergo in its thinking about the meaning of being.

In the meantime, and in preparation for our later evaluation of the argument, we will have to look more closely at how the rational mind goes about forming an image of God, locating the thing itself in thought, based upon the claim that he cannot be thought not to exist, and how such a thought works, given the mechanics of mind suggested by Anselm's visionary epistemology. In Anselm's view, if the rational mind is, as P 4 requires, to think the thing itself, and not just the signs that signify it, some likeness will have to be formulated in the vision of its thinking based upon the impression the reality itself has made upon thought. Of course, given our previous experience in the *Monologion,* we should not be surprised to find that reason forms its image of God by deforming its vision of creatures. The strategy for thinking the absolute difference between creator and creature in the *Monologion* requires that beings retain some semblance of being so that the supreme being can maintain its own identity in its difference from them. In M 28, such a possibility involved conceiving of beings in terms of their nothingness, while attributing some "almost nonexistent" existence to them, just as the mode of existence attributed to them in P 3, in its own way, serves to remove creatures from our ontological sight as what can be thought not to exist while at the same time granting them that degree of being needed to maintain the difference. Thus, while the sort of explicit annihilation of beings that takes place in the *Monologion* is not obviously at issue in the distinction of P 3, something of the rather literal diversion that keeps both being and beings in view at once, as it must keep beings in its sights even while diverting the eye of the mind toward God, may nonetheless be tacitly built into the strategy of the *Proslogion.*

At the very least, thinking through P 3's revised version of the ontological difference calls for a certain overlooking of creatures in a projection of our rational vision, of the trajectory of reason's inner line of sight, beyond what can be thought not to be, so as, however, to locate in thought what is other than them. This ontological oversight, which presumably sees beyond those beings that can be thought not to be, even if it does so precisely by looking away from them, is part and parcel of the rational elevation of the mind invited by a distinction that is "taken to heart" insofar as it hits upon, as the object of its projection, what cannot be thought not to be and sights it—indeed, sites it—through the ontological difference that categorically distinguished God from everything else. As we shall see, this cognitive act, which we are claiming relies upon the sort of mental maneuvers going on in the *Monologion*'s negative ontology, serves to distinguish God from all else by elevating him to his own ontological domain, to that "dwelling place" the *Proslogion* refers to as the domain of "inaccessible light." In any case, while in P 3 creatures may not appear to vanish completely, as they are attributed their specific measure of being, they must nonetheless be removed from reason's view, as they apparently block its vision of the reality that rational thought seeks to sight, and they are so removed by appealing in an even more precise way to what is now to be regarded as the ultimate difference.

Ontologically speaking, then, reason is actually invited to disregard beings precisely by granting them the being of what can be thought not to exist, so that the eye of the mind might sight what, in contrast to them, alone cannot be thought not to be. It is this sort of ontological oversight, enforced by the distinction drawn in P 3 and analogous to the departure of beings into the difference between them and the supreme being that occurs in the moment of truth in M 28, that clears the way for a rational vision of God. Against this strong measure of being claimed in P 3, in comparison to what exists such that it cannot be thought not to exist, what can be thought not to exist pales, as if to nothing. And in taking such a distinction to heart, or, in P 4's way of putting it, in "expressing" such a distinction "in the heart," the contemplative would, in effect, be putting into action the thinkability of the nonbeing of those beings that, even while existing, can be thought not to exist. In that event, they are literally overlooked: removed, in thought, from reason's view in order to clear the way for an insight into what alone cannot be thought not to exist, as thought is directed, by means of this ontological difference, to look beyond creatures to their creator. For it is only in the vision of what is other than beings, made possible by this distinguishing feature of God's being, that the rational mind can distinguish which one God is and so locate the thing itself in thought, such that it is compelled to think as it apparently must.

Our suggestion that this is accomplished by "clearing" the way for a vision of God, that is, by clearing beings out of the way, is designed to indicate—and we will pursue this prospect later—that there is a certain emptying of the mind taking place in the ontological annulment of creatures. As we argued earlier, what the *Monologion* calls the supreme being ultimately appears in the disappearance of beings, through the reversal that occurs in the ontological departure of creatures that leaves thought projecting into the void that remains after their withdrawal. And while the *Proslogion*'s characterization of what cannot be thought not to exist may seem more positive, as it aims to designate rather rigidly one and only one possible being, it is worth noticing that this conception of the thing itself, which presumably constrains thought such that it cannot think otherwise, is not as positive as it might appear. In fact, if we take the claim that creatures can be thought not to exist as an indication of the procedure involved in directing thought toward God, then were we to pursue the specific features Anselm takes to be entailed by his characterization of what cannot be thought not to exist, we may find that such a conception is formed by converting the void that rational thought is left with after its negation of creatures: by negating this negation of beings so as to fill the void through a process of double negation.

The aim of this complex maneuver would be to entertain a positive object of thought through the negation of a negation, by negating the "can be thought not to exist" of creatures. The time-space left empty by the ontological lapse of those beings that exist in a particular place at a particular time would be filled by inserting into this void a being that is "everywhere and always wholly," even as the claim that what cannot be thought not to exist must be "without beginning or end or multiplicity of parts" would be arrived at by negating those features that make it possible for us to think of any other being as not existing. In this way, the ontological emptiness left by the negation of beings would itself have been erased through a further negation that aims to direct our rational vision, in the conversion of the meaning of being, to God. But if God's own being seems, not coincidentally, to take on the characteristics of this void of beings that is presumably left behind as thought makes its way to what is beyond what can be thought not to exist, that is, if the supreme being is conceived in terms, however negatively, determined by the thinking away of beings, then P 3 may not be providing as positive a characterization of what the eye of the mind is trying to sight as we might at first think, even if it may, in some sense, seem to allow us to isolate a specific object of thought toward which we are to be directing our inner vision.

In any event, I want to insist that the insight into what cannot be thought not to be is accomplished through a certain ontological oversight that I think it is fair to characterize phenomenologically in terms of a projection of our rational vision beyond beings. In the trajectory of reason's line of sight, it is forced to overlook creatures if it is to catch a glimpse of what is beyond them. Such an elevation of the mind does not just amount to the movement to a higher category but involves a sort of open-ended projection of the inner line of vision of the eye of the mind that elevates it to what is presumably beyond creatures by projecting into, while projecting certain features onto, the void left by the ontological withdrawal of beings. And what is seen in this long-distance vision is not—as Anselm will himself confess—a clearly definable object that simply presents itself once beings are removed from our rational sight. Instead, it would seem to involve a redirection of thought that turns it away from the domain of beings in its projection toward a region of being that can be located but cannot be altogether objectified. Nevertheless, the inner vision made possible by Anselm's argument may not only be said to direct the eye of reason toward the appropriate matter for thought, but such a projection does have the desired result, that is, if properly effected, what is so thought cannot be thought not to exist, but—as we will later try to show—for rather different reasons than Anselm thinks. Either way, the point remains that it is this locating of a certain object of thought in the inner vision of the rational mind that compels it to think as it does based upon an insight into the thing itself and, thus, that it is such a vision of God that must lie at the heart of Anselm's argument.

If we had to characterize more concisely the nature of the elevation of the mind to the rational understanding of God that takes place in the *Proslogion,* I would say that it might best be thought in terms of a certain ecstatic clarity. By this, however, I mean to indicate the way in which the precision of a rational argument that clears beings out of the way of reason's sight so that it can direct its vision beyond them may bring the contemplative, within the domain of inner experience, to a certain ecstatic moment of insight, to the clarity of a vision that occurs in the lifting of one's inner sight toward, in the opening out and up to, that which transcends beings, or, as we have said in our analysis of M 28, to that which is before, beyond, and without beings. Needless to say, this vision *de profundis,* this transcending projection, that operates through a kind of ecstatic oversight, aims to overcome, with its long-range vision, the very gap that rational thought has opened up between creator and creature. In an arc of thought, as it were, reason aims to reach what is beyond beings, forcing the eye of the mind to look in its direction by enforcing the ultimate ontological difference. And the way this difference is drawn in P 3 serves to designate quite precisely the sole and proper object that this trajectory of thought aims to hit upon, even if such a distant insight will eventually turn out to involve a strange sort of seeing in the dark that claims to locate its object, but only regionally. Nonetheless, this ecstatic moment of vision is explicitly connected to the elation which the *Proslogion* calls "joy," and which, later in the text, will be associated with "the joy of the lord" promised in the vision of God in the afterlife. As we shall see, the strategy of the *Proslogion's* overall argument requires that reason enjoy in this life a taste of the "joy complete" (*gaudium plenum*) promised in the life to come—a tactic essential to the defense of reason going on in the text.

For the moment, however, the point we do not want to miss, since it is essential to the theology of reason developed in the remainder of the *Proslogion,* is that the sort of ecstatic clarity that apparently leaves rational thought open to a certain rapture would seem to operate through God's filling the void left by the ontological departure of creatures. Or, if this characterization seems most fitting to M 28, we might say that P 3 more positively directs the eye of the mind beyond all ordinary beings, calls upon thought to transcend what can be thought not to exist, so as to press its inner vision out beyond the scope of beings in order to sight what is everywhere and always wholly through a categorical elevation achieved in the contrast between them and what cannot be thought not to exist. In both cases, the cognitive maneuvers involve a moment of rational elevation, a moment of vision in contemplation, when the mind removes from reason's sight all that it is normally thinking, indeed, taking as its measure of being. The ontological conversion begins to set in at that moment when rational thought is able to remove from its inner view those beings that can be thought not to exist precisely because they exist here rather than there, at this time rather than at that time, in parts rather than as a whole, come from nothing and must be preserved by another, etc., in its attempt to behold what exists through itself alone, wholly everywhere and always, purely, properly, simply, immutably, indivisibly, etc. And this is a strictly ontological matter, a matter of the logic of being and of a certain conversion-experience that the rational mind may undergo in thinking such a thought. In fact, this is why we are reluctant to assume that any particular object, any ontical reality, appears in this vision, although we would also like to show that the *Proslogion* itself confesses that its insight into God depends upon a rather strange presentation of this ultimate object of thought, even if it tries to justify its strangeness on the basis of an inherent limitation in the nature of our inner sight that makes it difficult for us, at least in our current life, to envision such an extraordinary being.

But we will turn to that issue, of how and why, as P 14 will put it, God is both seen and not seen by those seeking him, as we continue our reading of the *Proslogion.* For now we want simply to repeat that were we to attempt to characterize the experience of thinking that is built into Anselm's argument as it draws us into its phenomenological conclusion, I think we could, with no little justification, speak, as the *Proslogion*'s preface does, of a certain elevation of the mind that takes place in its contemplation of what so exists that it cannot be thought not to exist. Its moment of vision in the experience of rational thinking, during which thought is apparently left with nothing to think but God, involves an ecstatic clarity in which reason projects its inner line of sight beyond creatures, thanks to the precision of the ontological distinction drawn in P 3. Such rational ecstasy—this standing out in the elation of the elevation of the mind—not only involves the conversion that turns thought away from the domain of beings, in a sort of staring with the eye of the mind into the beyond of creatures, but apparently also culminates in a flash of clarity that connects the rational mind to God when the arc of this trajectory of thought is completed, when it hits upon the appropriate object in what Anselm refers to, at the conclusion of P 4, as a moment of "illumination." Of course, given what we have said, this may well involve, if not a seeing in the dark, then at best a momentary flash of insight. While blinding, it may nonetheless be thought to illuminate, however dimly, a distant ground that does not present itself as one being among others but makes its appearance in the absence of creatures, indeed, in their withdrawal, by filling the void left as they are thought not to exist. Be that as it may, it is in this moment of vision, however negatively wrought, that "the thing itself" is understood. During this moment of rational intuition, thought does more than think about the thing by means of the signs that indirectly signify it and, instead, experiences a certain compulsion that the reality itself imposes upon the mind such that the rational thinker cannot think otherwise.

I do not mean to pretend to be able to capture the elevation of the mind involved in such a vision of God any better than Anselm has with the distinction he has drawn for us and would now attempt to draw us into. I only want to keep in mind that reason has, for him, a visionary element associated with it that may be lost sight of in working through the reasoning of his argument. The aim of the conclusion arrived at in P 3 is to divert the inner eye of the mind to God by directing our rational vision away from creatures. It is in this sense alone, given the precise nature of such ecstatic clarity, that we may speak of a mystical vision, albeit a rational one, embedded in the argument itself and of a certain rapture that reason may undergo. In fully understanding an argument that is designed to guide those thinking their own way through it to that moment of elevation in which the inner vision of the mind transcends creatures, rational thought enjoys a momentary and fragmentary vision of God. That this is the sort of "understanding" faith is seeking in the *Proslogion,* and that it must involve a certain moment of gratification, is clear, as we shall see, from the beginning to the end of the text. At the very least, the isolation of this rational insight into what cannot be thought not to exist, which we claim lies at the root of the argument, can alone serve to account, in Anselm's view of the nature of thinking, for what we might call its conviction-producing aspect, which results from the way in which, once thought has caught sight of such an imposing reality, it is apparently compelled to think as it does.

The logical compulsion involved in the ecstatic clarity that the argument's vision of God produces not only explains how so seemingly simple a proof could have exercised the influence it did on the history of thought, and why the tradition has been inclined to engage in the continual formulation and reformulation of the reasoning proper, so as to preserve for later generations the ontological insight achieved in and through the argument; it also suggests how it is that reason could come to be regarded as essentially relevant to theological matters in a tradition whose paradigm of truth was revelation. For what is at issue in Anselm's argument is nothing less than reason's revelation of God. This is why it does little good to criticize the discursive aspect of the argument, since those privy to its intuitive basis will simply reformulate the reasoning in line with the insight that supposedly lies at its root. Thus, we face, and will later face up to, the problem of how to criticize an insight. Presently, we mean only to suggest that a sufficiently fundamental interpretation of its reasoning, one which alone can prepare the way for an adequate criticism of the argument, must render explicit the sort of theological vision that is, in fact, conviction-producing in the ontological argument. This mystical aspect of Anselm's argument, which remains untouched by all merely discursive critiques of it, is not a matter of going beyond reason but of finding one's way to that moment of rational elevation in which the clarity produced by a certain logic grants us insight into that which requires for its sighting the ontological annulment of creatures. In effect, what we have been calling Anselm's rational mysticism involves an ecstatic moment of absolute clarity whose vision of God is so compelling, so indubitable, that when rational thought entertains the ontological difference, which leaves it with nothing to think but God, it is convinced that it cannot think otherwise.

In this respect, the critical contention, effectively asserted in P 4, that has sustained the ontological argument as such, is that once this object of thought is sighted, it cannot be thought not to exist. This is not because the rational mind has felt the presence of God in a moment of mystical union but because of the nature of its insight into the thing itself: into what exists truly, properly, simply, absolutely, immutably, perfectly, through itself alone, without beginning or end or multiplicity of parts, and is everywhere and always wholly. It is, of course, such characterizations of the being of God that led the tradition after Anselm to claim, as Anselm does, that no one understanding what God is can think that he does not exist, even if this comes to be taken to mean that existence pertains to his essence, or that the very conception of such a thing entails its existing. And while Anselm certainly concurs that when the mind entertains a true conception of God, enjoys an inner vision of the thing itself, it cannot think that he does not exist, the reason for this is not simply a matter of logical inference but of the experience involved in the mind's locating in the vision of its thinking which one God is.

For such thinking to have its conviction-producing point, it must not be a matter of our simply following the words of a proof or of our merely entertaining the sort of nominal conception to which such reasoning might blindly lead. Instead, each one must "elevate his own mind to the contemplation of God" in being directed to a rational insight into something than which nothing greater can be thought, so that we might experience the clarity that comes in the breakthrough from the words to the thing itself. This is why the argument must be cast in the form of a meditation, from which the fool is ultimately excluded. Accordingly, if we ourselves lose sight of the reality we are supposed to be thinking or slip into other forms of thought, or if the object of thought itself slips back into the dark after a momentary flash of clarity, it becomes possible to think that God does not exist. It is only during the moment of ecstatic inner vision, during the elevation of insight, that God cannot be thought not to be. And while we can understand how, for Anselm, this would be a matter of our "conception" of God, we must also understand that the subsequent tradition will give its own meaning to such "conceptions of the mind" and to the "insight" it will still insist is at the heart of the ontological argument.[58] It will have its own account of the nature of reason, in fact, any number of different accounts that will explain the various revisions of the argument that have come down to us, from Descartes and Spinoza, through Hegel and process philosophy, right up to the present day, in the interpretation of Anselm's argument in terms of that uniquely twentieth-century vision of reason that is captured in symbolic logic.

That Anselm himself aims to align his argument with what would have been the theological tradition to which he was heir, that the specific view of reason and, thus, the way his reasoning is designed to work, is meant to invoke the legacy of earlier medieval thought, especially Augustine, is clear from the fact that he refers, at the end of his argument, to the "illumination" he has received through it. Such talk suggests the deep foundation that his reasoning is claimed to enjoy not just in the vision of an inner revelation but also in an insight that is itself interpreted in light of a theological epistemology. If our raising of certain psychological issues is meant to be relevant to a later analysis of the manipulations of the mind that may be at work in the illumination Anselm reports, we will also want to show how these cognitive experiences are made to take on a certain look by surrounding the philosophical arguments with a theological narrative whose one flank we have already traced in our initial treatment of the prayer of P 1. Ironically, P 4's stressing of the effect that the revelation of the thing itself has upon thought is emphasized by the way Anselm concludes his argument with a reversal of the famous saying that was the final note of P 1. We will recall that in the opening prayer, after petitioning God to "show himself,"

Anselm insists that he does not expect the vision complete in this life but asks to understand only as much as is appropriate. Nor, one might suppose, does he expect his faith to be supplanted by reasoning, for, as he says at the end of the prayer of P 1:

> And neither do I seek to understand so that I may believe,
>   but believe so that I may understand.
> For this also I believe:
>   that *unless I believe,*
>   *I will not understand.* (S I, 100)

P 4, nonetheless, boldly claims at last:

> Thanks to you, good lord, my thanks to you. For what I first believed through your gift, I now so understand though your illumination that even if I did not want to believe that you existed, I could not fail to understand. (S I, 104)

This final prayer of thanks closes the argument and, in its way, serves to enclose it, clearly indicating that what began in P 2 with the petition for understanding that God "exists as we believe" and that he is "that which we believe" has now been fulfilled. In framing the argument of P 2–4 between two prayers, such closure suggests that we have a complete and completed movement of thinking in which the demands prayed for from the start have been met. In my view, of course, both petitions in the opening line of P 2 have been fulfilled, and have been fulfilled together. The same argument that shows that God exists in the way the faithful believe him to, that is, in his own distinctive way, is also sufficient to demonstrate that he is something than which nothing greater can be thought. More importantly, since the fulfillment of both petitions is based on it, the complementary request made in P 1 for God to illuminate our eyes, indeed, to show himself, has apparently also been granted, and in no mean way, for Anselm is not apt to speak lightly of illumination. On the contrary, he talks here, as he rarely does, but as he has prepared us for in P 1, as if a revelation had come to him, a revelation whose joy, the preface suggests, he aimed to offer to his readers in writing the *Proslogion.*

Needless to say, in my account, it is precisely such an illumination of God that lies embedded in and throughout Anselm's argument. It aims at reason's revelation of the supreme being, at the vision of God as he is brought before the eye of the mind in the moment of ontological insight. Such a vision may not be "face-to-face" but is no doubt more properly characterized as "from afar" (*vel de longe*), indeed, as P 1 puts it, as "from the depths" (*vel de profundo*).[59] It is nonetheless a matter of a certain vision of "the thing itself" and, in some sense, entails a seeking of its "face," if the latter involves those features that allow us to recognize someone in his unique identity. The power of the clarity resulting from Anselm's argument is evidently so imposing that it is claimed to have the force of an illumination not only of God, but from God—that is, by truth itself. It is so overpowering that even if we wanted to think otherwise, "did not want to believe," we should nonetheless be unable not to understand. In this sense, while the reference to "illumination" may well serve to emphasize both the vision involved and the "clear light of truth" by means of which the thing itself may be seen in thought—even as it suggests something of that flash of clarity that can fade from sight so quickly and may be as blinding as it is revealing—it is perhaps most of all designed to express a feeling of "necessity," of the unavoidable conclusion to which the argument has led us.

It is important to note, in what may appear to be the merely rhetorical flourish that concludes the argument, the historic relation that is being set up between faith and reason with this talk of illumination. Once we realize that this is a reference to the rational vision that has connected the human mind to God, it should be clearer that the suggestion is tacitly being made here, as it is elsewhere in Anselm's work, that the illumination which our reason now has access to may be part and parcel of a rational revelation of God that supplements the original revelation of faith. This is emphasized in the above passage by suggesting that the "gift" of faith, which does not require our own struggle to elevate our minds to a vision of God through the exercising of our reason and consequently remains essentially blind, is no more or less given to us by God than is the illumination of reason. As Anselm will elsewhere claim, this makes the rational revelation of the divine in our present life something like a mean between the blindness of faith and the vision complete reserved for the life to come.[60] Such rational illumination allows for a partial vision of God, however "from afar" and "from the depths" and however momentary its glimpse may be. Nonetheless, it is more like the vision to come than is the blindness of a faith that will itself be unnecessary when our experience of God is complete. In this way, the visions of reason in this life—in fact, the specific vision supplied by the argument of P 2–4—offer some foresight into the vision of God in the life to come.

If we are to develop the point of this claim, which is being made at a critical stage in the history of rationality, we will have to notice not only that Anselm's work stands as a monument to that moment in our history when theology becomes strictly rational, but also that this is a moment when reason becomes essentially theological, as it establishes its own efficacy based on its ability to provide the human mind with a vision of God. No doubt this theological empowerment of the authority of reason ultimately led away from Anselm's rational mysticism to the formality of scholasticism, which in turn prepared the way for the even more strictly methodological rationality we think of as characteristic of modern thought, when the "light of truth" is naturalized. But we should not be surprised to find Anselm's monastic rationalism indulging in a certain epistemological mysticism, exploiting the presumed connection of the rational mind to God as it is bathed in the light of divine illumination. As we shall see, the *Proslogion* proceeds to press this image of the "God of truth," when it returns to explain how it is that he dwells in what P 1 has already called "inaccessible light." The point just now is that if what is at issue in Anselm's argument is a rational revelation of God, then this says something about the nature and power of reason with respect to those issues that the tradition to which Anselm was heir would have regarded as matters of revelation. If the dominant epistemological paradigm is that of a revealed truth, that is, if the model of truth is revelation, then it serves as a defense of reason to show that it has a revelatory capacity and, indeed, enjoys exclusive rights to such visionary revelations in the case of God—at least in this life, if not in the next.

We will yet have to pursue the precise way in which reason is bound to such a vision of God, including the manner in which its claimed access to reality will have to be redeemed through the confession of a certain lack of vision, if we are to appreciate the contortions through which human rationality comes to be legitimated on the basis of an object of thought it cannot altogether see. At present, all we mean to suggest is that the joy claimed to be involved in the elevation of the mind to such vision, as well as—perhaps most of all—the talk of illumination, is no rhetorical flourish incidentally added to a rational argument; rather, like most other religious invocations in Anselm, it has a philosophical rationale. As part and parcel of the historic moment of the founding of a rational theology, it is essentially a matter of appropriating religious language to express a philosophical point. At the same time, this translation of religious images into rational ones imbues philosophical activity with a certain theological significance. In the case in point, the truth determination that the rational mind may undergo in its vision of God is to be counted as an illumination or revelation, as surely sent from God, who is the divine reason and the source of truth, as was the gift of the original revelation that the faithful receive through their faith. Indeed, as we already know, this supreme truth is itself associated with the birth of the word in God, that is, with his son, who came in the person of Christ and who, as will be suggested later, may well continue to come in the rational revelation of God in history.

Here we begin to touch upon a circle that we cannot afford to lose sight of—a self-generating circle that develops between philosophy and theology—in which reason provides a philosophical ground for faith while faith provides a theological ground for reason. In fact, the circularity of the relation between faith and reason will eventually lead us to suggest that there is a certain complicity between Anselm's God and the rationality that forms an image of him. The point remains that the talk of divine illumination, as if rational thought were so overwhelmed by the truth of its God that it is powerless to think otherwise, is actually asserting the power of reason, however much these claims to rational revelation are couched in a language of humility. This should be all the more clear if, as we claim, reason comes to power through the historical transference of what were religious images into rational ones that, in some sense, supersede them. In the present case, Anselm's argument presumes to provide a vision of God sufficiently powerful that the force of this rational revelation of God allows it to supplant the revelation of faith. It is so compelling, to paraphrase Anselm, that even if I did not want to believe, I would still be forced to understand. For where there is vision, there is no longer a need for blind faith; indeed, where rational understanding is so compelling, there is no room for decision on our part at all.

Once we appreciate how Anselm's epistemology and his claims about the visionary power of reason work to legitimate the use of reasoning in theology, it becomes clear that we can regard his famous argument neither as an exercise in logical cleverness nor as the expression of a mystical vision that claims to be beyond rational evaluation. Instead, a specific vision of God must be embedded in Anselm's reasoning as its consummate aim. This insight into God may best be recalled by insisting that there is a certain mysticism at work in the argument. The vision of God that it produces is, however, a rational matter, requiring that we think, in somewhat paradoxical terms, of a rational mysticism. As we have warned, given its presumed foundation in rational intuition, it barely scratches the surface of the argument to launch attacks against its discursive dimension, against the reasoning proper, that is, against its exterior. For at the innermost heart of its reasoning, preserved beneath its outer facade and protected by it, is a deep clarity that may well be regarded as Anselm's historic insight. As our history has shown, attacks on the exoteric dimension of the ontological argument only result, for those who feel that they nonetheless have attained the intuitive insight at its root, in repeated reformulations of its reasoning. To criticize the heart of the argument, to evaluate precisely what, for Anselm, must be taken to heart in his argument, is to criticize its ontological insight. This intuition, to which we have here attached Anselm's name—and perhaps rightly, insofar as he preserved it at a certain critical point in the tradition—really has the name of Western philosophy written all over it, for it has underwritten, virtually from the start, the strain of Western rationalism that lies closest to the heart of our philosophical history.

While we have, then, tried to isolate a certain inner vision that we claim resides at the root of Anselm's argument, and as an insight that has phenomenological grounds insofar as it can be documented in the inner experiences of rational thought, this does not mean that we think such rational intuition is beyond question. On the contrary, it is precisely this vision of God that must be isolated and criticized if we are to evaluate the argument. Before entering into those criticisms in our concluding remarks, which will be aimed at showing the limitations of Anselm's argument, we need to be aware of the limits that Anselm himself admits, in the remainder of the *Proslogion,* to his project of seeking a rational understanding of God—the limits, we might say, of his rational mysticism—as he attempts to protect not only his insight but reason itself by shrouding it in a confession.

∎ Anselm's Confession

In its way, P 5 takes up where P 4 leaves off, making it clear what it is we must be thinking when we are thinking of something than which none greater can be thought. Along with the rest of the *Proslogion,* it also takes up topics that should look less different from the *Monologion* than the first four chapters of the *Proslogion* might. P 5 begins with a question that determines what remains to be done in the *Proslogion,* and one to which Anselm responds in terms most reminiscent of his earlier work:

> What, then, are you, lord God, than whom none greater can be thought? What, indeed, are you but that which, as the highest of all, alone existing through itself, created everything else from nothing? For whatever is not this, is less than what can be thought. But this cannot be thought about you. Therefore, what good does the supreme good, through which all good exists, lack?
> You are, then, just, truthful, blessed, and whatever it is better to be than not to be. For it is better to be just than not just, blessed than not blessed. (S I, 104)

Anselm is obviously anticipating the way in which the form of argument that the title "something than which nothing greater can be thought" makes possible can be applied to a clarification of the nature of God, so as to answer the question, in specific terms, of "what" (*quid*) God is. He has already shown which one God is (*id quod est*), although not so much by means of a reflection on his "essence" as on the nature of his existence. To this extent, we may have some sympathy with those who claim that the argument for the existence of God is not completed at P 4 but requires the remainder of the text to show that the being demonstrated to exist in P 2–3 has all the features attributable to the radically Christian God. Certainly Anselm needs to demonstrate that the metaphysical reality that we have gained insight into through his argument, what we might call the ontological God of philosophy, is the theological God of Christianity. In this respect, it is not irrelevant that chapters 5–26 contain claims that are logically separable from the argument of P 2–4. We could accept the argument for a "supreme being," for what "alone exists through itself" such that it "cannot be thought not to exist," and thus accept the claim that it exists in a different way than do the beings with which we are ordinarily familiar, without committing ourselves to any essential characterization so specific as to take the shape of a God who is just or merciful, that punishes the wicked or spares them, let alone whose tri-unity allowed it to incarnate in the person of Christ. Consequently, even if P 2–4 has a right to claim to have shown that "God" exists, it remains a question—and one that P 5–26 aims to resolve—exactly which god that is.

While acknowledging the ambiguity involved here, I would still not be inclined to say that the demonstration for the existence of God only comes in the entire *Proslogion* rather than in P 2–4. Even if one rejects the arguments of P 5–26, this does not, if one accepts the demonstration of P 2–4, amount to a denial of the existence of God but only of a particular conception of God. In fact, were one to take the order of the overall argument of the *Proslogion* as any indication, the strictly theological conception of God would appear to be a kind of appendix to the metaphysical reality claimed to have been shown to exist by Anselm's ontological argument. This means that one could accept the philosophical conclusion that God exists as a result of the argument of P 2–4, undergo the rational intuition that allows for the appropriate ontological conversion, and still reject the specific theological conception of God developed in P 5–26. To reject the argument for the existence of God in the *Proslogion,* it would not suffice to reject the arguments of P 5–26, for it does seem that P 2–4 provides an adequate characterization of something than which nothing greater can be thought such that it has a right to be called "God," even if one then went on to disagree about which other features should be attributed to such a being. Evidently, Anselm wants to show that the ontological reality that Western thought has been thinking about almost from the beginning, what might also be called the God of reason, is the theologically conceived God of faith. Of course, what Anselm wants and what he accomplishes may not be the same; although the point remains that the denial of the existence of God must ultimately come in a critique of the fundamental characterization of his "being," not in a rejection of those arguments that serve as an appendix to Anselm's ontological insight, adding piecemeal those features that Anselm would like to be able to include in the conception, whether he has an argument for them, that is, whether they are grounded in rational insight or not.

We might just note, in this latter regard, how freely Anselm moves from the conclusion of P 2–4 to the claim in the above passage that S is the supreme being discussed in the *Monologion,* the being that exists through itself alone and created everything else from nothing. No doubt if something cannot be thought not to exist, it must not exist through another, or else it could be thought not to exist simply by thinking that this other had not brought it to be. Anselm, however, goes on to insist that the being that alone exists through itself made everything else from nothing. And this does not follow in any direct way, either from the claim that something cannot be thought not to exist or from the claim that it is something than which nothing greater can be thought, for it is perfectly conceivable, as Anselm himself has had us conceive in M 28, that such a being might alone exist.

Of course, Anselm may seem to have some reason for insisting that what exists such that it cannot be thought not to exist made everything else from nothing insofar as those beings that can be thought not to exist have just appeared in their nothingness in P 3. But while we may well sense something of the ontological supremacy that Anselm claims to accrue to what "exists through itself" and while it may be evident that creatures do not so exist, it is not altogether clear how it adds to the greatness of the supreme being to be what created everything else. While it might follow that something than which nothing greater can be thought must exist through itself alone—or else something greater could be thought—it does not clearly follow that it would be "less than what can be thought" were it not thought of as having created all else from out of nothing. If the supreme good (as Anselm now wants to call it, again rehearsing the characterizations of the *Monologion*) itself lacks nothing, it is not obvious how it could be made any greater or even that something greater is being thought, if we think it to be the creator of the world, whether we regard that creation to be full of goodness or not. Metaphysically speaking, which is what the notion of "greatness" is supposed to be based upon, it seems dubious to suggest that the supreme reality could be made in any way greater, that is, any more real, through its creation of ontologically inferior beings.[61] On the contrary, the claim that what alone exists through itself "made everything else from nothing" seems tacked on and dangles like a flag warning us that the transition is taking place from the kind of ontological argument that does not base itself on something providing the ground for beings, but on an insight into a reality made visible to us in the absence of beings, to the theological reconstruction of God that will be intertwined throughout the remainder of the text with this rational intuition.

If the ontological insight into what so exists that it cannot be thought not to exist is not, at least explicitly, achieved through a grounding claim—if something than which nothing greater can be thought is not shown to be the ground of beings, even if it is clarified in its difference from them—then the conception of the creator being suddenly foisted upon us in P 5 requires logically separable arguments that may, in fact, lack the sort of intuitive basis that the argument of P 2–4 offers. Even if we accept, for example, that it makes sense to contend that what exists such that it can be thought not to exist must exist through another and that this "other" must exist through itself, this would not entail that the relation between the being that exists through itself and those beings that exist through another is a causal one. Nor would it require the theological conception of a *creatio de nihilo,* rather than, say, a view such as emanationism, or, for that matter, pantheism. In this way, P 5 must be seen as a transitional chapter that begins to extend the philosophical insight into the nature of the "supreme being" in the direction of the theological conception of a "supreme good" that is just and happy, truthful and merciful, and "whatever it is better to be than not to be." Indeed, the talk of what is "better" rather than "greater" opens the door to value characterizations rather than ontological clarifications. Thus, the characteristics that will later be marshaled to the forefront to be associated with the ontological reality sighted in P 2–4 will develop a thoroughly theological conception, not just of a God of goodness and justice but of punishment and mercy, of incarnation and salvation. Such a conception of God will lead, finally, to the promise of eternal life and the "joy of the lord" in a world to come. And all of this, we want to stress, is an appendix to the argument of

P 2–4, neither necessary for showing that God exists nor, however, irrelevant for clarifying which god Anselm would like to claim he has shown to exist.

That chapters 5–26 appear to be, and have only appeared in our tradition as, an appendix to the argument of P 2–4 does not, however, mean that they are not essential to it.[62] On the contrary, I would like to suggest that the intertwining of these two distinguishable conceptions, the flipping back and forth throughout the remainder of the text between an ontological and a theological conception of God, belongs to the strategy of the *Proslogion*. No doubt, in P 5 we see the beginnings of Anselm's "theologizing" of this ontological reality as his conception of God is extended beyond the insight, an insight that apparently does not require Christianity, since later thinkers will be able to use the ontological argument to show other theologically conceived gods to exist. At the same time, however, as Anselm is making use of his philosophical insight to provide a foundation upon which to construct a specifically Christian conception of God, he is employing that theology, contained in the prayers with which he has surrounded his argument, to justify certain features of the reasoning itself, or, as we claim, of the cognitive experiences that ground the reasoning of P 2–4. On the one hand, then, given the structure of the text, the Christian God would seem to be an appendix to, perhaps a supplement of, the ontological insight. On the other hand, the theological narrative in which the *Proslogion* indulges, however supplementary it may appear to be, will turn out to be essential to the justification, indeed, to the supplementation, of its rational arguments, especially insofar as the latter have not altogether achieved what one might have expected.

There is no need to work our way through the arguments directed to the theological molding of the ontological conception of God. We have seen enough already if we are clear that the openended criterion mentioned in P 5, that S is "whatever it is better to be than not to be," allows Anselm to show that God has whatever characteristics he pleases, as long as he insists that they are better to have. Suffice it to say that if this sudden construing in P 5 of the ontological difference in terms of the creator/creature distinction raises certain questions, even more so should the movement from the ontology of something than which nothing greater can be thought to the theology that will be sprinkled throughout the remainder of the *Proslogion* and is in a way retroactively injected into the ontological intuition in the argument of P 2–4. In that case, it may seem little wonder that later in the text Anselm begins to doubt his vision, confessing its inadequacy. To a certain extent, this could be regarded as a matter of honesty on his part, if we assume that his theological conception of God cannot be grounded in phenomenological insight insofar as it is a construction built around the ontological conversion-experience. But that, I think, would be too generous a judgment, since it will turn out that Anselm has a way of making use of his ontological insight to justify a certain lack of insight, in which case, his confession may not be so much a matter of honesty or humility as part of a strategy that aims to get us to accept the claims being made, not just despite, but in light of their inadequacy.

We will, then, have to pursue our reading of Anselm's vision of the god shown to exist in P 2–4 into those areas of the text that are normally considered to be irrelevant to his argument. This is critical to our interpretation not only because Anselm may appear to be denying the possibility of a vision of God in this life later in the text, but also because, at the very points at which he does, he provides a rather explicit account of the nature of his philosophical insight. That account, however, must itself be glimpsed as it surfaces between the theological considerations at issue in P 5–26. In those chapters in which Anselm continues to address the metaphysical character of God, he would appear to be on more solid ground than in the chapters devoted to God's strictly theological nature. Indeed, he would seem to be standing on the ground of Western metaphysics itself. It is this ontological ground, which extends all the way from Canterbury to Elea and which supplies the mystical ground of Western thought, that we are most interested in isolating and eventually evaluating. At the same time, however, we must be careful that the theological speculations that lead to Anselm's questioning of the adequacy of his vision neither become confused with the ontological insight at issue in P 2–4 nor cast suspicion on our account of Anselm's argument. We do not want to let the theological issues distract us from our ultimate object of interest, namely, the ontological conception of God, whose critical evaluation has a greater range of application; nor, however, do we want to miss the way in which Anselm's confession functions to protect certain of his claims by shrouding them in darkness. Anselm's admitting to the limitations of his rational vision neither overturns nor undercuts the earlier illumination, nor does it merely serve to justify the problems he is having in his further speculations. Instead, it is designed to exploit the original ontological intuition by extending its vision of God through an insight into his nature that serves not just to justify Anselm's lack of insight but to turn his failure, his blindness, as it was called in P 1, into an insight of its own.

Thus, after having shown, between P 5 and P 13, that this being, which after P 4 is freely referred to as "God," is perceptive, although he does not have a body; is omnipotent, although he cannot do all things; is compassionate, although he is impassible; is just, although he spares the wicked; is alone limitless and eternal, although other things can also be said to be so; is, in short, omniscient, omnipotent, merciful, just, living, good, blessed, infinite, and eternal, Anselm begins to have his doubts or, at least, to express certain reservations that will lead to a critical transition in P 15, where it is argued that something than which nothing greater can be thought is greater than can be thought. In fact, the duplicity that begins to inform the text is first announced in the title of P 14: "How and why God is both seen and not seen by those seeking him." This topic and the opening paragraph of that chapter clearly take us back to P 1 and its talk of a vision of God. In some ways, it takes us back to the original title of the text as Anselm faces the question of how much the faithful can expect to accomplish in their search for understanding. The issue is raised in P 14 in a way that sets the stage for a pivotal transition aimed at transferring the promise of vision from this life to the next:

> Have you found, O my soul, what you were seeking? You were seeking God, and you found him to be something which is the highest of all, than which nothing better can be thought, and to be life itself, light, wisdom, goodness, eternal blessedness, and blessed eternity, and to exist everywhere and always. But if you have not found your God, how is he this which you have found, and which you have understood with certain truth and true certitude?
>
> But if you have found him, why is it that you do not experience what you have found? Why, O lord God, does my soul not experience you if it has found you? (S I, 111)

Here we encounter a strange confession, which might be regarded not just in P 14 but in the chapters to follow, as the confessions of a rational mystic. For it is clear what Anselm seeks and yet has not found, namely, an experience (*sentio*) of God. And the problem this raises is not just why one should seek God if he cannot be found but, more specifically, why one should pursue this sort of contemplation *sola ratione* if it does not bring one to what is apparently expected to be the point of its undertaking, namely, a mystical vision.

As we will find a few chapters later, as the lament is consummated in P 17, this "experience" of God that Anselm admits he has not arrived at really amounts to the vision complete, or, rather, to the full "perception" of God, which is not just a matter of intellectual vision but of that total mystical experience in which God is not just seen but heard, smelled, tasted, and touched with all the "senses of the soul":

Still, lord, you hide from my soul in your light and blessedness,
and so it still remains surrounded by its own darkness and misery.

For it looks around—and does not see your beauty.
    It listens—and does not hear your harmony.
    It smells—and does not sense your fragrance.
    It tastes—and does not know your savor.
    It touches—and does not feel your softness.

For you have in you, lord God,
    in your own ineffable manner,
    what you have given to the things created by you
    in their own sensible manner.
But the senses of my soul,
    because of the ancient weakness of sin,
    have become hardened and dulled and obstructed. (S I, 113)

When Anselm asks why he does not "see" God when he "looks
around," he seems to mean this quite literally. If God is "wholly
present everywhere," "within me and around me," he should be visible right before my eyes. I ought to be able to sense his omnipresence, to discern his all-pervasive harmony, to catch a whiff of his
ineffable fragrance, to taste his distinctive flavor, and to feel the inexpressible softness of his permeating presence. Presumably, the
senses would be capable of doing this were they not so dull, did they
not suffer from the "ancient weakness of sin" as a result of the Fall.
We must not forget, however, that Anselm's faith also includes the
expectation that our loss will be corrected when the senses are themselves redeemed in the resurrected body. As P 25 assures us, in the
joy of the life to come, the faithful will delight in "all the goods of
body and soul" when what "*is sown as a natural body* (*corpus
animale*) . . . *will rise as a spiritual body* (*corpus spirituale*)."[63] This
arisen body will not only have been transfigured such that its metaphysical senses will be cleansed so as to provide for a kind of supernatural sensuality that will allow it to experience those sensual
qualities God possesses in his own ineffable manner. There will also
be a totalizing of experience in which the various senses that are
now only in relative harmony with one another will be in complete
accord in the perfection of the partial and incomplete perception we
now have. In the "joy complete" (*gaudium plenum*), all the senses of
this "glorified body" (*corpori claritatis*) will be working together toward the revelation of a single object, perceiving all at once, hearing,
seeing, smelling, tasting, and touching, one and the same reality.[64]
Moreover, P 25 is not just an extended promise of all the faithful will
receive at that time, in "the fullness of their joy," but is designed to

suggest, as P 26 explains, that this is to be expected as the logically necessary completion in that complementary life of what in this life remains always partial and ultimately unfulfilling, whatever it might be.

Of course, P 1 has, in its own lament, documented our fall from the original vision of God and the subsequent "exile" into our present "blindness." Given the corruption of the fallen body, its inability to see what is right before its very eyes, this initial prayer suggests that we look the other way, that we turn inward and seek the vision of God, not with the eye of the body but with the eye of the mind, which, in this life, is the closest thing we have to a supernatural sense organ. This vision offered by the *oculus mentis* is supposed to provide us with a glimpse of the sort of metaphysical perception that all our senses will enjoy in the life to come. At the same time, however, over and above the limitations imposed upon us for a complete mystical experience in this life, Anselm also wants to show why we should expect even our intellectual vision of God to be similarly partial in our present condition; why, in certain respects—and we must keep both respects in view in what follows—God is both seen and not seen in our current vision of him. For not only is the rational vision we seek in this life presumed to be less than that for which we ultimately long, but it has its own inherent limitations.

With this in mind, Anselm completes his lament in P 18 in a manner that reverts not just to the form but to the language of the prayer of P 1:

And once more *confusion,*
> once again sorrow and grief stand in my way as I seek
> *joy and gladness!*
Even now my soul hoped for fulfillment,
> and once again
> it is overcome with need.
Even now I have sought my fill,
> and yet I hunger all the more.
I strove to ascend to the light of God,
> and instead descended into my own darkness.
Indeed, not only have I fallen back into it but feel myself engulfed
> by it.
I fell before *my mother conceived me.*
Surely in darkness *was I conceived,*
> and wrapped in it was I born.
For long ago all of us fell in him *in whom we have all sinned.*
In him—
> who easily possessed what he evilly lost for himself and for us—
> all lost that which
> when we desire, we do not know how to seek;
> when we seek, we do not find;
> when we find, is not what we were seeking.

Help me, *in accord with your goodness, lord.*
> *I sought your face,*
> *For your face, lord, will I search.*
Do not turn your face away from me.
Lift me from my self to you.
Cleanse, heal, focus, *illuminate* the eye of my mind *so that it*
> *may behold you.*
Let my soul regather its strength, O lord, and with the whole of its
understanding strive once more unto you. (S I, 113–14)

We should not miss the point that Anselm's confession of a lack
of vision serves as the occasion for a request for further illumination.
Ironically, that further insight comes as a result of his lack of vision
insofar as it follows from an explanation of why we should expect our
present understanding of God to be incomplete. The text continues:

> What are you, lord, what are you; what shall my heart under-
> stand you to be? You are life, you are wisdom, you are truth,
> you are goodness, you are blessedness, you are eternity, and you
> are every true good.
> But these are many, and my narrow understanding cannot
> behold them all in one single simultaneous intuition so as to
> delight in them all at once. How, then, lord, are you all these? Are
> they parts of you, or is each one of them the whole of what you
> are? For whatever is composed of parts is not altogether one
> but in a certain way many and different from itself and can be
> divided in fact or in thought. But this is foreign to you, than
> which nothing better can be thought.
> There are, then, no parts in you, lord, nor are you many, but
> you are so one and the same with yourself that in no way are
> you dissimilar with yourself. Indeed, you are unity itself, indi-
> visible by thought.
> Therefore, life and wisdom and the rest are not parts of
> you, but all are one, and each is wholly what you are and what
> all the others are. Since, then, neither you, nor the eternity
> which you are, have parts, nowhere and never is there a part
> of you or your eternity, but you exist as a whole everywhere, and
> your eternity exists as a whole always. (S I, 114–15)

Anselm emerges from his lament with the new illumination he
has apparently received. He now understands his limited vision to
be a revelation of the absolute unity of God, whose utter simplicity
his mind's eye cannot grasp in its fullness in "one single simultaneous intuition" insofar as human thought is limited to glimpses, to
seeing in aspects, what is one in God in an extraordinary kind of
partless wholeness. In effect, then, if P 17 has made it clear that the
sort of "experience" of God Anselm feels he is lacking is the total perception in which each of the various senses would all be correlated
and concentrated on a single object, P 18 is claiming that there is
an analogous partialness to our intellectual intuition, which will
also have to be corrected and completed, similarly "totalized," in the

vision of God in the life to come. If the desire to bring together our various rational insights into God, so as to "delight in them all at once," echoes the perceptual totalizing that Anselm expects to take place in his experience of God through the resurrected body, then in lamenting our limitation in this life to intellectual vision alone, it should be clear both that "seeing" is only one aspect of experience and that it is itself partial and quite limited in yet another regard. Our rational intuition can see only in part what is one in God in an absolutely indivisible simplicity.

What is being suggested here is that our understanding may be said to be in a position to behold (*intueatur*) God, as M 10 would have put it, "by means of reason" (*per rationem intuetur*) in partial "profiles" while, nonetheless, not exactly seeing "face to face," never beholding straight on but always from a distance and aspectively, from afar and perspectivally—in short, as P 1 puts it, from the depths (*de profundis*). The illumination of the eye of a mind that can only see from below—which is where it finds itself after the Fall and which is why it must strive to "look upward to the light"—results at best in a kind of seeing in the dark, or at least from the shadows. No doubt, it is to be expected that those who were "conceived in darkness" and "wrapped in its shadow" at birth would only be capable of the sort of insight that sees in and through such imperfect likenesses. This does not mean, however, that we are utterly excluded from a vision of God in this life, or else Anselm would not ask for it again in P 18 in the same terms as he did in P 1; nor, in that case, could he contend, as he does, that the vision we presently enjoy offers us some foresight into the experience of a future life. Rather than lacking a vision of God, it is as if we have too many, as if we have seen too much in the sense that we have required a discursive series of isolated insights that would have to be integrated into one simultaneous intuition in that vision complete whose joy can only be imagined on the basis of the fragmentary illuminations we now receive.

At the same time, the admitted "partiality" of our current visions raises the question of whether the various features of God that Anselm has discerned are mutually consistent with one another. Apparently this consistency is not guaranteed by these isolated visions themselves, as the different aspects are not seen in their absolute unity. But this is a problem that does not appear to bother Anselm here, although it has bothered him elsewhere in the *Proslogion*.[65] Instead, he insists that while we have glimpsed the truth of the thing itself, we have not seen the whole truth. We see in this life only to a certain extent, from afar and from the depths, and while such long-range vision provides us with a certain limited insight, the immediate intuition of God, which would bring the temporal series of aspectual visions together in the experience of his absolute and total presence, is reserved for eternity. In this way, in this life, God is both seen and not seen in the rational vision of those seeking him. Indeed, he is not seen in being seen and seen in not being seen. For God is not seen as he is "in himself," as he is glimpsed in intuitive visions that cannot be integrated so as to see him as a whole, although he is, in some sense, seen in these partial insights.

The not so obvious point of all this is that, insofar as P 18 is still responding to the question raised earlier about the extent to which the faithful can expect to achieve understanding in this life, it is actually proposing a rather more important and subtler sense in which God is "seen in not being seen." The claim that we cannot see the totality of God in one single simultaneous intuition is not just regarded as a revelation of his absolute unity but as evidence of his incomprehensibility. Our lack of insight, in other words, is supposedly providing us with a direct insight into God's "inaccessibility." The claim, then, that we cannot see God "as he is" is not only taken to be part and parcel of our present vision of him but, as such, is presumed to offer us a further revelation of his being. In this sense, God is ultimately seen in not being seen, that is, in the insight into his being beyond human comprehension. In fact, this point has determined the discussion since P 15 first offered its own philosophical insight into our lack of insight by arguing that it follows from the logic of something than which nothing greater can be thought that it is greater than can be thought, which in turn is treated in P 16 as a revelation of the theological claim that God "dwells in inaccessible light."

Put in these terms, the issue has actually been with us from the beginning of P 1, for it asks, in its first address to God, why, if he is present everywhere, we do not see him, and it answers with a biblical reference to the *lux inaccessibilis*.[66] It is this point, made in its own way in P 15 and literally repeated in P 16, that we want to press, not only because it provides the pivotal point on which the text turns, but also because it indicates that the same being that exists such that it cannot be thought not to exist can be shown, by nature, to be greater than what can be thought. Eventually, I will want to suggest that these two noetic claims about the nature of the thought of God are consistent with one another; that the reason something than which nothing greater can be thought cannot be thought not to exist is the same reason it is greater than what can be thought; although it is a rather different reason than the one on the basis of which and for the sake of which Anselm wants to suggest that something than which nothing greater can be thought, in some sense, cannot be thought. For the moment, however, we want to stress the manner in which the rather ironic illumination Anselm has just received—his insight into his lack of insight into God—serves to bring his various intuitions together, as the fact that they cannot be brought together is taken to reveal the incomprehensible unity of a being that is beyond human comprehension.

Through this confirmation of the inaccessibility of God, Anselm's multiple visions are effectively unified as the "uncomprehendible" features of an incomprehensible object. It is critical for him to convince us of this, since it is not enough to show that God is not seen in this life, or that even in being seen he is not altogether seen. Instead, Anselm must demonstrate that God has been glimpsed in a certain essential invisibility and that the disunity of our intuitions is evidence of the absolute unity of a being who by nature dwells in "inaccessible light." Anselm has, of course, been exploiting the model of perception, albeit through the image of an inner sight, to create the impression of an object of thought that is given in a series of one-sided perspectives but that cannot be comprehended as a whole. The question remains why, in the case of a conception in which we cannot bring its various elements together into a single intuition, we should assume that there is, nonetheless, some one object that has all these characteristics but which is itself "beyond" what can be thought, rather than that it is simply unintelligible.[67] This raises special difficulties for Anselm, who holds a psychological view of conceivability, even if it would seem that his causal theory of mind might lead him or at least allow him to make this assumption. For the presumed model of thought, in which the mind is determined in its thinking by the effect of reality upon it, would seem to be what allows Anselm to turn his lack of insight into a certain object of thought into an insight into that object's inaccessibility to thought by supposing that "the thing itself" is compelling him to think of it as unthinkable.

This epistemological model, drawn from the *Monologion,* is enhanced in the *Proslogion* by its theological promise of the metaphysical experience of a presently incomprehensible object in a life to come, just as the current obscurity of this divine self-concealment remains Anselm's final word on the matter. After all is said and done, after all the various features of God have been discerned, the claim to divine invisibility must be made to pervade whatever has been seen. To heap irony on irony—and in a way that continues to objectify his lack of insight—the image of an inaccessible light allows Anselm to contend that the nature of God's inconceivability is the result of his being the very element of intellectual sight and insight, that "light" of truth which remains "inaccessible" because it is too true for human thinking to think. Insofar as this *lux inaccessibilis* is associated with the light that illuminates the rational mind, even if it is too bright for the eye of reason to stare at directly, it will nonetheless be the case, as P 14 insists, that if human reason has seen any truth, it has seen God:

> Why, O lord God, does my soul not experience you if it has found you? Has it not found that which it found to be the light and the truth? But how did it understand this except by seeing the light and the truth?
>
> Could it understand anything at all about you except through *your light and your truth?* If it saw the light and the truth, it saw you. If it did not see you, it did not see the light or the truth.
>
> Or are the truth and the light what it saw, and yet it did not see you, since it saw you to a certain extent, but did not see you *as you are?*
>
> Lord my God, you who have formed and reformed me, tell my desiring soul what else you are other than what it has seen, so that it may see clearly what it desires. It strives so that it may see more, and it sees nothing beyond what it has seen except darkness. Indeed, it does not see *darkness, which is in no way in you,* but it sees that it can see no more because of its own darkness.
>
> Why is this lord,
> why is this?
> Is its eye darkened by its own weakness,
>   or dazzled by your brilliance?
> But surely it is both darkened within itself
>   and dazzled by you.
> Certainly, it is both darkened by its own shallowness
>   and overwhelmed by your immensity.
> Truly, it is both constricted by its own narrowness,
>   and overcome by your vastness.
> For how great is that light
>   from which shines every truth
>   that illuminates the rational mind!
> How vast is that truth
>   in which is all that is true,
> And outside of which
>   is only nothingness and falsehood!
> How immense is that which beholds
>   in one single intuition
>   all of creation,
> And by whom and through whom and how
>   all creatures were made from nothing!
> What purity, what simplicity,
>   what certainty and splendor,
>   are there!
> Surely it is more than can be understood by any creature.
>
>   (S I, 111–12)

When Anselm calls upon God to show him "what else you are" other than what he has seen so far, the subsequent images—of the vastness and depth of God's truth, in contrast to the weakness and shallowness of creaturely understanding—are supposed to provide the answer. In fact, they are designed to initiate the further revelation of God that will follow from them in the next chapter, namely, the seemingly paradoxical but for P 15 quite reasonable contention that something than which nothing greater can be thought is greater than can be thought—or at least thought by any creature. And while the conclusion of the above passage would seem to add yet another sense to the already ambiguous meaning of "greater," the psychological claim that God is "more than (*plus quam*) can be understood by any creature" remains a pivotal point in the text insofar as it establishes the need for a certain deferral of vision from this life to the next. This is not just so that we may be satisfied with the limited vision we presently enjoy, but so that this failure can provide a kind of epistemological promise of a life to come, in which the understanding of God that is presently impossible will not only become a possibility but an actuality.

P 15, then, marks the transition from our present and partial vision to the anticipation of the vision complete in eternity, incited through a strategy that redeems our lack of total vision by means of an argument that would not work were there a total lack of vision. As we have suggested, this critical transition ultimately depends upon a rather peculiar "insight," since it would appear to be based on a lack of insight. And we must, I think, allow ourselves to be struck by the way in which Anselm's vision of God apparently entails an admitted, indeed, a kind of inherent failure. We must be struck by the fact that Anselm's own treatment of the cognitive event of forming a true conception of God evidently includes an impression of a certain inconceivability, especially if this impression is said to be forced upon us by the very nature of what is being thought. We need, in that case, to ask whether there is any phenomenological justification for this lament of a rational mystic who, for all his philosophical labors, has not arrived at an experience of God or even at the vision of God that he ultimately anticipates, or whether this is all merely a matter of some theological apologetic designed to keep us hoping.

It would certainly be difficult to ignore Anselm's apparent satisfaction with all this, his sense that it is fitting that he has seen what he has seen and seen it only to the extent to which he has. The questions remain, however, why he is so content with his lack of vision and whether his confession, including his insight into his lack of insight, speaks against anything we have said about the vision of God that is embedded in his argument. It goes without saying that I would like to be able to show that Anselm's confession actually confirms our account of the nature of the "illumination" he proclaims himself, in P 4, to have received. What we would have to demonstrate is that the kind of cognitive experience at work in the single argument that spans P 2 and P 3 provides philosophical grounds for the later confession of the limitation of the rational mystic's vision of God, even if Anselm's seeming honesty, that he has only seen "incompletely," can be turned to use to legitimate his intellectual insight and to supply a certain apology for reason itself.

We are interested, then, in what all of this, including Anselm's confession, reveals about his vision of God in the *Proslogion*. In that case, the question becomes: How is a lack of vision consistent with Anselm's vision of God? And if we stay with these metaphors of vision, which may not be altogether metaphorical but a direct transference from outer to inner, then the phenomenology of visual perception might provide us, as it has Anselm, with some insight into the experience of such inner visions, into the psychologic, or, as we have said, the psychodynamics, involved in his vision of God. To show how the mental conversion at work in such a "distant" insight into God justifies Anselm's confession of the limitations of his rational mysticism, we will have to look more closely at certain features of the language of his laments, taking a clue in their reading from my contention that he is trading in the historical translation of religious images into rational ones. In that event, we will need to ask what it means, philosophically speaking, to claim that God "dwells in inaccessible light," how this claim is critical to the *Proslogion*'s overall argument, and whether Anselm's confession of a lack of vision speaks against anything we have said about the vision of God offered in P 2–4, or is instead part and parcel of that very insight.

Notice the vocabulary in which P 16 expresses the difficulties involved in seeing God, virtually repeating the language we have just encountered in P 14:

> Truly, lord, this is *the inaccessible light in which you dwell.* For truly there is nothing else that can penetrate it so as to look upon you there. Truly, therefore, I do not see it, since it is too much for me; and yet whatever I see, I see by means of it—just as an eye that is weak sees what it sees by the light of the sun, which it cannot look at in the sun itself. My understanding is not up to it. It shines too brilliantly; I grasp it not. Nor may the eye of my soul direct itself to it for long.
>
> It is dazzled by its splendor,
>> overcome by its vastness,
>> overwhelmed by its immensity,
>> confused by its extent.
> O supreme and inaccessible light,
>> O whole and blessed truth!

How far you are from me,
  who am so near to you!
How distant you are from my sight,
  whose sight I am so present to!
You are wholly present everywhere, and I do not see you.
In you I move and in you I am,
  and yet I cannot approach you.
You are within me and around me,
  and I do not experience you. (S I, 112–13)

Anselm begins here by invoking the traditional image of light as the element for sight, but which itself cannot be seen. Notice, however, that with the exception of the reference to "splendor"—and even then, if the intense "brilliance" of that blinding light is a matter of an excessive abundance "too much" for the eye of the mind to glimpse—the other three images are of size, of the unlimited extent of God. Or, to mix the metaphors of vision and of size, they are images of scope. By contrast, the vocabulary mustered to characterize the human mind in its thinking capacity depends upon images of restriction. These infuse the confession at P 14 as well as the explanation at P 18. The former laments the "littleness" or "brevity" (*brevitate*) of a human understanding overwhelmed by God's immensity, even as the clarification of why the human mind cannot gather into a single intuition what is one in God is attributed to its being constricted by its own "narrowness," which is overcome by God's amplitude, by the fullness of what is called, in the above passage, the "whole truth." In effect, then, the terms for God across the various passages suggest the scope of his immensity (*amplitudine / immensitate / capacitate*), whereas the terms for human understanding stress its lack of scope in a certain narrowness (*brevitate / angustia*) of vision.

Not only is this sense of the "uncircumscribability" of God as "simultaneously everywhere wholly," originally noted in P 13, complicated in P 18 by the claims about his utter simplicity and absolute unity, but the very narrowness of human vision lamented there seems in some sense to be requested. After the radical lament of P 17, which admits to the lack of a true and full "experience" of God, Anselm returns in P 18 to the language of vision developed in P 1:

I sought your face,
For your face, lord, will I search.
Do not turn your face away from me.
Lift me from my self to you.
Cleanse, heal, focus, *illuminate* the eye of my mind *so that it may behold you.* (S I, 114)

Here the request for focus, for sharpening (*acies*) the vision of the eye of the mind, would seem to invite the very limitation that

Anselm laments later in the same chapter. The focal nature of human thought, the fact that it must concentrate its attention on specific aspects of God, one at a time, is what keeps it from that "single simultaneous intuition" promised in the vision to come. It is, of course, this explanation of the inherent narrowness of human understanding that allows Anselm to have it both ways at once, to claim that God is both seen and not seen by those seeking him. It does not, however, altogether account for that subtler sense in which God is "seen in not being seen" insofar as our ultimate insight into him lies in a vision of his incomprehensibility. Consequently, we would not want to confuse the explanation of God's "inaccessibility" as a matter of our multiple visions of him with its confirmation in Anselm's own inner experience in the unifying insight into God's inconceivability. For the latter alone explains Anselm's explanation and can show why he is not just satisfied with his lack of insight but regards it as itself an insight, not just into the limitations of human thought but into the very nature of God.

If we press the images used to make Anselm's point to force to the surface the insight that lies beneath them and thus show the inner visual dynamic he is inadvertently documenting in his confession, then we must stress not just the metaphors of illumination or of the cleansing and healing of the fallen eye of the mind, or even those basic oppositions in Anselm's vocabulary—between light and dark, height and depth, then and now, the arisen and fallen, let alone in the final elevation of the resurrected body—that are marshaled to the forefront to explicate the claim about God's dwelling in "inaccessible light." Instead, it seems to me that the critical reference turns out to be the one that has guided Anselm's visionary epistemology from the start. The talk of "focus," of the "sharpening" of our mental vision so as to concentrate clearly on its object, is already at work in M 10's claims about the "acuteness" of vision (*acies cogitationes*) for which thinking strives in its attempt to envision likenesses of the things themselves in thought, as the rational mind aims to sharpen the outline, as it were, of its inner image of things. Were we then to ask how such concentrated vision can entertain a reality like the supreme being in thought, it seems clear that the ultimate characterization of God, or at least of how such a being appears to our rational mind's eye, inevitably leads to the notion of an inaccessible light of unlimitable scope. Both images, whether of light or of size, serve to suggest that whatever is presenting itself to thought does not appear as something that can be contained or confined as a determinate object. In this way, P 18 would seem to be suggesting, given the emphasis upon and limitation of human thinking, that the disclaimer of P 15, that God is greater than can be thought, amounts to the contention that he cannot be made a focal object of our inner vision and that this is itself part and parcel of our insight into him.

I take it to be no coincidence that Anselm's reflections on such matters are sandwiched between a dual account of God's ubiquitous presence, even as certain features at issue in these discussions will be explicitly associated with the claim that he cannot be thought not to exist. Were we to attend to the order of the text so as to highlight the topics quite literally surrounding Anselm's confession and infused into it, it would be clear that the ontological distinctiveness of God is what supports the entire discussion. Just before the announcement in P 14 that God is both seen and not seen by those seeking him, Anselm has switched back in P 13 from the theological considerations at issue in P 9–12 to more metaphysical concerns, to the claim that God is "limitless" and "eternal," is confined by no space or time, but is instead simultaneously everywhere wholly. After the discussion of our vision of God in P 14–18, Anselm returns in P 19–21 to reconsider and amplify the issues first raised in P 13 about God's eternal ubiquity, culminating in the *Proslogion*'s final flurry of metaphysical thinking, of which we have already taken note, in P 22. There the claim that something cannot be thought not to exist is correlated with its existing absolutely and simply, properly and immutably, eternally and inherently, as compared to what can be thought not to exist, which exists at some particular time, is changeable, has a beginning from nothing and can return to nothing unless kept to be by another. And what Anselm wants to conclude from this is not just that God "contains" all things or that, as P 20 begins, he "fills" and "surrounds" them all but that he is also "before and beyond" all beings. Thanks to his limitless immensity, God is able to be everywhere and always wholly, without, however, being constrained or divided by any place or time, or even being limited by, while being in every place and time. In short, he is, as P 21 suggests, a "centerless" center that, in being everywhere, is nowhere.

I mention these claims about the ontological peculiarity of God (which we have seen developed in detail in the earlier work) and the placing of the insistence on our lack of insight between them, because I think it is what leads Anselm to speak, with some phenomenological justification, of such a being's inaccessibility to human thought, while at the same time allowing him to suppose that he has caught a glimpse of God, paradoxically enough, in his very "invisibility." If P 13 argues that God is uncircumscribable in his being everywhere and always wholly and P 19–21 resumes its treatment of these topics, it is because such claims are meant to explicate the insistence that God is both seen and not seen by those seeking him.

The interminable immensity of God's eternal ubiquity would clearly place him beyond the scope of our inner vision, such that talk of God's "vastness" might indicate the extent to which he is, by nature, bound to exceed and elude the contracted insight of the eye of a mind that cannot confine as an object of its inner sight what is unconfinable precisely because it is everywhere. In short, God's peculiar omnipresence would seem to make him the kind of being that cannot be seen by a vision that must focus its sight here or there but cannot look everywhere.[68] More importantly, however, it is also an essential element of what makes him the sort of being that cannot be thought not to exist insofar as he alone is without beginning or end or multiplicity of parts, and is everywhere and always wholly. And our aim is to formulate the issue in view of this key factor that we have claimed captures the ontological distinctiveness of the supreme being so as to show how the characteristic of God that he "cannot be thought not to exist" is consistent with the contention made later in the text that he is "greater than can be thought."

The answer I am suggesting to the question Anselm is himself trying to answer—if we may read his admission of his lack of vision and his appeal to the image of an "inaccessible light" in terms of a phenomenology of the inner experience involved in his rational sighting of God—is that the supreme being can only and ultimately be "seen" in a certain diminishing of objectivity, in its relinquishment of objecthood, or, as I would prefer to say, through a "defocal" vision that does not concentrate its attention on a center of focus but sights God in his invisibility out of the corner of the eye of the mind without any focal object appearing to thought. And it is my contention that concealed in these confessions of a rational mystic is the confirmation of the kind of intellectual experience Anselm has had of God. In fact, Anselm's confession and his subsequent insistence that God dwells in inaccessible light may well reveal, albeit inadvertently, what I would regard as the most fundamental feature of his ontological vision. As we will recall, whether in the vision of God in P 2–4 or in M 28, creatures are not simply replaced by another object when they withdraw. On the contrary, precisely insofar as what can be thought not to exist is removed from reason's sight against the measure of what cannot be thought not to exist, the supreme being "appears" in the void of beings, in the emptiness left by their ontological disappearance. The absolute presence of being itself is thus secured in the absence of beings, as thought projects into the void whose features God takes on by filling. In this projection beyond beings of reason's line of sight, the supreme being could not be focused on as an object of thought but would, at best, have to be glimpsed in the peripheral vision of the eye of the mind. The focusing of attention on the nothingness left by the departure of beings releases thought from all focal determination in a dilation of the mind's eye, in a "defocusing" that opens up the scope of our own inner sight. This may well give the impression that one has caught sight of what is everywhere and always wholly in the vision of the absence of beings as whole, just as it may perhaps rightly be said to involve a "blinding" of our inner vision if we mean by this that no focal object appears to thought in thinking God. In that event, God would seem to appear to human thought at the limit of its insight, as if he were glimpsed in the impossibility of being seen.[69]

Our point, then, is that in the inner experience of thinking the supreme being through the negation of beings, the eye of the mind cannot refocus its attention so much as it must defocus, dilate, in stretching the limits of its vision, extending its sight to the extreme. In expanding its scope to the boundary of its inner field of vision, effectively reversing the order of normal perception, it may seem to catch a glimpse of what cannot be seen under normal conditions. In that case, however, there would appear to be a certain essential insight revealed in the mind's lack of insight, in the failure of an object of thought to appear. Consequently, I would suggest that the image of the inaccessibility of an omnipresent light that cannot be looked at directly, even if it can be seen peripherally, and the talk of a vision "from afar" both indicate the impossibility of precise focus as well as a certain distance from any clear objectification in what I would call, for lack of a better term, Anselm's defocal vision of God. If we are still going to speak in visual images—and I see no reason why we should not—it would seem appropriate to say that such a vision of God, given the invisibility of his omnipresence, must be of a nonfocal sort. The possibility that one might be able to glimpse out of the corner of the eye of the mind what cannot be thought not to exist in its being everywhere and always wholly would not require the sighting of a new object of focal vision (an object like those objects of focal sight that can be thought not to exist precisely because they are limited to a particular place and time, etc.) but must involve a yielding of the demand for such focal precision in the reversal of the normal order of vision that attempts to catch sight of the ground precisely in the absence of all figures of focus. As such, like the omnipresence of light, God is not exactly seen, is both seen and not seen, and ultimately is seen in not being seen. As Anselm says from the start, God is seen "from afar" and "from the depths" (*vel de longe, vel de profundo*), although I would imagine that this double metaphor of distance, and of the long-range vision associated with it, not only implies a projection of reason's line of sight but suggests a certain diminishing of objectivity and the concomitant impossibility of any focal determination of the object of thought.

On this phenomenological reading, the image of an "inaccessible light" effectively characterizes both the element of illumination and the failure of an object to be grasped by thought. In short, it captures precisely the illumination of an object of thought that does not appear. This is not, of course, inconsistent with our earlier claim that Anselm is objectifying his lack of insight, "reifying" it, in his contention that it is the thing itself that forces upon thought the confession that such an object is greater than can be thought. Instead, it reveals the manner in which he achieves the objectification of an incomprehensible object by construing it as an object that is beyond objectification, even as it documents Anselm's own sense that this conclusion has been arrived at as a result of an insight into the very nature of what is being thought. Nor, therefore, is any of this regarded by him as a matter of vagueness. On the contrary, it is presumed to be a quite precise way of clarifying the elusive presence that most properly characterizes the inaccessibility of God and that Anselm himself might just as well have called, as other mystics have, the divine darkness. He prefers, although no less paradoxically, to attribute the invisibility of God to a superabundance of light and any darkness to our limited understanding. And this seems fitting, since such a dark vision of God, this seeing in the dark that becomes even darker in the voiding of beings, is supposed to be the result of the blinding clarity that the thought of the supreme being apparently has upon the rational mind. For if it is against this measure of true being, revealed in the lightening flash of the illumination of being itself, that beings are voided, then it might seem clear enough that the ontological excessiveness of God would require that the eye of the mind close, or at least squint, in its loss of all focal determination. In effect, the eye of reason would have to close itself off to all focal presentations in order to open itself to what cannot be so seen and can just barely be caught sight of in the stretching of the scope of its vision, in forcing our rational insight to its limit in what we might well refer to as a liminal vision of God.

All I am suggesting is that the extreme that ruptures the categories of rational thought in the ontological reversal of M 28 is recaptured in the distinction of P 3. When translated to a quite literal, albeit inner, visual level, both ultimately involve a blanking out, a "blinding," of our inner vision. Such blank vision, in which we look without seeing or see without seeing anything, involves the removal of all ordinary objects from thought. It is this sort of inner experience, achieved in the emptying from our inner sight of all focal objects, that is essential to the elevation of the mind at work in the cognitive insight incited by Anselm's ontological argument, which directs our line of vision toward a certain domain by forcing it to look beyond beings. And something of this is being confessed, or captured, in the insistence that God's "dwelling place" is beyond human thought, that God resides in a region of being that can only be located regionally—that can be sited, even projected toward, but in which, nonetheless, he cannot be altogether seen as an object of thought.

We still have to show just how such an essentially empty vision can be conviction producing, that is, why such an "object" of thought convinces rational thought that it cannot fail to be. For the moment, we will note that, if we may mix the *Proslogion*'s preferred image with M 7's memorable exploitation of the image of light, we could say that the talk of the inaccessible light serves to document quite precisely the sort of visual dynamic that happens to the eye of the mind in its rational vision of being itself. Such imagery would seem to indicate that it is in the dark of the mind, as it turns its back on the whole domain of beings, that the "illumination" of and by the supreme being takes place, even as this insight cannot establish or settle on an object of thought but can, at best, sight God, in a certain moment of ecstatic insight, in his invisibility. As such, the vision is itself said to be as blinding, even if in a more profound sense, as the blindness of the faithful, who, in another sense, have not seen God. For us, of course, the claim about the blinding effect that the scope of the supreme being has upon reason suggests the defocal features of Anselm's inner vision of God: that the eye of reason cannot exactly locate its object. In either case, such imagery clearly indicates, however inadvertently, the inner visual dynamic, or, if one prefers, the phenomenologic of being itself as it appears to the eye of the rational mind. Acknowledging this elusive dynamic, indeed, this dynamic of elusion, is, for Anselm, apparently essential to a careful characterization of our mental experience of God and may well be what calls for an ontological "conversion" in our thinking, in a reversal of our inner sight, that is elicited, if not entirely secured, through the practice of rational meditation.

In the end, we will try to show how Anselm has accomplished this cognitive experience of what cannot be thought through certain categorical abuses that manipulate the mechanics of the mind so as to induce a vision of what cannot be seen. In anticipation of that discussion, we want to conclude our present considerations by reemphasizing that Anselm's confession functions as a tactic for dealing with God's failure to appear, and that the concession of a psychological incomprehensibility, denying that any conception of the supreme being, including a rational one, can envision him "as he is," does not stop Anselm from attempting to provide a "likeness" of the divine. On the contrary, confessing the impossibility of conceiving of what is beyond human conception is part of the attempt to form an image of God, allowing Anselm to construct a rational likeness that simultaneously applies and denies specific features to him, including the feature of incomprehensibility. Of course, one might still wonder why Anselm's admitting that he has been unable to secure, by means of reason, a comprehensive and comprehensible vision of God does not lead him to the philosophical conclusion that there is no such object, not even of thought, or at least to question his assumption that there is an object that is eluding his thought. Clearly, this has something to do with his religious commitments. It must be equally clear, however, that the way in which those commitments invade the rhetoric of the *Proslogion* remains part and parcel of the staging of the text in terms of a specific theological scenario. This formal difference is what perhaps most distinguishes the *Proslogion* from the *Monologion,* for while the earlier work presumes to proceed *sola ratione,* the later work operates with the aid of prayer.

It is through these prayers that a certain theological significance can come to be attached to the particular cognitive experiences that the *Proslogion*'s rational arguments produce. In the case in point, for example, were we to ask why, according to the *Proslogion,* we should think that there is any unified object of thought at issue, given what Anselm has claimed about its failure to appear, the answer must be that the presumption of an object that is beyond human thought is ultimately secured through the deferral of vision from this life to the next based on a theological appeal. Needless to say, in my view, there is good reason to think that Anselm's negative ontology, which sights being itself through a manipulation of our understanding of beings, would have to be supplemented by a theological scenario that transfers the promise that the supreme being will appear as itself to a future time, so as to make sense of the possibility that what cannot appear as an object of thought may be regarded as an object that is presently eluding our thought. In effect, a philosophically incomprehensible God must be established as a possible object of thought through the theological postponement of his appearance to some future life when what can now only appear at the threshold of our understanding will show itself "face-to-face," even as the promise of that vision complete in the afterlife is based on the foresight that reason presumably enjoys in the partial visions available to it in our fallen condition. This circular strategy alone serves to establish the legitimacy of an inconceivable object of thought that cannot, despite our obvious lack of understanding, be finally judged to be unintelligible insofar as the temporal deferral of vision can create the impression that what presently cannot be thought will someday become wholly and entirely accessible as an object, not just of thought but of experience.

Or perhaps even then objectivity, and the separation from its object that such vision requires, may not be the order of the day. For in the joy complete, God will not simply become an object seen from close up, since he will still be too abundant. In the total delight, in the unending and unerring mystical experience of God, such joy will be too great to come to those who rejoice. Instead, they will enter wholly into that joy. And this fullness of joy, which remains a promise deferred for eternity, is the *Proslogion's* last word on the matter, as the text ends in P 26 as it began: praying for the vision of God.

> My lord and my God, my hope and the joy of my heart, tell my soul if this is the joy that you express to us through your Son: *Ask and ye shall receive, so that your joy may be full.*
> For I have found a joy that is full, and more than full. For when, with a full heart, a full mind, and a full soul, the whole man is full of that joy, joy beyond measure remains. Therefore, not all of that joy shall enter into those who rejoice, but those who rejoice shall enter wholly into that joy.
> Speak, O lord, tell your servant in his inner heart if this is the joy into which your servants will enter, who enter *into the joy of their lord.* But surely that joy, in which your elected ones will rejoice, *no eye has seen, nor ear has heard, nor has it arisen in the heart of man.* (S I, 120–21)

Having seen Anselm's repeated tendency to take back with one hand what he has given with the other, it might sound here as if the deferred vision will itself not, even in the next life, be altogether complete, since while we may well enter wholly into that joy, it is not clear that the whole of that joy will be available to us. In the fullness of vision, "joy beyond measure remains," that is, the object of our joy will apparently still elude our complete grasp. In any event, Anselm does not conclude that he must simply await the life to come to receive the knowledge and joy and love for which he longs. Instead, he will go on to pray that, in the meantime, through continuous striving, he may proceed through his partial visions in this life toward that mystical experience which can come only in eternity.

The projection of such a time, and the connection of our presently truncated visions of God to the prospect of the unified vision in eternity, is obviously designed to give our current lack of experience of God a certain meaning. In fact, as we shall see, it gives a specific meaning to time itself. Such a proposal suggests a particular historical mission for rational theology in its attempt to secure the ongoing revelation of the invisible God in history by means of reason, that is, through the practice of a rational meditation whose illuminations, as P 4 insisted, are as surely sent from God as is the gift of faith. It is, of course, no surprise that, in the end, a rational mystic would invoke the "God of truth," nor that he would seek absolution for reason through a confession that admits its shortcomings while redeeming its efficacy through a strategy of deferral. Thus, Anselm actually concludes the *Proslogion* by praying not just for the fulfillment of the promise of a total mystical experience in the life to come but for the daily revelation of that joy for those faithful seeking understanding, so that their rational vision of God—and thus their knowledge, their love, and their joy—may be increased while they wait:

> I pray, O God,
>> that I may know you
>> and love you,
>> so that I may rejoice in you.
> And if I cannot fully in this life,
>> at least let me advance,
>> day by day,
>> until that fullness comes.
> Let the knowledge of you increase in me here,
>> and there come to fullness.
> Let love for you grow
>> and there be fulfilled,
> so that here my joy may be great in hope,
>> and there in the fullness of reality.
>
> Lord, you have commanded,
>> indeed, counseled,
> that we call upon you,
>> through your Son,
> and you promise that we shall receive,
>> *so that our joy may be full.*
> I ask, O lord,
> for what you counsel *through* our *wonderful counselor.*
> May I receive what you promise through your truth,
>> *so that my joy may be full.*
> God of truth,
>> I beseech you:
>> may I receive,
>> *so that my joy may be full.*
>
> Until then,
>> let my mind meditate on it,
>> let my tongue speak it,
>> let my heart love it,
>> let my mouth preach it,
>> let my soul hunger for it,
>> let my flesh thirst for it,
>> let my whole substance desire it,
> until that time when *I enter into the joy of my lord,*
> who art God,
>> three in one,
>> *blessed for all ages.* Amen. (S I, 121–22)

The anticipation of joy that set the stage for the *Proslogion* in its preface now closes the curtain on its conclusion—which means that it has effectively pervaded, even if behind the scenes, the whole of the interior design of the text. This taste of a joy that is promised and yet remains unfulfilled, that is left in the mouth that proclaims it, in the heart that longs for it, in the soul and body that hunger and thirst for it, apparently requires, first and foremost, that the mind meditate on it. Needless to say, in my view, the *Proslogion* aims to offer just such a meditation. Through its rational contemplation, thought may not only try to imagine what "no eye has seen or ear heard" as it envisions the expectation of the fullness of joy, when these same senses will see, taste, touch, feel, and hear God, but must, in such incipiently mystical meditation, "foresee," that is, enjoy some foretaste of the ecstatic experience that it will someday enter wholly into.

The text appropriately concludes, then, on a note of what I am inclined to call an incipient mysticism. This is to say that the book aims not to conclude at all but, instead, to close in a way that keeps it open to what is presumed to be beyond it. Indeed, it ends where it began: initiating a present movement of thought in anticipation of that eternal future in which is promised the mystical experience that will redeem a paradise lost in our prehistoric past. But unlike the opening prayer of P 1, this final passage does not stress our fallen condition and the separation from God to which Adam subjected those of us in exile. Instead, it stresses the continuity between this life and the next, the way the day-to-day understanding that comes from the pursuit of this God of reason—and comes through his son— may develop into, perhaps provides some basis for, the election of those whose joy is destined to be complete. In that case, however, this first step on the road to glory, taken through the historic initiation of a rational theology that is inevitably mystical, entails a leap that is quite a bit more daring than its concealment in terms of the traditional rhetoric of salvation may let on.

| NOTES

1. S I, 97. We have already taken note of a similar reference in the instructions Anselm offers for the reading of his prayers and meditations (S III, 3) in note 8 of the preceding chapter.

2. S I, 93–94.

3. Eadmer, *The Life of St. Anselm,* 29–30.

4. Eadmer, 14–15.

5. S I, 93.

6. Eadmer, 30–31. The "original" version of the *Proslogion,* according to this story, is lost to us. The version we have is a reconstruction of the text based on a second set of tablets that were found broken into pieces.

Why the original would have been stolen, or the second version destroyed, is anybody's guess. No doubt it says something, even if we are not sure what, about the reception of Anselm's work among his brethren.

7. S I, 104.

8. Gillian R. Evans, for example, suggests this in her *Anselm and Talking about God*, 40–42.

9. The poetic rendering of the prayers is suggested by Schmitt's version of the Latin text as presented in his German translation of the *Proslogion* and further interpolated by Benedicta Ward in her English translation (see *The Prayers and Meditations of St. Anselm with the Proslogion*, 238–67, as well as her "Translator's Note," 19–21). We will take certain liberties in our formal presentation in an attempt to capture the poetic affect of Anselm's prose, while we will continue to cite page locations from the *Opera omnia*. Italicized words or phrases within Anselm's text indicate biblical citations. Locations for those citations are given in the margin of Schmitt's Latin, which accompanies my own English translation of the *Proslogion*, both of which are provided after my interpretation.

10. For discussion of this and other mystical images from early medieval thought, see Anselm Stolz, *The Doctrine of Spiritual Perfection*.

11. S I, 122.

12. M 78 had already distinguished between "living" and "dead" faith, although perhaps more to the point and directly parallel with the conclusion of P 1 is the claim on which M 77 closes: "It is evident then that just as one cannot strive for [this being] unless he believes in it, so is it of no avail to believe in [this being] unless one strives for it" (S I, 84). Cf. Psalm 13: "The lord looks down from heaven to see if there is anyone who understands and seeks him."

13. S I, 120.

14. S I, 104.

15. See Schmitt's introduction to the 1968 edition of the *Opera omnia*, 1, 64*.

16. The best-known proponent of this view is Karl Barth, in his *Anselm: Fides Quaerens Intellectum*. A derivation of it has been expounded by D. P. Henry, who thinks the investigation of "a whole series of attributes" begins in P 3. See his "*Proslogion* Chapter 3."

17. The latter point has been stressed by Stolz in, for example, "Anselm's Theology in the *Proslogion*," and more recently by Richard Campbell in *From Belief to Understanding*.

18. S I, 98.

19. S I, 125.

20. It could well be that the profound precision of this very designation was part of the revelation itself, and not only in Anselm's understanding of the fittingness of the name but of all that could be shown by means of it.

21. Anselm's response begins by insisting that he will respond not to the "fool," on whose behalf Gaunilo wrote, but to the "catholic" (S I, 130). This allows him to appeal throughout the replies to certain views that, if Gaunilo held them, would be inconsistent with his faith.

22. See, in this connection, Aquinas's critique of Anselm's argument in the *Summa theologica* (1.2.1). I might just mention here that the account Aquinas provides in his *Summa contra gentiles* (1.10) may have helped to perpetuate a certain misunderstanding of P 2, begun by Gaunilo, of which we will take note shortly. In another respect, which we will also address,

Jonathan Barnes, in *The Ontological Argument,* thinks the talk of "something of such a nature" gives away the argument in the sense that it reveals its central error.

23. *Memorials of St. Anselm,* 336.

24. It is difficult not to recall, in this connection, Rudolf Berlinger's remark that Anselm's key phrase operates between "something" (*aliquid*) and "nothing" (*nihil*) (*Philosophie als Weltwissenschaft,* 1:164).

25. Gaunilo apparently took or, as Anselm claims, mistook the example to suggest more than this. See Anselm's insistence in reply 8 that Gaunilo has overextended its point. We, however, think that Gaunilo's remarks in objection 5 are to the point, at least insofar as he insists that we do not understand "something than which nothing greater can be thought" as we do or can unreal things, but understand the words alone. Indeed, Anselm himself seems to take pride, for example in reply 5, in the presumed fact that from the sound of the utterance alone (*hoc ipso quod sonat "quo maius cogitari non possit"* [S I, 135]), the matter can be clarified. Certainly, Gaunilo missed the self-clarifying nature of the expression and surely missed the central point of the argument of P 2; but Anselm misses Gaunilo's objection to the emptiness of a merely verbal conception.

26. This means that Anselm's argument does not require that we begin with an understanding of the "essence" of God (as Aquinas supposes), or (as later "ontological arguments" require) that we even have a positive "conception" of God. Instead, Anselm's argument begins from the words of a phrase which is itself not even obviously designating a specific feature of God nor needs to be understood, at least so Anselm thinks, in any but a nominal or "semiotic" manner.

27. As I have noted in my earlier work on Anselm, Adolf Kolping, in his *Anselms Proslogion-Beweis der Existenz Gottes,* 69, has drawn attention to something like the need for the suppressed premise we have labeled as premise 4, although William Rowe has only recently clarified its importance.

28. See, in this connection, S I, 101, *priores recensiones,* 16, which indicates that the line claiming that "if it exists in the understanding alone, it can be thought to exist in reality also, which is greater," begins in certain manuscripts: "For whatever (*quidquid*) exists in the understanding alone . . ." Moreover, line 17 apparently has included after it in certain versions the following gloss: ". . . therefore whatever (*et ideo quicquid*) exists in the understanding alone is [something] than which a greater can be thought."

29. S I, 130–32.

30. Obviously, the enhanced status that the independent is assumed to have in Anselm's thought has been with us since the beginning of the *Monologion,* with its emphasis on the supremacy of what is and is whatever it is "through itself" (*per se*). It may be worth noting that talk of the thing existing "in itself" (*in seipsis*), as a mark of its greater reality, is echoed in the more frequently employed notion—for example, in P 2—of something's existing "in reality" (*in re*). The latter refers to the existence "in themselves" of things (*res*), to the kind of ontological status, indeed, ontological independence, that "things" enjoy in contrast to the dependency of the "likenesses" of things in the understanding, which are dependent not only on the mind but also on the things themselves; even if those things are not as truly "in themselves" in themselves as they are in God, whose mark of supremacy is his absolute independence.

31. I refer here especially to Norman Malcolm and Charles Hartshorne. See the former's "Anselm's Ontological Arguments" and the latter's *Anselm's Discovery*.

32. Richard Campbell has suggested that premise 1—that "God is something than which nothing greater can be thought"—is a factual claim in the sense that it depends upon a "speech-act" someone must perform (*From Belief to Understanding,* 30ff.). As will eventually become clear, we are sympathetic with the insistence upon the "contingency" of such a claim, even if it is not based upon the contingent fact that a certain language-game happens to be played. In the end, Campbell would seem to attribute more necessity to the playing of such language-games than we will. Suffice it to say that Anselm would not have thought of premise 1 as contingent upon a natural language in the sense of a historically developing sign-system. Nor, we might mention in passing, would we regard premise 2, which claims that the fool understands S, to be intended as a factual matter. Obviously, any interesting criticism of this premise rests upon questioning the intelligibility of the key phrase, not upon whether some specific fool happens to be able to understand it, or, to press Campbell's fideistic suggestion, happens to hear Anselm perform this speech act while overhearing him praying. Furthermore, while we are also sympathetic with Campbell's reminder that understanding for Anselm is always "owned" (see his "Anselm's Background Metaphysics"), that it is always somebody's understanding, the fact that rational insight has a "psychological" ground would not make it, for Anselm, any less necessary.

33. S I, 134.

34. The same pattern of argument is apparent in Gaunilo's famous parody, in which a lost island, which is said to be superior to all others, is shown to exist, since if it did not, "whatever other lands exist in reality would be more excellent than it" (S I, 128).

35. Charles Hartshorne, for example, has suggested that the modal argument he is seeking may well be in Anselm's replies.

36. For an example of a "modalized" account of the argument of P 2, see William Rowe's version in "The Ontological Argument," originally published in his *Philosophy of Religion,* which is based, we should note, on the alteration of Anselm's key phrase.

37. See Jonathan Barnes's criticism in *The Ontological Argument,* and Richard Campbell's defense in *From Belief to Understanding.*

38. For a detailed discussion, see Jerome Shaffer, "Existence, Predication, and the Ontological Argument," reprinted in *The Many-Faced Argument.*

39. S I, 129.

40. S I, 131.

41. One would, then, have to take such differences into consideration when creating counterexamples of concepts into which one has simply built the concept of existence. See, in this connection, Rowe's creation of the category "magican," which he defines to include only those magicians who actually exist. This is not to deny that it is possible that Anselm has himself, however covertly, implanted something in the concept of God from which existence (or, as Rowe also rightly notes, the impossibility of nonexistence) grows. But it is to admit that if he has, it is propagated through a far subtler seed. If anything, and as unlikely as it may sound at this stage, we will ultimately try to show that Anselm has secured the inconceivable nonexistence of

S, not through the inclusion of existence in the concept but through its exclusion, by rendering such categories irrelevant.

42. See Anselm's remarks near the conclusion of reply 1 (S I, 131–32).

43. See Malcolm's and Hartshorne's accounts. Ironically, the tradition of ignoring the importance of P 3 goes back as far as the so-called Hereford *Proslogion* (*Anselm Studies* 1:258–73), which, in its "summary" of the text, omits any mention of P 3, even though it deals with the question it raises in P 4.

44. R. LaCroix, *Proslogion II and III: A Third Interpretation of Anselm's Argument.* This view has also been defended by Jasper Hopkins.

45. See my "The Identity of Anselm's Argument" as well as my *An Introduction to Anselm's Argument.* See also the various discussions of the issue that ensued upon the publication of Richard Campbell's similar account of the argument in *From Belief to Understanding.* It would seem that the historical conditions had been set up in such a way by previous discussions, elicited by the debate over the Malcolm/Hartshorne proposal, that both Campbell and I were independently led to the one alternative that had been overlooked. See my "What Is It for God to Exist?" as well as the aforementioned "Reunderstanding Anselm's Argument" for further discussion and citations.

46. D. P. Henry, *"Proslogion* Chapter 3."

47. In this respect, D. P. Henry's claim that P 3 begins a list of distinguishing attributes of God is to the point, even if it misses another.

48. See Stolz, "'*Vere esse*' im *Proslogion* des hl. Anselm," for a discussion of this tradition. In fact, a prayer once attributed to Anselm but since shown to be likely to have been written by one of his followers (and which also, like P 22, comments on the famous self-designation of God in Exodus) reads: "I, he said, am who I am. And this is beautifully said. For that alone truly exists whose existence is immutable. Accordingly, he whose existence is so excellent, so singular, alone truly exists in comparison to which all other existence is nothing" (J. P. Migne, *Patrologia Latina,* 148:712). See, in this connection, the comments of A. Wilmart, who compiled the prayers for the critical edition of Anselm's works, concerning this prayer (*Auteurs spirituels et textes devots du moyen âge latin,* 193) as well as Ward's comments about Elmer of Canterbury, the presumed author of the above prayer (*Prayers and Meditations of St. Anselm,* 283ff.). I might just mention, to set the record straight, that when I said in my earlier book on Anselm that this prayer was "unfortunately" not included in the Schmitt edition (56), I did not mean, as Jasper Hopkins took me to, that it was unfortunate that Schmitt did not include material that had been shown to lack authenticity, but that it was unfortunate for my account that such a stunning case of the use of *vere esse* had been shown not to be Anselm's, even if, as Wilmart and Ward suggest, as written by one of his disciples, it is in some sense nonetheless "Anselmian."

49. I might just mention that Richard Campbell and I, even at this stage, have in general come to similar conclusions about Anselm's argument. There is a point, however, and it is not far off—as it is relevant to our view of the implications of this reading of the single argument of P 2–3 and, in certain respects, of the basis for the identification of God with S—at which our accounts diverge. In the end, the main limitation of Campbell's approach, from my point of view, is that it does not include any interpretive apparatus that would allow him to distinguish between what Anselm thought he was doing and what Campbell thinks Anselm is doing. This obscures the differences between their respective epistemologies, including their views of logic and language, and is, no doubt, what forces Campbell to avoid the claims about the argument made in P 4, where Anselm appeals to his own visionary account of the nature of thinking. In effect, then, while I very much appreciate the extent of Campbell's reading of the argument of P 2–3, we cannot endorse the way in which his interpretation forces him to segregate Anselm's argument from the remainder of the *Proslogion,* since in so doing, he succeeds in ripping the argument out of its original—and that means originally mystical—context, even as he fails to provide any analysis of the prayers that surround the reasoning. For the moment, however, we can still recommend his account of P 3 (*Faith Seeking Understanding,* 90–150, especially 126ff.), since I think it, to this point, reflects the original intentions of the text.

50. Here, I suppose, one might say that it is critical not to confuse the comparative with the superlative, although matters are a bit more complicated than that. This may be why a certain confusion has persisted in Jasper Hopkins's criticisms of my position. For a detailed discussion, see my "Reunderstanding Anselm's Argument," 399ff. I might just mention that his most recent attack (in the introduction to his new translation of Anselm's *Monologion* and *Proslogion,* which consists of a serial critique of three accounts of Anselm's argument, namely, Richard Campbell's, my own, and G. E. M. Anscombe's) could not make any clearer the extent to which he has failed to appreciate the connection between M 28 and P 3 and, thus, the radical point each is attempting to make. In response to Campbell's account, Hopkins insists: "What Anselm calls *true existence* varies with the context. In M 31 he refers to the Divine Word as true Existence (*veritas essentiae*). This point is an extension of his assertion, in M 28, that *in comparison with* the supreme spirit other things do not exist. (This point is associated with P 22, not with P 2 and 3)" (*A New, Interpretive Translation of St. Anselm's Monologion and Proslogion,* 307n.9). With respect to my account, he amplifies the above parenthetical remark by claiming that P 22 "has no more to do with the argument of *Proslogion* 2–4 than does the claim in *Proslogion* 15 that God is greater than can be thought" (24). Ironically, we will eventually want to show that the claim of P 15 has everything to do with the argument of P 2–4, as does P 22.

In any case, more fundamental than the failure to appreciate the relation of M 28 to P 3, and thus of P 3 to P 22, is the lack of appreciation of the philosophical subtleties of M 28 itself and of what is at issue in its pivotal claim that God alone exists. While Hopkins admits that the meaning of "true existence" varies with the context (and we are, of course, insisting that the relevant context for the *vere esse* in the title of P 2 is in reference to God), when it comes to M 31, which explicitly asserts that the supreme being alone enjoys true being, he claims that the appeal I have made to it simply compounds my error. For while I am, with Stolz, suggesting that the "true being" of God refers to his distinctive existence (a reading Hopkins himself endorsed in his earlier book on Anselm), Hopkins informs us that in M 31 Anselm is not speaking of what "truly exists" but of what exists "most truly" (311n.35). This, however, is simply to miss the point while making it. In M 31, Anselm is indeed discussing what exists most truly, namely, the supreme being, but the point is that he does not there speak in these terms, that is, he does not there refer to what *est verissime,* as

Hopkins would lead one to believe, but to what enjoys "true and simply be-ing" (*vera simplicemque essentiam*), which, I have contended, connects the reference to "true being" in M 31 to the reference to "absolute and simple being" in M 28. In this context, and in view of the ontological reversal of M 28, Anselm does not, in M 31, speak of God in the comparative or the super-lative but in terms of the absolute positive, that is, he does not refer to what exists "more truly" or "most truly" but simply and absolutely to what alone enjoys "true" being.

At the same time, all the controversy about the various uses of *vere esse* in Anselm should not distract us from what I take to be the philosophi-cal—not merely philological—justification for my reading of the relation of P 2 to P 3 based on Anselm's understanding of what it is for God to exist. Even if the word "truly" did not appear in the title of P 2, the fact that Anselm intended to demonstrate the absolutely unique existence relevant to God alone would be clear from a procedure that carries the argument on in P 3. Hopkins only confirms his failure to grasp the radical nature of the ontological insight in M 28, as well as its relationship to P 3, when he in-sists that Anselm holds to the doctrine of the analogy of being, warning us that "Anselm dare not be confused with someone such as Nicholas of Cusa, who teaches that there is no comparative relation between creator and creature, that God exists *most* greatly of all without existing *more* greatly than anything" (20). But this surely is the point of Anselm's assertion that God alone exists, even if he must, for strategic reasons, attempt to moder-ate this claim while insisting upon it. M 31, as we have seen, as part and parcel of what I have called the reinstatement of beings after their ontologi-cal obliteration, aims precisely to assert this ontological asymmetry, first produced by M 28, in its claim that creatures are a likeness of God, but not the other way around. In this sense, properly speaking, while it may be said that beings exist less truly than God, the point in M 31 is that God does not exist more truly than creatures but simply and absolutely and alone truly ex-ists. And it is my contention that all that is entailed by the *Monologion*'s ontological vision of God has been packed into the conclusion drawn in P 3, even if we will need to do some further unpacking to show this.

51. S I, 49.

52. S II, 10.

53. This may turn out to be the paradigm case, as God is so often for Anselm, in which reason's supposed access to reality, including its claim to enjoy access to the essential reality of things in other cases, is grounded— the exception that not only proves but also provides the rule.

54. S I, 45. We need not go into the reasons why Anselm would have thought that there can be one and only one such being. Suffice it to say that any other such being would have to have the same characteristics, in which case, since nothing could be accidental, there would be no basis for distin-guishing between the two. Anselm, of course, thinks that he has already shown that there can be only one being that "exists through itself" in his initial arguments in the *Monologion* and that this feature is entailed by the claim that something "cannot be thought not to exist."

55. Hopkins's new translation has pointed to an ambiguity in the "*sic esse deum*" of the concluding line (*Qui ergo intelligit sic esse deum, nequit eum non esse cogitare*), which he regards as referring not to the way in which God exists, as it has in the previous line (. . . *id ipsum sic esse ut nec cogitatione queat non esse*), but to the fact that "God is such [a being]," namely, than which none greater can be thought. This reading is encouraged by the fact that the *sic* in the final line occurs without a *sic . . . ut* construction. Such a grammatical transformation aims to render the second clause as a claim about the one who is doing the understanding, not about the nature of the being of God. As I have pointed out elsewhere, it is not, however, clear why Hopkins takes this as a reference to an earlier line rather than to the line immediately preceding this one. Even if the concluding line should be read to be claiming that "God is such [a being]," it is not clear why the sort of being he is then presumed to be is not the sort that "itself so exists that it cannot even for thought not exist." Instead, Hopkins skips back to the line before this one to insist that the concluding line is claiming that God is something than which nothing greater can be thought.

Needless to say, I would be happy enough with the characteristically "disambiguated" reading that Hopkins provides, since it would serve to stress the necessary identification of God with S, that is, it would emphasize that the argument ultimately turns on understanding that God is such a being. Thus these last three lines would capture the whole of the argument: the first beginning from the key claim with which it begins in P 2, the second expressing the conclusion of the single argument that spans P 2–3, and the third demanding that the argument bring us to a true understanding of the nature of God as "such a being," namely, as one that is something than which nothing greater can be thought precisely because it alone exists such that it cannot be thought not to exist. Just how this understanding results in the conclusion we want to claim follows from the argument, given all the aspects at work in it, should emerge from our own highlighting of another grammatical transformation at play in these final lines.

56. We should, then, not be altogether unsympathetic with those who would claim that God's nonexistence is logically impossible, and that this feature is unique to the sort of being Anselm claims to have sighted, so long as we realize that his contentions in P 3 and elsewhere depend upon a psychological account of logic. Thus, one would have to admit that, for Anselm, conceptions of the mind are mental formations or psychological events such that the inconceivability of something is determined by the inability of the mind to form a conception of it. Consider, in this connection, reply 1 and its talk of what cannot "in actuality or in thought" (*nec actu nec intellectu*) not exist (S I, 131). If the claim we are about to make looks inconsistent with this, it may be because there is an inconsistency in Anselm on the meaning of what it is for something to be "unthinkable." In this respect, G. B. Matthews's critique ("On Conceivability in Anselm and Malcolm") of Malcolm's reading of the "cannot be thought" in P 3—that Anselm's contention that something "cannot be thought not to exist" must be a psychological claim, or else in P 15 when Anselm claims that God is greater than can be thought, the conclusion that he cannot be thought would mean that he is logically impossible—while making a point against Malcolm, may be missing a point that needs to be made against Anselm.

57. I would distinguish this sense of a "psychological" account from what might be called psychopathological accounts of the ontological argument, which may attribute the argument to a guilt complex or to the need one might have, as a result of being rejected by his mother, for a dependable ground, etc. See, as an example of this sort of account, Lewis Feuer, "God, Guilt, and Logic: The Psychological Basis of the Ontological Argument." We are thinking, instead, of a set of cognitive experiences that surround the logic of the argument, not as if the reasoning were caused by certain psychological experiences but as if certain psychological experiences were produced by its reasoning. The compulsion of such experiences would, of course, not be irrelevant to a tradition of logic that assumed itself to be trading in the psychological forms of thought. I might add that Anselm's further "psychologizing" of the traditional modal categories, through the inclusion of the term "thought" (in which, that is, what is impossible is not the nonexistence of God, but the thought of his nonexis-tence) certainly serves the function that Henry has rightly pointed out, namely, to distinguish God from all else, including other "necessary beings" (*Logic of St. Anselm*), even if he has not drawn the same conclusion from this (in his account in "*Proslogion* Chapter 3") as we would.

58. One critical difference is that whereas those later arguments begin with a concept of God, Anselm begins from the words of his key phrase and leads us to a certain conception of the mind. The fact that the *Proslogion* argument does not begin from a concept of God has led Jean-Luc Marion to deny that Anselm offers what will later in the tradition be characterized as an ontological argument. See his "Is the Ontological Argument Ontological?" Marion, however, can maintain such an account only by ignoring P 4 and skipping over to the later claim that God is greater than can be thought. We will have reason to disagree with his account of this later portion of the *Proslogion* as well.

For a somewhat different view than mine of the relation of Anselm to the modern tradition, see Gerald Galgan's *God and Subjectivity*.

59. S I, 100.

60. S II, 40.

61. Robert Sokolowski, in *The God of Faith and Reason,* has made something like this point in the name of Anselm in claiming that God plus the world can be no greater than God. Obviously, if the creator were made any greater by his creation, then, as something than which nothing greater can be thought, he could not be thought without it. In this sense, one might say that to maintain his own identity God must create ontologically inferior beings. As Anselm himself will say in P 20 in considering how it is that God is "beyond" all things, "they could not in any way exist without you, whereas you would be in no way less even if they returned to nothing" (S I, 115).

We might also note, in this regard, the problem with Jasper Hopkins's insistence that it is not until P 5 that Anselm has a right to contend that there is one and only one being than which none greater can be thought. He thinks this must be based on the claim that S "alone exists through itself and creates all else from nothing" (see his *New, Interpretive Translation of St. Anselm's Monologion and Proslogion,* 10ff.). But while the initial characterization—which does constitute a claim to uniqueness insofar as Anselm thinks there can only be one being that exists *per se*—is entailed by the claim that something cannot be thought not to exist, the additional contention that it created all else from nothing is not entailed by its being something than which nothing greater can be thought. Moreover, Hopkins's account ignores the fact that the talk in P 5 of "the highest all" (*summum omnium solum existens per seipsum*) is itself a reference to the second half of P 3, which, as we have suggested, could be presumed to support the claim that all other beings must come from nothing, or at least do not exist through themselves, insofar as they can be thought not to exist.

62. As we have indicated, the tradition of extracting and segregating Anselm's argument from the remainder of the *Proslogion* is virtually as old as the text itself. During Anselm's lifetime, P 2–4, together with Gaunilo's response and Anselm's replies, circulated separately under the title *Sumptum ex eodem libello* (S I, 123).

63. S I, 118. The scriptural reference is to 1 Cor. 15:44. We might remind the reader that the biblical citations Anselm weaves into his text are indicated in our translation by italics.

64. It is worth noting that this centering on the sensual presence of God may also be thought to occur in the sacrament of the eucharist. In his "Prayer Before Receiving the Body and Blood of Christ" (S III, 10), Anselm speaks (again with reference to Paul, this time to Phil. 3:21) of the cleansing of our "lowly body" (*corpus humilitatis*) in its transfiguration in accord with the "glorified body" of Christ at the resurrection, and of the "eternal joy" that is promised to follow from this. In a similar vein, the ninth-century writer Paschasius Radbertus claims, in his *Liber de corpore et sanguine domini,* that "if the five senses of the body are inwardly converted to what are spiritually intelligible, because we know aright or perceive aright, the divine spirit which is in us is also enhanced by the same grace and teaches and increases those senses of ours to perceive them. So also, of course, to entice inwardly to the mystical reality not only taste but also sight and hearing as well as smell and touch, in some manner it reveals that nothing is felt in them save the divine" (II, 2). I should take this opportunity to thank Irv Resnick not only for providing me with the latter passage, but also for his comments on my translation of Anselm.

65. For example, in the question of the relation between God's justice and his mercy in P 8–11.

66. S I, 98 (1 Tim. 6:16).

67. Needless to say, the sense in which God has failed to appear "as a whole" is not the sense in which an object of perception appears as a whole through our multiple perspectives on it. In the visual perception of an object, an intuition of the "singleness" of the object is given in the intuition of its aspects. It is, apparently, just this "single" intuition, that is, the intuition of singleness, that Anselm lacks in the intuition of God's various features.

68. In fact, the original occasion for the introduction of the notion of God's inaccessibility in P 1 is based upon the question of his omnipresence: "Lord, if you are not here, where should I seek you in your absence? And if you are everywhere, why do I not see you in your presence? Surely *you dwell in inaccessible light*" (S I, 98).

69. On the dilation of the eye of the mind with respect to the vision of the creator in the diminishing of creation, I would refer the reader once again to the passage cited earlier from St. Gregory on Benedict's mystical experience. For a concrete illustration of the defocal element of visual perception and of its recent exploitation in the visual arts, see my "Overpowering the Center: Three Compositions by Mondrian."

| **Rational Theology and
the Historical Revelation of God**

Ironically, the full import of the scarcely spoken assumptions at the root of such meditational works as the *Monologion* and *Proslogion* surfaces later in Anselm's own writings, when those assumed conditions no longer obtain. Once Anselm can no longer presuppose the practices of a sympathetic monastic community, once he is confronting a hostile world that does not share his interest in elevating the mind to the contemplation of God or his confidence in reason, in short, once Anselm loses his innocence, he must make clear the assumed conditions for the practice of rational understanding that are at issue in his work. For example, in the more apologetic writings of the 1090s, such as the *Letter on the Incarnation of the Word,* where Anselm is responding to the criticisms of Roscilinus, or in *Why God Became Man,* where he is attempting to explain the incarnation to a more general audience, Anselm must provide an interpretation, or at least an indication, of how he thinks reasoning works insofar as he can no longer assume the good faith of dialecticians or assume that they see reason as an element in the ascent to the vision of God.[1]

In fact, with respect to the *Cur deus homo,* a text whose radical rational theology presumes to demonstrate the necessity of a God-man not just *sola ratione* but *remoto Christo*—that is, without reference to Christ, "as if he had never been heard of"[2]—Anselm finds himself defending the right of reason to be employed in theological matters. In a commendation of the work to Pope Urban II, Anselm insists:

> Since the apostles, many of our holy fathers and teachers have said such a great deal about the rational ground of our faith—

not only to confound the foolishness and break the hardheart-
edness of unbelievers, but to nourish those whose hearts, once
cleansed by faith, might take joy in its rational ground, after
whose certitude we ought to hunger—that while we would not
expect, in our time or in the future, anyone to equal them in
their contemplation of the truth, one should in no way be
viewed with reprehension if, stable in faith, he desires to engage in the investigation of its rational ground. Indeed, since
"the days of man are short," not only were [the holy fathers]
not able to say all that they could have if they had lived longer,
but the rational ground of truth is so vast and so deep that it
cannot be exhausted by mortals, even as, within his church,
with which the lord promised to stay "until the end of the
world," he does not cease to impart the gifts of his grace. And—
to mention just one passage in which the sacred page invites us
to rational investigation—when it says, "unless you believe,
you will not understand," it clearly instructs us to direct our
attention to understanding, in that it teaches the manner in
which we ought to proceed to such understanding. For since I
understand the understanding of which we are capable in this
life to be midway between faith and direct vision, I take it that
the more one advances to understanding, the closer they are
to the sight for which we all long.

Comforted, then, by these considerations, even though I am
a man of meager knowledge, I strive to be in some way elevated,
to the extent to which supernal grace deigns to grant it to me, so
that I may behold the rational ground for what we believe. And
when I expose something that I have not seen before, I disclose
it freely to others so that I may learn, through the judgment of
another, what I ought to securely maintain.

Consequently, my father and lord, Pope Urban, who is loved
with reverence and revered with love by all Christians, and
whom the providence of God has established as the supreme
pontiff within his church, since I can to no one more fittingly, I
present the enclosed work for the scrutiny of your holiness, so
that, by your authority, what is here to be accepted might be
approved, and what is to be corrected might be amended. (S II,
39–41)

Obviously, the vocabulary of this passage carries us across the
course of Anselm's thought that we have covered, from its mention
of a meditation on the rational ground of faith to the talk of nourish-
ing the hearts of the faithful with the joy of rational elevation, right
through to the characterization of the role of understanding in its
dealings with that vast and profound truth, as midway between the
blindness of faith and the vision complete in the life to come.[3] Not so
obvious, however, is the most extreme claim suggested here, which
is barely detectable in its concealment within a list of reasons for
reasoning. Not only does the passage aim to place its readers, historically speaking, between the original revelation, to which the
apostles and church fathers were closer, and the Second Coming,

when Christ returns to claim his faithful and to which Anselm no doubt assumed his historical audience to be near, but it also reminds us of Christ's promise to remain with his church "until the end of the world." In the present context, the claim that he "does not cease to impart the gifts of his grace" can only be regarded as suggesting that, in the sort of disclosure of truth that reason allows for, we receive a kind of continuous historical revelation of and from God. Unlike the revelation of faith, which is once and for all, the revelation of God through reason is ongoing, like the day-to-day clarification of the God of truth Anselm prays for in P 26 or the illumination he thanks God for at the conclusion of P 4, even if the grace that grants both faith and understanding is the gift of the same truth that is the second person of the Trinity.

On this account, it would be no coincidence, although it would again be a rather extreme allusion in the midst of an only apparent humility, that Anselm has found a way to commend his project of a rational theology to the pope by designating the latter as the one whom "divine providence" has empowered, no doubt to determine what is providential. By commending his work to the final arbiter of revelation, Anselm would seem to be suggesting that his own writings are of such a nature that no one could be more fitting to judge them than the one authorized by God to determine what is or is not consistent with providential history. Moreover, as the passage leading to this conclusion would seem to indicate, in submitting his work to the head of the body of believers that is the church, Anselm's claim that the aim of writing and circulating his text is both to reveal to others what he has discovered and to allow it to be accessed by them implies that the project of rational theology is not just a personal matter but a collective dialogue that may result in securing an ongoing revelation of God in history through rational dispute. While it is noteworthy, then, that Anselm had to defend the use of reason in theological matters to others in the church, even more remarkable, although less noticeable, is the way in which he is defending it, namely, through the prospect of the continuous rational revelation of God in history.

Needless to say, this latter claim is supposed to provide the justification for a strictly rational theology, even if it raises the question of whether Anselm's later texts do any such thing or whether the *Monologion* and the *Proslogion* alone constitute his properly theophantic works—in which there is a revelation of God by means of reason—against whose standard he makes his claims about what theology should be up to. Is it, in other words, Anselm's mystical approach in the *Proslogion* that provides the basis for his own later, more apologetic, indeed, more scholastic, works? And does its rational revelation of God, secured through monastic contemplation, still serve to justify the later application of reason in this other, more worldly context after Anselm has left the prayer cell and is defending the faith to the world at large? In short, is the *Proslogion* Anselm's most historic work because it provides a rational vision of God that supplies a foundation for the use of reason, not only in his later writings but also in the scholasticism they ultimately bred? And is this why the text called for a new genre of writing to present its rational mysticism in the form of a philosophical prayer that begins by redefining the role of reason in a mystical history? The one thing that is clear is that the *Proslogion's* intertwining of prayer and proof shows on its face the extent to which Anselm stands between traditions, between the two extremes of monastic mysticism and scholastic rationality. As both the original title of the *Proslogion* and the above passage would indicate, the aim of Anselm's work is the development of an understanding that seeks a form of rational insight that is continuous with the face-to-face vision in the life to come. It is not only a middle ground between the blindness of faith and the vision complete but is already on the way to "the joy of the lord," such that the rational meditator is nourished in this life by a taste of the vision promised in the next.[4]

While the point of such a rational mysticism has, I trust, by now become sufficiently clear, the more pressing question is why Anselm confines his mysticism to the rational even while confessing its limitations. No doubt, the answer to this is connected to a question that we have already addressed, namely, why Anselm's rationality must be mystical, that is, why the approach of proceeding *sola ratione* must contain these visionary features. I have suggested that Anselm retains these mystical elements in his work because of the tradition from out of which he is thinking and in view of the new tradition he aims to found. Given the historical situation, Anselm had to advance the method of seeking God by means of reason alone—perhaps to establish the basis for a renewed revelation of God after his failure to appear at the millennium—by grounding rational thought not simply in human deductive powers but in the visionary fulfillment that is the mark of truth for the sort of illuminatory epistemology he had inherited. In this respect, Anselm must be seen as the paradigm of a historically creative thinker, preserving a tradition through its transformation, advancing the possibility of a purely rational theology by showing that and how reason provides an access to truth that remains genuinely "theo-logical." The above passage not only documents Anselm's view of the prospect for another kind of historical appearance of God through ongoing rational discourse but also provides some evidence of the awkward position he was in and of the suspicion that surrounded his procedure of using reason to interrogate the beliefs of the faithful.

As the pivotal thinker in medieval philosophy, flanked by Augustine, whose unsystematic but illuminating argumentation aims essentially at whetting our intuitions, and Aquinas, whose systematic reasoning expressly lacks vision, we find in Anselm a blending of logical rigor with mystical insight and a middle ground between an epistemology of direct illumination and the formal rationality whose inferences are, in their own way, as blind as faith. Clearly, the breadth of Anselm's thought from the sheerly analytical to the purely poetic is more extreme than in either of these two other giants of medieval philosophy, as the rigor of his reasoning is more unrelenting than anything we find in Augustine, while the poetry of his prayers demonstrates a passion that has no place in Aquinas. And putting aside, at least for the moment, the question of whether such breadth can serve as a lesson for a future philosophical theology, we want to insist that the basis for this blending of the analytic and the poetic may provide a response to the question we have not yet answered as to why Anselm's mysticism remains at the level of the rational. That response, however, requires us to appreciate that there must be an essentially poetic aspect to reason if, as Anselm claims, our conceiving of things, their expression in our thought, while tied to reality, does not simply involve the passive entertaining of static ideas. Instead, it demands the active formation, the creative formulation, in thought of images that allow the mind to sight the thing itself in the vision of thinking. In that case, we will have to pursue the question of how it is that reason is, for Anselm, in the business of image formation, even as we will have to show, no doubt in contrast to our ordinary assumptions about mysticism, that the production of images of God is at the heart of at least the sort of mystical vision Anselm achieves.

The understanding of Anselm's early writings that I have proposed should, then, not only allow us to consider the general relation between rationality and religious vision and to ask how the latter is generated by his famous argument; it will also force us to raise the question of the role that the historical formation of images of God might play in a philosophical theology, and just how such formations are possible. If what reasoning aims to accomplish, according to Anselm, is not just to draw deductive conclusions from a prescribed set of ideas but to struggle to form true likenesses of the things themselves in the mind, to scribe the reality itself in the vision of its thinking, then the dynamics of reasoning and the collective process of argumentation and disputation must be thought in its relation to the perfection of our inner vision. The question is how Anselm presumes to accomplish this in the case of God. For he does not appeal to illumination simply in terms of the direct contact of the mind with the second person of the Trinity,[5] nor does he expect another "face-to-face" revelation of God until the Second Coming. Instead, he proposes a certain rational revelation of God that may occur across a historical time that is itself timed by the coming of Christ, who, despite his failure to appear at the millennium, apparently continues to come, to impart the "gifts of his grace" to the faithful, until the end of the world.

Anselm's visionary epistemology stresses the human mind's active struggle to elevate its thinking to God by means of those formations of rational thought that allow it to entertain a likeness of the thing itself, while at the same time exploiting the passive determination of thought by reality in its inner vision of things, in the case in point, in the partial illuminations of the inner eye of the mind that the God of truth continues to impart while we await the end of history. We have so far only intimated why the rational mind must be inspired by prayer to such a vision of God, although we have tried to provide a sense of the nature of thinking as it is developed in the *Monologion* sufficient to allow us to appreciate what it might be to seek a rational vision of the things themselves within us. Later we will see more specifically how the poetic element of Anselm's thought, his creative use of language, induces us to such vision, not just in the prayers proper but in the formations of thought at work in the naming of God as "something than which nothing greater can be thought." The point just now is that the aim of Anselmian contemplation and of what we mean by his rational mysticism is neither a matter of some direct contact with God nor of proceeding blindly, as faith does no less than mere inference. For we do not need or mean to claim any direct revelation, since nothing in our view of Anselm's argument hinges on the immediate presence of God. On the contrary, everything hinges on the idea, or, as Anselm would say, on the generation of an image of God, once this likeness is regarded as a matter of inner experience, as the object of a certain kind of mental vision. What we are interested in, then, is the psychodynamics of Anselm's conception of God, given his visionary epistemology— the psychologic of the thought of God as Anselm thinks it and of the cognitive formations to which the rational mind must be inspired in forming such an image of the divine.

This, of course, is what I have argued is most at issue in the *Proslogion,* including in the process of reasoning that we call the ontological argument, although it is evident that this sort of mental construction or rational reconstruction of the human mind's conception of God is at work in the *Monologion* as well. In either case, the point is to give birth to an inner expression of the supreme being in the thought of one meditating on this unique matter, even if such presumed uniqueness has required us to attend to how the normal processes of rational thought must be disrupted or at least disturbed in thinking through this absolutely distinctive object of thought. The paradox remains that the only object the rational mind can sight as an "individual" is an object it cannot know or clearly see as it is—at least not yet. Such a view is not unique to Anselm, nor is he the only thinker in the history of Western thought to redeem reason through a confession of its limitations. But to appreciate exactly how he deals with such issues, we will have to understand why the overall strategy of the *Proslogion,* given its vision of God, requires the postponement of the vision complete until eternity, and how this deferral can serve to legitimate reason based on an object of thought, an object for its eyes only, that does not appear.

If we are to concentrate in what follows on a critique of Anselm's ontological argument as a matter of reason's revelation of God in a vision based upon the ecstatic clarity that rational thought can come to concerning his distinctive existence, then we must neither regard this famous proof as a mere exercise in logical cleverness nor assume it to be the expression of a mystical insight that is beyond rational evaluation. In my view, there is a specific vision of God embedded in Anselm's argument, but as its ultimate rational aim. While this visionary element may best be characterized by insisting that a certain mysticism is at work in its reasoning, the vision of God that the argument seeks is a logical matter, requiring that we think, in somewhat oxymoronic terms, of a rational mysticism. In this sense, not just the point of the argument but its entire strategy is founded upon the deployment of what M 10 calls "rational understanding," although the sorts of experiences of thinking this involves must be placed, as the *Proslogion* more clearly does, in the context of the practice of a mystical contemplation in which such understanding refers to a specific kind of mental vision. The reason I have insisted upon this, however, is not just because I believe such meditative thinking, and the rational insight it allows for, provides the basis for the ontological argument but because it is quite possible that these rational visions are not as fundamental as Anselm thinks. In that case, if we are to evaluate the argument at its deepest level, it will have to be in terms of the significance attached to those inner visions and associated with monastic contemplation, with the very "excitation" of the mind that begins in the prayer of P 1 and is intermittently extended throughout the text.

If it is primarily in and through the prayers of the *Proslogion,* which serve to enforce its mystical master-narrative, that rational thought is provided with a specific context for reading the cognitive experiences it is undergoing, then this poetic narrative forms an essential preface to the ontological argument. It initiates the circle of prayer and proof, in which a theological metanarrative provides the structure for our philosophical experience. Consequently, while we have tried to isolate an insight at the root of Anselm's reasoning that has phenomenological grounds in that it can be documented in the experiences of rational thought, it is precisely this religious vision that must be criticized if we are to provide a sufficiently penetrating evaluation of the argument. This can only be done by showing how such a vision of God has been produced. Given the depths of its foundation, it barely scratches the surface of the argument to launch attacks against its discursive dimension. For at the heart of the reasoning proper, preserved beneath and protected by its outer facade, is a conviction-producing clarity that, as history has shown, tends to result in the argument's repeated reformulation. At least in the minds of some, the intuitive insight at the root of the argument lives on, despite all attacks on its reasoning.

Getting at this deeper dimension of Anselm's argument to effect a more convincing critique of it has required us to take a rather complex approach to its interpretation. And just as our account has involved a certain balance between those four different approaches that we have loosely called the objective, the hermeneutical, the phenomenological, and the deconstructive, so too must our evaluation. It goes without saying that an objective interpretation of the argument is essential to the clarification of its logical elements—an aspect one would, no doubt, be expected to address in any philosophical criticism—while a hermeneutical approach is crucial to the philological establishment of the text that allows us to identify the single argument spanning P 2–3. In fact, if the logical evaluation of Anselm's reasoning will not play as exclusive a role in our account as it does in most, it is because we believe that critiques of Anselm have suffered from their failure to locate the whole of the argument. Only once we have identified its ultimate conclusion can we see how it is designed to afford a certain vision of God and thus move from the logical aspect of the argument to its phenomenological ground; just as our deconstructive account—which attempts to show how such rational experiences have been produced—can itself only then be confirmed in an objective criticism of the logic of the argument's reasoning.

Traditional criticisms of Anselm's argument have suffered from the fact that it has never been fully understood and therefore has been, in a strange way, protected from attack at the level of its basic insight. This has been oddly complicated by the fact that the intuition we claim to be at the root of the reasoning has, in some sense, remained operative in the very tradition that mislocated the argument. As we will show, the reasoning of P 2 has all along been drawing, however unconsciously, the same conclusion as the argument of P 3. In this way, those recent commentators who now claim that the essence of Anselm's argument is in P 3 may have unwittingly discovered that the argument of P 2 cannot stand alone but depends upon an insight that only becomes clear in P 3. This is not to deny that the tradition has all along been drawing its own unconscious inference, drawing out the implications of the fragment of the argument that survived and thus thinking on the basis of an insight it is not acknowledging—indeed, as our critique of the reasoning of P 2 will show, of which it could not altogether afford to be aware. In that case, however, if we have retrieved the original argument and identified its proper conclusion, we are at least, and at last, in a position to evaluate it at the level of an intuition that has finally been rendered explicit. Of course, arriving at this level of the argument, at its phenomenological basis, would seem to raise the question of how it is possible to criticize an insight, and for that we need to call upon other aspects of our interpretive approach. By having a closer look at the rational inducement of such cognitive visions and at the psychological nature of the experience itself, we should be able to see whether there is not, in fact, a questionable complicity at work between reason and the image of the God of which it has its vision. In so doing, we may be able to get at what remains "unthought" in the argument and, perhaps, in the tradition of rational onto-theology it serves to found.

Our ultimate phenomenological aim, then, in isolating a specific cognitive experience at the heart of Anselm's reasoning is to raise the question of whether it is to be counted as veridical, whether the insight into being itself, produced through a certain conversion essential to the ontological argument, is a valid experience of thinking. This phenomenological element is not, despite my emphasis on the practice of rational contemplation, just a medieval issue. It is an issue for anyone who has ever been struck by the power of so simple an argument. For among the strangest features of the ontological proof is the fact that some of the subtler minds in our history have found it thoroughly convincing, while other equally profound thinkers have found it altogether unconvincing, and vehemently so—as if it were as insipid an argument as the *insipiens* it is supposedly addressing—while yet others have disagreed with themselves, at some time having been convinced by it, at another time not.[6] This, I think, is not just because philosophers can never agree on anything, including with themselves. Instead, it says something about the elusively "insightful" nature of the argument and of the basis for our continuing fascination with it.

To appreciate what might be at issue in the strong attraction that the argument has had for some but not for others (an element Anselm himself touches on in P 4), we will have to attend to what I call its conviction-producing aspect. While the discussion of the logic of Anselm's argument should, no doubt, give us an opportunity to treat such issues in terms of the soundness or unsoundness of a reasoning process that may not appear to have changed in its procedures since the eleventh century as much as it has changed in its nature, this must not distract us from the question of why the *Proslogion,* and especially its famous argument, has had the sort of lasting attraction it has in our history. Needless to say, the answer to this question will in part involve the contention that the argument is grounded in a certain transhistorical insight that its reasoning is designed to elicit. In that case, the continual attempt to revise the argument long after it, as well as the historical world to which it belongs, may have appeared to be dead and gone can be seen to be grounded in its phenomenological aspect, in the argument's inducing, indeed, producing, certain cognitive experiences that may remain intuitively effective throughout its discursive reformulations and that can be reproduced by structuring the text of the argument differently so as to accommodate the insight to its new historical surroundings. In this sense, the rational intuition at the heart of the ontological argument has been literally carried on through acts of preservation right up to the present day in the various attempts to retrieve the argument, including its translation into that most modern of modern languages: symbolic logic. This quantum leap that reason has recently taken from natural to artificial languages has implications for both logic and the philosophy of mind that are so far-ranging and range so far beyond the scope of the present study that they can scarcely be intimated in what follows. At the same time, in that perverse reading against the grain of the text that will allow us to attack its reasoning from behind, we will not only press the essentially psychological—or, as we will want eventually to say, psycholinguistic—element of the argument, but will also address certain narratological issues. This should at least raise the question of whether such reasoning, symbolic or otherwise, would have any meaning at all without the surrounding narrative, even if in Anselm's case the theological story that reason recites in the dark of its own groundlessness is quite a bit different from the one it these days tells itself to legitimate its logistics.

In that event, we may well find that the rational experiences of thinking documented in the *Proslogion* do not have the same meaning for us that they did for Anselm. This, in turn, will not rule out the possibility of a revision of his work if our aim in interpreting his early writings is to learn something from them that may be as relevant to the future of philosophical theology as their founding of a rational theology was to its past. Such a historic appreciation of Anselm, however, will require that we take advantage of all four approaches in our critique of his thought in a balance that results not simply in the summation of them all but in that behind-the-scenes appreciation which we have presumed to follow from understudying his writing. We would, then, like the order of our evaluation to follow the order of interpretation. Beginning with a logical critique of Anselm's argument, we will be led through this attack, at some points from behind, to the more phenomenological and, in this sense alone, psychological claims surrounding its reasoning. After this destructive assault, we will try to determine what historical validity the argument may nonetheless be said to enjoy in view of a certain deconstructive renovation that should not only put us in a position to suggest where we stand, historically speaking, but may well force a revision of our understanding of the historical mission we have seen Anselm propose for a genuinely philosophical theology.

| Evaluating Anselm's Argument

We never really completed our discussion of the reasoning of P 2, since we not only withheld any evaluation of it in our account but also left hanging the question of the possible ambiguity between conceptual and factual uses of "exist" within the argument itself. Needless to say, we postponed our evaluation in order to continue the discussion unimpeded, even though I am of the view that P 2 is riddled by any number of problems, including a rather innocent but fatal flaw that centers around this distinction of which Anselm was apparently unaware. We need not belabor the point, not only because it has been made by others[7] but because we will want to concentrate on certain implications of the distinction that have been overlooked. Nonetheless, we must begin by noticing that given the very nature of the argument itself, as a conceptual analysis of "something than which nothing greater can be thought," it would seem that the conclusion of P 2 can itself be nothing more than a conceptual clarification, like the reminder that nonfictional characters exist both in the understanding and in reality, which is not to be regarded as a factual claim when it is taken to be clarifying a type of thing. Consequently, one could agree with the strictly conceptual conclusion that something than which nothing greater can be thought exists both in the understanding and in reality and still not admit that anything, in fact, exists.

Some indication of the conceptual force of the argument and conclusion of P 2 is, I think, revealed in what we have called the modal element of its reasoning, which has it that matters cannot be otherwise, that is, that S cannot exist in the understanding alone. Such "impossibility" may suggest that we are not dealing simply with matters of fact but with conceptual issues, like the case of a nonfictional character that cannot exist in the understanding alone precisely because if it did, it would no longer be a nonfictional character. Of course, as we have just said, we could well agree that this conceptual claim is true and nonetheless insist that there are, in fact, no nonfictional characters, that none actually exist, or, as we put it, that nothing is a nonfictional character. Similarly, as far as the argument of P 2 goes, we could agree that given the nature of something than which nothing greater can be thought, it cannot exist in the understanding alone—for if it did it would not be something than which nothing greater can be thought—and still contend that there is nothing of such a nature, as P 2 itself puts it. For if Anselm begins his argument by getting us to think of a type of thing, of the nature of "something than which nothing greater can be thought," then if we are shown that existence must be said to pertain to the type of thing it is, or at least that the attribution of nonexistence leads to contradiction, then we can conclude that such a kind of thing cannot exist in the understanding alone, insofar as existence is relevant to its type, without our needing to concede that there is anything of that type.[8]

Once we concede the possibility that P 2's conclusion may be other than the one Anselm thinks—as it never occurred to him that there is a distinction between factual and conceptual uses of "exist"—we may well be inclined to look back at the argument of P 2 itself to see just where the slippage occurs that allows for a result so riddled with ambiguity. And when we do, we may find that conceptual uses of "exist" are not as comparable to factual uses as they might appear to be. For the former do not so much show or express what is the case about the world as they clarify how our concepts are laid out. They are, in other words, grammatical clarifications.[9] In effect, then, to employ a conceptual use of "exist" is not to attribute a certain kind of existence to some possible object but to clarify how a term is to be used and thus how we are to think about, or what can sensibly be said about, for example, nonfictional characters in contrast to fictional characters. The claim that nonfictional characters exist both in the understanding and in reality simply reminds us that, in a certain conceptual or linguistic system, if the term "nonfictional" is to be applied to anything, that thing must at some time have existed in reality. But, then, to say that nonfictional characters exist in reality is not to say that there are any such things but to say that whether there are any or not, they would have to be conceived of as existing insofar as existence is relevant to their conception.

If an analogous sort of conceptual analysis is going on in P 2, then not only should it show up in the argument, but it would have certain implications for its reasoning, if, as we have suggested, conceptual cases of existence have a logic of their own. And we would, no doubt, expect it to show up in the *reductio*. In fact, we earlier noted a certain questionable moment related to the ambiguity between conceptual and factual uses of "exist" in that section of the reasoning of P 2 that aims to show that S cannot exist in the understanding alone by contending that if it did, a greater could be thought. For convenience, let me repeat here my schematization of the argument:

1. God is something than which nothing greater can be thought.
2. "Something than which nothing greater can be thought" is understood when it is heard.
3. Whatever is understood exists in the understanding.
4. Whatever exists in the understanding either exists in the understanding alone or exists both in the understanding and in reality.
5. That than which a greater cannot be thought cannot exist in the understanding alone:
   a. Assume it exists in the understanding alone.
   b. Then it can be thought to exist in reality also, which is greater.
   c. Thus, if it exists in the understanding alone, it is that than which a greater can be thought.
   d. But then, that than which a greater cannot be thought is that than which a greater can be thought; which is absurd.
   e. So premise 5 is shown.
6. Therefore, without doubt, something than which a greater cannot be thought exists both in the understanding and in reality.

In our earlier discussion of the move made in 5 a–b, we conceded that for the comparison between what exists in the understanding alone and what exists in reality to have sufficient force, Anselm would not need to assume the factual existence of anything. If it is greater to exist in reality than in the understanding alone, then, for example, we would be thinking of something greater if we were thinking of nonfictional rather than fictional characters, whether or not any such characters actually existed. At this level of the argument, it is strictly a matter of what can be thought.

Our attention, however, to this virtue of Anselm's argument—that it need not, as Gaunilo's version does, appeal to any matters of fact—may have distracted us from a problem concealed in the space between the assumption for the *reductio* and its next step.[10] While beginning predictably enough by supposing the opposite of what is to be shown (namely, that S exists in the understanding alone), the reasoning of the *reductio* proceeds with a presumed comparison to what "can be thought to exist in reality also," as if it follows from the formal supposition that S can be thought to exist in the understanding alone. Needless to say, unless it is conceivable that S exists in the understanding alone, it is not the case that something greater is being thought when we think of it or of anything existing in reality; indeed, there would be no comparison at issue at all. But supposing that S exists in the understanding alone is quite a bit different from conceiving of it as existing in the understanding alone. The one is a logical supposition, while the other is a psychological proposition.

Here it may help to recall the basic difference between Gaunilo's version and Anselm's own argument. Anselm protests against Gaunilo's characterization of his reasoning as contending that "that which is greater than everything" must exist if "whatever else exists" is not to be greater than it. I have suggested that Anselm objects to such a revision because, given Gaunilo's transformation of the key phrase, it is conceivable that that which is greater than everything exists in the understanding alone, since all we need do is imagine that nothing else exists. In that case, it is not a conceptual contradiction to assume that it does not exist, but only a factual impossibility, given that something else exists. In short, "that which is greater than everything" both can not-exist and can be thought not to exist. In Anselm's account of his own argument, however, the claim made in the name of something than which nothing greater can be thought is much stronger than this, as is emphasized in his own revisions of P 2 in reply 1, which stress its modal character, resulting in the contention that S both cannot not-exist and cannot be thought not to exist. The contradiction in P 2 is not generated by appealing to anything else, let alone to some fact about the world to which S is to be compared, but by appealing to the way the conception of S existing in the understanding alone, when compared to the conception of it or anything existing in reality, is the conception of something than which a greater can be thought, in which case, the nonexistence of S is shown to be conceptually, not just factually, impossible.

No doubt, the criterion of conceivable greatness, rather than factual greatness, provides the subtle but critical twist to Anselm's argument, as the "can be thought" of something than which nothing greater can be thought—and thus the form of the argument it allows for—lends it a certain conceptual force. But this may turn out to be a self-defeating power if it rules out the conceivability of S existing in the understanding alone. While Anselm's argument avoids the factual assumption that something other than S actually exists, P 2 must depend upon generating a contradiction in view of the very conception of something than which nothing greater can be thought. It does this, of course, by substituting for the factual claim that something exists the contention that something greater can be thought than S existing in the understanding alone; that is, the claim is not that there would be something greater than S if it did not exist, but that something greater can be thought than S existing in the understanding alone. This, however, requires that the presumed comparison operate at the level of conceivability, such that for something greater to be thought than S existing in the understanding alone its existence in the understanding alone must be conceivable. Unless there is some conceivable alternative to its being thought to exist in reality, there simply will be no comparison being made, in which case, something greater is not being thought when we think of S or anything as existing in reality. In short, something greater than S existing in the understanding alone cannot be thought if S cannot be thought to exist in the understanding alone.

Although it may already be clear that I would eventually like to suggest that the conceptual force of P 2 amounts to the demonstration of the inconceivability of S existing in the understanding alone, we can make our present point in terms of its claim to the impossibility of S existing in the understanding alone. In fact, one might think that our complaint about the logic of a comparison based on an unthinkable alternative is itself limited to the *reductio* as it stands, as it would be rather easy to revise the argument in such a way as to avoid this pitfall.[11] And while we are more interested in Anselm's own argument than in opening the Pandora's box of revisions of it that could be offered, I have suggested, in my own account of the basic principle standing behind the critical claim of P 2, a way in which a contradiction might be generated without comparing the conception of S existing in the understanding alone with the conception of it or anything existing in reality. If the general principle Anselm exploits is that, for any X, if X exists in the understanding alone, a greater can be thought, then what he is claiming is simply that something than which nothing greater can be thought cannot exist in the understanding alone, or else it would be something than which a greater can be thought. On this basis, he need not conceive of S existing in the understanding alone so as to compare it to what exists in reality to determine which is greater, but he may establish the general principle, presumably from other cases, and then apply it to the case of S.

This, however, raises the question of whether, even if we concede the general principle, it might not only properly apply to what can exist in the understanding alone; that is, it is not clear that it can be intelligibly applied to S if S cannot exist in the understanding alone and, indeed, cannot even be thought to exist in the understanding alone. While it may make sense to claim that if something exists in the understanding alone, a greater can be thought, it is not altogether clear what it would mean to contend that if something could exist in the understanding alone, a greater can be thought. For while we may well have enough trouble understanding logically just what it means to say that if what is not the case were the case, or could be the case, such and such would follow, it is not clear what it means to think—let alone know what would follow from the claim—that if what cannot be the case could be the case, certain things would follow.[12] I suppose one might assume that all that is required is that we can think to be the case what cannot be the case. But if the "cannot" at issue does not express a factual, but a conceptual, impossibility, then this requirement would itself reveal the assumption that Anselm must be making, namely, that we can think that S exists in the understanding alone such that we can intelligibly determine what would follow from it.

We are, of course, raising two different, but related, issues. The one is a question of comparison, the other a question of relevance. In either event, we need to remember that Anselm's argument requires recourse to a rather strange sort of case for it to work. To avoid the Kantian contention that existence is not pertinent to the determination of a concept, we have had to consider some unusual examples in which it apparently is. But when we do, we must appreciate that they are not like ordinary cases in any number of ways—not just in the ones to which Anselm would no doubt like to draw our attention—and that this is precisely why these conceptual arguments may be put to work on their behalf. In effect, while Anselm wants to exploit the extraordinary case, he also wants to assume that the logic of ordinary cases can be applied to it. It is, however, not at all clear that the logic of factual cases of existence applies in conceptual cases.

For example, the presumption, in ordinary factual cases, that something can be thought as existing or as not existing would not apply to conceptual cases; that is, we cannot think of existence-relevant concepts as we would existence-neutral concepts. If a mirage turns out to exist, it can no longer be thought of as a mirage, in which case, it makes no sense to compare an existent with a nonexistent mirage, nor, therefore, is it clear that it makes sense to say that a mirage would have been greater had it existed in reality. Similarly, if we are asked to conceive of a nonfictional character that never existed, we cannot presume to be able to compare him to a nonfictional character that has at some time existed; for if something has never existed, it is simply not a nonfictional character, nor could we intelligibly think that a nonfictional character that does not exist would not be as great as one who does. And while we might suppose that we are thinking that nonfictional characters are greater than fictional characters if the former exist in reality, this is possible in that case precisely because there is a thinkable alternative to nonfictional characters, that is, P 2's general principle may seem relevant to the fictional/nonfictional distinction.

Whether it is relevant to "something than which nothing greater can be thought"—and, thus, whether the latter is altogether analogous to the nonfictional character case—is a topic we will address shortly. Before turning to the question of relevance, we want to press another point out of the problems involved in the comparison in P 2 in order to show just what may be hidden in the inference at issue there. To do that, we must notice not only that the conceiving of S as existing in the understanding alone may be impossible but that the elements of the comparison would seem to be incompatible insofar as 5a speaks of what "exists" in the understanding alone, while 5b speaks of what "can be thought" to exist in reality. Thus, 5a appears to assert an ontological claim, while 5b appeals to what is conceivable. In this way, one might assume that the conception of S existing in the understanding alone is not an issue, since Anselm has a right, given the *form* of the argument, to suppose that S exists in the understanding alone as a supposition he aims to show is impossible. This, however, would only be admissible if the *content* of his argument did not depend upon a conceivability that is not entailed by the formal assumption. In other words, once having made the logical supposition that S exists in the understanding alone, Anselm cannot proceed as if he were entertaining a conception of S existing in the understanding alone. Moreover, if we are, in any case, to be comparing two conceptions such that something greater will be thought when we think the one rather than the other, not only can we not compare a conception with a supposition, but we cannot compare a conception with a state of affairs; that is, we can no more compare the "supposition" that S exists in the understanding alone with the "conception" of something that exists in reality than we can the "thought" of what exists in reality with the "fact" of S existing in the understanding alone. Instead, we would have to compare the conception of S existing in the understanding alone with the conception of S existing in reality. As it stands, however, the former conception is not supplied by the supposition for the *reductio,* nor can it be validly inferred from it.

To correct for this, Anselm could begin his *reductio* not with the supposition that S exists in the understanding alone but with the assumption that S can be thought to exist in the understanding alone. In that case, rather than assuming that the supposition that S exists in the understanding alone guarantees its conceivability, he would have to suppose the conception of S existing in the understanding alone. In some sense, the form of argument that the phrase "something than which nothing greater can be thought" elicits surreptitiously invites this assumption, just as it leads to the talk of what "can be thought" to exist in reality also. And while the argument may well speak as if what were at issue is the fact of S existing in the understanding alone, insofar as it is operating at the level of what can be thought, it is actually trading on the conception. Ironically, the conceptual element is masked at this point in the argument as a result of the conditions set up by its key phrase in that the "can be thought" in step 5b does not belong to the content of the comparison, but to the form of the argument. Anselm is not claiming that S is greater if it "can be thought to exist in reality," but that something greater "can be thought" than what exists in the understanding alone, namely, what exists in reality. In that case, it may appear that we are comparing fact with fact, or the thought of a certain state of affairs (it can be thought that S or something exists in reality) with the thought of another state of affairs (it can be thought that S exists in the understanding alone), to determine which is greater. But the argument, as it stands, has simply created the appearance of comparability by treating the supposition for the *reductio* as if it were a conception whose content could be compared to another conceivable state of affairs while maintaining the appearance that the comparison of one "fact" to another operates strictly at the level of what "can be thought" thanks to the form of argument that the content of the key phrase allows.

In any event, the contention that S can be thought to exist in the understanding alone must either be regarded as the explicit assumption for the *reductio,* or we must assume that Anselm is himself implicitly assuming that if something can be supposed to be the case, it can be thought to be the case. Given this suppressed assumption, that is, given the appropriate premise in 5a, even if the argument went through, it would follow only that S cannot be thought to exist in the understanding alone, from which we could not conclude that S exists in reality unless we also assumed that what cannot be thought cannot be the case. Obviously, while the original assumption trades on the confusion of a logical with a psychological condition, the latter presumption trades on an assumed connection between a psychological and an ontological condition. What all this suggests, as far as we are concerned, is that the conceptual conclusion that S exists both in the understanding and in reality amounts to the claim that S cannot be thought to exist in the understanding alone, that is, that it cannot be thought not to exist. Indeed, if we wanted to press the point, we might say that the contradiction generated by the claim that S exists in the understanding alone is nested in the contradiction generated by the conceptual impossibility of it being thought to exist in the understanding alone, that is, in the inconceivability of S as not existing. In that case, however, P 2 would be covertly, although no doubt unknowingly, drawing the same conclusion as P 3.

What we are trying to get at here should not be too surprising given our earlier contention that conceptual uses of "exist," while having the same apparent grammatical form as factual uses, amount to the claim that something cannot be thought except as existing. To say that nonfictional characters cannot exist in the understanding alone and still be nonfictional characters is to say that they cannot be conceived of as existing in the understanding alone because then one would be conceiving of a fictional character. If this is all that could be shown in the name of something than which nothing greater can be thought (that is, that it cannot be conceived to exist in the understanding alone or else one is conceiving of something than which a greater can be thought), it would mean that Anselm could not make the move to his conclusion, since he would not have shown that S cannot exist in the understanding alone, but only that it cannot be thought to exist in the understanding alone. Moreover, if the latter claim were recast in terms of existence and nonexistence, it would amount to the contention that S cannot be thought not to exist. If to say that something "exists in the understanding alone" is to say that it does not exist (in reality), then to say that it cannot be thought to exist in the understanding alone is to say that it cannot be thought not to exist. In that case, P 2 would hinge upon the same "insight," indeed, would actually be generating its contradiction based upon the same claim as P 3; but it has made it in terms that conceal the talk of inconceivable nonexistence in a conceptual use of "exist" and with a vocabulary that looks different because it speaks of what "exists in the understanding alone," rather than simply of what does "not exist" in reality.

Perhaps, then, those more recent proponents who contend that the essence of the argument is in P 3 are right, even if they have not noticed that what is claimed there is simply a repetition of a covert inference at work in P 2. At the same time, they may also be right to think that the best approach is to attempt to render P 3 independent of P 2. As the text stands, at least as I have interpreted it, not only does the argument of P 3 depend upon the argument of P 2, but the success of the conclusion of P 3 would explicitly undermine what must be an implicit assumption in the *reductio* of P 2. For the conclusion of the reasoning of P 3 is that S cannot be thought not to exist, that is, that it cannot be thought to exist in the understanding alone. In this regard, it may well benefit the argument of P 2 to be separated, as it has been historically, from the conclusion to which it inevitably leads in P 3. Of course, according to those recent interpreters, P 3 is making a logical, not a psychological, point. As they would put it, the claim that S cannot be thought not to exist means that God's nonexistence is logically impossible.[13] This modern translation of Anselm's "cannot be thought" allows these interpreters to avoid the textual fact that the talk of "existence" in P 3 carries over from P 2 while it provides them with a way of concealing the grammatical fact that the modal claim of P 3, unlike the modal claim of premise 5 in P 2, is modifying "thought," not existence. What cannot be the case, according to P 3, is not that God not exist but that he be thought not to exist.

If Anselm's argument makes any claim to the impossibility, logical or otherwise, of God's nonexistence, it is in P 2's contention that S cannot exist in the understanding alone, not in P 3, which is explicitly dealing with the question of thought. I would, of course, suggest that the modal element of P 2 is itself covertly rooted in the claim that only becomes explicit in P 3, that S cannot be thought not to exist—a root that is also exposed in reply 1. Nonetheless, it seems clear from P 4 that Anselm thinks he is making a psychological claim in P 3, as is equally evident from P 15, where the insistence that God is "greater than can be thought" is meant to express a psychological point, not to suggest that God is logically impossible.[14] As we have tried to show, Anselm's appeal in P 4 to his own epistemology clearly indicates that the argument is operating on the basis of a certain psychological compulsion. And while many would still be bothered by the leap from the logical to the real that the recent way of interpreting P 3 would require, even more would be concerned by the leap from the psychological to the ontological that we contend is at the heart of Anselm's argument.

All these problems could be attributed by defenders of Anselm to the ontological peculiarity of God and to the uniqueness of his case. No doubt they would want to insist that this is precisely why our presumably analogous examples of conceptual existence are inadequate, since they do not get at the radicalness of the absolutely distinctive being of God, who "cannot be thought not to exist" for even more extreme reasons. As we have put it, in the case of a nonfictional character, existence may be said to have been added to the concept, whereas in the case of God, existence would seem to grow out of it. As such, the fact that, for example, we cannot even conceive of God as existing in the understanding alone may be regarded as an expression of his extraordinary being, which is inevitably reiterated and only fully articulated in P 3. So much the less, one might argue, for human thought if its normal procedures are violated by the supreme being, who, as Anselm is himself at pains to show in P 15 and following, is even greater than can be thought.

On the other hand, there would be no little irony in God's exceeding the normal categories of human thought if it turned out that the reasoning of Anselm's argument, which is presumably an expression of this extraordinary being, were undermined by the power of its own conclusion; if, ultimately, the strategy that maintains that the matter at issue cannot be thought otherwise results in its being impossible to think it at all. In this respect, the inconceivable alternative traded on in the comparison at issue in P 2 may not be altogether unlike the disappearing difference in M 28, which is itself reworked into the distinction of P 3. Such extraordinary distinctions may be the result of a self-defeating logic derived from the application of ordinary categories of thought to what is claimed to exceed them, just as the appeal to uniqueness must be made if we are to pretend that the inevitable distortion of those categories is a result of their being filled by something that does not fit them. To this extent, it would be critical to the *Proslogion*'s overall argument that if what we say of God at some point fails to make sense, it can be accounted for based on the inadequacy of human thought. In that case, the insight into our lack of insight into something than which nothing greater can be thought—that is, the insight that something than which nothing greater can be thought is greater than can be thought—would have to be part and parcel of our understanding of it, even as the thought formations that allow the rational mind to entertain such an extraordinary being would require categorical distortions that might well lead to a certain vision of God.

To make our way from the logical to a phenomenological evaluation of Anselm's argument, we not only need to examine why God cannot be thought not to exist but to show that the reason he cannot be thought not to exist in P 3 is the same reason he is said to be greater than can be thought in P 15. In short, we need to demonstrate that God cannot be thought not to exist for the same reason that he cannot be thought. As we will recall, the basic insight at the root of the argument—its conclusion, as interpreted for us by Anselm himself in P 4—depends upon the psychological contention that the human mind cannot think otherwise when it enjoys a vision of the thing itself within the rational mind. This epistemological implication of the ontological explication of God raises a variety of questions that are finally solved, at least to Anselm's satisfaction, by sealing the argument in a presumably unassailable conclusion to which there is no conceivable alternative. The point seems to be that we cannot think God not to exist because of the nature of the being so thought, not just as what cannot be thought not to exist, but, as Anselm interprets it in his replies, because this feature would itself entail something that exists without beginning or end or multiplicity of parts, and that is everywhere and always wholly. We took this as only one indication that reason must have a quite specific and rather extraordinary being in mind for any of what is claimed to be true, and that the precision of the distinction drawn in P 3 (which, as we have tried to show, condenses into it a certain pattern of thought from the *Monologion*) must allow the rational mind to locate that "uniquely singular and singularly unique" reality in thought. Only then can the "truth" of that being impose itself upon our thinking, such that, as P 4 concludes, whoever really understands the thing itself cannot think that it does not exist. And it is this compelling insight into the reality itself (*res ipsa*) based on a distinctive and identifying feature (*proprium dei*), this ontological intuition into what cannot be thought not to exist as a vision of the one God is (*id quod deus est*) and on the basis of which the mind cannot think otherwise, that we would contend ultimately constitutes the conviction-producing aspect of Anselm's argument.

The critical question then becomes: Why is it that God cannot be thought not to exist? And there are two answers we must consider, Anselm's and our own; or, rather, Anselm's answer and the more destructive conclusion that might be drawn from our analysis of it. Anselm would have us think that he has shown that something than which nothing greater can be thought cannot be thought not to exist because of the nature of the thing itself. And while we might agree with this in the sense in which the same may be said of non-fictional characters, there is admittedly something different about the case of God. In my view, however, what is different is that something than which nothing greater can be thought ultimately cannot be thought not to exist not so much because, like the nonfictional character case, we have a positive conception of it to which existence pertains as because, in striving to think such an extraordinary being,

Anselm succeeds in thinking nothing at all. By thinking God through the strategies of a negative ontology that proceed by means of disappearing differences and by negating those features under which we could ordinarily think of something as existing or not existing, the rational mind is rendered unable to think that such a being does not exist, but not so much because it has been shown or can think that it exists. Were we simply to conclude, then, that P 2 demonstrates the conceptual relevance of existence to the notion of something than which nothing greater can be thought, we would be missing the point of just how it goes about demonstrating this through an essentially negative strategy. The direct demonstration of P 2 operates by assuming the logic of ordinary cases in premises 1–4, so as to commit us to the claim that S either exists in the understanding alone or exists both in the understanding and in reality. It then proceeds, in view of the presumably extraordinary logic of "something than which nothing greater can be thought" displayed in the *reductio* (5 a–e), to conclude that if the one alternative is excluded—that is, if we have shown that S cannot exist in the understanding alone—the other is "without doubt" the case, namely, that it exists both in the understanding and in reality. Similarly, in P 3 the options seem to be that something either exists such that it cannot be thought not to exist or exists such that it can be thought not to exist. Having shown the latter to be inapplicable to S, the former is concluded. In either case, Anselm has essentially backed into the conclusion of his arguments: in P 2 he concludes that S exists by showing that it cannot not-exist, while in P 3 he concludes that God cannot be thought not to exist by showing that it cannot be the case that he can be thought not to exist.

Consequently, if something than which nothing greater can be thought cannot be thought not to exist, whether covertly in P 2 or overtly P 3, it is not because existence has been shown to be included in the concept but because nonexistence has been shown to be excluded from it. Moreover, while this negative strategy may appear to produce positive results in the conclusion that God exists "everywhere and always wholly," "without beginning or end," or "multiplicity of parts," etc., on the basis of which Anselm presumes to locate a specific reality in thought insofar as such a being "cannot be thought not to exist," these characteristics are themselves simply negations of the conditions under which we normally can conceive of anything as existing or not-existing. If something exists in a specific place or time and if it has begun to exist but not as yet ceased to exist, we know what it means to say that it exists; just as if it has come to an end or been decomposed into its various parts, we know what it means to say that it no longer exists. But if we negate all these categories that normally define the conditions for determining whether something exists or not, with what are we left? There may well be no basis for denying that it exists, but that may be because there is also no meaning to claiming that it does; that is, existential categories may simply have been rendered irrelevant by removing the conditions under which they can be applied and a determination of existence made.

We know that P 3 itself insists that no such determination of existence can be made in the case of God. Of course, Anselm takes this as an indication of the psychological fact that the human mind is not free to judge its creator insofar as it cannot think otherwise, and he imagines this to mean that thought cannot think of God as not existing when it is determined in its thinking by the nature of the thing itself, even if this very nature later forces the confession that the human mind cannot think it. It is no coincidence, then, that Anselm must try to deal with the problem of thinking the unthinkable by means of certain logical contortions that generate suitably extraordinary categories. For example, while ordinarily the determination that any spatial or temporal object exists or does not exist could be expressed by saying that it exists "somewhere" or "nowhere," or "at some time" or "never," the *Monologion* goes to great lengths to show that there is, in each case, yet a third option that, in an only apparently paradoxical way, incorporates both of the other two. It argues that God is "everywhere" and means by this that he is "in every place" while being "no place," just as he exists "always" in the sense that he is "at all times" without being limited to any particular time. These contentions, however, are achieved by applying the categories of space and time to the supreme being while denying that the laws governing these categories apply to him. In other words, if normally something subject to spatial categories is either somewhere or nowhere, Anselm must show that both options both apply and do not apply to God. By claiming that God is everywhere, we affirm that he is somewhere while denying it (as in every place he is some place, but, as not limited to that place alone, is nowhere), even as we deny that God is nowhere while affirming it (he is not no place if he is somewhere, although everywhere is no particular place). Nor is it a coincidence that such arguments must operate by a complex process of multiple, indeed mutual, eliminations, where one category is used to eliminate another at one stage of the argument, while the other category is used to eliminate it at another.

In any number of cases, Anselm must show that the normal categories of thought do not properly apply to God by means of a negative process that backs into its conclusions by excluding alternatives while strategically reapplying or misapplying the very categories that are claimed not to apply. Such a logic, however, raises questions of relevance. In fact, rather than taking Anselm's route to showing that it makes sense to think that there is something that is everywhere, one might be inclined to assume that the omnipresence of God would be better expressed by saying that the *categories*—and not just, as Anselm assumes, the *laws*—of space and time do not apply to such a being. That suggestion, however, would not only undermine Anselm's account, but it might well remind us that not every negation implies the possession of the opposite characteristic; nor, therefore, will an argument by process of elimination be warranted unless the options at issue are relevant. If neither of a pair of options applies to something, the denial of one does not require the application of the other. In a world in which the only colors are red and blue, to say that something is not red is not necessarily to claim that it is blue, for it may be colorless. Or if we are thinking of something to which color concepts do not apply, say, the number 2, then it cannot be red; but this is not because it is another color. In this way, we could say that it cannot be not-red, i.e., any other color, just as we might say that it cannot be thought to be in some particular place, but not because it is everywhere or, for that matter, nowhere. For to say that a number is nowhere would simply mean that spatial categories do not apply to it.

Similarly, when it comes to existence, the contention that something cannot be thought not to exist could be an expression of the fact that the categories of existence and nonexistence cannot be intelligibly applied to it, in which case it would not entail that such a thing can be thought to exist, but that it can no more be thought to exist than not to exist.[15] And while this may seem to run against our claims about the conceptual use of "exist" in P 2, it is consistent with our warning about the strategy by means of which Anselm presumes to have demonstrated the relevance of existence to the concept of something than which nothing greater can be thought by excluding its conceivable nonexistence. If something cannot be thought not to exist and yet it might still be possible that it cannot be thought to exist, existence may well not be relevant to the concept of "something than which nothing greater can be thought" in the same sense in which it is to the concept of a nonfictional character. In the latter case, we might say that existence is both relevant to, and part of, the positive conception of such a thing. In the case of S, however, the apparent importation of existence into the concept— and therefore the appearance that it is an existence-relevant concept—is based upon the exclusion of nonexistence, which may occur for different reasons. That is, unlike the nonfictional character case, in which nonexistence is excluded, at least in a certain sense, as a result of the inclusion of existence in the concept, in the case of S, the strategy is quite the opposite: existence is concluded to belong to the concept because nonexistence has been excluded from it. But while the inclusion of existence in a concept does require the exclusion of nonexistence, at least from the concept, the exclusion of nonexistence does not guarantee the inclusion of existence but may instead be the result of the categorical irrelevance of both.[16]

While we have been treating S as if it belonged to a special existential category, insofar as it is not existence neutral (that is, cannot be thought as something that may or may not exist), the appearance that it is therefore an existence-relevant concept (that is, that existence or nonexistence belongs to its conception) may result from an argument that exploits the fact that it is existence irrelevant (that is, something to which existence and nonexistence do not apply). No doubt, even assuming that it is incumbent upon Anselm to show that "something than which nothing greater can be thought" is categorically relevant to the issue of existence, the question remains whether I have any reason to think that it is not. Certainly such a conclusion would be consistent with the claim that Anselm is thinking nothing, indeed, that there is no positive conception of something than which nothing greater can be thought in the understanding. Of course, one might imagine that this is to miss the whole point, not only of my own account of the argument but also of the rational theology of both the *Monologion* and *Proslogion,* which is to generate a rational vision of God, just as one may assume that we can think both the conclusion of Anselm's argument and this classical vision of God. What I am suggesting, however, is that there is something strange about the production of this presumably positive image of "something than which nothing greater can be thought" and about the characteristics that are supposed to make the argument about its inconceivable nonexistence seem plausible, namely, the insight into the time-spacelessness of being itself, as a whole with no parts, without beginning or end, and which cannot be thought not to be precisely because it exists everywhere and always wholly, and through itself alone. And while we aim to press the attack on this fundamental ontological insight that has fueled our tradition virtually from the start and that surfaces with a particular clarity in Anselm's ontological argument, we might begin by noticing that no positive conclusion is drawn in P 3. For to say that S cannot be thought not to exist expresses a negative psychological situation—that thought cannot think that God does not exist—that allows for no positive transformation.

This is because the double negation that results in the argument's vision of God is a negation of the already negated being of creatures as what "can be thought not to exist." It is, in other words, a negation of the ontological negation of beings. Thanks to the intrusion of the word "thought" into the traditional modal category, the double negative does not, however, return us to their positive being. Instead, through the reversal of a second negation, it turns us toward the presumably incomparable being of God. We have been taking this as an indication of Anselm's overall strategy, which is not just to sketch an image of God by negating all those factors that would be the conditions for the possibility of creaturely existence or nonexistence, but to do so in a way that makes those very negative features appear to be the measure of true being. Needless to say, he cannot do this without reversing the meaning of "being," for if he did not, the supreme being would violate the conditions for existence as we normally conceive them. Thus, Anselm's vision of God must include a conversion in our understanding of being that is captured at the extreme in M 28, where it is claimed that God alone exists, and that is recaptured in P 3 in the distinction between what exists such that it can be thought not to exist and what exists such that it cannot be thought not to exist. But if, as we contend, the latter is for Anselm a psychological claim, then just as the argument of P 3 would both expose and undermine the hidden heart of P 2, it is possible that the turning point of the *Proslogion* at P 15 and Anselm's confession concerning what it is to think something that is greater than can be thought may similarly reveal both the heart and the breaking point of the argument of P 3.

We have tried to show in our reinterpretation of Anselm's argument that the precision of the distinction drawn in P 3 is designed to effect a transformation in our understanding of the meaning of being by distinguishing God from all else so as to direct the eye of the rational mind to the proper object of thought. As all those beings that can be thought not to exist withdraw from our inner sight against the measure of what cannot be thought not to exist, the way is cleared for a rational vision of the supreme being. Phenomenologically analyzed, however, the ontological disappearance of ordinary beings in thought and in the projection into the void left by their being thought not to exist forces the eye of the mind to dilate in its attempt to think what is everywhere and always wholly, in an opening that expands the scope of its vision beyond the limits of the ordinary focus of thought. As a result of the defocal vision incited by watching the ontological withdrawal of all creatures, such a dilated mind is not in a position to refocus on any specific object, although Anselm must insist that there is nonetheless an object of thought which, for its own reasons, cannot appear, or rather, appears and is glimpsed in its very "invisibility." God is claimed to "dwell in inaccessible light" and as such to be "not seen in being seen and seen in not being seen." In effect, in this unfocused condition, the eye of reason can sight no determinate object, and Anselm confesses this, indeed, takes it as a further revelation of the extraordinary being of God: his unfathomable "breadth" eludes the "narrowness" of our focal vision.

My point, however, is that it will be impossible for thought to think what it is, in that case, "thinking" as not existing because, strictly speaking, it is not thinking anything insofar as there is nothing, no object, presenting itself to thought, even if Anselm would like to convince us that there is something that thought is "not-thinking" and that must be "seen in not being seen." The fact, then, that God cannot be thought is the reason he cannot be thought not to exist. For if the categories under which we would ordinarily determine the existence or nonexistence of something are rendered irrelevant by a conversion of the meaning of being, then the rational mind may seem to be confirmed in its impression that it cannot think otherwise, or rather that it must think as it does based upon, as Anselm's epistemology would have it, the impression that this extraordinary object of thought has made upon it. To convince us of this, Anselm must find a way to contend—and we will try to demonstrate more precisely the complexity of this maneuver in the next stage of our criticism—that this is an impression that has been made upon thought by an object that cannot be thought, or that appears by failing to appear insofar as it appears to thought as what eludes it. What I am proposing, however, is that Anselm can have this conviction-producing experience of God as what cannot be thought not to exist and that this can compel the rational mind to think as it does precisely because of the strategy involved in his negative ontology. In thinking God by means of the empty vision produced by the negation of a certain image of creatures, rational thought projects into the void left by the ontological withdrawal of beings, leaving it not only with nothing to think but God, but—as I have tried to show is inadvertently confessed later in the *Proslogion*—with nothing to think at all and, therefore, with nothing that can be thought not to exist.

We will return to the implications of such a vision of emptiness later, when we attempt a final critique of this "insight" into God that I claim lies at the heart of Anselm's argument. For now we might just conclude our initial evaluation by noting that the conclusion that Anselm is thinking nothing is consistent with our earlier warning that "something than which nothing greater can be thought" is a negative notion, like "not-man," moving the mind to a conception that is not there. According to Anselm's own analysis, there are certain negative names such that, even when they are understood, there is nothing in the understanding corresponding to them. It is just this problem that Gaunilo encounters with Anselm's key phrase, since while one might be said to understand the terms that compose it, it is not clear that there is anything in the understanding corresponding to it.[17] Needless to say, this is not only contrary to premise 3 in our schematization of P 2, but it also casts suspicion on the transition from premise 2 to premise 3 to the critical and suppressed premise 4. If it is only the words that are understood, which Anselm insists in his replies is all the fool need admit, then if one cannot validly infer from this that there is something that exists in the understanding corresponding to this string of words, it will not turn out that we are committed to the claim that "something than which nothing greater can be thought" either exists in the understanding alone or exists both in the understanding and in reality, since these options do not apply to the name itself. This is, of course, why Anselm must try to get from the terms of the phrase, which are what is understood in premise 2, to something that "exists in the understanding" in premise 3.

A proper emphasis on what we have earlier called Anselm's semiological starting point would not only serve to distinguish his argument from later versions of the ontological proof insofar as he begins from the "signs" alone, not from a conception of God, but would reveal what is perhaps the most obviously illicit maneuver made in P 2, namely, the move from premise 2 through premise 3 to premise 4. Ironically, the very categorical irrelevance that we have suggested Anselm may be exploiting would be nowhere more evident than in the case in which the words alone exist in the understanding, since it does not follow, if words may be said to exist in the understanding, that they either exist in the understanding alone or exist both in the understanding and in reality. No doubt, in some sense we might be willing to say that words only exist in the understanding, although I do not think we could mean by this that they exist in the understanding alone as opposed to existing in reality, but that they are not of such a nature that they exist either in the understanding alone or both in the understanding and in reality, any more than fictional characters are. Similarly, unless we already know that S is the name of something (if, for example, S names nothing, as does the term "nothing," which is one of Anselm's other examples of negative names), one cannot infer that "it" either exists in the understanding alone or exists both in the understanding and in reality; for "nothing" does not exist in the understanding alone in the way, say, that my dream house does. And since "something than which nothing greater can be thought" would appear to be a negative expression, we cannot suppose that it enjoys the privileges afforded to positive conceptions, especially if it turned out that this string of words was ultimately self-defeating, that is, was the expression of and for something that could not be thought, and, in this sense, was the name of nothing. For not only must certain self-contradictory notions be sufficiently "intelligible" to discern that they are nonsense, but—and we will return to this linguistic issue at the conclusion of our conclusion—the words of a phrase may, in some sense, be understood without there being any intelligible conception of such a thing in the understanding.

In my view, then, the reasoning of P 2 is riddled with problems virtually from beginning to end, for premise 2 is as ambiguous in its claim that something than which nothing greater can be thought is understood as is the claim to existence in premise 6; while premise 3—that whatever is understood exists in the understanding—is apparently false, unless it is referring to the words themselves. In that case, premise 4 is either false or irrelevant if we never get beyond the words in our understanding of S, which, of course, means that it is only true for those kinds of things in our understanding to which existence and nonexistence in reality are pertinent. But even if we let the argument pass to premise 5, the *reductio* is, if not self-defeating, then at best capable of sustaining a conceptual conclusion, which would result in P 2 in effect making the same claim as P 3, namely, that S cannot be thought to exist in the understanding alone, that is, that it cannot be thought not to exist. And to pursue our criticism of this fundamental "insight" in view of what we have already said of it and of the *Proslogion* as a whole, we must turn, first, to a closer evaluation of the claims made on its behalf not only in P 4 but also in the remainder of the text and, finally, to the question of how Anselm could have accomplished all that he has by thinking nothing at all.

▌ The Rites of Reason

Critiques of Anselm's argument have concentrated on the logic of P 2 and, more recently, of P 3 but have rarely attended to, let alone evaluated, the claims made in P 4, not to mention in the remainder of the *Proslogion*. This is in part because traditional interest has centered around the reasoning of P 2, in part because, even with the recent attention to P 3, P 4 tends to be regarded as an appendix responding to certain problems raised by the conclusion of the argument, even as it provides a kind of closure, thanks to its final prayer, that seems to insulate it from the rest of the text. But this appendix, in its claims about the nature of thinking, actually completes the argument by sealing it in a self-confirming circle that legislates the conditions under which it operates and those under which it does not. In showing how the fool thought what the argument has shown cannot be thought, P 4 insists upon a specific way of thinking, as it requires that we understand "the thing itself," not simply think the words that signify that thing. And this would appear to suggest that the argument turns on Anselm's theory of signs, as the contentions about the nature of thinking in P 4 lead us back to the linguistic epistemology articulated in M 10.

Not inappropriately, then, those who have given any serious attention to P 4 have done so by concentrating on its philosophy of language. Unfortunately, this has not so much led to an evaluation of Anselm's view as either to an uncritical presentation of it or to the substitution of his account of language for a more contemporary one.[18] Thus, both Heideggerian and Wittgensteinian philosophies of language have recently been called to the aid of the argument. Indeed, one interpreter has employed Wittgenstein to update Anselm's argument while appealing to Heidegger to explicate his notion of truth.[19] And while the latter appeal, to borrow an image from the former thinker, may be like buying two copies of the morning paper to verify its claims—since both Heidegger and Anselm may be so deeply implicated in the history of Western ontology that they do not confirm in their agreement anything but this implication—it seems to me that if Heidegger has anything to contribute to our understanding of such issues, it is in his critique of the "onto-theo-logical" nature of metaphysics. In fact, this well-known slogan of the later Heidegger is not unconnected to the claim, made much earlier in his career, that the essence of metaphysics lies precisely in its thinking nothing—even if Heidegger, in so claiming, is trying to make sense of the tradition and of this "nothing" that not only lies at the root of Western metaphysics but even closer to the heart of the thought of "being."[20]

On the other hand, those who would attempt to interpret Anselm by speaking in Wittgensteinian terms of "language-games" and the "grammatical" claims that may be made to clarify them— who would perhaps be inclined to account for what we have been calling conceptual claims as grammatical truths revealing something about the practice of a certain language-game that people play—fail to mention that Anselm holds, and that his argument as it stands depends upon, the very Augustinian view of language that Wittgenstein is presumably attacking. Moreover, these interpreters have a tendency to deny the ultimate groundlessness of our linguistic practices.[21] As we know, Anselm does not think that language is based on the relation between signs in a signifying system or on the uses to which those signs may be put in the practice of their actual employment, but thinks that the meaning of words requires recourse to a domain of ideal significations.[22] Consequently, while he admits that we can generate sense through the signs themselves, it is exactly in this way that we fail to think properly. Thus, P 4 requires us to distinguish between thinking by means of signs and thinking the things themselves, that is, grasping the true "signification" of those signs. And while some have rightly interpreted Anselm's argument in view of his own philosophy of language, they have tended to take his claims at face value rather than considering whether his argument actually achieves what he claims it must.

Clearly, Anselm's reasoning in P 2–3, according to his own self-interpretation in P 4, requires that its "signs" bring us to some insight into the reality they signify if the argument is to work. Ironically, we would seem to be heading toward the opposite conclusion, namely, that there is no "thing itself" that Anselm's argument allows us to think, as it begins from the words "something than which nothing greater can be thought" and never gets any further— if, that is, it does not ultimately provide us with a clear vision of the matter at issue but with a vision of nothing, of the void left when thought thinks away what can be thought not to exist. For whatever we can be said to have concluded about this "something than which nothing greater can be thought" is based on the self-clarifying nature of the expression itself, not on an insight into, or even a likeness of, the thing appearing in or to thought. In fact, we might go so far as to say that the key to the argument lies in the absence of anything being thought or presenting itself to thought. There is not even a proper conception, in the sense in which Anselm uses this term, of something than which nothing greater can be thought in the understanding, although the negative nature of the key phrase keeps the mind open for the nominal maneuvers that the argument leads thought through. The verbal formula functions to set thought in motion as if there were something to think, implying in its very formulation that there is "something" than which nothing greater can be thought, even if it only exists in the understanding. In the end, however, our thought is never directed to any such object of thought but to an empty vision that depends entirely and solely upon the name itself.

In this way, we will eventually suggest that, contrary to his own account, Anselm's argument consists of, and depends solely upon, signs and what they can produce—although the latter is not a matter, as he would insist, of getting from the name to the thing itself, whether in reality or in thought. Instead, if the point is to manipulate the mind into applying its normal thought-functions to an object that cannot be thought by exploiting what in ordinary cases Anselm claims to be the formative tendencies of human thinking, then the movement of his argument is more a matter of getting from the name to, or rather associating the name with, nothing. In that case, we might say, in light of Anselm's claims in P 4 about thinking as an "expressing in the heart," that there is no heart to the argument, nothing to take to heart. Or, rather, there is this nothing, which, when taken to heart, has the desired effect.

Anselm himself, in his own way, confesses this later in the *Proslogion,* when he begins to insist in P 14 and following that something than which nothing greater can be thought is beyond what can be thought insofar as the human mind cannot form a unified image of it, while we have tried to show that the reason why God cannot be thought not to exist and the reason he cannot be thought are one and the same. In both cases, Anselm can make the claims he does on "experiential" grounds because, strictly speaking, in the moment of insight, he is thinking nothing—which is why the vision of God must ultimately be deferred until after death. It is this latter tactic that allows Anselm to convert his admitted failure into the claim that there is something he is not able to think, as his lack of insight is supposed to supply a positive confirmation of a being that is greater than can be thought. Of course, if something than which nothing greater can be thought is beyond what can be thought, there would be no apparent reason to think that there is something that is (not) being thought, unless Anselm can make sense of this through the deferral of vision to the afterlife, in the projection of the possibility that what presently eludes our thinking will someday appear in all its ontological—or perhaps I should say, ontical—glory.

It is precisely at the point of this ambiguity that I want to take advantage of certain Heideggerian clues about the onto-theo-logical nature of metaphysics before turning to a final evaluation of Anselm's claims about the nature of language and thought. As is well known, Heidegger thinks that the history of Western metaphysics, at least since Plato, has failed to take heed of the ontological difference, namely, that if there is a difference between being and beings, then being is not itself a being. The presumed result of this metaphysical confusion is that being is construed in most of our tradition as if it were a supreme being that is both the ground of beings (ontological) and the highest being (theological), rather than, as Heidegger's own phenomenological reformulation would have it, as the way in which phenomena appear. Putting aside for the moment this phenomenological account of the meaning of being, to which we will return later, it should be clear that our view of Anselm is at critical points riddled with the ambiguity of the ontological difference: of whether what he calls "being itself" should be thought of as a particular being or whether it is to be thought of as other than beings.

On the one hand, part of the thrust of our account of Anselm's ontological argument is precisely that it is ontological rather than ontical; that is, that it involves a reversal in our thinking about the meaning of being that is more fundamental than the demonstration of the existence of any particular being. On the other hand, while it may seem clear that Anselm thinks that being itself resides in a particular being, namely, in the individual he calls God, his own account of the thought of the supreme being in what we are calling his confession admits that no particular object of thought, no ontical reality, has actually appeared to thought. If we are contending that Anselm's argument trades on this confusion of the ontical and the ontological, then the question remains how he produces the appearance of an object of thought while admitting that no particular being has appeared to thought. And the answer, of course, is through the theological scenario. While in this life it is admitted that no ontical reality appears to human thought in its thought of God, this ontological reality—a designation that for Heidegger would show the very confusion at issue—is secured through the deferral of its appearance to an afterlife, when being promises to show itself as the being it is.

If we may assume that the fundamental cognitive contortion at work in Anselm's thought is the double reversal that claims that the supreme being is beyond beings—indeed, is beyond being—even as it is claimed to be a being, then we might say that the afterlife is of the essence of such an onto-theo-logical metaphysics. Only the expectation of another life can create the possibility that what currently cannot appear as a comprehensible object of thought will someday present itself as the unique individual it is claimed to be. At the same time, this theological promise of the totalizing of our fragmentary intuitions not only supplies reason with an object of thought, albeit one that cannot appear, but this deferral of thought also serves to incite a certain experience of God. In the postponement of the vision complete, we are afforded not just an anticipation of joy but the joy of a certain anticipation based upon our present insight into the essential invisibility of God, as if in the confession of our blindness we were allowed a dark glimpse of what cannot be seen until the afterlife.[23]

In that event, we must attend to the way certain experiences, including the insight into our lack of insight, have been produced not only through the arguments themselves but also through the poetic narrative of the prayers that creates the context for the text and, as such, actually supplies the rhetorical ground for its reasoning. For

Anselm's theological scenario, which begins in P 1 with its excitation of the mind to the contemplation of God and must be intermittently repeated throughout the text, is not just designed to get us to read the rational experiences of thought that the arguments will put us through in a particular light; it is ultimately designed to justify our lack of rational insight by suggesting that while a certain distorted vision is all we have in this life, our myopic condition is only temporary and will be corrected in an eternal life to come. In contrast to this attempt to generate an object out of an empty experience, I would suggest that it is a category mistake to think that the defocal vision in the dark, this blind sight achieved through the manipulation of our inner vision by thinking nothing, could ever be converted into the vision of some focal object, and that the confession and deferral serve to mask the lack of anything being thought in the attempt to claim that something is revealed to thought in its failure to appear. In that case, Anselm's thought is founded on a vision of nothing that is then, through his confession, converted into a deferred vision of something. The theological God is the object invisibly inserted into this ontological void through the confession of his failure to appear, although he is claimed to be caught sight of in a partial vision that promises to be completed in a future life, indeed, that provides evidence of a life to come when alone "our joy may be full."

In this way, the rational reconstruction of God in Anselm's positive theology is founded upon an insight produced by the strategies of his negative ontology, even as this theology fills the emptiness of his ontological vision with its own image of God. And while the positive theology serves to correct for the empty vision afforded by the negative ontology, this void is filled by a theological conception that is in turn protected by the very emptiness of the ontological insight that seemingly justifies the claim that God is greater than can be thought. In short, ontology and theology work together to hone a specific vision of God. Of course, in a sense this is what the founding of a rational theology is all about, as its point is to lead us to a certain conception of "the essence of divinity," just as it is no doubt precisely at this historic juncture that the question of the relation between faith and reason in Anselm's thought is properly raised. In fact, of most interest to us is the way Anselm's confession of a lack of vision, and its deferral to an afterlife based on the theological narrative, is actually part and parcel of a defense of reason based upon the confession of its limitations. For a certain legitimation of rationality is occurring through this rationalization of divinity as surely as reason's need for an object of thought is being met through the theological promise of totality. What is most critical to us at this point, then, is not just the way Anselm's ontology is theological or his theology ontological but the manner in which both are irreducibly and unavoidably "logical," since what the negative ontology and the positive theology have in common, what brings them together such that they can work in complicity with one another, is the way both are determined *"sola ratione."*

We would like to show that the intertwining of the theological and the ontological conceptions of God in the *Proslogion* is part of a self-generating circle that it is attempting to establish between faith and reason, a self-confirming circle that is best uncoiled by exposing the mental manipulations that rational thought is capable of, and the way in which it may achieve the desired effect in certain self-evident, we might even say, self-induced, "inner experiences." Before turning our attention to the nature and function of the theological narrative, we must first be clear about the extraordinary maneuvers that reason has undergone in securing its vision of God. The "ontological" argument, whether in the *Proslogion* or in its prototypical form in the *Monologion,* is essentially a matter of a reversal in the meaning of being, effected through reasoning, that leads to a vision of God in thought and, as such, becomes a "theo-logical" argument. Its "logical" element ultimately involves reason's visionary power, which is why it may well be regarded as an a priori argument. This means that it can appear to run its course in the mind alone insofar as it is strictly a matter of a conversion experience that proceeds *sola cogitatione,* by means of thinking alone. In that case, the ontological argument is essentially theological, insofar as a specific vision of God is embedded within it, and equally psychological in that the mind is lead, by a certain way of thinking, to those mental experiences which have suggested to us that the ground of the argument lies in some rational, and, therefore, in a strictly phenomenological sense, "psycho-logical" insight in which thought is compelled to think as it does—so long as it is thinking in a particular way—about a particular object of thought. To this extent, one might say that the key to Anselm's argument lies in his philosophy of mind, which alone can account for the compulsive ground of the argument.

Put in slightly different terms, however, the logical element of the ontological argument, with regard to its root in the psychological compulsion of a certain inner experience, might be said to have a psychotic aspect to it. The hidden power of the argument lies in an insight that reverses the meaning of "reality" as it seeks to effect the mental elevation designed to force us to lose contact with "the things themselves," with what ordinarily supplies us with our measure of being—namely, beings—by thinking them not to be, so as to direct our vision toward an object of thought that cannot appear. In this sense, the argument induces a certain ontological psychosis that must lose contact with reality so as to legitimate reason itself, even if Anselm tries to apply his causal epistemology to a case in which it is doubtful that we are entertaining a likeness of some original rather than a purely productive image of God. It is, however, critical to appreciate that there is nothing inconsistent about claiming that reason produces for itself and from itself an object of thought that is nonetheless "binding" upon it. Instead, I would suggest that this is precisely the point.

Obviously, as P 4 insists, Anselm's argument depends entirely upon a certain way of thinking, not just as a piece of reasoning but as reasoning that itself must be grounded in the insight into a specific and unique reality, although he later confesses that no object has actually appeared to thought—an event that must consequently be interpreted as if something has shown itself, or shown something of itself, by not appearing. However blinding, reason's illumination of and by an invisible God is required as a justification, within the context of a tradition whose paradigm of truth is revelation, for Anselm's proposal to proceed *sola ratione*. What Anselm does not admit, even in his confession of the presumed limitations of human reason, is that he is proceeding on the basis of a certain faith in reason. He works from a specific conception of rationality that is only justified by the metaphysics he is assuming: a metaphysics of inner experience—of reason's presumed access to reality in an inner vision that is determined by what it is thinking—which is itself grounded in the conception of God he aims to demonstrate by means of such rational vision. This may well suggest not just that Anselm's overall strategy is circular but that reason must have already had a hand in manipulating the experiences that are supposed to be grounding it; that there is a certain complicity between Anselm's onto-theo-logical image of God and rational thought. In that case, despite, or perhaps in light of, Anselm's repeated claims to the contrary, human rationality, and its apparently privileged accesses to reality, would not be the result of the human mind being an image of God but of the fact that Anselm's god is an image, indeed, an artifact of human reason, as his likeness is formed, we might even say, produced, in the process of rational reconstruction that is philosophical theology.

If Anselm's image of God is the product of a certain way of thinking, then the essence of his argument is, in fact, revealed in P 4. Its most critical result would be to get us involved in its way of thinking—a way that is essential to the historic conversion of faith to reason and to the task of an ongoing rational revelation of God in history. This amounts, however, to the conversion to the production or, as Anselm would no doubt prefer to put it, to the formation of images of God by reason alone. In the case in point, reason has found a way to convert the emptiness of its ontological experience into a theological image of the divine, and in a vision in which reason supplies itself with an object of thought in the form of a God that does not appear. In this filling of the void, I think it is fair to say that reason creates an experience for itself, produces an experience on which to ground itself. Its creation of a rational image of God provides the basis for its form of thinking in a certain inner vision, even if it can accomplish the necessary maneuvers irrespective of any confirming experience insofar as the confession in the *Proslogion* functions to seal reason's self-confirming vision in its lack of vision, as its very failure is made to count as success. In its own strange way, reason meets its requirement for an object of thought by supplying itself with a kind of missing ground, just as it fulfills its inherent need to give grounds for the giving of grounds precisely through the tactic of confession and deferral, by postponing its ultimate confirmation while confirming itself in this very postponement.

In a quite different sense, then, Anselm's thought is proceeding *sola ratione,* for reason does all this alone, without any "other," insofar as it posits an other that cannot appear. This, however, simply amounts to the hermetic sealing of reason and its God in an airtight argument, that is, in the vacuum created by the vicious circle that has found a way to exclude all foreign material by confirming itself through an inner experience in which nothing appears. As such, the confession of a rational mystic—that God is not seen in being seen and seen in not being seen—serves as the ultimate apology for reason, designed, through such blind vision, to get thought caught up in a self-confirming circle in which reason circles itself in the construction of an object for its eyes only, even as it closes its circle with faith. For God's elusion of rational thought, as well as the invocation of the "joy of the lord" anticipated on the basis of our presently inadequate vision, not only belongs to the theological scenario that provides a narrative foundation for reason but is in turn presumably confirmed by the ontological insight supplied by Anselm's argument. In effect, human reason creates its own ground through the theological narrative of the prayers as much as through its philosophical arguments, as it confesses the inadequacy of its vision of God, but not because there is nothing to ground it or because it has seen nothing but nothing, but because its own blindness is part and parcel of its insight into an incomprehensible theological object. To this extent, our "fallen" rationality has guaranteed its success from the start insofar as its failure to see God is its ultimate achievement.

This basic maneuver, in which thought creates the appearance of an object that cannot appear, could not be made any more apparent than it is in the rhetorical form of the *Proslogion,* which its very title announces. As we know, Anselm concocted the terms *"Monologion"* and *"Proslogion"* when he retitled these exemplary texts that were to initiate the practice of a strictly rational meditation, presumably suggesting that they are companion volumes. But their basic formal difference should be as striking as any similarities. Clearly, both involve a speaking (*logos*). In the first case, however, it is a speaking alone (*mono*), in a "monologue" that the solitary reasoner carries on with himself as a kind of rational soliloquy. In this sense, the *Monologion,* as it proclaims from the start, does proceed *sola ratione,* but in the dual sense that it uses reason alone, most notably without the aid of Scripture, and consequently that reason is alone in its thinking—is doing whatever it does by itself and to itself.

In contrast, the *Proslogion* is not a monologue; nor, however, is it a dialogue. Instead, it is an address, an allocution, a speaking to or before or in the face of (*pro*) someone else, namely, God. Obviously, this audience has a special role to play in such an allocutionary act. Rhetorically, the *Proslogion* is an address, a formal speech, and in the rather literal sense that it does not so much treat itself as a matter of writing as of speaking. It is, however, neither a lecture nor an oration nor an encomium but is instead a hortatory address. And while the invocation of P 1 may well be designed to arouse the brethren to undertake the task of contemplation, there can be no doubt that the more fundamental exhortation is the one that calls upon God to "show yourself," just as there can be no doubt that the text as a whole is primarily addressed to God. In fact, it is spoken before God, and this is why it is entitled *Proslogion,* as a speech that formally proceeds as if in the presence of another.[24]

This form of address, it seems to me, not only provides us with the key to the point of the poetic narrative of the *Proslogion* but also indicates its essential difference from the *Monologion.* Lacking both the form and the content of a "theo-logical" address, that is, of a prayer that speaks to God as if he were present, the *Monologion* provides no obvious justification for proceeding by means of reason, nor is it clear how its procedure is relevant to those in the monastery. It simply assumes that the brethren are eager for such an approach, when, in fact, we know that the text was coolly received, at least by the most important brethren to Anselm.[25] The *Proslogion,* however, not only incorporates the more familiar references to Scripture but also places the text within the context of spiritual reading, making such rational thought appear to be relevant to the meditational movement toward God to which monastic existence is itself addressed, as is clear from what we have already shown. What we must not fail to notice is that the *Proslogion* achieves all of this not simply through its rational arguments but through a form of address that finds a way to produce an "other" that does not appear. The rhetorical form of the hortatory address creates the appearance of an other that, while not the interlocutor of a true dialogue, remains nonetheless an essential, albeit silent, partner. It is this element of the silent other—who is created through the speech act itself, through the allocutionary act, and who, as silent, "appears" in the text as the one who is addressed but never answers, indeed, who is produced through the form of address itself—that provides a model for the sort of self-production we have drawn attention to in the case of reason. The formal structure of the text, in its implication of an other whom it is presumably addressing but who by nature (or at least in view of the part it plays in such an address) can never answer, is reproduced within the *Proslogion* in reason's providing itself with an object of thought that cannot appear, even though it presumably dwells in the inaccessible light of truth, that is, of reason itself.

We would, of course, not want to forget that the content of the theological narrative is also designed to provide a foundation for reason, for the method of proceeding *sola ratione,* as it not only invokes the "God of truth" but also confirms the procedures through the "foretaste" of joy that such a rational revelation of God presently offers. In a sense, it is this joy that supplies the immediate psychological ground for reason and the ultimate justification for the arguments of the *Proslogion.* It is the topic around which the narrative turns, as does the text itself. For Anselm's "little work," which apparently does not deserve to be called a "book,"[26] begins in its preface, even before the narrative proper, by justifying its own writing in terms of the hope of being able to produce in others the joy it brought to its author and ends with the promise of the "joy complete" (*gaudium plenum*) in a life to come—both of which serve to point the reader outside of the text. And while we would want to suggest that what is at issue in such joy is the ecstasy involved in an unfocused inner vision incited by a certain excess of reason, and while we will postpone for the moment the question of whether this experience is altogether "extratextual," we would insist that, in all this, rational thought has nonetheless retained the upper hand. Despite the passion of the prayers and their apparent excesses, reason has kept its head; in fact, it has taken control of the *Proslogion's* religious images insofar as it has found a way to interpret philosophically the scriptural passages it cites, as even the "joy of the lord" is ultimately marshaled to reason's aid.

The intertwining of theology and philosophy in the very form of the *Proslogion* is designed to elicit a philosophical reading of its religious language while providing a religious vision of its rational arguments. It is, however, critical to realize that reason is ultimately controlling the narrative for its own purposes. The strange and rather lopsided complementarity between prayer and proof, in the philosophical appropriation of intermittent citations from Scripture in complicity with a religious interpretation of philosophical thought, aims to get us to view certain cognitive manipulations of the mind in a specific way through an effectively rationalized theological narrative. To this extent, while it is a commonplace to claim that philosophy is the handmaiden of theology in the Middle Ages, only a proper understanding of the nature of the bondage at work here could show how and why the servant overtook her master in the development of history. Indeed, modern thought, presumably liberating philosophy from the shackles of theology, continues the exploitation of theological narratives as the foundation for reason while it repeats the ontological argument as the founding event of rational thought, from Spinoza to Hegel and beyond.

As important as Anselm's apparent employment of reason to rationalize the doctrines of faith may be, his less apparent legitimation of reason through a theological narrative is even more far-reaching. If, as we have said from the start, Anselm is a central figure in the history of Western thought as the pivotal figure in medieval philosophy, then he is not only the father of scholasticism, but, in a more direct manner than we might imagine, he is also a patriarch of modern thought, as is most obvious in its dependence upon his famous argument. While it may appear that philosophy is a slave to theology in Anselm's work insofar as reason is supposed to defend the doctrines of faith, Christian theology is marched to the forefront to serve as a defender of reason. Moreover, it submits to reason's principles of justification, most notably in the implication (however often it is denied) that faith itself stands in need of a ground, and one that can be supplied by a "God of truth," who now becomes the preferred object of thought because his nature compels reason to think in a certain way. In view of this possibility of grounding reason in an insight into the ultimate reality, the ontological argument becomes attractive to the rational theology characteristic of modern philosophy because of its epistemological orientation. It seeks certainty and finds it in a God that supplies reason with an indubitable object of thought. The thought of a thought that cannot be thought otherwise obviously appeals to reason as the thought of an ultimate ground, that is, as the ground of reason itself. This compelling insight into a reality, or rather into the thought of a reality that is binding upon thought—as ancient as the name of "being" and as recent as the attempt to redress it in the "necessity" of a formal modal logic—has allowed the ontological argument to be reformulated throughout modernism, and right up to the present day, in an ever more rational garb. As such, theology, at least of this philosophical sort, is characteristically rational in the modern era, not because modernism wants to supply a rational basis for faith but because it aims to provide a theological basis for reason.[27]

As we have already indicated, Anselm is neither the first philosopher to exploit what from the start has been regarded as the compelling insight into being itself in its ultimately unthinkable difference from nothing, nor would he be the last to defend reason by confessing its limitations. On the contrary, we would suggest that Anselm's ontological argument touches the ground of Western thought itself as it runs its course on the track of this distinction without a difference from Parmenides to perhaps the greatest rational theologian in the Anselmian tradition, Hegel, and right up to the present day, not only in the process theology that the latter inspired but also in the presumably postmetaphysical atheological thinking of the philosopher who first informed us of the onto-theo-logical character of metaphysics. And while it may sound extreme to suggest that a single argument can take us to the heart of Western metaphysics, we are supposing that it does so by crystallizing an insight that actually belongs to the ontological origin of our tradition, a transhistorical insight that has been repeated throughout the tradition and is historically preserved in Anselm's argument. It is this insight that allows for the reformulation of the ontological argument in modern thought, long after the medieval world appeared to be dead and gone, and that can even be retrieved, albeit in his own way, by a thinker like Heidegger, for whom logic is, in certain respects, a thing of the past. In this regard, what we have been calling the phenomenological element of the argument may be even more far-ranging than we might at first imagine, which is why we will have to return to its detailed evaluation shortly.[28] For the moment, the point is that reason remains enthralled by its insight into a supreme being, is entranced by this "onto-logic," because it provides a compelling ground for reason itself in the psychological compulsion that claims that rational thought cannot think otherwise about a specific object of thought, even if such an incomprehensible object can only be thought through the cognitive excesses that seem bound to lead to a certain ecstasy of reason.

Anselm's approach is still grounded in a tradition of contemplative experience, but one that has meanwhile come to be determined by the ecstasies of a rational mysticism. The object of worship is now revealed to reason in its own trance of truth, as the dilated eye of the mind stares into the void of beings, enrapt by the seizure of an illumination in which thought cannot think otherwise. Of course, our remystification of Anselm's thought is not meant to suggest that it is a matter of some mindless mysticism. On the contrary, we regard his moment of vision as a matter of an inner experience produced by reason's own drawing of the ultimate ontological difference. In the end, we would suggest not only that, in its joy, reason is essentially ecstatic over itself, as it is entranced by a self-induced clarity, but that this is produced by reason's construction of an absolute difference through which it is grounded and in which it settles. Rational thought has found its way to a kind of quiet for which it apparently longs and in which it is determined entirely by the matter it is thinking. The joy of reason, in drawing a distinction that ends all differences, delivers it into a repose not altogether unlike the one presumed to be promised in the life to come, when thought need no longer think, form images and imitations, but sees fully and directly, indeed, does not even see, but enters wholly into the joy of the lord, as if reason were consumed by its consummate object.

It is, however, this "passive" confirmation—in a resting of reason, ending all striving in the perfection and completion of its partial vision, when it no longer has to envision likenesses—that we need to question. For if rational thought has arrived at its ultimate object in a vision of the incomprehensible, it has done so through its own formation of a rather graphic image of God. And we cannot help but wonder whether Anselm's theory of signs, as it is applied in P 4, as well as the linguistic epistemology that goes along with it, does not in fact function in the opposite way as is claimed; whether, once again, they are not being misapplied in the present case to create the impression that the argument has achieved the opposite effect it actually has. While Anselm's argument depends entirely upon the causal claim that the reality itself determines thought such that it cannot think otherwise, we might well wonder whether this taking to the extreme of one side of his epistemology is not a way of masking the fact that in the case of God, we are not rather at the other extreme, encountering the mind's active formation of rational images that are the expression of no reality whatsoever. For if Anselm's vision of God is in effect a vision of nothing, if there is no reality appearing to thought, and if Anselm himself admits this, then his likeness of God would have to be regarded as an image that has been constructed by reason alone and from the ground up.

In that event, we might say that reason is never more productive, or "purer," indeed, that it is never more poetic, than in its formation of images of God. If rational thought may be said to be as creative in its arguments as the prayers are in their rhetorical narrative, then this is because both create the desired effect through a use of language that produces the object it is addressing. Part of our aim, then, in drawing attention to reason's commandeering of the narrative of faith has been to expose human rationality in its ungrounded condition, so as eventually to suggest the ultimate defenselessness of any genuinely philosophical theology, once reason itself is shown to be a creative force that can only be grounded in its own self-productions. What this means at the moment, however, is that Anselm's account of rational thought, itself modeled on a restrictive notion of imagination, does not explain how it works, if, in fact, the logic of such onto-theo-logical thinking has been operating in a more productive manner than any of its practitioners would be willing to admit. In that case, the *Monologion*'s view of the nature of reason would be doing more to conceal what the founding of rational theology is all about than to reveal it, just as surely as the claims made in P 4 would be leading us away from the heart of the ontological argument; unless, of course, we were prepared to reread Anselm's own rhetorical model of thinking—as a matter of "inner locution"—with new eyes.

| The Theographic Image

If the ontological argument can take us to the very foundation of Western thought, it is because it is not simply a relic left from the history of philosophy. Instead, this argument must be regarded as one of the shrines of Western metaphysics in which a particular image of God is not only kept but through which that image is protected. In fact, insofar as its reasoning enshrines within it Anselm's consummate vision of God, which itself holds the remains of an insight that has repeated itself throughout our tradition, it may be simplest to think of the argument as a kind of rational icon, or, perhaps, as a theological iconoscope: a rational "projector" designed to display a specific image of the invisible God on the screen of the mind. And however this image of God is produced, including in the depiction that forms its likeness in reverse, through a negative image that runs its reels in the dark of the mind, there is a rather vivid impression made upon rational thought by the movement of

Anselm's negative ontology. Of course, our claim has been that it is this inner experience elicited by Anselm's ontology that lies at the root of his famous argument and that insofar as the argument itself lies at the virtual epicenter of Western metaphysics, it should allow for a certain exposure of the ground of Western thought—as if the "psychologic" at the heart of Western ontology were most clearly evident in the mystical meditations of the medieval monastery.

While I would like to stress the element of image-production in Anselm's work, this feature is obscured not only by his own epistemology but also by the fact that the rational image of God has become an idol of philosophical theology. In that case, a critique of Anselm's thought requires the exorcising of this rational idol—which dominates his theology as surely as it came to dominate philosophy—by revealing the logical apparatus that serves such cognitive apparitions, exposing the tactics on the basis of which they have been conjured, and showing the manner in which these visions of God serve to fill a void in reason's own self-image. In the end, however, we want to make use of our account of the founding of rational theology to suggest certain elements pertinent to philosophical theology that may be indicated by these logically, or, as I would like to suggest, linguistically induced experiences, even if, to do so, we will yet have to criticize the phenomenological ground of the argument that may seem to remain even after the "destruction" of its reasoning. For while our account of the rites of reason that are enacted in the *Proslogion* was articulated with reference to Heidegger's claims about the theological nature of metaphysics, this does not mean that we do not have our doubts about the ontological element of the ontological argument and the "intuition" that supposedly grounds it, or about any phenomenological attempt to refound the argument in a way that might appear to avoid metaphysics by means of an appeal to experience. Our aim is not, as it is for Heidegger, to destroy the metaphysical image of God so as to get back to its true ground in ontology, for we are not suggesting that metaphysics must be overcome so that we can retreat to the originally ontological ground of our tradition. On the contrary, our conclusion would suggest that if metaphysics must be abandoned, it is because it is a development of the questionable ontological tactics that generate the tradition of which Anselm and his famous argument are products, namely, the one that runs, with various alterations, from Parmenides to Plato through Plotinus into Augustine and, eventually, the negative theology of Pseudo-Dionysius.[29]

In this way, a full evaluation of Anselm's argument requires the exposure not only of its metaphysical element but also of the ontologic on which his theological vision thrives. As we have already indicated, this is of more than antiquarian interest to us. Not only does such ontological thinking continue to dominate modern metaphysics, but its basic turns of thought are still with us in contemporary philosophy in presumably postmetaphysical forms. In fact, they have reappeared in forms that are expressly designed to reissue such traditional thoughts in supposedly untraditional ways. For example, in what might well be regarded as the founding document of postmodern philosophy, Heidegger himself begins an attempt, as it is put on the first page of *Being and Time,* to reformulate the ancient question of being in phenomenological rather than metaphysical terms and, in so doing, to retrieve the hidden ontological treasure presumably buried by our tradition. And while we cannot afford to go into the details of Heidegger's strategy for reviving the tradition in the name of its destruction, in effect, propping up the classical texts of Western metaphysics from Plato to Nietzsche by placing them between their ontological bookends, namely, Parmenides, on the one end, and Heidegger himself on the other, we do need to mention a certain tactic for revitalizing the tradition that could be thought to provide the possibility of yet another resurrection of Anselm's ontological argument.

It is no coincidence that in Heidegger's own phenomenological ontology, the problem of nothing and of how it can be thought is treated in view of the nothingness of beings and, like M 28, involves an experience in which they are "nihilated."[30] Of course, Heidegger is supposing that we can interpret this phenomenologically, rather than metaphysically, by locating an "experience of nothing" that is itself to be regarded not only as a legitimate but as a legitimating experience of thought. In his view, beings take on a certain ontological appearance in the experience of anxiety, which involves their "slipping away as whole into nothing" as they pale into utter insignificance, and through whose withdrawal "the question of being" is forced to our lips as thought is left projecting into the void. In an attempt to evade the logical problems associated with the distinction between being and nothing that have riddled the tradition, to reground that tradition phenomenologically, Heidegger appeals to a privileged "mood" that is claimed to operate prior to all cognition and that apparently does not involve a disappearing other to being but rather an elusive other that in some sense cannot be conceived or objectified, even if it can be experienced. In this key experience, which is supposed to unlock the ontological heart of metaphysics, a prerational thought thinks "nothing," not in cognitive terms of its unthinkable difference from being, nor, for that matter, as altogether other than being but, more like negative theology, as closer to being than beings.

In treating the original distinction between being and nothing not as a rational manipulation but as a phenomenological revelation, Heidegger must find a way to rehabilitate the thought of nothing, whose very nothingness is essential to this distinction without a difference that founds the unique features that being has traditionally enjoyed precisely insofar as it alone is without a proper "opposite." Like Anselm, however, Heidegger distracts us from the presumably unthinkable difference between being and nothing by relocating it in the distinction between being and beings, which is still drawn, not unlike the creator/creature distinction, on the basis of the nothingness of beings. In either case, both manage to conceal the preontological difference between being and nothing in the ontological difference itself, even if Anselm thinks the difference between being and beings metaphysically, while Heidegger rethinks it phenomenologically, that is, not in view of the metaphysical negation or conceivable annihilation of those beings that have been created *ex nihilo*, but in the phenomenological experience of the "nihilation" of (the meaning of) beings that occurs in anxiety. Nonetheless, each in his own way tries to graft the thought of nothing onto the ontological difference when, in fact, the opposite is the case. They are actually grafting the difference between being and beings onto the preontological difference between being and nothing while concealing this root by concentrating on the relation between beings and nothingness.

In any event, being is not originally determined in, but is presupposed by, what Heidegger no doubt rightly calls the "ontological" difference. For being must come to the ontological difference already distinguished from nothing if it is to dominate the distinction on both sides, whether in speaking of "being itself" or of "beings."[31] This preontological difference between being and nothing, which precedes the delimitation of being and thus is more original than the difference between being and beings, is, however, no difference at all. That, at least, is how traditional ontologic can work its magic. By following the logic of a distinction without a difference that is flaunted as such, the basic features of being are determined through a difference that is claimed to be unthinkable insofar as one of its elements cannot be thought. Without an other to determine it, insofar as its opposite "is not" but can nonetheless serve to delimit being in contrast to an other that, as "nothing," can in no way limit it, "being itself" comes to take on its peculiar set of characteristics. Buried in a long history and hidden beneath its apparent maneuvers, this ontologic remains at the heart of Anselm's thought, and it is not far-fetched to suggest that Heidegger inherited certain strategies directly from medieval ontology, as he did some of his most basic terminology.

The point just now is that the similarities between Anselm's onto-theology and Heidegger's phenomenological ontology may be sufficient to raise the possibility of a revival of the ontological argument based upon a postmetaphysical thinking that aims to get beyond metaphysics by getting before it, so as to reroot it ontologically. In fact, I have mentioned Heidegger's phenomenological updating of these traditional tactics both to stress the long history of ontologic and to suggest that just as an ultimate critique of the ontological element of the argument cannot be achieved logically—for as long as the fundamental intuition survives phenomenologically, one may simply reformulate the reasoning—the "experience of being" can seem so compelling that, for some, if logic proves to fail us in capturing this ultimate insight, they may eventually be inclined not to reformulate the argument but to reject reason itself in favor of a form of thinking that is better equipped to remain true to the "originary experience" that founds our ontological tradition. Of course, we do not doubt that Anselm's argument is, in the respects we have indicated, grounded in a certain experience of thought any more than we want to deny that Heidegger's point in insisting upon what he calls the ontological difference is that being cannot be thought of as a being, supreme or otherwise. To a certain extent, Anselm's negative ontology would seem to be suggesting this as well, as does all negative theology. The point is that in not having as yet fully criticized the phenomenological intuition at the root of Anselm's argument in view of its ontological insight, we have not undermined its mystical ground but, instead, may appear to have provided it with just such a ground. For there is undeniably a moment of ecstatic clarity in the inner experience that the argument produces, just as such "ecstatics" play a critical role in Heidegger's account of anxiety as the premier ontological experience in which thought projects beyond beings into nothing.

The problem is that if we have aimed to describe the "lived experience" that the mind undergoes in thinking through a certain rational image of God, then one may well concede that its formation is not causally grounded in an object that presents itself to thought while nonetheless insisting that we distinguish between metaphysically induced experience and phenomenologically reduced experience. Something of this distinction is, no doubt, already at work in our own account insofar as we have tried to isolate a particular phenomenological experience while at the same time trying to strip away the metaphysical-theological garb in which it has been dressed. In that case, after such a "destruction" of Anselm's onto-theo-logical metaphysics, and still seeking what remains "unsaid" in his thought, one might want to suggest that the historical validity of his argument lies elsewhere: that, in the early work, before Anselm turns to apologetics and the rationalization of Christian doctrine, there is a moment of the most excessive rationality in which he exceeds metaphysics, momentarily avoiding—or rather quite literally voiding—the onto-theo-logical image of God as a being, at least among others, even as he ultimately aims to exceed the image of God as the creator insofar as he thinks of being itself as before and without beings.

This crucial moment is dramatically apparent in the ontological reversal that takes place in M 28, which, as the prototype, is repeated in Anselm's ontological argument. Its understanding of being not only rests upon the drawing of the ultimate difference between being itself and all other beings, which is captured in P 3, but its moment of vision forces rational thought to project beyond beings, beyond all that can be thought not to exist, and, as such, to project into the void left by the ontological departure of creatures. Furthermore, Anselm makes a point of insisting upon the voiding of whatever image of God he produces and at a particular point explicitly exceeds the vision of God as if he were a being among others, as he ultimately thinks of the divine in terms of a domain of inaccessible light.[32] That the *Proslogion* regards the dwelling place of divinity as a region of self-concealment, and thus as an element in which God appears without showing himself, would seem to suggest, especially given the concessions made in his confession, that Anselm's god may be thought dimensionally but cannot be sighted as an object. And one might take this as an indication of the ontological revelation of the holy that these days invites talk of an ontical atheism, which some think may get us closer to the divine than any traditional metaphysical theism. In the moment of rational elevation in which the mind is blinded by an inaccessible light, in the ecstatic clarity that comes in the breaking open of thought to a domain beyond all objects, as the rent in the blindness of faith reveals a new blindness of reason, Anselm may seem to be teaching us how to see in the dark. For one might find in this voiding of all images of God the trace of a truth that may be worth retrieving or at least retracing in Anselm's early writings, as the traces of his, however momentary, "mysticism."

What we are concerned about, then, is that the ontological argument might be thought to find a new phenomenological ground exactly where our critique of it has left us: in the experience of nothing. After the attack on its reasoning, and precisely on the basis of its deconstruction, which shows Anselm to be thinking nothing at all in the moment of insight, one might try to lay claim to this experience as a legitimate experience of thought. According to Heidegger's own destructive model of interpretation, it would seem that one could undermine the metaphysical aspect of Anselm's argument while retaining its phenomenological element. We might distinguish the ecstatic experience of nothing, as a nonobjective experience in which thought projects toward a domain beyond beings, from the theological contention that there is a being that is the invisible object of such a vision and that shows itself by not appearing. In that event, if we have claimed that the basis of the ontological argument lies in the thought of nothing, then the question would appear to be whether such an empty vision or, if one prefers, such a vision of emptiness is a legitimate "religious experience"; indeed, whether it is not the premier experience of mysticism, rational or otherwise. For a postmetaphysical thinking might well find God in this vision of the void—as if the experience of nothing, or of a "pure," or purely empty, "consciousness," were itself a fundamental religious experience—while avoiding metaphysics, that is, without going on either to reify the void or to reground beings in it, but instead leaving thought in the dark of a presumably illuminating nothingness.[33]

In this respect, one need not know anything about Heidegger to appreciate that the experience of nothing might be taken to lie at the heart, if not so obviously, of metaphysics, then far more evidently of mysticism, and especially of the negative theology that is characteristic of a dominant strain of medieval thought. The point, in either case, is that if we have faced Anselm's rationalism, it is time to face his mysticism insofar as a full evaluation of the ontological argument requires us to raise the question of how it is possible to criticize an insight if, as we are claiming, a certain conviction-producing experience lies at the root of its reasoning. And we can only hope that our earlier account of the rites of reason may alert us to the possibility that a phenomenological ontology can no more depend upon experience than it can on intuition, not only because both have for so long been riddled with metaphysics, but insofar as it can be shown that a rational metaphysics is capable of creating, and thus grounding itself in, its own self-induced experiences of thinking. In my view, we might well suspect that the ontologic that gives birth to metaphysics is capable of doing the same.[34]

Any talk of mysticism raises certain questions. We might ask, for example, whether there is a domain of experience, inner or otherwise, that is essentially purified of all theory and thus may provide an originary ground, that is, a ground that is original and is not the by-product of thinking. Such an absolute ground would have to be given in its self-evidence and present itself as unmediated by the language in which it is articulated or by the rational arguments on the basis of which it has been clarified. In short, it would be expressed in its truth precisely insofar as our thought could give voice to it, according to Anselm's model, as an expression of the impression that this pregiven reality makes upon a mind that consequently cannot think otherwise. Or are we instead dealing with a psychologic that has made use of both reason and language to manipulate the mind into an ontological conversion-experience? For while one may claim to be getting beyond reason and language, or before them, this could be a matter of getting to a condition after reason, postrational, even postmetaphysical, in the sense that it may involve the distortion of the categories of rationality or of metaphysics, not through their transfiguration but simply through their disfigurement. As such, the assumption of a promised land that is prior to or beyond language and cognition could appear to be confirmed by an experience that thought may have within the domain of its own linguistic rationality by distorting its normal patterns, and thus would be an experience that operated primarily on the basis of reason.

Put in terms of our earlier account of the various approaches to the interpretation of a text, we might ask if there are any "pretextual" experiences, as a phenomenological account would suggest, that occur, as Anselm himself presumes in his preface, prior to writing, or whether the sorts of rhetorical experiences the *Proslogion* works to incite in the reader are textually induced. In that case, it would provide no absolute ground or get us beyond either reason or language if the experiences at issue were a matter of working within the domain of rationality in a subversive manner by means of the honing of certain linguistic images, such that the experience that is produced may be interpreted in terms of a mystical metanarrative. And while we are not in a position to supply an argument for any claims about mystical experience in general, we do have a particular case at issue just now, and to whose understanding certain recent discussions may contribute.[35] The question is whether the mysticism inherent in Anselm's negative ontology itself brings us to an insight into a reality that ultimately exceeds language and rational thought or is operating wholly within the domain of language and cognition, in fact, primarily on this basis. Put differently, the question remains: How, if Anselm has accomplished all that he has by thinking nothing, has he gone about getting us to think it in the rather precise way in which he has?

Of course, one might insist that while a phenomenological retrieval of the ontological argument would have to appeal to a certain experience of nothing that, as a "mood," gets us prior to all theory, that is, to all language and concepts, Anselm himself neither thinks in terms of what is given directly to intuition—as all thought, in his view, takes place by means of likenesses—nor does he speak as if anything could present itself to the mind except through the mediation of a primal word. To deal, however, with the issue of the direct causal relation he claims between thought and reality (not to mention with the directness of a certain thought to itself in the immediacy of its conviction-producing self-evidence), we will need to return to Anselm's view of the nature of thinking and to his image of an image as the vehicle of thought, as well as to the linguistic ontology that provides the basis for his account of rational thought as an expressing of reality in the mind by means of likenesses. For this linguistic model of thinking—indeed, both Anselm's ontology of the image and his rhetorical view of thinking as an act of inner locution—depends, as we have seen in so many cases, upon claims that are self-defeating.

In the case of his ontology of images, which fuels his vision of thinking as an entertaining of likenesses, while Anselm does insist upon the formative nature of thought in its own striving to form likenesses of the things themselves, he does so on the basis of an image of imagination that ties thought to experience in such an essentially passive way that its creative element is all but obliterated. Imagination, according to Anselm, can do no more than form and reform likenesses of those originals that have left their direct impression on the mind in experience. In the paradigm case (which, while modeled on this image of imagination, is of a thinker who does not imagine but is a pure reason), the true expression in thought is an exact duplication of the original as a perfect likeness of it that is caused by it as an impression that God's thought makes directly upon itself. And while he promises to make a similar impression on us in our experience of him in the afterlife, this sort of determination of thought by the thing itself is already foreshadowed in the compelling effect that God presently has on our rational minds as a thought that cannot be thought otherwise.

It is no coincidence that this linguistic model of rational thought, in which reality is said to be expressed in the human mind thanks to a primal word, must ultimately work to defeat the very semiotic element of language upon which it depends. While M 10 begins from a theory of signs so as to establish the notion of signification, it aims to arrive at an inner locution that, while it may be said to be the word of a thing insofar as it expresses that thing in thought, is essentially related neither to the spoken (whether out loud or silently) nor, as is not mentioned, to the written sign.[36] Consequently, Anselm's philosophy of language must be developed in apparent contrast to his theory of signs. Certainly, he still speaks of the word or expression of a thing in thought as enjoying something like a signifying relation to reality, that is, he exploits the sign-function, presumably as signifying something other than itself. But he must deny that these primal words are signs precisely because his account must apply to a primordial language user who has no use for either spoken or written signs (insofar as he expresses himself only to himself) or for a system of signs (insofar as he expresses himself and all else by means of a single word). Thus, for Anselm, language is founded on a "natural" word and has nothing essentially to do with the conventional signs on which the very notion of signification would seem to be based.[37]

But what, we might ask, is linguistic expression that does not occur in a sign-language? Is Anselm's account of imagination as an expressing in the mind of the likenesses of things such an example? And can this image of imagination provide us with an adequate model of reason, indeed, of our own linguistic rationality? Even more to the point, how would our view of Anselm's argument change if we did not allow him the philosophy of language and thought through which P 4 requires us to interpret it? What would the argument look like if we did not assume the linguistic ontology that connects thought and being by means of a primal word, but instead supposed that language and signification—and perhaps even thought—were essentially tied to a system of signs, to words capable of generating meaning in reference neither to things nor to the truth of being, but through the commerce between the signs themselves?

In a certain way, the entire argument, as well as the often repeated question it raises about the relation between thought and reality, hinges on this "grammatical" issue insofar as it depends upon the distinction between word and sign that Anselm proposes in P 4's appeal to the linguistic epistemology developed in M 10. Obviously, if we are right that Anselm is thinking nothing, then his own account of the nature of language and thought is misleading, just as he may be reversing their relation to reality. In other words, P 4, which claims that thought is compelled to think as it does by the thing itself, may be concealing the fact that, unlike the cases Anselm offers in the *Monologion* to construct his paradigm of knowledge, there is no reality of which the thought of God is a likeness. Instead, reason has indulged its own productive capabilities to construct the image of an object that is binding upon thought, a rational image of a rational reality that rational thought cannot think otherwise, but as a purely constructed image that it projects for itself. In fact, it is not clear what sense it makes, according to Anselm's own account, to regard the thought of God as the likeness of an original that cannot appear to thought, even if his confession becomes a strategic part of reason's construction of its ultimate object as unthinkable. A causal model of rational thought would seem to break down in the case of something that is greater than can be thought, raising the question of just how Anselm could have succeeded as he has in showing all that he has in view of what he has not seen. For how, in that event, has the *Proslogion* gone about constructing its image of God, indeed, how can reason form any conception of or in any sense understand that which is expressly claimed to be incomprehensible?

The answer is: through the name "something than which nothing greater can be thought." This linguistic expression serves to generate an image of God, but quite in contrast to Anselm's own philosophy of language, not because it moves thought from the phrase to a conception in the mind, let alone to the reality; for when the mind does try to construct a rational image of something of such a nature, it is ultimately faced with the conception of an inconceivable being. Instead, Anselm is able to generate linguistically a vision of God that operates on the basis of his semiological starting point. We do not entertain any likeness of the thing itself—if that is what a "conception of the mind" is for Anselm—but are limited to a certain nominal understanding of "something than which nothing greater can be thought." This is not to say that we only understand the sound of the words but rather that signs can function, even in Anselm's view, quite independently of mental conceptions.

Such a nominal way of thinking allows us to think God in terms of the signs alone, without any reality or likeness appearing to thought. In fact, given the nature of the designation at issue, we are ultimately forced to remain at the level of signs, without any movement to the "word" that Anselm would regard as the true signification of the thing itself in thought. It is nonetheless effective in its production of a strictly linguistic image of God insofar as the phrase itself functions as a self-clarifying expression. But it is not on the basis of a conception—at least not in the sense that Anselm's epistemology would think such a notion, that is, in a way that disjoins the inner locutions from the linguistic signs by connecting them directly to the impression that the thing itself has made upon the mind—that the argument operates. As we have seen, according to Anselm's own account of negative terms, there would be no likeness in thought in the case of a name like "something than which nothing greater can be thought." Instead, the argument of the *Proslogion* begins from, and remains at, the level of the linguistic expression itself, thinks the thing, as P 4 would put it, only insofar as the signs signifying it are thought, generating its contradictions in the name of this name, while such a nominal image of God, and the vision of nothing it produces, can only take on the meaning it does as an element in a more extensive narrative.

In this way, the whole of Anselm's argument, indeed, the whole of the *Proslogion,* lies in the claim of the name in premise 1: that God is something than which nothing greater can be thought, just as this designation itself depends upon a certain language-game that had been played for some time before Anselm.[38] If Anselm distinguishes between two different ways of thinking, then, despite his insistence to the contrary, it is not by thinking the thing itself that rational thought proceeds as it does in the *Proslogion* but precisely by remaining always and only at the level of signs, doing whatever thinking it does through this presumably revealing, if not revealed, name of God. And while it may be obvious that this linguistic expression is the key even to its rational arguments—as obvious, no doubt, as that the event of the "naming" of God is essential to all theology, philosophical or otherwise—it is important to be clear about just what Anselm has accomplished by means of this linguistic image. While the key phrase may appear to provide a constructive definition of God that allows rational thought to reconstruct a mental image or a rational likeness of the God of faith, "something than which nothing greater can be thought" is a rather unusual designation. It is unusual not only given the procedural element contained in the expression itself but also in that it ultimately names an incomprehensible object. By following the procedures built into this self-clarifying expression, in undertaking the reconstructive process instigated by the verbal formula that is supposed to allow us to construct a rational image of God, we are admittedly led to the image of something of which we cannot form a unified image in thought.

While we are reminding ourselves, then, that the *Proslogion* generates whatever conception of God it does by means of language, and thus that its philosophical image of God is a linguistic image, provided not just by the theological narrative but by the naming of God as something than which nothing greater can be thought, we must not forget that Anselm's depiction of such a being depends upon the demonstration of its incomprehensibility. This in itself would seem to be sufficient to raise the question of how reason can entertain a vision of what, at least presently, cannot be thought. The answer I am proposing is: semiotically, or, if one prefers, nominally.

That is, Anselm provides the rational mind with a "conception" of something that is greater than can be thought through the linguistic maneuvers that are achieved by means of his key phrase. Obviously, reason cannot, in the relevant sense, entertain the conception of an inconceivable being, least of all based upon a negative name.[39] Consequently, Anselm must insist that his rational naming of the holy offers, at best, its own kind of iconographic revelation of what refuses all names and is beyond all images or conceptions. Indeed, it is Anselm himself, although no doubt with another meaning in mind, who in P 1 requests a sign through which to seek the unknown god.[40] And that sign, we have suggested, is given in the name of God on the basis of which the *Proslogion* thinks whatever it does about him.

But what kind of a designation is "something than which nothing greater can be thought," and how does it serve to signify an inconceivable object? It is, we claim, a linguistic image that forms whatever understanding of God it does strictly on the basis of the signs themselves and that, if it can be said to have a rational content, is the result of our own essentially linguistic rationality. At the same time, this is not to say that the key phrase is not quite well designed to lead rational thought to a rather distinctive cognitive experience, or that it is not perfectly suited to leave the impression that these experiences are of an object that is eluding it. Not only is the nominal concept of something than which nothing greater can be thought developed through a series of linguistic moves—which includes the rational arguments based on the verbal formula—but the ecstatic clarity at issue in the most critical of those arguments serves to clear the mind of all likenesses of beings that can be thought not to exist. In this way, Anselm accomplishes an inner vision of God, albeit strictly negatively. Far from supplying rational thought with a likeness of the thing itself, the argument that leads us to the distinguishing feature proper to God alone, which is supposed to allow the mind to distinguish him from all else so that the reality may determine our thinking about it, actually achieves the opposite effect. For the psychological compulsion associated with the thought of what "cannot be thought not to exist" lies in the way it renders the mind incapable of focusing on any object of thought.

The *Proslogion*'s arguments, including its ontological argument, are fundamentally "semio-logical" in the sense that they proceed by determining what is consistent—or, to stress their necessarily negative approach, what is inconsistent—with the key phrase itself while creating the impression that they serve to clarify, that is, to signify some reality, albeit one that cannot appear to thought, indeed, that appears in its failure to appear insofar as it is seen in its invisibility. In effect, then, Anselm is producing whatever insight into God he does through the linguistic expression itself by running the rational mind through a course of logical maneuvers in the name of "something than which nothing greater can be thought." This includes a certain experience of emptiness that can be read in terms of the deferral of vision proposed by the mystical metanarrative of the prayers with which the *Proslogion* surrounds its reasoning and which is completely consistent with the key phrase signifying nothing. In that case, any conception we enjoy of something than which nothing greater can be thought, any vision of the thing itself in thought, let alone as greater than can be thought, must be an essentially linguistic event and cannot be modeled on the formation of likenesses, based in perception, that occurs in at least a certain kind of imagination, even though the latter is exploited by Anselm to create a misleading account not only of the nature of reason but also of the nature of language. In short, if there is any mental formation associated with the key phrase, it is strictly psycholinguistic.

Our point is that if Anselm claims to have arrived at a vision of a domain beyond all names and images, he has done so by means of an image, and a linguistic one at that. Moreover, this need to produce an image of the incomprehensible may well provide the response to a question we have thus far left unanswered, namely, why Anselm's mysticism must be rational. It is, we would suggest, because it depends upon a certain image of God, and the logical maneuvers that the mind may be put through by means of it, to produce a vision of nothing that can in turn be rationalized in view of the logic of "something than which nothing greater can be thought." One might say that the key to Anselm's key phrase lies in the way it sets the mind in motion toward a thought it cannot form. In that case, his mystical vision exploits the formative tendencies of rational thought to induce a specific psycholinguistic experience that results from the cognitive misinformation, or misformation, produced by the name itself, including in the demand (eventually made explicit, but all along implicit in the formal procedures built into the verbal formula) that reason entertain a conception of what cannot be thought. In so manipulating the plastic elements of the mind, in semiotically setting off a thought formation that cannot be completed—and both the thought of what cannot be thought not to exist as well as of what is greater than can be thought involve the same mental misfiring that empties the mind linguistically of all concrete content—indeed, in calling upon the rational mind to envision the invisible, certain cognitive experiences are undoubtedly produced by concentrating on this nominal image of God. But they are experiences of nothing, induced on the basis of a verbal icon that ultimately defies rational thought.

It is quite clear that such idolizing of the incomprehensible, which attempts to lay claim to the ineffable through the linguistic image, remains among the basic strategies in our tradition for insuring the absoluteness of an absolute. What is not so clear is what we should call the sort of divine imaging, which can include its own ban on images, that is in fact going on in Anselm's work.[41] It would not only require a more linguistic understanding of imagination than the one Anselm has provided us with but would also seem to demand a more constructive model of thought, or at least an account of the production of images that are not themselves mere reproductions. How are we to think of this linguistic tracing of an image of the holy which is not the likeness of an original but an original image, a "pure" image, untainted by any contact with reality? We could, I suppose, think of it in traditional terms as "theology," were we able to regard the latter less as a matter of reason and more as a matter of words; or we could call it iconography if we wanted to stress the importance of the production of images for Anselm's project, although this would no doubt play into his hands in stressing the need to look beyond them. Perhaps, then, it might be best to employ the term "theography," where the "graphic" may suggest not only the word but also the depiction of the divine that the written sign itself, although not necessarily alone, is capable of painting or drawing, sketching or outlining, in the case in point, through a linguistic image which is not, in my view, a matter of some inner visual event but the product of a semiotic imagination. In that case—and all the more so if language is treated as a productive element of thought— theology, in its rather familiar garb as a "naming of the holy," as theography, would not be a matter of taking divine dictation. Instead, as in the case of Anselm's rational theology, it would involve a naming that produces a historical image of the holy. The *Proslogion*'s own memorable theographic act, its philosophical construction of God as "something than which nothing greater can be thought," would not then provide a "master name" as a name to end all naming but would be the name of a beginning: the "first name" of God as a name designed to begin the ongoing, apparently collective task of a rational depiction of divinity.

In its own ambiguous way, Anselm's *Proslogion* belongs to this tradition of naming the holy, but as a matter of the rational revelation of God through the linguistic designation that, at least to a certain extent, refuses to allow the divine to remain in the protective shroud of mystery, as it calls upon the faithful to undertake the historical task of pursuing an understanding of God that is determined by rational dispute. Insofar as Anselm's own philosophical image of God serves this subversive purpose—as it calls for the historic interruption of faith in order to resite it, through a kind of historical transference, in reason—it sets a new goal for what it thinks, and tries to get others to think, as "theology." However misleading it may otherwise sound, we might regard Anselm's proposal that the rational meditator reason for himself and write for others about the divine as setting the mission for a rational theology that seeks not some single, final, and proper name, as if it could be looking for the "last name" of God. Despite recent contentions, the appeal to the "proper" is not, in our tradition, so much a matter of seeking the master name of God, or rather, insofar as it is, it more often serves as a device for claiming that no name properly applies to him. For there is no more absolute truth than the one that cannot be uttered and that, instead of calling for a name that names the holy, protects it in the claim that God has no proper name. In this sense, there is no more absolute metaphysics—even if it is expressly not onto-theological—than negative theology, which, in the name of the nameless, proposes a ban on all images, symbolic or rational, so as to dress the unthinkable in the cloak of absolute mystery. As such, however, "mystery" itself becomes the ultimate master name, a name designed to master all naming.[42]

By contrast, the claim that the holy can and must be named is not a "traditional gesture" and least of all in Anselm's case insofar as he calls for a rational renaming of God. Needless to say, I would not want to deny that Anselm also participates, in his own way, in what I have called the idolizing of the incomprehensible. But the more historic demand, the one that has been most effective in our history, is Anselm's call for the production of new images of the divine, in his case, rational images, even if they are designed to revitalize, through a kind of ongoing historical revelation, the more static image of God that faith entertains. Of course, neither would we be willing to assume, as Anselm does, that these are simply two different images of one and the same god, any more than we would want to suggest that there is some reality standing behind either or any of them. On the contrary, we are not thinking of such images as likenesses of an original but as original formations, pure constructions, through which a revelation of the divine may well take place in the naming of the holy, but one that is both essentially historical and strictly phenomenological, as it occurs in a groundless epiphany behind which nothing stands and that only happens through the image itself, indeed, through multiple images.[43] In this way, there is nothing appearing in these multiple appearances, nothing over and above the pure show, no single reality hiding invisibly behind the polyphany of images, linguistic or otherwise. Nor, then, could we regard such historical appearances as aspectival manifestations of something that withdraws from total revelation but will reveal itself completely later, whether this is deferred to some future time in history or to an eternal life to come. Instead, the holy would only appear in and through the complex of images honed by theographic acts, in the original image, which is not the image of some original but an image that is itself an original: the image that is the origin of God.

To say that these theographic images are original is, of course, not to say that they come from nowhere but simply to deny that they have any causal basis in reality. No doubt another lesson that the *Proslogion* should be teaching us in its own recycling of traditional imagery is that such divine names originate from a collective history in which there can be no first historical act but only acts that later become historic through their creative preservation.[44] This in turn raises the question of what we propose to preserve as still historically valid in Anselm's early writings. For we would like to think that a study of the founder of rational theology might have something to teach us about the nature of philosophical theology and the prospects for its future. The one thing that is clear, whatever else Anselm may have thought he was doing, is that his work expressly called for a new beginning, and at a historical time when it was needed, given the failure of Christ to appear at the millennium. His writings attempt to secure their own kind of Second Coming through the ongoing, collective, rational revelation of God, which could only be pursued by changing our way of thinking about theological matters. Consequently, if we have followed Anselm's performance in understudying his work, then the question it poses for those of us approaching the second millennium is whether we still want to play a part in this act, to perform in this play, which is the drama, or perhaps the inevitable comedy of errors, that is philosophical theology.

Both the asking and the answering of such a question may well begin from a rereading of the original script for a philosophical theology that Anselm has provided in his *Proslogion*. This new reading—with a certain behind-the-scenes appreciation that was not possible for its original audience but is only available to those watching from the wings—should put us in a position to raise the question of whether we want to close down the show or simply cancel the matinee, awaiting a new opening night when we are better prepared, indeed, have taken the time to prepare the revisions that would have to be made not only for a new cast but for a new audience as well. In this connection, our own reading of the *Proslogion* has at least suggested that one of the things that might help to guide a re-writing of this classical script is an awareness that, for our time, what may be most analogous to the new beginning that Anselm pro-posed for theology in the conversion from faith to reason would be our historical conversion from the necessity of reasoning as the ground of philosophical theology to an emphasis on the groundless or, as I have called it, the pure image. This is not to rule out the pos-sibility that such historic images might not themselves enjoy the clarity of their own kind of truth without representation. Pursuing this suggestion, however, would require an elaboration quite dif-ferent than Anselm would no doubt want to give of the constitution of a collective truth that is itself produced and creatively reproduced through ongoing work, such that we might articulate the historical nature of the appearance of the divine in view of the production through theographic acts of a complex of free and open images that can contribute to their own productive future.[45] I mention it now only as an indication that the aim of our critique of Anselm is not to deny that there can still be something like philosophical theology but to suggest that it must be essentially different from the rationalizing of Christian doctrine that some would these days pro-pose we pursue in his name.

The current invocation of Anselm to justify a rational apologetic betrays the radicalness of his thought and fails to appreciate the cre-ative demand he was making on his own historical time. To show an appreciation of how extreme his rational proposals would have been to those in the monastery, and the historic ramifications they in fact had as theological matters became subject to rational dispute, means that we would repeat his philosophical radicalness in the-ology not by doing the same thing he did but by being as extreme with respect to our historical situation as Anselm was with respect to his. By contrast, the idea of using reason to control theological thinking while using Christian beliefs to confine the limits of what reason can think about the divine is not so much an example of philo-sophical theology as of theological philosophy.[46] A genuinely philosophi-cal theology, of the historical sort Anselm himself timidly proposed, would have to keep thinking about what is holy in whatever ways it could and thus in terms of whatever determination of "the essence of divinity" came to be possible, but always with an awareness of the ultimate defenselessness of philosophy as a productive activity that can only be grounded in its own self-constructions. In this respect, Anselm would be a historic figure in the development of such a philo-sophical theology, not because he tried to provide a rational defense for the doctrines of faith but because he was not afraid, in so doing, to create his own image of God.

| N O T E S

1. G. R. Evans also suggests, in *Anselm and Talking about God,* that later in his career, Anselm became more and more aware, as his own life and work became more and more "worldly," that others were not of the same mind as he, indeed, that they may not be using their mind in the same way and for the same purposes. One might argue that there is already some indication of this in the *Proslogion*'s change of format from the dispassionate rationality of the *Monologion* to the prayerful form that provides an interpretation of reason in relation to the vision of God in its first chapter—as if the brethren had missed the visionary element of reason in the *Monologion* such that it had to be made explicit in the *Proslogion.* Of course, one might take this change to be a merely rhetorical move based on the fact that the brothers in the monastery had a certain expectation of what texts should do and that the *Monologion* violated that expectation, in which case the *Proslogion* had to be recast to fit their needs. Consequently, the form of the *Proslogion* could be regarded as a retreat from, or compromise of, Anselm's rational theology, or at least a concession that reason was forced to make to theology as a result of the cool reception with which the *Monologion* apparently met. Needless to say, I would like to think that the change of format—from one in which the rational meditator reasons with himself to one in which the contemplative addresses God directly, requesting a rational revelation of him—is based on the philosophical epistemology already articulated in the content of the *Monologion* and implicit in its form (but lost sight of in the concatenation of multiple arguments) as well as by the experience Anselm had had in the vision of God that came to him between books that night at matins. If there is any rhetorical point to the change of format, it serves a philosophical rather than a sociological purpose.

2. S II, 42.

3. For Schmitt's reminder about the use of *"speciem"* in Augustine in reference to the "face-to-face" vision of God, see his note to lines 9–12 at S II, 40. For another treatment of such issues by Anselm, see the beginning of his *Letter on the Incarnation of the Word* (S II, 3ff., available in English in the Hopkins/Richardson translation, 3:9ff.; see especially 11–12), also addressed to Pope Urban II, which includes an interpretation of the conditions under which the faithful should presume to undertake the task of reasoning about theological matters. There Anselm's characterization of the steps of spiritual ascent includes a consideration of the relation between faith, moral practice (including nutritional as well as ethical "denial of the flesh"), and intellectual vision. The latter is said to involve an experience of the thing itself, not by "hearing," presumably about it, but by "seeing"; while anyone who questions such vision is compared to those who cannot see the sun because, like bats, they only come out at night. Clearly, such "prefaces" have come a long way from the earlier ones; indeed, they show something of the road that Anselm has followed from the monastery to the domain of church politics.

4. As we have noted, the *Cur deus homo* also exploits the "incomplete" nature of this life as an argument for a life to come and, at least here and there, retains the rhetoric of revelation.

5. As, for example, Augustine at times does. See especially his *De vera religione.*

6. Here one might think of Spinoza's appeal in his book on Descartes's philosophy in which he longs for humanity simply to agree on this most agreeable argument or of Hegel's contention that it is the preferred argument for the existence of God, in contrast to Schopenhauer's characterization of it as a "charming joke," not to mention Bertrand Russell's revelation on the way to the tobacco shop.

7. Most notably by Jerome Schaffer in his "Existence, Predication and the Ontological Argument," reprinted in *The Many-Faced Argument.*

8. As I mentioned earlier, some interpreters have detected an illicit move in P 2's substitution of *"id"* for *"aliquid"* in its key phrase. Jonathan Barnes presses the claim about the transition from the indefinite to the definite description to make a rather more technical point (*The Ontological Argument*, 80), while Richard Campbell has defended the logic of this move in P 2 (*From Belief to Understanding*, 32ff.). From my point of view, however, Campbell's defense may itself perform an illicit move in supposing that Anselm has a right to assume "some arbitrary individual" of which the singular proposition is asserted when the question is whether "something than which nothing greater can be thought" refers to a particular thing or to a type of thing. For another approach, see Brian Leftow, "Individual and Attribute in the Ontological Argument." See also, in connection with certain other points we are making, his "'Existence in the Understanding' in *Proslogion* II."

9. Of course, someone like Campbell might well agree but would not admit that the way language is used is simply a matter of the way we design our concepts (see *From Belief to Understanding*, 38–39). My differences with Campbell on this score, despite my many other agreements with him, should become clear later. While I appreciate his appeal to the linguistic ground of the argument, he speaks as if all language-games were natural events, whereas I understand the "naming of God" to be part of a historical language-game that involves creative linguistic acts in the most radical sense of the term. The unnaturalness of the phrase "something than which nothing greater can be thought" is only one indication of this, since, despite the fact that it is composed of words drawn from ordinary language, their creative combination yields, as we shall see, a rather extraordinary linguistic image that must itself be accounted for in view of the sort of cultural artifact it is. Perhaps something of this is admitted in Campbell's final conclusion (226) that, with respect to what he thinks of as the "speech-act" on which the argument is based, which speaks of God as "something than which nothing greater can be thought," that is, with respect to the question of whether we are willing to utter it, "[a] measure of choice remains."

10. I am indebted to Arthur Skidmore for certain ways of putting the problem in what follows, as we have come to similar conclusions from different directions.

11. For example, William Rowe's modalized revision of P 2 and of its key phrase, which he ultimately admits is the "son" of Anselm's argument ("Response to Dicker," 203), not the original, would seem to avoid this assumption.

12. Suppose, for example, that it is true of numbers that, for any *n,* a larger can be thought. Does it make sense to say of what cannot be a number, for example, the color blue, that if blue could be a number, something larger than it could be thought? Or rather, in saying this, even if it made some sense, would the sense it made be saying anything about blue?

13. Others have effectively reread the argument of P 2 in similar terms. We have already mentioned Rowe, while R. M. Adams might seem to avoid certain problems we have raised by reading the "can be thought" of P 2 as "is logically possible" ("The Logical Structure of Anselm's Arguments").

14. As indicated earlier, this point has been made by Matthews in his "On Conceivability in Anselm and Malcolm," while D. P. Henry has insisted that the inclusion of "thought" in the formula is designed to distinguish God from other "necessary beings" as well as to avoid the suggestion that there is some "incapacity" in God. See his *Medieval Logic and Metaphysics,* 108–11.

15. This would, no doubt, explain why some have claimed to be able to formulate arguments to show the inconceivability of the existence of God based on Anselm's principles. D. P. Henry, for example, has suggested that the principles at work in P 2 could be used to show that S cannot exist both in the understanding and in reality. He contends that if S exists at least in the understanding, it cannot be thought to exist in reality, or else a greater would be thought (*Medieval Logic and Metaphysics,* 117).

16. Rowe has taken note of this negative factor in P 2. Its implications, as well as the differences between his argument and Anselm's, have been discussed in his exchange with Georges Dicker (*Faith and Philosophy* 5 [1988]: 193–206). In my view, however, Rowe's conclusion—that the illicit premise in the argument is the question-begging assumption that S can exist in the understanding (according to his reading, that S is possible)— would appear to concede the legitimacy of what I take to be, and what he himself has located as, a key and hidden assumption in P 2, which I have rendered as premise 4, namely, that whatever exists in the understanding either exists in the understanding alone or exists both in the understanding and in reality (and which he would render as: if something is possible, then it is either an existing or a nonexisting thing). For this premise is designed to establish the relevance of categories of existence and nonexistence to the category at issue. The illicit move in P 2 is, then, made by means of the literal "con-fusion" of an epistemological category with an ontological category, as if the epistemological category "exists in the understanding" were of the same order as the ontological category "exists in the understanding alone," such that in conceding the former, we are exclusively committed to the aforementioned two options. But something can "exist in the understanding," in the sense of "be understood," without it following that we are committed to the ontological conclusion that it either exists in the understanding alone or exists both in the understanding and in reality. As we shall suggest, the latter would not apply, for example, to the words of the key phrase itself. Put otherwise, to say that God's existence is possible—as defenders of the ontological argument since Leibniz have admitted must be shown—is to say more than that the concept of God is intelligible. Instead, it is to claim that existential categories are relevant to it. In effect, then, even if the unintelligibility of a concept assures us that the question of existence is irrelevant, the intelligibility of a linguistic expression does not insure that the categories of existence or nonexistence are relevant; although I do not mean to imply by this that "something than which nothing greater can be thought" is intelligible. We have yet to indicate the precise sense in which we think the phrase "is understood."

17. See Gaunilo's reply 4 (S I, 126–27). For a discussion of the antinomic nature of Anselm's key phrase that connects it directly to P 15's conclusion that S is greater than can be thought, see J. Vuillemin's "Id quo nihil cogitari potest. Über die innere Möglichkeit eines rationalen Gottesbegriffs."

18. For an example of the former, see V. Warnach, "Wort und Wirklichkeit bei Anselm von Canterbury," as well as his "Zum Argument in *Proslogion* Anselms von Canterbury." See also Gillian Evans's *Anselm and Talking about God,* Marcia Colish's *The Mirror of Language,* as well as her "St. Anselm's Philosophy of Language Revisited," and Wolfgang Gombocz's "Anselm über Sinn und Bedeutung."

19. While Campbell depends primarily on Wittgenstein in his *From Belief to Understanding,* he does, with McGill, mention the relevance of Heidegger's account of language (219) and has recently written on the relation between Heidegger's and Anselm's view of truth. See his "Freedom as Keeping the Truth." McGill had appealed to the linguistic element of the argument in *The Many-Faced Argument* (104–10), although he fails to work out the implications of the Heideggerian view of language for Anselm's argument.

20. On "The Onto-theo-logical Nature of Metaphysics," see Heidegger's *Identity and Difference.* On the thought of "nothing" in relation to the question of being, see his "What Is Metaphysics?" including its subsequent introduction ("The Way Back into the Ground of Metaphysics") and "Postscript," as well as what amounts to the introduction to *An Introduction to Metaphysics,* entitled "The Fundamental Question of Metaphysics."

21. I have already mentioned Campbell in this connection. I might note, however, that while I am sympathetic with the sort of linguistic account he attempts, I think that it does more to undermine the argument than to provide any grounds for it. Despite Wittgenstein's potentially misleading image of the "bedrock" of our linguistic practices (*Philosophical Investigations,* #217), it must be remembered that Anselm is not clarifying ordinary language, nor, for that matter, ordinary religious language, but the language-game of Christian theology. His "name" of God is a cultural artifact, grounded, I would suggest, not so much in reality, or even in the things people ordinarily do or say, as in a specific textual tradition. No doubt one can play the game of grounds here, suggesting that this only shows how deeply rooted Anselm's language is in a collective history. But it seems to me not altogether un-Wittgensteinian to be suspicious of such highly specialized language-games that, while parasitic on ordinary language, themselves have no need to follow its conventions but rather tend to operate by "correcting" it through the extraordinary usage of ordinary language. In the end, we will suggest another account of the way in which the argument is grounded linguistically. Our basic disagreement with Campbell's reading of the force of the argument involves the fact that while turning our attention to these linguistic issues, he seeks a new ground for the argument in a language that is somehow naturally related to reality, whereas we will stress the ultimate groundlessness of such nominal images of God.

22. In this regard, we might say that if Anselm's philosophy of language is most similar to any recent account, it would seem to be Husserl's rather than Heidegger's; although the latter may depend in certain respects upon the former. As is well known, such a view of language has been subjected to extensive criticism by Derrida in his *Speech and Phenomena.* For a discussion of the connection between Derrida's critique of Husserl and Wittgenstein's critique of the traditional view of language, see Newton Garver's introduction to the aforementioned work.

23. For a phenomenological discussion of the type of joy that may be thought to be associated with such anticipation, see S. Strasser's *Phenomenology of Feeling*.

24. Derrida has recently drawn attention to a similar format in the writings of Pseudo-Dionysius. See his "How to Avoid Speaking: Denials."

25. On Lanfranc's reception of the *Monologion,* see R. W. Southern, *St. Anselm and His Biographer,* 57.

26. S I, 94.

27. For some suggestions concerning the legitimation of reason in modern thought through metanarratives, see Jean-François Lyotard's *The Postmodern Condition.*

28. This is not to deny that there is, shall we say, a scholastic tradition of resurrections of Anselm's argument, that is, a tradition interested only in the reasoning itself, working from blind inference, without concerning itself with the insight involved. This may well seem to be all the more the case as the argument enters into the reinterpretations that translate it into symbolic logic.

29. For some suggestions in this connection, see Beckaert, "A Platonic Justification for the Argument *a Priori*"; Michael P. Slattery, "Parmenides: Anselm *eminenter*"; and Vincent J. Ferrara, "Some Reflections on the Being-Thought Relationship in Parmenides, Anselm and Hegel." Obviously, the development of the "history of being" that underwrites Anselm's claims about a supreme being and the logic of the history this name propels are beyond the scope of this study. Suffice it to say that, in my view, the ontological argument is properly, if coincidentally, so called precisely because it is among the founding moments in the development of the logic of being as what is without an other. I would suggest that the rational arguments that lead, early on in our tradition, to the thought of being as setting a certain standard of reality insofar as its opposite is nothing, that is, in that it has no opposite, eventually yield, given the contradictions that can be shown to be involved in such reasoning, the thought of what is "beyond" being. Like this original nothing, it is admitted to be unthinkable, but in a rather literal sense as what must be thought in a form of "unknowing" that is capable of elevating the mind beyond both being and nothing in an ecstatic experience that can be, if not elicited, then at least prepared for through those tactics of thought that are eventually canonized under the title of the *via negativa.* All of this must be seen to belong to the complicated development of an ontological strategy that may have begun with the Eleatic arguments but eventually developed along certain Neoplatonic lines into a Christian tradition that cherishes "being itself" (*esse per se*) as the first name of God, even if, by the time of Anselm, the treatment of such "divine names" had at its disposal the tactics of a negative ontology that is not altogether unlike the mystical theology of Pseudo-Dionysius. Indeed, it is precisely the joining of these elements—as distant as the original rationalization of being may seem to be from the ecstasies of unknowing—that lies at the heart of Anselm's rational mysticism.

I say this despite recent attempts to exempt Anselm from traditional critiques of the ontological argument by insisting that his argument is not "ontological," even though I would agree that Anselm's argument differs in any number of ways from the arguments Kant had in mind when he so dubbed them. I have already mentioned J.-L. Marion in this regard. For another approach, see Thomas Losoncy's "Saint Anselm's Rejection of the 'Ontological Argument.'" See also, in response to his account, my "A Classical Misunderstanding of Anselm's Argument."

30. See Heidegger's 1929 lecture "What Is Metaphysics?" (which has become famous for its claim that "the nothing itself nothings" [*Das Nichts selbst nichtet*]), as well as the later introduction, "The Way Back into the Ground of Metaphysics," and "Postscript," between which the original essay was sandwiched in the 1940s. We might just note that if, as Heidegger insists, metaphysics is but a moment, albeit a long one, in the "history of being," then the thought of being, which precedes metaphysics (if the latter begins with Plato), may well be "destined" to lead to it, but precisely in the sense that it provides the logical, or, in our phenomenological sense of the term, psycho-logical ground of Western thought. The latter, of course, remains evident in Platonic metaphysics in the famous divided line, in which the various levels of reality are correlated with different states of consciousness, even as *Being and Time* itself, despite its claims to the contrary, provides an essentially psychological account of anxiety. In this connection, it could be shown, I think, that the various stages of Heidegger's rewriting of the experience of anxiety progressively "ontologize" it, indeed, may well be said to "metaphysicalize" it. The last gasp of Western metaphysics is perhaps most audible in Heidegger's own thought in the later introduction and postscript to "What Is Metaphysics," which finds its way back to the "ground" of metaphysics by means of an ontological conversion that turns "nothing" into "the veil of being."

31. When Heidegger addresses the question of the delimitations of being in Greek philosophy in *An Introduction to Metaphysics*, he thinks in terms of the difference between being and becoming, being and appearance, being and thinking, being and value, but not in terms of the original and primary difference between being and nothing. Instead, the discussion of "nothing" is reserved for the introduction to this introduction to metaphysics insofar as it is relevant to what is claimed to be the basic question (*Grundfrage*) of metaphysics: Why are there beings and not rather nothing? In short, "nothing" is associated with beings, but precisely so as to direct us to the way in which the question of being remains concealed in this question about beings and their nothingness.

32. One might argue that both the ontological conversion of M 28 and the historic moment of the theological "epoche"—of the suspension of the God of faith as a historic beginning for rational theology—require a certain suspending of all images of God. I would suggest, however, that Anselm is in effect operating with a double image of God, indeed, a double vision of "the God of faith and reason," and a doubling that is not simply a result of our mental myopia. To this extent, he may be thought to be working between images, although, in my view, this "between" is itself achieved by means of an image.

33. For a discussion of the relation between Eastern and Western thought in this regard, see H. Waldenfels, *Absolute Nothingness*.

34. It has, of course, been so criticized from the "first critique" of ontology by Gorgias to, as Heidegger would say, the "end of metaphysics" in Nietzsche. And while Heidegger can, in *An Introduction to Metaphysics*, perversely embrace Nietzsche's claim that "being" is an empty expression by regarding it as documentation of the fact that Nietzsche is himself the

"victim" of a tradition that has been progressively forgetting being, he cannot account in this way for what, in his own account of the history of Western thought, would have to be counted as a premetaphysical critique of Eleatic ontology in Gorgias. In either case, for reasons that will be suggested in what follows, the issue is quite appropriately framed by Nietzsche—and with this Gorgias would surely agree—at the level of language, namely, of the emptiness of the word "being." The whole thrust of traditional ontologic depends upon the assumption that while "nothing" does not refer to anything, "being" does. That is, the basis for the privileging of being depends upon problematizing the distinction between being and nothing, as if it were unlike other distinctions, because while the one side of the difference refers to something that is, the other side refers to what is not. The uniqueness of this distinction, then, arises only if one assumes that words must refer to something, in which case, "nothing" becomes problematic, indeed, becomes what we have called a disappearing other to being. To what extent this model of difference—indeed, this model difference—becomes the model for other differences (in which one element dominates the other through a logic of suppression) is another issue. Ironically, the case in point would itself appear to suggest that what is regarded as the primary element of a difference gets its primacy through its other, that is, in the case of this difference, the uniqueness of "being" is actually based on the peculiarity of "nothing." And while Heidegger's own emphasis on "the nothing" may be regarded as an acknowledgment of this, its transfiguration into "the veil of being" can hardly help but remind us of another Nietzschean diagnosis of the logic of Western metaphysics: better nothingness than nothing. In any event, for a discussion of Nietzsche's account of the nature of metaphysics and of how the latter goes about transforming nothing into something by means of the magic wand of the word, see my "The Metaphysician as Poet-Magician."

35. The controversy to which I refer is the one incited by, among others, Steven Katz in his *Mysticism and Philosophical Analysis* and later in his *Mysticism and Religious Traditions.* A book-length response has recently appeared, edited by Robert Forman, under the title *The Problem of Pure Consciousness.* See also Wayne Proudfoot, *Religious Experience,* and, most recently, Nelson Pike's *Mystic Union.*

36. Classically, a distinction was drawn between the spoken, written, and mental sign.

37. This makes it all the more ironic that M 10 gives as the sole example of a word that is identical to what it signifies the letter *a,* which, in referring to an element of the sign system, signifies itself.

38. The exact turn of phrase had already been used by Seneca, while both Boethius and Augustine employed similar expressions (see S I, 102). Campbell refers to the claim Anselm is here making as a "speech-act" that he performs, presumably in reiterating a move in a religious language-game. In a sense, I agree but want to suggest that Anselm is performing a more radically creative act than Campbell may be inclined to admit, and, indeed, that he is not performing a religious, but a theological act, even if it involves the sort of rhetorical or allocutionary speech—or written—act that we have previously discussed. Furthermore, it is not clear, as Campbell implies, that Anselm utters this phrase while in prayer. Instead, it would seem to be an act performed somewhere between prayer and proof, that is, between the prayer of P 1 and the proof in P 2. In any case, if Anselm did not make up the name but inherited it from the tradition, the creativity of his linguistic act would not lie in his utterance of the phrase but in the use to which he found he could put it.

39. For a discussion of Anselm's attempt to explain away this problem, see the aforementioned article by Vuillemin and his comments concerning the role of a metalanguage in expressing the claim that something is inexpressible. One may well entertain the conception that something is inconceivable, but this is not to entertain a conception of something that is inconceivable.

40. S I, 98.

41. At this point, someone like J.-L. Marion would no doubt insist that we distinguish between an idol and an icon. For a general discussion of the difference, see his *God Without Being*. Given Marion's own account, however, I think it can be shown that the incomprehensible is an idol designed in fact to stop thought, to arrest and freeze it, not an icon that aims to get us to look beyond it, as Marion would say, to the "invisable." In fact, as this appeal to the invisable should indicate, the very notion of an icon is always already based on the idolizing of the incomprehensible. Further discussion of this in the present context would require a detailed critique of Marion's reading of the later portions of the *Proslogion* (in his "Is the Ontological Argument Ontological"?) and its account of the invisibility of God.

42. For a recent version of this, see John Caputo's *Radical Hermeneutics*. We might say that the general tendency is to suppose that there are only two options: either one can name the holy finally and completely (the proper name), or one must posit mystery as what cannot be named except iconographically, that is, through a name that names the nameless. But there is a third alternative: that the holy is produced by naming, in which case there is nothing being named or eluding the name, nor would there be any final name in the sense that a new name can always be uttered—that is, a new image produced—even if not at will.

43. As we have suggested, Anselm's thought could itself be said to offer multiple images of God, indeed, to require a double vision of God that allows it to work between the god of faith and the god of reason, so as to play the one image off of the other. For us, these are not two views of the same god, as they would be for Anselm, nor do we suppose our myopia could be corrected in a future life.

44. The name "something than which nothing greater can be thought" could offer no better example. It would, no doubt, have been lost to the annals of history had Anselm not rendered it historic. Only after Anselm do we look back to see where the phrase originates. More importantly, however, I would not want my comments about the history of ontologic to leave the impression that we are to think of this history as a matter of some generic idea of "being" rather than of a specific set of images that are recycled from a concrete textual tradition. If anything, the close reading we have given to Anselm's texts is based upon the assumption that the history of philosophy is not a history of general ideas but of specific images and arguments. It is, in short, not so much a history of ideas as a history of texts. For it is in committing itself to writing that philosophical thought commits itself to the specific ideas it does; that is, it is in writing alone that thought becomes concrete and establishes the specificity of what it thinks.

45. For some preliminary suggestions concerning the nature of the advent of such a collective truth, see my "Heidegger on Community," as well as my "Heidegger's Contribution to a Phenomenology of Culture." This discussion would have to be carried on in view of what might be called the deontological aspect of at least a certain phase of Heidegger's later thought, and with specific regard to Heidegger's account of the nature of divinity.

46. Such an approach would seem to be suggested by Thomas Morris in his *Anselmian Explorations.*

| **Text and Translation:
Anselm's *Proslogion***

The translation that follows would not have been possible were it
not for existing translations. I have tried to take advantage of them
as well as of the unique opportunity provided by this series to offer a
translation that is not so much designed to stand alone as to come at
the end of, and to appear entirely within the context of, an extensive
interpretation. In short, since this translation is not designed to
compete with other translations so much as to complete our reading
of Anselm, I have not just felt free to offer a rather free translation
but to borrow freely from the insight of other translators. I have,
needless to say, also been freed by a format that includes the original text with my translation.

I have taken the Latin text from F. S. Schmitt's German translation of the *Proslogion*. The difference between the Latin version he
provides with his translation and the one he had offered in the *Opera omnia* is primarily a matter of form. I have further interpolated
the format he proposes, leaving Schmitt's presentation in the Latin
text, while trying in my English version not so much to highlight, as
he does, the formal structure of the words as to highlight the rhythm
and flow, indeed, the passion of those passages in which Anselm
breaks into prayer. Especially in those cases, I understand the aim
of my translation to be to produce the poetic affect of Anselm's prose,
not simply to reproduce in English a literal version of the Latin. Indeed, a truly literal rendering is often made impossible by the very
singsong rhymes of which Anselm is so fond and which depend upon
the sound of the Latin words.

I have also followed Schmitt's method of indicating the scriptural citations that are woven into Anselm's text. Some translators
have seen fit to use quotation marks, while others have noted each
citation, whether in a separate footnote or in brackets within the

text itself. Both practices, however, tend to break up the flow of Anselm's writing. The best solution, I think, is the use of italics. While this also tends to distinguish the biblical citations from Anselm's text rather than to incorporate them into it, it does serve to remind us of the force with which such phrases from Holy Writ would have rung in the ears of a monastic reader.

Finally, one may wonder why I have not, as tradition would have it, included along with my translation of the *Proslogion* Gaunilo's response on behalf of the fool and Anselm's reply. As far as I am concerned, while this exchange, in its addressing of the issues in a purely rational fashion, may well show the historic change that *has taken place* and therefore may well be relevant to analyzing the arguments involved, it does not show the change *taking place* if, as I have claimed, the latter is dependent upon Anselm's distinctive interlacing of prayer and proof. In this regard, I have wanted the prayer that the *Proslogion* itself must be understood to be to have the last word, which, in addressing God rather than Gaunilo, is, of course, *Amen.*

| Prooemium

Postquam opusculum quoddam velut exemplum meditandi de ratione fidei cogentibus me precibus quorundam fratrum, in persona alicuius tacite secum ratiocinando quae nesciat investigantis edidi: considerans illud esse multorum concatenatione contextum argumentorum, coepi mecum quaerere, si forte posset inveniri unum argumentum, quod nullo alio ad se probandum quam se solo indigeret, et solum ad astruendum quia Deus vere est, et quia est summum bonum nullo alio indigens, et quo omnia indigent ut sint et ut bene sint, et quaecumque de divina credimus substantia, sufficeret.

Ad quod cum saepe studioseque cogitationem converterem, atque aliquando mihi videretur iam posse capi quod quaerebam, aliquando mentis aciem omnino fugeret: tandem desperans volui cessare velut ab inquisitione rei, quam inveniri esset impossibile. Sed cum illam cogitationem, ne mentem meam frustra occupando ab aliis, in quibus proficere possem, impediret, penitus a me vellem excludere: tunc magis ac magis nolenti et defendenti se coepit cum importunitate quadam ingerere. Cum igitur quadam die vehementer eius importunitati resistendo fatigarer, in ipso cogitationum conflictu sic se obtulit quod desperaveram, ut studiose cogitationem amplecterer, quam sollicitus repellebam.

Aestimans igitur quod me gaudebam invenisse, si scriptum esset, alicui legenti placiturum, de hoc ipso et de quibusdam aliis sub persona conantis erigere mentem suam ad contemplandum Deum et quaerentis intelligere quod credit, subditum scripsi opusculum. Et quoniam nec istud nec illud, cuius supra memini, dignum libri nomine aut cui auctoris praeponeretur nomen iudicabam, nec tamen eadem sine aliquo titulo, quo aliquem, in cuius manus venirent, quodam modo ad se legendum invitarent, dimittenda putabam: unicuique suum dedi titulum, ut prius *Exemplum meditandi der ratione fidei,* et sequens *Fides quaerens intellectum* diceretur. Sed cum iam a pluribus cum his titulis utrumque transcriptum esset, coegerunt me plures, et maxime reverendus archiepiscopus Lugdunensis, Hugo nomine, fungens in Gallia legatione Apostolica qui mihi hoc ex Apostolica praecepit auctoritate, ut nomen meum illis praescriberem. Quod ut aptius fieret, illud quidem *Monologion,* id est soliloquium, istud vero *Proslogion,* id est alloquium, nominavi.

| Preface

After having written at the urging of several of my brethren a short work, as an example of meditation on the rationality of faith, in the person of one who seeks by silently reasoning with himself that of which he is ignorant, considering that it was composed of a complex sequence of interconnected arguments, I began to ask myself whether it might be possible to discover a single argument that required nothing for its proof but itself alone and would alone be sufficient to demonstrate that God truly is, and that he is the supreme good, needing no other, but which all need for their being and well-being, and whatever else we believe concerning the divine substance.

But as often and as eagerly as I turned my thought to this, it sometimes appeared to me that what I was seeking might be almost in my grasp, while at other times it altogether eluded the keenest vision of my mind, so that finally, in desperation, I was about to give up, as if I were looking for something that was impossible to find. When, however, I had resolved to shut this thought out altogether, so as not to keep my mind, in being occupied by the pointless, from other thought with which I might make progress, it then began, in my unwillingness and resistance, to force itself upon me more and more insistently. And then one day, when I was totally exhausted from resisting its troubling persistence, what I had despaired of finding appeared in the midst of the very conflict of my thinking, so that I eagerly embraced the thought that, in my anxiety, I had repelled.

Considering, then, that what had given me joy to discover, if it were written down, would afford pleasure to those who might read it, I have written the following short work, on this and various other topics, in the person of one striving to elevate his own mind to the contemplation of God and seeking to understand what he believes. And while I judged neither this one nor the other that I mentioned above worthy to be called a book, or to have the name of its author precede it, neither did I think they should be sent off without some title by which anyone into whose hands they might come would be invited in a certain way to their reading. Thus, I gave to each its own title, so that the first was called *An Example of Meditating on the Rationality of Faith,* and the sequel, *Faith Seeking Understanding.* But after both had already been copied with these titles by a number of people, some urged me—and especially the reverend archbishop of Lyons, named Hugo, serving as the apostolic legate in Gaul, who directed me on the basis of his apostolic authority—to prefix my name to them. So that this might be done more fittingly, I have, then, given the name *Monologion,* that is, a soliloquy, to the former work, but named this one *Proslogion,* that is, an address.

CAPITULUM I

Excitatio mentis ad contemplandum Deum

Eia nunc, homuncio,
    fuge   paululum occupationes tuas,
    absconde te modicum a tumultuosis cogitationibus
                  tuis.
    Abice   nunc   onerosas curas, et
    postpone   laboriosas distentiones tuas.
    Vaca   aliquantulum Deo, et
    requiesce aliquantulum in eo.

Mt 6:6   *Intra in cubiculum* mentis tuae,
        exclude omnia praeter Deum et quae te iuvent ad
            quaerendum eum, et
ibid.   *clauso ostio* quaere eum.
    Dic nunc, totum *cor meum,*
    dic nunc Deo:
    Quaero vultum tuum,
Ps 26:8   *vultum tuum, Domine, requiro.*
Eia nunc ergo tu, Domine Deus meus, doce cor meum,
    ubi et quomodo te quaerat,
    ubi et quomodo te inveniat.
Domine, si hic non es,
        ubi te quaeram absentem?
     Si autem ubique es,
        cur non video praesentem?
1 Tm 6:16 Sed certe habitas *lucem inaccessibilem.*
Et ubi est lux inaccessibilis?
Aut quomodo accedam ad lucem inaccessibilem?
Aut quis me ducet et inducet in illam,
    ut videam te in illa?
Diende quibus signis,
      qua facie   te quaeram?
Numquam te vidi, Domine Deus meus,
      non novi   faciem tuam.
Quid faciet, altissime Domine,
quid faciet iste tuus, longinquus exsul?
Quid faciet servus tuus anxius amore tui et longe
Ps 50:13   *proiectus a facie tua?*
Anhelat videre te   —et nimis abest illi facies tua.

Chapter 1
An excitation of the mind
to the contemplation of God

Come, now, O insignificant man,
  flee a while from your busy tasks,
  put aside for a moment the confusion of your thoughts,
  discard now your distracting cares and
  postpone your busy labors.
Free yourself a little for God, and
  rest a while in him.
Enter into the inner chamber of your mind,
  exclude everything, besides God and what can be of help in
  seeking him, and
  close the door to seek him.
Speak, now, *my* whole *heart,*
Say now to God:
  I seek your face,
  For your face, O lord, I search.

Come, now then, you, O my lord God, teach my heart
  where and how to seek you,
  where and how to find you.
Lord, if you are not here,
  where should I seek you in your absence?
And if you are everywhere,
  why do I not see you in your presence?
Surely *you dwell in inaccessible light!*
  But where is the inaccessible light,
  and how can I approach such unapproachable light?
Who will lead me to and bring me into it,
  so that I may see you there?
By what signs,
  in what profile, should I seek thee?

Never have I seen you, lord my God,
  I have not known your face.
What shall he do, O lord most high,
  what shall this far-flung exile do?
What shall your servant do,
  anxious for your love,
  but *cast far from your face?*
Breathless from the struggle to see you,
  your face is too far off.

Accedere ad te desiderat— et inaccessibilis est
                      habitatio tua.
Invenire te cupit   —et nescit locum tuum.
Quaerere te affectat   —et ignorat vultum tuum.
Domine, Deus meus es et Dominus meus es—
    et numquam te vidi.
Tu me fecisti et refecisti et omnia mea bona tu mihi
                      contulisti —
    et nondum novi te.
Denique ad te videndum factus sum—
    et nondum feci, propter quod factus sum.
O misera sors hominis, cum hoc perdidit, ad quod factus
                         est!

O durus et dirus casus ille!
Heu, quid perdidit et quid invenit,
    quid abscessit et quid remansit!
Perdidit beatitudinem, ad   quam factus est,
et invenit miseriam,   propter quam factus non est.
Abscessit,   sine quo nihil felix est,
et remansit, quod per se non nisi miserum est.

Ps 77:25   *Manducabat* tunc *homo panem angelorum,* quem nunc
                      esurit;

Ps 126:2   manducat   nunc *panem dolorum,*   quem tunc
                      nesciebat.

Heu publicus   luctus   hominum,
    universalis   planctus filiorum Adae!
Ille ructabat   saturitate—
nos suspiramus esurie.
Ille abundabat—
nos mendicamus.
Ille feliciter   tenebat et misere   deseruit—
nos infeliciter egemus et miserabiliter desideramus.
et heu, vacui remanemus!
Cur non nobis custodivit, cum facile posset,
    quo tam graviter careremus?
Quare sic nobis obseravit lucem
    et obduxit nos tenebris?
Ut quid nobis abstulit vitam
    et inflixit mortem?

He desires to come close to you,
    but your dwelling place is inaccessible.
He longs to find you,
    but does not know where you are.
He aspires to seek you,
    but does not know your face.

O lord, you are my God,
    and you are my lord,
    yet never have I seen you.
You have made and remade me
    and have given me whatever goods I have,
    and still I do not know you.
I was made to see you
and have still not accomplished that for which I was created.

O miserable lot of mankind
    when he lost that for which he was made!
O that hard and hapless fall!
    What was lost and what was gained,
    what departed and what remained?
He lost the beatitude for which he was made,
    and found the misery for which he was not made.
He lost that without which nothing is happy,
    and gained what is itself nothing but misery.
Then *man feasted on the bread of angels,* for which we now hunger,
    now we eat *the bread of pain,* which he knew not.

O the common affliction of mankind,
    the universal lament of the sons of Adam!
He tasted fullness;
    we sigh with hunger.
He abounded;
    we beg.
He happily had and miserably deserted;
    we unhappily lack and long in our misery.
Alas, we remain empty!
Why could he not have kept for us what would have been so easy
                             then,
    but now so hard to lose?
Why did he deprive us of the light
    and shroud us all in darkness?
Why did he take away our life,
    inflicting death upon us?

Aerumnosi, unde sumus expulsi,
      quo   sumus impulsi!
      Unde praecipitati,
      quo   obruti!
A patria   in exsilium,
a visione Dei in caecitatem nostram.
A iucunditate immortalitatis in amaritudinem
      et horrorem mortis.
Misera mutatio! De quanto bono in quantum malum!
Grave damnum,
gravis dolor,
grave totum!
Sed heu me miserum, unum de aliis miseris filiis
      Evae elongatis a Deo!
      quid incepi, quid effeci?
      Quo tendebam, quo deveni?
      Ad quid aspirabam, in quibus suspiro?

Ps 121:9   *Quaesivi bona—et ecce turbatio!*

Jer 14:19   Tendebam in Deum—et offendi in me ipsum.
      Requiem quaerebam in secreto meo—et *tribulationem et*

Ps 114:3   *dolorem inveni* in intimis meis.
      Volebam ridere a gaudio mentis meae—et cogor *rugire*

Ps 37:9   *a gemitu cordis mei.*
      Sperabatur laetitia—et ecce, unde densentur suspiria!

Ps 6:4   Et o *tu,*   *Domine, usquequo?*

Ps 12:1   *Usquequo, Domine, oblivisceris nos,*
      usquequo   avertis faciem tuam a nobis?

ibid., 4   Quando *respicies et exaudies* nos?

ibid.;   Quando *illuminabis oculos* nostros et *ostendes* nobis

Ps 79:4; 8   *faciem tuam?*
      Quando restitues te nobis?

O wretched ones,
 from where are we expelled,
 to where are we impelled?
 from where have we been cast down,
 to where are we sinking?
From the homeland into exile,
 from the vision of God into our blindness.
From the delight of immortality
 to the bitterness and horror of death.

O miserable mutation,
 from so much good to so much evil!
The grief of loss,
 the grief of pain,
 the grief of it all!
O my misery!
One more miserable son of Eve,
 far removed from God.
What have I undertaken,
 what have I accomplished?
For what was I striving,
 to what have I come?
To what did I aspire,
 for what do I sigh?

I sought goods,
 and, behold, confusion.
I reached for God,
 and tripped over myself.
I sought rest in my solitude,
 and *tribulation and pain have invaded* my inwardness.
I wanted to laugh in the joy of my mind,
 and am forced *to cry out with the groan of my heart.*
I hoped for gladness,
 and, behold, these sighs oppress me.

And *you, O lord,*
 how long?
How long will you forget us?
How long will you turn your face away from us?
When *will you look upon us and hear* us?
When *will you illuminate our eyes* and *show* to us *your face?*
When will you restore yourself to us?

Respice, Domine, exaudi, illumina nos, ostende nobis
    teipsum.

Restitue te nobis, ut bene sit nobis, sine quo tam male
    est nobis.

Miserare labores et conatus nostros ad te, qui nihil valemus
                       sine te.

Ps 78:9 Invitas nos, *adiuva nos.*

Obsecro, Domine, ne desperem suspirando, sed respirem
          sperando.

Obsecro, Domine, amaricatum est cor meum sua
               desolatione,
      indulca illud tua consolatione.

Obsecro, Domine,
    esuriens incepi quaerere te, ne desinam ieiunus
                  de te.
    Famelicus accessi, ne recedam impastus.
    Pauper veni ad divitem, miser ad misericordem,
    ne redeam vacuus et contemptus.

Job 3:24 Et si, *antequam comedam, suspiro,* da vel post suspiria
          quod comedam.

Domine, incurvatus non possum nisi deorsum aspicere;
        erige me, ut possim sursum intendere.

Iniquitates meae supergressae caput meum obvolvunt
Ps 37:5   me, *et sicut onus grave* gravant me.

Evolve me, exonera me, ne *urgeat puteus* earum *os suum*
Ps 68:16   *super me.*

Liceat mihi suspicere lucem tuam,
    vel de longe,
    vel de profundo.

Look upon us, O lord,
    hear us,
    illuminate us,
    show to us yourself.
Restore yourself to us
    so that good may be with us, you,
    without whom so much evil is ours.
Have pity on our labors in striving toward you, you,
    without whom we can do nothing.
You incite us, now *assist us!*

I pray, O lord,
    that I not suffocate on my sighs,
    but instead am revived by my hope.
I pray, O lord,
    that the bitterness of heart in my desolation
    may be sweetened by your consolation.
I pray, O lord,
    that as I began to seek you in hunger,
    I may finally finish my fast.

I approached in famine;
    do not make me withdraw unfed.
I come as a pauper
    to one who is wealthy,
a wretch to one rich in compassion;
    do not turn me away empty and in scorn.
And if, *before I eat, I sigh,*
    after the sighing, grant me that on which to feast.

Lord, I am so bent over
    that I can only look down;
Elevate me,
    so that I may strive to look up.
My iniquities are piled over my head
    and cover me;
Like a heavy burden,
    they weigh me down.
Relieve me, release me,
    so that *this pit of sin*
    does not bury me.
Let me look upward to your light,
    if only from afar,
    if only from the depths.

Doce me quaerere te et
ostende te quaerenti; quia
    nec quaerere te possum, nisi tu doceas,
    nec invenire,   nisi te ostendas.
Quaeram te desiderando,
    desiderem quaerendo.
Inveniam amando,
    amem inveniendo.
Fateor, Domine, et gratias ago, quia creasti in me hanc

Gn 1:27   *imaginem tuam,* ut tui memor te cogitem,
    te amem.
Sed sic est abolita attritione vitiorum,
    sic est offuscata fumo peccatorum,
ut non possit facere, ad quod facta est, nisi tu renoves et
    reformes eam.

Non tento, Domine, penetrare altitudinem tuam,
quia nullatenus comparo illi intellectum meum; sed
desidero aliquatenus intelligere veritatem tuam, quam
credit et amat cor meum. Neque enim quaero intelligere
ut credam, sed credo ut intelligam. Nam et hoc credo:

Is 7:9   quia *nisi credidero, non intelligam.*

Teach me to seek you and
    show yourself in my seeking;
    for neither can I seek you unless you lead the way
    nor find you unless you show yourself.
Let me seek you in longing
    and long for you in seeking;
Let me find you by loving
    and love you by finding.

I acknowledge, lord, and give thanks,
    that you created in me *your image,*
    so that I may remember you, think of you, and love you.
But it has been so effaced and worn away by my faults,
    is so clouded by the smoke of sin,
that it cannot do what it is made to
    unless you renew and reform it.

I do not strive, lord, to penetrate your heights,
    for my understanding is in no way equal to it;
but I do desire to understand to some extent your truth,
    which my heart believes and loves.
And neither do I seek to understand so that I may believe,
    but believe so that I may understand.
For this also I believe:
that *unless I believe,*
I will not understand.

CAPITULUM II

Quod vere sit Deus

Ergo Domine, qui das fidei intellectum, da mihi, ut, quantum scis expedire, intelligam, quia es sicut credimus, et hoc es quod credimus. Et quidem credimus te esse aliquid quo nihil maius cogitari possit.

An ergo non est aliqua talis natura, quia *dixit insipiens in corde suo: non est Deus?* Sed certe ipse idem insipiens, cum audit hoc ipsum quod dico: «aliquid quo maius nihil cogitari potest», intelligit quod audit; et quod intelligit, in intellectu eius est, etiam si non intelligat illud esse.

Aliud enim est rem esse in intellectu, aliud intelligere rem esse. Nam cum pictor praecogitat quae facturus est, habet quidem in intellectu, sed nondum intelligit esse quod nondum fecit. Cum vero iam pinxit, et habet in intellectu et intelligit esse quod iam fecit.

Convincitur ergo etiam insipiens esse vel in intellectu aliquid quo nihil maius cogitari potest, quia hoc, cum audit, intelligit, et quidquid intelligitur, in intellectu est.

Et certe id quo maius cogitari nequit, non potest esse in solo intellectu. Si enim vel in solo intellectu est, potest cogitari esse et in re; quod maius est. Si ergo id quo maius cogitari non potest, est in solo intellectu: id ipsum quo maius cogitari non potest, est quo maius cogitari potest. Sed certe hoc esse non potest. Existit ergo procul dubio aliquid quo maius cogitari non valet, et in intellectu et in re.

Ps 13:1; 52:1

Chapter 2
That God truly is

Therefore, lord, you who give understanding to faith, grant me that I might understand, to the extent you know to be beneficial, that you are as we believe and that you are that which we believe. And we believe that you are something than which nothing greater can be thought.

Or is there, then, not something of such a nature, since *the fool said in his heart that there is no God?* But certainly this same fool, when he hears what I say, namely, something than which nothing greater can be thought, understands what he hears; and what is understood is in his understanding, even if he does not understand it to be.

For it is different for a thing to be in the understanding than for that thing to be understood to be. When, for example, a painter pre-conceives of what he is to make, he indeed has in his understanding what he has not yet made, but he does not yet understand it to be. Once he has painted it, however, he both has in his understanding and understands to be that which he has now made.

Even the fool, then, is convinced that something than which nothing greater can be thought at least is in his understanding, since he understands this when he hears it, and whatever is understood is in the understanding.

But certainly that than which a greater cannot be thought cannot be in the understanding alone. For if it is in the understanding alone even, it can be thought to be in reality also—which is greater. If, therefore, that than which a greater cannot be thought is in the understanding alone, that than which a greater cannot be thought is itself that than which a greater can be thought. But certainly this cannot be. Therefore, without doubt, something than which a greater cannot be thought exists both in the understanding and in reality.

CAPITULUM III

Quod non possit cogitari non esse

Quod utique sic vere est, ut nec cogitari possit non esse. Nam potest cogitari esse aliquid, quod non possit cogitari non esse; quod maius est quam quod non esse cogitari potest. Quare si id quo maius nequit cogitari, potest cogitari non esse: id ipsum quo maius cogitari nequit, non est id quo maius cogitari nequit; quod convenire non potest. Sic ergo vere est aliquid quo maius cogitari non potest, ut nec cogitari possit non esse.

Et hoc es tu, Domine Deus noster. Sic ergo vere es, Domine, Deus meus, ut nec cogitari possis non esse. Et merito. Si enim aliqua mens posset cogitare aliquid melius te, ascenderet creatura super creatorem et judicaret de creatore; quod valde est absurdum. Et quidem quidquid est aliud praeter te solum, potest cogitari non esse. Solus igitur verissime omnium et ideo maxime omnium habes esse, quia quidquid aliud est, non sic vere, et idcirco minus habet esse.

Ps 13:1; 52:1   Cur itaque *dixit insipiens in corde suo: non est Deus,* cum tam in promptu sit rationali menti te maxime omnium esse? Cur, nisi quia stultus et insipiens?

Chapter 3
That it cannot be thought not to be

And surely it so truly is that it cannot be thought not to be. For something can be thought to be that cannot be thought not to be, and this is greater than what can be thought not to be. If, then, that than which a greater cannot be thought can be thought not to be, that than which a greater cannot be thought is itself not that than which a greater cannot be thought—which is contradictory. Therefore, something than which a greater cannot be thought so truly is that it cannot be thought not to be.

And this is you, lord our God. You so truly are, then, lord my God, that you cannot even be thought not to be. And this is fitting. For if some mind could think of something better than you, the creature would rise above the creator and judge of the creator, which is completely absurd. Indeed, whatever else is, other than you alone, can be thought not to be. You alone, then, most truly of all, and thus most greatly of all, possess being—for whatever else is does not so truly possess being and thus is to a lesser degree.

Why, then, did *the fool say in his heart that there is no God,* when it is so evident to a rational mind that you of all things are to the highest degree? Why, indeed, unless because he was stupid and a fool?

CAPITULUM IV

Quomodo insipiens dixit in corde,
quod cogitari non potest

Verum quomodo dixit in corde quod cogitare non potuit;
aut quomodo cogitare non potuit quod dixit in corde,
cum idem sit dicere in corde et cogitare?

Quod si vere, immo quia vere et cogitavit, quia dixit
in corde, et non dixit in corde, quia cogitare non potuit:
non uno tantum modo dicitur aliquid in corde vel cogitatur. Aliter enim cogitatur res, cum vox eam signifi-
cans cogitatur, aliter cum id ipsum quod res est intelligitur.
Illo itaque modo potest cogitari Deus non esse, isto vero
minime. Nullus quippe intelligens id quod Deus est,
potest cogitare quia Deus non est, licet haec verba dicat
in corde, aut sine ulla aut cum aliqua extranea
significatione. Deus enim est id quo maius cogitari non
potest. Quod qui bene intelligit, utique intelligit id
ipsum sic esse, ut nec cogitatione queat non esse. Qui
ergo intelligit sic esse Deum, nequit eum non esse
cogitare.

Gratias tibi, bone Domine, gratias tibi, quia quod
prius credidi te donante, iam sic intelligo te illuminante,
ut, si te esse nolim credere, non possim non intelligere.

Chapter 4

How the fool said in his heart what cannot be thought

But how has he said in his heart what he could not think, or how could he not think what he said in his heart, when to say in the heart and to think are one and the same?

For if he truly—or rather, because he truly—both thought, because he said it in his heart, and did not say it in his heart, because he could not think it, something is not said in the heart or thought in only one way. For in one sense, a thing is thought when the word signifying it is thought; in another sense, when that which the thing itself is is understood. In the first sense, then, God can be thought not to exist; but in the second sense, not at all. For no one understanding what God is can think that God does not exist, even though he may say these words in his heart either without any or with some foreign signification. For God is that than which a greater cannot be thought. Whoever really understands this clearly understands that it itself so exists that not even for thought can it not exist. Therefore, whoever understands that God is such, cannot think him not to exist.

Thanks to you, good lord, my thanks to you. For what I first believed through your gift, I now so understand though your illumination that even if I did not want to believe that you existed, I could not fail to understand.

CAPITULUM V

Quod Deus sit quidquid melius est esse quam non esse: et solus existens per se omnia alia faciat de nihilo

Quid igitur es. Domine Deus, quo nil maius valet cogitari? Sed quid es, nisi id quod summum omnium solum existens per seipsum, omnia alia fecit de nihilo? Quidquid enim hoc non est, minus est quam cogitari possit. Sed hoc de te cogitari non potest. Quod ergo bonum deest summo bono, per quod est omne bonum?

Tu es itaque iustus, verax, beatus, et quidquid melius est esse quam non esse. Melius namque est esse iustum quam non iustum, beatum quam non beatum.

CAPITULUM VI

Quomodo sit sensibilis, cum non sit corpus

Verum cum melius sit esse sensibilem, omnipotentem, misericordem, impassibilem quam non esse: quomodo es sensibilis, si non es corpus; aut omnipotens, si omnia non potes; aut misericors simul et impassibilis?

Nam si sola corporea sunt sensibilia, quoniam sensus circa corpus et in corpore sunt: quomodo es sensibilis, cum non sis corpus, sed summus spiritus, qui corpore melior est?

Sed si sentire non nisi cognoscere aut non nisi ad cognoscendum est — qui enim sentit cognoscit secundum sensuum proprietatem, ut per visum colores, per gustum sapores — : non inconvenienter dicitur aliquo modo, sentire quidquid aliquo modo cognoscit.

Ergo, Domine, quamvis non sis corpus, vere tamen eo modo summe sensibilis es, quo summe omnia cognoscis, non quo animal corporeo sensu cognoscit.

Chapter 5

That God is whatever it is better to be than not to be, and that, alone existing through himself, he makes everything else from nothing

What, then, are you, lord God, than whom none greater can be thought? What, indeed, are you but that which, as the highest of all, alone existing through itself, created everything else from nothing? For whatever is not this is less than what can be thought. But this cannot be thought about you. Therefore, what good does the supreme good, through which all good exists, lack?

You are, then, just, truthful, blessed, and whatever it is better to be than not to be. For it is better to be just than not just, blessed than not blessed.

Chapter 6

How he is perceptive, even though he is not a body

Since, however, it is better to be than not to be perceptive, omnipotent, compassionate, impassible, how are you perceptive if you are not corporeal, or omnipotent if you cannot do everything, or both compassionate and impassible at one and the same time?

For if only what is corporeal is perceptive, since the senses center around the body and are in the body, how can you be perceptive when you are not a body but a supreme spirit, which is better than the body?

But if to sense is nothing other than to know, or for the sake of nothing other than knowing—for he who perceives knows in accord with that sense what is proper to it, such as colors through sight, flavors through taste—then it is not unfitting that whatever in some way knows, may, in some way, be said to perceive.

Therefore, lord, although you are not bodily, you truly are supremely perceptive in the way in which you know supremely all things, without knowing, as an animal does, by means of corporeal senses.

CAPITULUM VII

Quomodo sit omnipotens, cum multa non possit

Sed et omnipotens quomodo es, si omnia non potes? Aut si non potes corrumpi nec mentiri nec facere verum esse falsum, ut quod factum est non esse factum, et plura similiter: quomodo potes omnia?

An haec posse non est potentia, sed impotentia? Nam qui haec potest quod sibi non expedit et quod non debet potest. Quae quanto magis potest, tanto magis adversitas et perversitas possunt in illum et ipse minus contra illas. Qui ergo sic potest, non potentia potest, sed impotentia. Non enim ideo dicitur posse, quia ipse possit, sed quia sua impotentia facit aliud in se posse; sive aliquo alio genere loquendi, sicut multa improprie dicuntur.

Ut cum ponimus «esse» pro «non esse», et «facere» pro eo quod est «non facere», aut pro «nihil facere». Nam saepe dicimus ei, qui rem aliquam esse negat: sic est, quemadmodum dicis esse; cum magis proprie videatur dici: sic non est quemadmodum dicis non esse. Item dicimus: iste sedet, sicut ille facit, aut: iste quiescit, sicut ille facit; cum «sedere» sit quiddam non facere et «quiescere» sit nihil facere.

Sic itaque, cum dicitur habere potentiam faciendi aut patiendi quod sibi non expedit aut quod non debet, impotentia intelligitur per potentiam; quia quo plus habet hanc potentiam, eo adversitas et perversitas in illum sunt potentiores, et ille contra eas impotentior.

Ergo, Domine Deus, inde verius es omnipotens, quia nihil potes per impotentiam, et nihil potest contra te.

Chapter 7

How he is omnipotent even though he cannot do many things

And yet, how are you omnipotent if you cannot do everything? If you can neither be corrupted nor tell a lie nor make the true be false, so that what has been done is undone, and other similar things, how are you capable of everything?

Or is the ability to do these things not a matter of power but of impotence? For he who is able do these things is capable of doing what is an impediment to himself and what he ought not to do. And the greater the extent to which he is able to do this, the greater the extent to which adversity and perversity are a possibility for him, and the less his capability against them. Therefore, one who is able in this way is not enabled by power but by a lack of power. For in that case, it is not said that he is able because he himself is able but because his own lack of ability enables something else to have power over him—or as might be expressed by means of some other manner of speaking in which, as we often do, we speak improperly.

For example, we use "to be" for "not to be" and "to do" for "not to do" or for "to do nothing." For we often say to one who denies something to be: "So it is, just as you say it is," when it would appear to be more proper to say: "So it is not, just as you say it is not." Similarly, we say: "This one sits, just as that one does"; or: "This one rests, just as that one does," when to sit is not to do anything and to rest is to do nothing.

In this way, then, when it is said that someone has the power to do or to suffer what is an impediment to himself or what he should not, power is to be understood as a lack of power, since the greater extent to which one has this power, the more powerful are adversity and perversity over him, and the more powerless he is against them.

Therefore, lord God, you are then more truly omnipotent because you can do nothing through a lack of power, and nothing can have power over you.

CAPITULUM VIII

Quomodo sit misericors et impassibilis

Sed et misericors simul et impassibilis quomodo es? Nam si es impassibilis, non compateris; si non compateris, non est tibi miserum cor ex compassione miseri, quod est esse misercordem. At si non es misercors, unde miseris est tanta consolatio?

Quomodo ergo es et non es misericors, Domine, nisi quia es misericors secundum nos, et non es secundum te? Es quippe secundum nostrum sensum, et non es secundum tuum. Etenim cum tu respicis nos miseros, nos sentimus misericordis effectum, tu non sentis affectum.

Et misericors es igitur, quia miseros salvas et peccatoribus tuis parcis; et misericors non es, quia nulla miseriae compassione afficeris.

Chapter 8

How he is merciful and impassible

But how are you both merciful and impassible at one and the same time? For if you are impassible, you do not feel compassion; if you do not feel compassion, you do not have a heart full of pity in its commiseration with the miserable, which is what it is to be merciful. But if you are not merciful, from where do the miserable derive such consolation?

How, then, are you both merciful and not merciful, lord, unless because your heart is full of mercy with respect to us but not with respect to you? Indeed, you are so according to our sentiments, but not according to yours. For when you look upon us in our misery, we feel the effect of your compassion, but you do not feel the affect.

You are, then, both full of mercy because you save the miserable and spare those who sin against you, and not full of mercy because you in no way feel the affect of compassion for the miserable.

CAPITULUM IX

Quomodo totus iustus et summe iustus parcat malis, et quod iuste misereatur malis

Verum malis quomodo parcis, si es totus iustus et summe iustus? Quomodo enim totus et summe iustus facit aliquid non iustum? Aut quae iustitia est merenti mortem aeternam dare vitam sempiternam? Unde ergo, bone Deus, bone bonis et malis, unde tibi salvare malos, si hoc non est iustum, et tu non facis aliquid non iustum?

An quia bonitas tua est incomprehensibilis, latet hoc in *luce inaccessibili* quam *inhabitas?* Vere in altissimo et secretissimo bonitatis tuae latet fons, unde manat fluvius misericordiae tuae. Nam cum totus et summe iustus sis, tamen idcirco etiam malis benignus es, quia totus summe bonus es.

1 Tm 6:16

Minus namque bonus esses, si nulli malo esses benignus. Melior est enim qui et bonis et malis bonus est, quam qui bonis tantum est bonus. Et melior est, qui malis et puniendo et parcendo est bonus, quam qui puniendo tantum. Ideo ergo misericors es, quia totus et summe bonus es. Et cum forsitan videatur, cur bonis bona et malis mala retribuas, illud certe penitus est mirandum, cur tu totus iustus et nullo egens malis et reis tuis bona tribuas.

O altitudo bonitatis tuae, Deus!
et videtur, unde sis misericors, et non pervidetur.
Cernitur, unde flumen manat, et non perspicitur fons, unde nascatur.
Nam et de plenitudine bonitatis est, quia peccatoribus tuis pius es;
et in altitudine bonitatis latet, qua ratione hoc es.
Etenim licet bonis bona et malis mala ex bonitate retribuas,
ratio tamen iustitiae hoc postulare videtur.

Chapter 9

How he who is wholly just and supremely just spares the wicked; and that it is just to have pity on them

But how is it that you spare the wicked if you are totally just and supremely just? For how is it that one who is wholly and supremely just does something that is not just? Or what kind of justice is it to give everlasting life to one who is deserving of eternal death? How, then, good God—good to both the good and the evil—how is it that you save the evil, if this is not just, but do nothing that is not just?

Or, since your goodness is incomprehensible, is this hidden in *the inaccessible light* which *you inhabit?* Truly, in the most lofty and secret element of your goodness is hidden the fount from which the stream of your mercy flows. For while you are wholly and supremely just, you are nonetheless also benign to the wicked, since you are wholly and supremely good.

You would then be less good if you were benign to none of the evil. For he who is good to both the good and the evil is better than one who is good only to the good. And he is better who is good by both punishing and sparing the wicked than only by punishing them. For that reason, then, you are merciful because you are wholly and supremely good. And while we may see why you should repay good with good and evil with evil, it is no doubt astonishing that you, who are wholly just and in need of no one, should allot good to those who are wicked and guilty before you.

O God, the depth of your goodness!
    So evident from where your mercy comes,
        and yet so hard to see.
So obvious whence its streaming flows;
        so hard to see the source from which its comes.
For it stems from a plenitude of good
        that you are kind to those who sin against you;
but it is hidden in the depths of your goodness
        what the reason for this is.
And though when you repay good for good and evil for evil,
        both out of goodness,
        it can be seen to follow from the nature of your justice;

Cum vero malis bona tribuis:
 et scitur, quia summe bonus hoc facere voluit,
 et mirum est, cur summe iustus hoc velle potuit.
O misericordia, de quam opulenta dulcedine et dulci
 opulentia nobis profluis!
O immensitas bonitatis Dei, quo affectu amanda es
             peccatoribus!
Iustos enim salvas iustitia comitante;
istos vero liberas iustitia damnante.
Illos meritis adiuvantibus,
istos meritis repugnantibus.
Illos bona, quae dedisi, cognoscendo,
istos mala, quae odisti, ignoscendo.
O immensa bonitas, quae sic omnem intellectum excedis,
 veniat super me misericordia illa, quae de tanta
  opulentia tui procedit!
Influat in me, quae profluit de te.
Parce   per clementiam,
ne ulciscaris per iustitiam.

Nam etsi difficile sit intelligere, quomodo misericordia tua non absit a tua iustitia, necessarium tamen est credere, quia nequaquam adversatur iustitiae quod exundat ex bonitate, quae nulla est sine iustitia, immo vere concordat iustitiae. Nempe si misericors es, quia es summe bonus, et summe bonus non es, nisi quia es summe iustus: vere idcirco es misericors, quia summe iustus es.

 Adiuva me, iuste et misericors Deus, cuius lucem quaero, adiuva me, ut intelligam quod dico. Vere ergo ideo misericors es, quia iustus.

when you allot good to the evil,
    I know the supremely good has willed it to be thus,
    and yet I wonder how the supremely just
    could let it thus be willed.

O mercy,
    from what abundant sweetness and sweet abundance you stream
    forth to us!
O the immensity of the goodness of God,
    with what affection must even sinners love you!
For you save the just ones
    whom justice commends,
and free the unjust
    whom justice condemns.
The first are saved
    through the help of their merits,
The others are saved
    despite their demerits.
Acknowledging in the one the good
    which you gave them,
Ignoring in others the evil you hate.

O immense goodness
    that so exceeds the understanding of us all!
May that mercy come over me
    which from you so abundantly proceeds.
Let flow into me
    what flows out of you.
Spare
    in clemency;
do not avenge in justice.

For though it may difficult to understand how your mercy is not incompatible with your justice, it is still necessary to believe that what flows from goodness is not at all opposed to justice but could in no way be without it, indeed, truly coincides with justice. For surely if you are merciful because you are supremely good, and are not supremely good unless you are supremely just, then truly you are merciful because you are supremely just.

    Help me, O just and merciful God, whose light I seek, help me to understand what I am saying. Truly, therefore, you are merciful because you are just.

Ergone misericordia tua nascitur ex iustitia tua?
Ergone parcis malis ex iustitia? Si sic est, Domine, si
sic est, doce me quomodo est.

An quia iustum est te sic esse bonum, ut nequeas
intelligi melior, et sic potenter operari, ut non possis
cogitari potentius? Quid enim hoc iustius? Hoc utique
non fieret, si esses bonus tantum retribuendo et non
parcendo, et si faceres de non bonis tantum bonos et
non etiam de malis. Hoc itaque modo iustum est ut parcas malis, et ut facias bonos de malis.

Denique quod non iuste fit, non debet fieri; et quod
non debet fieri, iniuste fit. Si ergo non iuste malis misereris, non debes misereri; et si non debes misereri, iniuste misereris. Quod si nefas est dicere, fas est credere
te iuste misereri malis.

CAPITULUM X
Quomodo iuste puniat et iuste parcat malis

Sed et iustum est, ut malos punias. Quid namque iustius, quam ut boni bona et mali mala recipiant? Quomodo ergo et iustum est ut malos punias, et iustum est
ut malis parcas?

An alio modo iuste punis malos, et alio modo iuste
parcis malis? Cum enim punis malos, iustum est, quia
illorum meritis convenit; cum vero parcis malis, iustum
est, non quia illorum meritis, sed quia bonitati tuae
condecens est.

Nam parcendo malis ita iustus es secundum te et
non secundum nos, sicut misericors es secundum nos et
non secundum te. Quoniam salvando nos, quos iuste
perderes, sicut misericors es, non quia tu sentias affectum, sed quia nos sentimus effectum: ita iustus es, non
quia nobis reddas debitum, sed quia facis quod decet te
summe bonum.

Sic itaque sine repugnantia iuste punis et iuste
parcis.

Is not your mercy then born of your justice? Do you not then spare the evil out of justice? And if this is so, lord, if it is so, teach me how it is.

Is it because it is just for you to be so good that you cannot be understood to be better, and to be operating with so much power that you cannot be thought to be more powerful? For what is more just than this? But surely this would not be if you were good only through retribution and not by sparing, and if you made good only those who are not good, and not those who are evil as well. In this way, then, it is just that you spare the evil, and from the evil make good.

In the end, what is not just ought not to be; and what ought not to be is unjust. If, then, it is not just for you to be merciful to the evil, you ought not to be merciful; and if you should not be merciful, your mercy is unjust. But if it is irreverent to say this, then it is right to believe that it is just for you to have mercy on the wicked.

Chapter 10
How he justly punishes and justly spares the wicked

But it is also just that you punish the wicked. For what is more just than that the good receive good and the evil evil? How, then, is it both just that you punish the evil and just that you spare the evil?

Or do you in one way justly punish the evil and in another way justly spare the evil? For when you punish the evil, it is just because it meets their merits; when, however, you spare the evil, it is just not because of their merits but because it is meted out of your goodness.

For by so sparing the evil you are just with respect to yourself, not with regard to us, just as you are full of mercy with regard to us but not with respect to yourself. Thus, just as you are full of mercy not because you feel its affect but because we feel its effect, so, by saving us, whom you might justly abandon, you are just not because you return to us what would seem to be required but because you do what is seemly of you as supremely good.

Without inconsistency, then, you both justly punish and justly spare.

CAPITULUM XI

Quomodo universae viae Domini
misericordia et veritas, et tamen iustus
Dominus in omnibus viis suis

Sed numquid etiam non est iustum secundum te, Domine, ut malos punias? Iustum quippe est te sic esse
iustum, ut iustior nequeas cogitari. Quod nequaquam
esses, si tantum bonis bona et non malis mala redderes.
Iustior enim est qui et bonis et malis, quam qui bonis
tantum merita retribuit. Iustum igitur est secundum te,
iuste et benigne Deus, et cum punis et cum parcis.

Ps 24:10   Vere igitur *universae viae Domini misericordia et*
Ps 144:17 *veritas* et tamen *iustus Dominus in omnibus viis suis.*
Et utique sine repugnantia; quia quos vis punire, non
est iustum salvari, et quibus vis parcere, non est iustum
damnari. Nam id solum iustum est quod vis, et non
iustum quod non vis.

Sic ergo nascitur der iustitia tua misericordia tua,
quia iustum est te sic esse bonum, ut et parcendo sis bonus. Et hoc est forsitan, cur summe iustus potest velle
bona malis. Sed si utcumque capi potest, cur malos
potes velle salvare: illud certe nulla ratione compre-
hendi potest, cur de similibus malis hos magis salves
quam illos per summam bonitatem, et illos magis dam-
nes quam istos per summam iustitiam.

Sic ergo vere es sensibilis, omnipotens, misericors et
impassibilis, quemadmodum vivens, sapiens, bonus,
beatus, aeternus, et quidquid melius est esse quam non
esse.

CAPITULUM XII

Quod Deus sit ipsa vita qua vivit,
et sic de similibus

Sed certe quidquid es, non per aliud es quam per
teipsum. Tu es igitur ipsa vita qua vivis, et sapientia
qua sapis, et bonitas ipsa qua bonis et malis bonus es; et
ita de similibus.

Chapter 11

How all the ways of the lord are full of mercy and truth, and yet the lord is just in all his ways

But is it not also just with respect to yourself, lord, that you punish the evil? Certainly, it is just for you to be so just that you cannot be thought to be more just. But this you would by no means be if you only returned good to the good and not evil to the evil. For he is more just who returns to both the good and evil, not only to the good, what they merit. Therefore, it is just with respect to yourself, O just and benign God, both when you punish and when you spare.

Truly, then, *all the ways of the lord are full of mercy and truth* and yet *the lord is just in all his ways.* And surely this is not inconsistent; since it is not just for those you will to punish to be saved, and it is not just for those you will to spare to be damned. For that alone is just which you will, and that is not just which you do not will.

So, then, is your mercy derived from your justice, since it is just for you to be so good that you are good also by sparing. And this is perhaps why the supremely just can will good for the wicked. But if it can in any way be grasped why you can will to save those who are evil, it surely can in no way be comprehended why, of those who are alike in evil, you save some rather than others through your supreme goodness, and damn these rather than those through your supreme justice.

So, then, are you truly perceptive, omnipotent, merciful, and impassible, as well as living, wise, good, blessed, eternal, and whatever it is better to be than not to be.

Chapter 12

That God is the very life by which he lives, and likewise for similar attributes

But certainly whatever you are, you are not through another rather than through yourself. Therefore, you are the life itself by which you live, the wisdom through which you are wise, the very good by which you are good to both the good and evil, and likewise for similar attributes.

CAPITULUM XIII

Quomodo solus sit incircumscriptus et aeternus, cum alii spiritus sint incircumscripti et aeterni

Sed omne quod clauditur aliquatenus loco aut tempore, minus est quam quod nulla lex loci aut temporis coercet. Quoniam ergo maius te nihil est, nullus locus aut tempus te cohibet, sed ubique et semper es. Quod quia de te solo dici potest, tu solus incircumscriptus es et aeternus. Quomodo igitur dicuntur et alii spiritus incircumscripti et aeterni? Et quidem solus es aeternus, quia solus omnium, sicut non desinis, sic non incipis esse. Sed solus quomodo es incircumscriptus ?

An creatus spiritus ad te collatus est circumscriptus, ad corpus vero incircumscriptus? Nempe omnino circumscriptum est, quod cum alicubi totum est, non potest simul esse alibi; quod de solis corporeis cernitur. Incircumscriptum vero, quod simul est ubique totum; quod de te solo intelligitur. Circumscriptum autem simul et incircumscriptum est, quod, cum alicubi sit totum, potest simul esse totum alibi, non tamen ubique; quod de creatis spiritibus cognoscitur. Si enim non esset anima tota in singulis membris sui corporis, non sentiret tota in singulis.

Tu ergo, Domine, singulariter es incircumscriptus et aeternus, et tamen et alii spiritus sunt incircumscripti et aeterni.

Chapter 13

How he alone is unlimited and eternal, although other spirits are unlimited and eternal

But all that is in any way confined by place or time is less than that which no law of place or time constrains. Since, therefore, nothing is greater than you, no place or time contains you, but you are everywhere and always. And since this can be said of you alone, you alone are unlimited and eternal. How, then, are other spirits also said to be unlimited and eternal? No doubt you are alone eternal, since, alone of all things, even as you will not cease, so too you did not begin to be. But how are you alone unlimited?

Or is it that a created spirit is limited in comparison to you but not in comparison to a body? Surely, that which, while existing somewhere as a whole, cannot at the same time be elsewhere, is by all means limited—which is clear of bodies alone. That is unlimited, however, which is simultaneously everywhere wholly—which can be understood of you alone. That, however, is at the same time limited and unlimited which, while it is wholly somewhere, can simultaneously be wholly elsewhere but not everywhere—which is known to be true of created spirits. For if the soul were not wholly in each of the members of its own body, the soul as a whole would not have feeling in each of them.

Therefore, you, lord, are uniquely unlimited and eternal, and yet other spirits are both unlimited and eternal.

CAPITULUM XIV

Quomodo et cur videtur et non
videtur Deus a quaerentibus eum

An invenisti, anima mea, quod quaerebas? Quaerebas
Deum, et invenisti eum esse quiddam summum omnium, quo nihil melius cogitari potest; et hoc esse ipsam
vitam, lucem, sapientiam, bonitatem, aeternam beatitudinem et beatam aeternitatem; et hoc esse ubique et
semper. Nam si non invenisti Deum tuum: quomodo est
ille hoc quod invenisti, et quod illum tam certa veritate
et vera certitudine intellexisti?

Si vero invenisti: quid est, quod non sentis quod
invenisti? Cur non te sentit, Domine Deus, anima mea,
si invenit te? An non invenit, quem invenit esse lucem
et veritatem? Quomodo namque intellexit hoc, nisi vi-
dendo lucem et veritatem? Aut potuit omnino aliquid
Ps 42:3   intelligere de te, nisi per *lucem tuam et veritatem tuam?*
Si ergo vidit lucem et veritatem, vidit te. Si non vidit te,
non vidit lucem nec veritatem.

An et veritas et lux est quod vidit, et tamen nondum
1 Jn 3:2   te vidit, quia vidit te aliquatenus, sed non vidit te *sicuti
es?*

Domine Deus meus, formator et reformator meus,
dic desideranti animae meae, quid aliud es, quam quod
vidit, ut pure videat quod desiderat. Intendit se ut plus
videat, et nihil videt ultra hoc quod vidit, nisi tenebras;
1 Jn 1:5   immo non videt *tenebras, quae nullae sunt in te,* sed videt se non plus posse videre propter tenebras suas.

Cur hoc, Domine,
cur hoc?
Tenebratur oculus eius infirmitate sua,
aut reverberatur   fulgore tuo?
Sed certe et tenebratur   in se,
          et reverberatur a te.
Utique   et obscuratur   sua brevitate,
          et obruitur   tua immensitate.
Vere et contrahitur angustia sua,
          et vincitur   amplitudine tua.

Chapter 14

How and why God is both seen and not seen by those seeking him

Have you found, O my soul, what you were seeking? You were seeking God, and you found him to be something which is the highest of all, than which nothing better can be thought, and to be life itself, light, wisdom, goodness, eternal blessedness, and blessed eternity, and to exist everywhere and always. But if you have not found your God, how is he this which you have found, and which you have understood with certain truth and true certitude?

But if you have found him, why is it that you do not experience what you have found? Why, O lord God, does my soul not experience you if it has found you? Has it not found that which it found to be the light and the truth?

But how did it understand this except by seeing the light and the truth? Could it understand anything at all about you except through *your light and your truth?* If it saw the light and the truth, it saw you. If it did not see you, it did not see the light or the truth.

Or are the truth and the light what it saw, and yet it did not see you, since it saw you to a certain extent, but did not see you *as you are?*

Lord my God, you who have formed and reformed me, tell my desiring soul what else you are other than what it has seen, so that it may see clearly what it desires. It strives so that it may see more, and it sees nothing beyond what it has seen except darkness. Indeed, it does not see *darkness, which is in no way in you,* but it sees that it can see no more because of its own darkness.

Why is this, lord,
why is this?
Is its eye darkened by its own weakness,
    or dazzled by your brilliance?
But surely it is both darkened within itself
    and dazzled by you.
Certainly, it is both darkened by its own shallowness
    and overwhelmed by your immensity.
Truly, it is both constricted by its own narrowness
    and overcome by your vastness.

Quanta namque est lux illa,
   de qua micat omne verum,
   quod rationali menti lucet!
Quam ampla est illa veritas,
   in qua est omne quod verum est et
   extra quam non nisi nihil et falsum est!
Quam immensa est, quae uno intuitu videt,
   quaecumque facta sunt, et a quo et per quem et quomodo de nihilo facta sunt!
Quid puritatis, quid simplicitatis, quid certitudinis et
   splendoris ibi est!
Certe plus quam a creatura valeat intelligi.

CAPITULUM XV

Quod maior sit quam cogitari possit

Ergo, Domine, non solum es quo maius cogitari nequit, sed es quiddam maius quam cogitari possit. Quoniam namque valet cogitari esse aliquid huiusmodi: si tu non es hoc ipsum, potest cogitari aliquid maius te; quod fieri nequit.

For how great is that light
>from which shines every truth
>that illuminates the rational mind!
How vast is that truth
>in which is all that is true,
And outside of which
>is only nothingness and falsehood!
How immense is that which beholds
>in one single intuition
>all of creation,
And by whom and through whom and how
>all creatures were made from nothing!
What purity, what simplicity,
>what certainty and splendor,
>are there!
Surely it is more than can be understood by any creature.

Chapter 15
That he is greater than can be thought

Therefore, lord, not only are you that than which a greater cannot be thought, but you are something greater than can be thought. For since something can be thought to be of this kind, if you are not yourself this, something greater than you can be thought, which cannot be.

CAPITULUM XVI

Quod haec sit lux inaccessibilis, quam inhabitat

2 Tm 6:16 Vere, Domine, haec est *lux inaccessibilis, in qua habitas.* Vere enim non est aliud quod hanc penetret, ut ibi te pervideat. Vere ideo hanc non video, quia nimia mihi est; et tamen quidquid video, per illam video, sicut infirmus oculus quod videt, per lucem solis videt, quam in ipso sole nequit aspicere. Non potest intellectus meus ad illam. Nimis fulget, non capit illam, nec suffert oculus animae meae diu intendere in illam.

Reverberatur fulgore,
vincitur   amplitudine,
obruitur   immensitate,
confunditur   capacitate.
O summa et inaccessibilis lux,
  o tota et beata veritas,
quam longe es a me, qui tam prope tibi sum!
Quam remota es a conspectu meo, qui sic praesens sum
   conspectui tuo!
Ubique es tota praesens — et non te video.
Acts 17:28 *In te moveor et in te sum* — et ad te non possum accedere.
Intra me et circa me es — et non te sentio.

Chapter 16
That this is the inaccessible light which he inhabits

Truly, lord, this is *the inaccessible light in which you dwell*. For truly there is nothing else that can penetrate it so as to look upon you there. Truly, therefore, I do not see it, since it is too much for me; and yet whatever I see, I see by means of it—just as an eye that is weak sees what it sees by the light of the sun, which it cannot look at in the sun itself. My understanding is not up to it. It shines too brilliantly; I grasp it not. Nor may the eye of my soul direct itself to it for long.

It is dazzled by its splendor,
    overcome by its vastness,
    overwhelmed by its immensity,
    confused by its extent.
O supreme and inaccessible light,
    O whole and blessed truth!
How far you are from me,
    who am so near to you!
How distant you are from my sight,
    whose sight I am so present to!
You are wholly present everywhere, and I do not see you.
In you I move and in you I am,
    and yet I cannot approach you.
You are within me and around me,
    and I do not experience you.

CAPITULUM XVII

Quod in Deo sit harmonia, odor,
sapor, lenitas, pulchritudo suo
ineffabili modo

Adhuc lates, Domine, animam meam in luce et beatitudine tua, et idcirco versatur illa adhuc in tenebris et
miseria sua.

Circumspicit enim —	et non videt	pulchritudinem tuam.
Auscultat	— et non audit	harmoniam tuam.
Olfacit	— et non percipit	odorem tuum.
Gustat	— et non cognoscit	saporem tuum.
Palpat	— et non sentit	lenitatem tuam.

Habes enim haec, Domine Deus, in te tuo ineffabili
    modo,
qui ea dedisti rebus a te creatis suo sensibili modo;
sed obriguerunt, sed obstupuerunt, sed obstructi sunt
    sensus animae meae vetusto languore peccati.

Chapter 17

That harmony, fragrance, savor, softness, beauty, are in God in his own ineffable manner

Still, lord, you hide from my soul in your light and blessedness, and so it still remains surrounded by its own darkness and misery.

For it looks around—and does not see your beauty.
It listens—and does not hear your harmony.
It smells—and does not sense your fragrance.
It tastes—and does not know your savor.
It touches—and does not feel your softness.

For you have in you, lord God,
in your own ineffable manner,
what you have given to the things created by you
in their own sensible manner.
But the senses of my soul,
because of the ancient weakness of sin,
have become hardened and dulled and obstructed.

CAPITULUM XVIII

Quod in Deo nec in aeternitate eius,
quae ipse est, nullae sint partes

Jer 14:19   Et iterum *ecce turbatio,*
        ecce iterum obviat maeror et luctus quaerenti
Ps 50:10   *gaudium et laetitiam!*
        Sperabat iam anima mea satietatem — et ecce iterum
          obruitur egestate!
        Affectabam iam comedere — et ecce magis esurire!
        Conabar assurgere ad lucem Dei — et recidi in tenebras
          meas.
        Immo non modo cecedi in eas, sed sentio me involutum
          in eis.
        Ante cecidi, quam *conciperet me mater mea.*
Ps 50:7   Certe in illis *conceptus sum,*
        et cum earum obvolutione natus sum.
Rom 5:12 Olim certe in illo omnes cecidimus, *in quo omnes pecca-*
        vimus.
        In illo omnes perdidimus, qui facile tenebat et male sibi
          et nobis perdidit, quod
          cum volumus, quaerere nescimus;
          cum quaerimus, non invenimus;
          cum invenimus, non est quod quaerimus.
Ps 24:7   Adiuva me tu *propter bonitatem tuam, Domine.*
        Quaesivi vultum tuum,
        vultum tuum, Domine, requiram;
Ps 26:85 *ne avertas faciem tuam a me.*

Ps 12:4   Releva me de me ad te. Munda, sana, acue, *illumina*
Sg 6:12   oculum mentis meae, *ut intueatur te.* Recolligat vires
suas anima mea, et toto intellectu iterum intendat in te,
Domine.

    Quid es, Domine, quid es, quid te intelliget cor
meum? Certe vita es, sapientia es, veritas es, bonitas es,
beatitudo es, aeternitas es, et omne verum bonum es.

    Multa sunt haec, non potest angustus intellectus
meus tot uno simul intuitu videre, ut omnibus simul
delectetur. Quomodo ergo, Domine, es omnia haec? An

Chapter 18

That neither in God nor in his eternity, which he himself is, are there any parts

And once more *confusion,*
    once again sorrow and grief stand in my way as I seek
    joy and gladness!
Even now my soul hoped for fulfillment,
    and once again
    it is overcome with need.
Even now I have sought my fill,
    and yet I hunger all the more.
I strove to ascend to the light of God,
    and instead descended into my own darkness.
Indeed, not only have I fallen back into it but feel myself engulfed
    by it.
I fell before *my mother conceived me.*
Surely in darkness *was I conceived,*
    and wrapped in it was I born.
For long ago all of us fell in him *in whom we have all sinned.*
In him—
    who easily possessed what he evilly lost for himself and for us—
    all lost that which
    when we desire, we do not know how to seek;
    when we seek, we do not find;
    when we find, is not what we were seeking.

Help me, *in accord with your goodness, lord.*
    I sought your face,
    For your face, lord, will I search.
Do not turn your face away from me.
Lift me from my self to you.
Cleanse, heal, focus, *illuminate* the eye of my mind so that it may
    behold you.
Let my soul regather its strength, O lord, and with the whole of its
understanding strive once more unto you.

What are you, lord, what are you; what shall my heart understand
you to be? You are life, you are wisdom, you are truth, you are goodness, you are blessedness, you are eternity, and you are every true
good.
    But these are many, and my narrow understanding cannot be-
hold them all in one single simultaneous intuition so as to delight in
them all at once. How, then, lord, are you all these? Are they parts of

sunt partes tui, aut potius unumquodque horum est totum quod es? Nam quidquid partibus est iunctum, non est omnino unum, sed quodam modo plura et diversum a seipso, et vel actu vel intellectu dissolvi potest; quae aliena sunt a te, quo nihil melius cogitari potest.

Nullae igitur partes sunt in te, Domine, nec es plura, sed sic es unum quiddam et idem tibi ipsi, ut in nullo tibi ipsi sis dissimilis; immo tu es ipsa unitas, nullo intellectu divisibilis.

Ergo vita et sapientia et reliqua non sunt partes tui, sed omnia sunt unum, et unumquodque horum est totum quod es, et quod sunt reliqua omnia. Quoniam ergo nec tu habes partes nec tua aeternitas, quae tu es: nusquam et numquam est pars tua aut aeternitatis tuae, sed ubique totus es, et aeternitas tua tota est semper.

CAPITULUM XIX
Quod non sit in loco aut tempore, sed omnia sint in illo

Sed si per aeternitatem tuam fuisti et es et eris, et fuisse non est futurum esse et esse non est fuisse vel futurum esse: quomodo aeternitas tua tota est semper?

An de aeternitate tua nihil praeterit, ut iam non sit, nec aliquid futurum est, quasi nondum sit? Non ergo fuisti heri aut eris cras, sed heri et hodie et cras es. Immo nec heri nec hodie nec cras es, sed simpliciter es extra omne tempus. Nam nihil aliud est heri et hodie et cras quam in tempore; tu autem, licet nihil sit sine te, non es tamen in loco aut tempore, sed omnia sunt in te. Nihil enim te continet, sed tu contines omnia.

you, or is each one of them the whole of what you are? For whatever is composed of parts is not altogether one but in a certain way many and different from itself and can be divided in fact or in thought. But this is foreign to you, than which nothing better can be thought.

There are, then, no parts in you, lord, nor are you many, but you are so one and the same with yourself that in no way are you dissimilar with yourself. Indeed, you are unity itself, indivisible by thought.

Therefore, life and wisdom and the rest are not parts of you, but all are one, and each is wholly what you are and what all the others are. Since, then, neither you, nor the eternity which you are, have parts, nowhere and never is there a part of you or your eternity, but you exist as a whole everywhere, and your eternity exists as a whole always.

Chapter 19
That he is not in place or time, but all things are in him

But if through your eternity you have been and are and will be—and to have been is not the same as to be in the future, and to be is not the same as to have been or to be in the future—how is it that your eternity always exists as a whole?

Or does nothing of your eternity pass away such that it no longer is, or will be something in the future as if it were not already? It is not, then, that you were yesterday or will be tomorrow, but yesterday and today and tomorrow you are. Or rather: you are, neither yesterday nor today nor tomorrow, but simply are, outside all time. For yesterday and today and tomorrow are nothing except in time; but you, although nothing would be without you, are nonetheless not in place or time, but all are in you. For nothing contains you, but you contain all.

CAPITULUM XX
Quod sit ante et ultra omnia etiam aeterna

Tu ergo imples et complecteris omnia; tu es ante et ultra omnia. Et quidem ante omnia es, quia, *antequam fie-* Ps 89:2 *rent, tu es.* Ultra omnia vero quomodo es? Qualiter enim es ultra ea quae finem non habebunt?

An quia illa sine te nullatenus esse possunt, tu autem nullo modo minus es, etiam si illa redeunt in nihilum? Sic enim quodam modo es ultra illa.

An etiam, quia illa cogitari possunt habere finem, tu vero nequaquam? Nam sic illa quidem habent finem quodam modo, tu vero nullo modo. Et certe quod nullo modo habet finem, ultra illud est quod aliquo modo finitur.

An hoc quoque modo transis omnia etiam aeterna, quia tua et illorum aeternitas tota tibi praesens est, cum illa nondum habeant de sua aeternitate quod venturum est, sicut iam non habent quod praeteritum est? Sic quippe semper es ultra illa, cum semper tibi sis praesens, seu cum illud semper sit tibi praesens, ad quod illa nondum pervenerunt.

CAPITULUM XXI
An hoc sit saeculum saeculi sive saecula saeculorum

passim An ergo hoc est *saeculum saeculi* sive *saecula saeculo-rum?* Sicut enim saeculum temporum continet omnia temporalia, sic tua aeternitas continet etiam ipsa saecula temporum. Quae saeculum quidem est propter indivisibilem unitatem, saecula vero propter interminabilem immensitatem. Et quamvis ita sis magnus, Domine, ut omnia sint te plena et sint in te: sic tamen es sine omni spatio, ut nec medium nec dimidium nec ulla pars sit in te.

Chapter 20
That he is before and beyond all things, even eternal ones

Therefore, you fill and surround all things; you are before and beyond them. Indeed, you are before all things because *before they came to be, you are.* But how are you beyond all things? For in what way are you beyond those things that will not have an end?

Or is it because they can in no way be without you, but you are in no way less, even if they turn back into nothing? So are you, then, in a certain way, beyond them.

Or is it also because they, but not you, can be thought to have an end? As such, they do indeed, in a certain way, have an end; but you, in no way at all. And certainly what in no way has an end is beyond that which is in some way ended.

Do you also in this way surpass all things, even eternal ones, because both your and their eternity is wholly present to you, while they do not yet possess that of their own eternity which is yet to come, just as they no longer possess that which is already past? So, then, are you always beyond them, since you are always present to yourself or since that is always present to you which they have not yet reached.

Chapter 21
Whether this is the age of the age or the ages of the ages

Is this, then, *the age of the age* or *the ages of the ages?* For just as an age of time contains all temporal things, so your eternity also contains even the very ages of time. It is, indeed, a single age on account of its indivisible unity; but ages on account of its interminable immensity. And while you are so great, lord, that all things are full of you and are in you, you are so without all spatial determination that there is in you neither center nor half nor any part.

CAPITULUM XXII

Quod solus sit quod est et qui est

Tu solus ergo, Domine, es quod es, et tu es qui es. Nam quod aliud est in toto et aliud in partibus, et in quo aliquid est mutabile, non omnino est quod est. Et quod incepit a non esse et potest cogitari non esse et, nisi per aliud subsistat, redit in non esse; et quod habet fuisse quod iam non est, et futurum esse quod nondum est: id non est proprie et absolute. Tu vero es quod es; quia quidquid aliquando aut aliquo modo es, hoc totus et semper es.

Et tu es qui proprie et simpliciter es; quia nec habes fuisse aut futurum esse, sed tantum praesens esse, nec potes cogitari aliquando non esse. Et vita es et lux et sapientia et beatitudo et aeternitas et multa huiusmodi bona, et tamen non es nisi unum et summum bonum; tu, tibi omnino sufficiens, nullo indigens, quo omnia indigent ut sint, et ut bene sint.

Chapter 22
That he alone is what he is and who he is

You alone, then, lord, are what you are and you are who you are. For what is one thing as a whole and another in its parts, and in which there is something mutable, is not altogether what it is. And what began from nonexistence, and can be thought not to be, and returns to not being unless it subsists through some other; and what has a past which is no longer, and a future which is not yet—it does not exist properly and absolutely. But you are what you are, since whatever you are at any time or in any way, this you are wholly and always.

And you are the one who is, properly and simply; for you have neither past nor future but only present existence, nor can you be thought not to be at any time. And you are life and light and wisdom and beatitude and eternity and many goods of this kind, and yet you are nothing but the one and supreme good; you, altogether sufficient unto yourself, needing no one, but whom all need for their being and well-being.

CAPITULUM XXIII

Quod hoc bonum sit pariter Pater et Filius et Spiritus Sanctus: et hoc sit unum necessarium, quod est omne et totum et solum bonum

Hoc bonum es tu, Deus Pater; hoc est Verbum tuum, id est Filius tuus. Etenim non potest aliud quam quod es, aut aliquid maius vel minus te esse in Verbo, quo te ipsum dicis; quoniam Verbum tuum sic est verum, quomodo tu verax, et idcirco est ipsa Veritas sicut tu, non alia quam tu; et sic es tu simplex, ut de te non possit nasci aliud quam quod tu es.

Hoc ipsum est Amor unus et communis tibi et Filio tuo, id est Sanctus Spiritus ab utroque procedens. Nam idem Amor non est impar tibi aut Filio tuo; quia tantum amas te et illum, et ille te et seipsum, quantus es tu et ille; nec est aliud a te et ab illo, quod dispar non est tibi illi; nec de summa simplicitate potest procedere aliud, quam quod est de quo procedit.

Quod autem est singulus quisque, hoc est tota Trinitas simul, Pater et Filius et Spiritus Sanctus; quoniam singulus quisque non est aliud quam summe simplex unitas et summe una simplicitas, quae nec multiplicari nec aliud et aliud esse potest.

Lk 10:42 *Porro unum est necessarium.* Porro hoc est illud unum necessarium, in quo est omne bonum, immo quod est omne et unum et totum et solum bonum.

Chapter 23

That this good is equally Father and Son and Holy Spirit; and this is the one necessity, which is every and all and alone good

You are this good, O God the Father; it is your word, that is, your Son. And in that word by means of which you express yourself there cannot be anything other than what you are or something greater or lesser than you. For your word is as true as you are truthful, and is, therefore, the very truth you are, not other than you. And you are so simple that there cannot be born of you anything other than what you are.

This is itself the love, one and common to you and your Son, that is, the Holy Spirit proceeding from you both. For this same love is not unequal to you or to your Son, since the extent to which you love yourself and him, and he you and himself, is as great as you and he are; nor is that which is not unequal to you and him other than you and him; nor can anything proceed from supreme simplicity other than what that from whom it proceeds is.

But what each is singly, this the Trinity is as a whole at once, Father and Son and Holy Spirit; for each one singly is not other than the supremely simply unity and supremely unified simplicity which can neither be multiplied nor pluralized.

Moreover, *one thing is necessary*. And this is that necessary one in which is every good; or rather, which is every and one and all and alone good.

CAPITULUM XXIV
Coniectatio, quale et quantum sit hoc bonum

Excita nunc, anima mea, et erige totum intellectum tuum, et cogita, quantum potes, quale et quantum sit illud bonum. Si enim singula bona delectabilia sunt, cogita intente quam delectabile sit illud bonum, quod continet iucunditatem omnium bonorum; et non qualem in rebus creatis sumus experti, sed tanto differentem, quanto differt creator a creatura.

Si enim bona   est vita creata:
     quam bona   est vita creatrix?
Si iucunda   est salus facta:
     quam iucunda   est salus, quae facit omnem salutem?
Si amabilis   est sapientia in cognitione rerum
                              conditarum:
     quam amabilis est sapientia, quae omnia condidit ex
                              nihilo?
Denique si multae et magnae delectationes sunt in rebus
     delectabilibus:
     qualis et quanta delectatio est in illo, qui fecit ipsa
     delectabilia?

Chapter 24
A projection of the kind and quantity of this good

Arise now, my soul, and elevate the whole of your understanding and think, to the extent to which you can, of what kind and quantity that good may be. For if particular goods are delightful, just think how delightful that good is which contains the pleasure of all goods; and not of the kind we are acquainted with in created things, but as different as the creator differs from a creature.

For if created life is good,
how good is the life that creates?
If the haven of what has been made is pleasing,
how pleasant is the safety of what makes all things be safe?
If wisdom in our knowledge of created things is lovely,
how lovely is the wisdom of what forms them out of nothing?
And if there are such great delights in things that are delightful,
what kind and quantity is the delight in him who made those
same delights?

CAPITULUM XXV

Quae et quanta bona sint fruentibus eo

O, qui hoc bono fruetur:
quid illi erit et
quid illi non erit!
Certe quidquid volet, erit,
et quod nolet, non erit.
Ibi quippe erunt bona corporis et animae, qualia
nec oculus vidit
nec auris audivit

1 Cor 2:9   *nec cor hominis* cogitavit.

Cur ergo per multa vagaris, homuncio, quaerendo bona
animae tuae et corporis tui?
Ama unum bonum, in quo sunt omnia bona   — et
sufficit.
Desidera simplex bonum, quod est omne bonum — et
satis est.

Quid enim amas, caro mea,
quid desideras, anima mea?
Ibi est,
ibi est quidquid amatis,
quidquid desideratis.

Mt 13:43   Si delectat pulchritudo: *fulgebunt iusti sicut sol.*

Si velocitas aut fortitudo aut libertas corporis, cui

Mt 22:30   nihil obsistere possit: *erunt similes angelis dei;* quia

1 Cor 15:44 *seminatur corpus animale, et surget corpus spirituale,*
potestate utique, non natura.

Si longa et salubris vita: ibi est sana aeternitas et

Wis 5:16   aeterna sanitas; quia *iusti in perpetuum vivent et*

Ps 36:39   *salus iustorum a Domino.*

Ps 16:15   Si satietas: satiabuntur, *cum apparuerit gloria*
Dei.

Ps 35:9   Si ebrietas: *inebriabuntur ab ubertate domus*
Dei.

Si melodia: ibi angelorum chori concinunt sine fine
Deo.

Si quaelibet non immunda, sed munda voluptas:

ibid.   *torrente voluptatis suae potabit eos* Deus.

Si sapientia: ipsa Dei sapientia ostendet eis
seipsam.

Chapter 25
What and how great the goods are of those who enjoy it

O he who will enjoy this good;
> what will be his and
> what will not be his!

Surely, whatever he will want, will be;
> and whatever he will not want, will not be.

Indeed, all the goods of body and soul will be there, and of such kind that
> *neither eye has seen,*
> *nor ear has heard,*
> *nor has been* thought *in the heart of man.*

Why, then, do you wander among them, insignificant man,
> seeking the goods of your body and soul?

Love the one good, in which all goods are,
> and it will be sufficient.

Desire the simple good, which is every good,
> and it will be enough.

For what, O my flesh, do you love;
> what, O my soul, do you desire?

There it is,
> whatever you love,
> whatever you desire.

If beauty delights you: *the righteous will shine like the sun.*

If the speed or strength or freedom of a body that nothing can resist: *they will be like the angels of God;* for *it is sown as a natural body, and will rise as a spiritual body*—in power, of course, not in nature.

If a long and healthy life: there is a wholesome eternity and an eternal wholesomeness; for *the just shall live forever and the welfare of the just is with the lord.*

If satiety: they will be satisfied, *when the glory of God becomes visible.*

If intoxication: *they will be made drunk by the overabundance of the dwelling of God.*

If melody: there choirs of angels join in singing to God without end.

If any kind of pleasure, not impure but pure: *God will give them to drink from the torrent of his pleasure.*

If wisdom: the very wisdom of God will reveal itself to them.

Si amicitia: diligent Deum plus quam seipsos, et invicem tamquam seipsos, et Deus illos plus quam illi seipsos; quia illi illum et se et invicem per illum, et ille se et illos per seipsum.

Si concordia: omnibus illis erit una voluntas, quia nulla illis erit nisi sola Dei voluntas.

Si potestas: omnipotentes erunt suae voluntatis, ut Deus suae. Nam sicut poterit Deus quod volet, per seipsum, ita poterunt illi quod volent, per illum; quia sicut illi non aliud volent quam quod ille, ita ille volet quidquid illi volent; et quod ille volet, non poterit non esse.

Mt 25:21; Si honor et divitiae: Deus suos *servos bonos et*
ibid., 23 *fideles supra multa constituet;* immo *filii Dei* et dii
Mt 5:9; *vocabuntur* et erunt; et ubi erit Filius eius, ibi erunt
Ps 81:6 et illi, *haeredes quidem Dei, cohaeredes autem*
Rom 8:17 *Christi.*

Si vera securitas: certe ita certi erunt numquam et nullatenus ista vel potius istud bonum sibi defuturum, sicut certi erunt se non sua sponte illud amissuros, nec dilectorem Deum illud dilectoribus suis invitis ablaturum, nec aliquid Deo potentius invitos Deum et illos separaturum.

Gaudium vero quale aut quantum est, ubi tale ac tantum bonum est?

Cor humanum, cor indigens, cor expertum aerumnas, immo obrutum aerumnis: quantum gauderes, si his omnibus abundares? Interroga intima tua, si capere possint gaudium suum de tanta beatitudine sua.

Sed certe, si quis alius, quem omnino sicut teipsum diligeres, eandem beatitudinem haberet, duplicaretur gaudium tuum, quia non minus gauderes pro eo quam pro teipso. Si vero duo vel tres vel multo plures idipsum haberent, tantundem pro singulis quantum pro teipso gauderes, si singulos sicut teipsum amares. Ergo in illa perfecta caritate innumerabilium

If friendship: they will care for God more than themselves, and for each other as themselves, and God for them more than they for themselves; for they will care for him and themselves and one another through him, and he for himself and them through himself.

If concord: there shall be a single will for all, since there will be nothing but the will of God alone.

If power: they will be omnipotent in their will, like God in his. For just as God is able to do through himself what he wills, so they will be able to do through him what they will; for just as they will not will anything other than he, so he shall will whatever they will. And what he shall will cannot fail to be.

If honor and riches: God *will establish over many things his good and faithful servants*—or rather, *sons of God,* and gods *they will be called,* and they will be. And where his Son will be, there will they be also, *heirs indeed of God and coinheritors with Christ.*

If true security: surely they will be as sure that this or, rather, these goods will in no way ever fail them as they can be sure that they will not let go of it through their own free will, nor that a caring God will remove it, against their will, from those who care about him, nor that something more powerful than God will separate God from them involuntarily.

And yet, of what sort and how great is the joy, where such and so much goodness is?

O human heart, heart in need, a heart well versed in suffering, indeed, overcome by distress: how much would you rejoice if you overflowed with all of these? Ask your inwardness whether it can contain its joy over even its own great blessedness.

But certainly, if someone else, for whom you cared in every way as for yourself, enjoyed the same beatitude, your own joy would be doubled, since you would rejoice no less for him than for yourself. And if two or three or many more were to enjoy the same, you would rejoice for each one of them as much as for yourself, if you loved each as yourself. Therefore, in that perfect love of innumerable good

beatorum angelorum et hominum, ubi nullus minus diliget alium quam seipsum, non aliter gaudebit quisque pro singulis aliis quam pro seipso.

Si ergo cor hominis de tanto suo bono vix capiet gaudium suum: quomodo capax erit tot et tantorum gaudiorum? Et utique, quoniam quantum quisque diligit aliquem, tantum de bono eius gaudet: sicut in illa perfecta felicitate unusquisque plus amabit sine comparatione Deum quam se et omnes alios secum, ita plus gaudebit absque existimatione de felicitate Dei quam de sua et omnium aliorum secum.

Sed si Deum sic diligent *toto corde, tota mente, tota anima,* ut tamen totum cor, tota mens, tota anima non sufficiat dignitati dilectionis: profecto sic gaudebunt *toto corde, tota mente, tota anima,* ut totum cor, tota mens, tota anima non sufficiat plenitudini gaudii.

Mt 22:37

ibid.

angels and men, when no one will care less for another than for himself, each will rejoice for each other no differently than for himself.

If, then, the heart of man can scarcely contain its own joy over its own so great good, how will it be able to contain so many and such great joys? And especially since to the extent to which anyone cares for someone, he will to that degree rejoice over their good, just as in that perfect happiness each and every one will love God incomparably more than himself and all others with him, so he will rejoice immeasurably more in the happiness of God than of himself and of all others with him.

But if they so care for God with their *whole heart, whole mind, and whole soul,* such that even a whole heart, whole mind, and whole soul is insufficient for the grandeur of such belovedness, surely they will rejoice with a *whole heart, whole mind, and whole soul* such that their whole heart, whole mind and whole soul will not be sufficient for the fullness of joy.

CAPITULUM XXVI
An hoc sit gaudium plenum quod promittit Dominus

Deus meus et Dominus meus, spes mea et gaudium cordis mei, dic animae meae, si hoc est gaudium, de quo nobis dicis per Filium tuum: *Petite et accipietis, ut gaudium vestrum sit plenum.*

Jn 16:24

Inveni namque gaudium quoddam plenum, et plus quam plenum. Pleno quippe corde, plena mente, plena anima, pleno toto homine gaudio illo: adhuc supra modum supererit gaudium. Non ergo totum illud gaudium intrabit in gaudentes, sed toti gaudentes intrabunt in gaudium.

Dic, Domine, dic servo tuo intus in corde suo, si hoc est gaudium in quod intrabunt servi tui, qui intrabunt *in gaudium Domini sui.* Sed gaudium illud certe, quo gaudebunt electi tui, *nec oculus vidit, nec auris audivit, nec in cor hominis ascendit.*

Mt 25:21

1 Cor 2:9

Nondum ergo dixi aut cogitavi, Domine, quantum gaudebunt illi beati tui. Utique tantum gaudebunt, quantum amabunt; tantum amabunt, quantum cognoscent. Quantum te cognoscent, Domine, tunc, et quantum te amabunt? Certe *nec oculus vidit, nec auris audivit, nec in cor hominis ascendit* in hac vita, quantum te cognoscent et amabunt in illa vita.

ibid.

Oro, Deus, cognoscam te,
    amem te,
  ut gaudeam de te.
Et si non possum in hac vita ad plenum, vel proficiam
    in dies, usque dum veniat illud ad plenum.
Proficiat hic in me notitia tui — et ibi fiat plena;
crescat amor tuus — et ibi sit plenus,
ut hic gaudium meum sit in spe magnum,
et ibi   sit in re plenum.
Domine, per Filium tuum iubes, immo consulis petere et
    promittis accipere,

Jn 16:24

  ut gaudium nostrum plenum sit.

Chapter 26
Whether this is the fullness of joy
that the lord promises

My lord and my God, my hope and the joy of my heart, tell my soul if this is the joy that you express to us through your Son: *Ask and ye shall receive, so that your joy may be full.*

For I have found a joy that is full, and more than full. For when, with a full heart, a full mind, and a full soul, the whole man is full of that joy, joy beyond measure remains. Therefore, not all of that joy shall enter into those who rejoice, but those who rejoice shall enter wholly into that joy.

Speak, O lord, tell your servant in his inner heart if this is the joy into which your servants will enter, who enter *into the joy of their lord.* But surely that joy, in which your elected ones will rejoice, *no eye has seen, nor ear has heard, nor has it arisen in the heart of man.*

I have not yet said or thought, then, how much, O lord, those blessed ones will rejoice. No doubt, they will rejoice as much as they will love and will love as much as they will know. How much will they know of you then, O lord, and how much will they love you? Surely, *no eye has seen, nor ear has heard, nor has it arisen in the heart of man* in this life how much they will know and love you in that life.

I pray, O God,
    that I may know you
    and love you,
    so that I may rejoice in you.
And if I cannot fully in this life,
    at least let me advance,
    day by day,
    until that fullness comes.
Let the knowledge of you increase in me here,
    and there come to fullness.
Let love for you grow
    and there be fulfilled,
so that here my joy may be great in hope,
    and there in the fullness of reality.

Lord, you have commanded,
    indeed, counseled,
that we call upon you,
    through your Son,
and you promise that we shall receive,
    so that our joy may be full.

Is 9:6 Peto, Domine, quod consulis *per admirabilem consilia-*
             rium nostrum;
     accipiam, quod promittis per veritatem tuam,
Jn 16:24   *ut gaudium meum plenum sit.*
     Deus verax, peto accipiam,
ibid.   *ut gaudium meum plenum sit.*

Meditetur	interim	inde mens mea,
loquatur		inde lingua mea.
Amet		illud cor meum,
sermonicetur		os meum.
Esuriat		illud anima mea,
sitiat		caro mea,
desideret		tota substantia mea,

Mt 25:21 donec *intrem in gaudium Domini mei, qui est* trinus et
Rom 1:25 unus Deus *benedictus in saecula. Amen.*

I ask, O lord,
for what you counsel *through our wonderful counselor.*
May I receive what you promise through your truth,
 so that my joy may be full.
God of truth,
 I beseech you:
 may I receive,
 so that my joy may be full.

Until then,
 let my mind meditate on it,
 let my tongue speak it,
 let my heart love it,
 let my mouth preach it,
 let my soul hunger for it,
 let my flesh thirst for it,
 let my whole substance desire it,
until that time when *I enter into the joy of my lord,*
who art God,
 three in one,
 blessed for all ages. Amen.

▌ Latin Texts

Schmitt, F. S., ed. *Proslogion.* Stuttgart (Bad Cannstatt): Friedrich Frommann Verlag, 1962.

———. *Sancti Anselmi Opera omnia,* 6 vols. Edinburgh: Thomas Nelson and Sons, 1938–61; reprinted in two volumes, Stuttgart (Bad Cannstatt): Friedrich Frommann Verlag, 1968.

Schmitt, F. S., and R. W. Southern, eds. *Memorials of St. Anselm.* Oxford: Oxford University Press, 1969.

▌ English Translations

Charlesworth, M. J. *St. Anselm's Proslogion.* Oxford: Oxford University Press, 1965.

Deane, S. N. *St. Anselm: Basic Writings.* La Salle, Ill.: Open Court, 1903.

Fairweather, Eugene. *A Scholastic Miscellany: Anselm to Occam.* Philadelphia, Pa.: Westminster Press, 1956.

Hopkins, Jasper. *A New, Interpretive Translation of St. Anselm's Monologion and Proslogion.* Minneapolis, Minn.: The Arthur J. Banning Press, 1986.

Hopkins, Jasper, and Herbert Richardson. *Anselm of Canterbury.* 3 vols. Lewiston, N.Y.: The Edwin Mellen Press, 1974–76.

Ward, Benedicta. *The Prayers and Meditations of Saint Anselm with the Proslogion.* Harmondsworth, Middlesex: Penguin Classics, 1973.

▌ Secondary Sources

Abelson, Raziel. "Not Necessarily." *Philosophical Review* 70 (1961): 67–84.

Adams, Robert M. "The Logical Structure of Anselm's Arguments." *Philosophical Review* 80 (1971): 28–54. (Reprinted in *The Virtue of Faith.* Oxford: Oxford University Press, 1987.)

Allen, R. E. "The Ontological Argument." *Philosophical Review* 70 (1961): 56–66.

Alston, William P. "The Ontological Argument Revisited." *Philosophical Review* 69 (1960): 452–74.

Angelet, Benoit. "*Idem dicere in corde, et cogitare*—Or: What We Still Can Learn from an Existential Anselm." *Aquinas* 30 (1987): 93–108.

Aspenson, Steven S. "In Defense of Anselm." *History of Philosophy Quarterly* 7 (1990): 33–45.

Back, Allan. "Anselm on Perfect Islands." *Franciscan Studies* 43 (1983): 188–204.

Barnes, Jonathan. *The Ontological Argument*. New York: Macmillan, 1972.

Barth, Karl. *Anselm: Fides quaerens intellectum*. Translated by I. W. Robertson. Richmond, Va.: John Knox Press, 1960.

Basham, R. Robert. "The 'Second Version' of Anselm's Ontological Argument." *Canadian Journal of Philosophy* 6 (1976): 665–83.

Beckaert, A. "A Platonic Justification for the Argument *a Priori*." In *The Many-Faced Argument: Recent Studies of the Ontological Argument for the Existence of God*, edited by John Hick and Arthur McGill, 111–18. New York: Macmillan, 1967.

Bencivenga, Ermanno. *Logic and Other Nonsense: The Case of Anselm and His God*. Princeton, N.J.: Princeton University Press, 1993.

Berlinger, Rudolf. "Das höchste Sein: Structurmomente der Metaphysik des Anselm von Canterbury." In *Tradition und Kritik*, edited by W. Arnold and H. Zeltner. Stuttgart (Bad Cannstatt): Friedrich Frommann Verlag, 1967.

———. *Philosophie als Weltwissenschaft*. Vol. 1. Amsterdam: Rodopi, 1982.

Brecher, Bob. "Aquinas on Anselm." *Philosophical Studies* 23 (1975): 63–66.

Brecher, Robert. *Anselm's Argument: The Logic of Divine Existence*. Brookfield, Vt.: Gower, 1985.

Brown, T. P. "Professor Malcolm on 'Anselm's Ontological Arguments.'" *Analysis* 22 (1961): 13–14.

Brunton, J. A. "The Logic of God's Necessary Existence." *International Philosophical Quarterly* 10 (1970): 276–90.

Campbell, Richard. "Anselm's Background Metaphysics." *Scottish Journal of Theology* 33 (1980): 317–43.

———. "Anselm's Theological Method." *Scottish Journal of Theology* 32 (1979): 541–62.

———. "Freedom as Keeping the Truth: The Anselmian Tradition." *Anselm Studies* 2 (1984): 297–318.

———. *From Belief to Understanding*. Canberra: Australian National University Press, 1976.

———. "On Preunderstanding St. Anselm." *The New Scholasticism* 54 (1980): 189–93.

Caputo, John. *Radical Hermeneutics*. Bloomington: Indiana University Press, 1987.

Charlesworth, M. J. *Introduction to and Analysis of St. Anselm's Proslogion*. Oxford: Oxford University Press, 1965.

Coburn, R. C. "Professor Malcolm on God." *Australasian Journal of Philosophy* 41 (1963): 143–62.

Colish, Marcia L. *The Mirror of Language*. New Haven, Conn.: Yale University Press, 1968.

———. "St. Anselm's Philosophy of Language Revisited." *Anselm Studies* 1 (1983): 113–23.

Davis, Stephen T. "Anselm and Gaunilo on the 'Lost Island.'" *Southern Journal of Philosophy* 13 (1975): 435–48.

———. "Anselm and Question-Begging: A Reply to William Rowe." *International Journal for Philosophy of Religion* 7 (1976): 448–57.

———. "Does the Ontological Argument Beg the Question?" *International Journal for Philosophy of Religion* 7 (1976): 433–42.

———. "Loptson on Anselm and Rowe." *International Journal for Philosophy of Religion* 13 (1982): 219–24.

Decorte, Jos. "Saint Anselm of Canterbury on Ultimate Reality and Meaning." *Ultimate Reality and Meaning* 12 (1989): 177–91.

Derrida, Jacques. "How to Avoid Speaking: Denials." In *Languages of the Unsayable: The Play of Negativity in Literature and Literary Theory,* edited by Sanford Budick and Wolfgang Iser. New York: Columbia University Press, 1989.

———. *Speech and Phenomena: And Other Essays on Husserl's Theory of Signs.* Translated by David B. Allison. Evanston, Ill.: Northwestern University Press, 1973.

Devine, Philip E. "'Exists' and St. Anselm's Argument." *Grazer philosophische Studien* 3 (1977): 59–70.

Dicker, Georges. "A Note on Rowe's Response to Dicker." *Faith and Philosophy* 5 (1988): 206.

———. "A Refutation of Rowe's Critique of Anselm's Ontological Argument." *Faith and Philosophy* 5 (1988): 193–202.

Downey, James Patrick. "A Primordial Reply to Modern Gaunilos." *Religious Studies* 22 (1986): 41–50.

Duclow, Donald F. "Anselm's Proslogion and Nicholas of Cusa's Wall of Paradise." *Downside Review* 100 (1982): 22–30.

Eadmer. *The Life of St. Anselm.* Edited and translated by R. W. Southern. Oxford: Oxford University Press, 1972.

Engel, S. M. "Kant's 'Refutation' of the Ontological Argument." *Philosophy and Phenomenological Research* 24 (1963): 20–35.

Engelbretson, George. "Anselm's Second Argument." *Sophia* 23 (1984): 34–37.

Evans, Gillian R. *Anselm and a New Generation.* Oxford: Oxford University Press, 1980.

———. *Anselm and Talking about God.* Oxford: Oxford University Press, 1978.

———. "The Hereford Proslogion." *Anselm Studies* 1 (1983): 253–73.

———. "St. Anselm and Knowing God." *Journal of Theological Studies* 28 (1977): 430–44.

Evans, Gillian R., ed. *A Concordance to the Works of St. Anselm.* Millwood, N.Y.: Kraus International Publications, 1984.

Ferrara, J. Vincent. "Some Reflections on the Being-Thought Relationship in Parmenides, Anselm and Hegel." *Analecta Anselmiana* 3: 95–111.

Feuer, Lewis S. "God, Guilt, and Logic: The Psychological Basis of the Ontological Argument." *Inquiry* 2 (1968): 257–81.

Findlay, J. N. "Some Reflections on Necessary Existence." In *Process and Divinity,* edited by by W. L. Reese and E. Freeman, 515–27. La Salle, Ill.: Open Court, 1964.

Forgie, J. William. "The Modal Ontological Argument and the Necessary a Posteriori." *International Journal for Philosophy of Religion* 29: 129–41.

———. "Theistic Experience and the Doctrine of Unanimity." *International Journal for Philosophy of Religion* 15 (1984): 13–30.

Forman, Robert. *The Problem of Pure Consciousness.* Oxford: Oxford University Press, 1990.

Galgan, Gerald J. *God and Subjectivity.* Bern: Peter Lang, 1990.

Gellrich, Jesse. *The Idea of the Book in the Middle Ages.* Ithaca, N.Y.: Cornell University Press, 1985.

Gilbert, Paul. "Id est summum omnium quae sunt." *Revue philosophique de Louvain* 82 (1984): 199–223.

Gombocz, Wolfgang L. "Anselm über Sinn und Bedeutung." *Anselm Studies* 1 (1983): 125–41.

Gregory, Donald. "On Behalf of a Second Rate Philosophy: A Defense of the Gaunilo Strategy against the Ontological Argument." *History of Philosophy Quarterly* 1 (1984): 49–60.

Hartmann, R. S. "Prolegomena to a Meta-Anselmian Axiomatic." *Review of Metaphysics* 14 (1961): 637–75.

Hartshorne, Charles. *Anselm's Discovery.* La Salle, Ill.: Open Court, 1965.

———. "Further Fascination of the Ontological Argument." *Union Seminary Quarterly Review* 18 (1963): 244–55.

———. "How Some Speak and Yet Do Not Speak of God." *Philosophy and Phenomenological Research* 23 (1962): 274–76.

———. "The Logic of the Ontological Argument." *Journal of Philosophy* 58 (1961): 471–73.

———. "Necessity." *Review of Metaphysics* 21 (1967): 290–96.

———. "Ten Ontological or Modal Proofs for God's Existence." Chap. 2 of *The Logic of Perfection.* La Salle, Ill.: Open Court, 1962.

———. "What Did Anselm Discover?" *Union Seminary Quarterly Review* 17 (1962): 213–22.

———. "What the Ontological Proof Does Not Do." *Review of Metaphysics* 17 (1964): 608–09.

Hasker, William. "Is There a Second Ontological Argument?" *International Journal for Philosophy of Religion* 13 (1982): 93–101.

Hegel, G. W. F. *Lectures on the Philosophy of Religion.* Edited and translated by Peter C. Hodgson. Berkeley and Los Angeles: University of California Press, 1984

Heidegger, Martin. *An Introduction to Metaphysics.* Translated by Ralph Mannheim. New Haven, Conn.: Yale University Press, 1959.

———. *Identity and Difference.* Translated by Joan Stambaugh. New York: Harper and Row, 1969.

———. "Postscript." In *Existence and Being,* edited by W. Brock, translated by R. F. C. Hull and Alan Crick. San Rafael, Calif.: Gateway, 1949.

———. "The Way Back into the Ground of Metaphysics." In *Existentialism from Dostoyevski to Sartre,* edited and translated by W. Kaufmann. New York: New American Library, 1975.

———. "What Is Metaphysics?" In *Basic Writings,* translated by D. F. Krell. New York: Harper and Row, 1977.

Hendley, Brian. "Anselm's *Proslogion* Argument." In *Sprache und Erkenntnis im Mittelalter,* edited by Jan P. Beckmann. Berlin: W. de Gruyter, 1981.

Henle, P. "Uses of the Ontological Argument." *Philosophical Review* 70 (1961): 102–9.

Henry, D. P. *The Logic of St. Anselm.* Oxford: Oxford University Press, 1967.

———. *Medieval Logic and Metaphysics.* London: Hutchinson, 1972.

———. "*Proslogion* Chapter 3." *Analecta Anselmiana* 1:101–5.

————. "The Proslogion Proofs." *Philosophical Quarterly* 5 (1955): 147–51.
————. "St. Anselm and Nothingness." *Philosophical Quarterly* 15 (1965): 243–46.
————. "St. Anselm's Nonsense." *Mind* 72 (1963): 51–61.
————. "Was St. Anselm Really a Realist?" *Ratio* 5 (1963): 181–89.
Henze, D. F. "Language-Games and the Ontological Argument." *Religious Studies* 4 (1968): 147–52.
Herrera, Robert A. *Anselm's Proslogion: An Introduction.* Lanham, Md.: University Press of America, 1979.
————. "The *Proslogion* Argument Viewed from the Perspective of *De casa diaboli.*" *Spicilegium Beccense* 2: 623–29.
————. "St. Anselm: A Radical Empiricist?" *Analecta Anselmiana* 2:45–56.
Hick, John, and Arthur McGill, eds. *The Many-Faced Argument: Recent Studies of the Ontological Argument for the Existence of God.* New York: Macmillan, 1967.
Holt, Dennis C. "Timelessness and the Metaphysics of Temporal Existence." *American Philosophical Quarterly* 18 (1981): 149–56.
Hopkins, Jasper. "Anselm and Talking about God." *The New Scholasticism* 55 (1981): 387–96.
————. *Anselm of Canterbury.* Vol. 4. Lewiston, N.Y.: The Edwin Mellen Press, 1976.
————. "On an Alleged Definitive Interpretation of Proslogion 2–4: A Discussion of G. Schufreider's *An Introduction to Anselm's Argument.*" *Southern Journal of Philosophy* 19 (1981): 129–39.
————. "On Understanding and Preunderstanding St. Anselm." *The New Scholasticism* 52 (1978): 243–60.
Illich, Ivan. *In the Vineyard of the Text.* Chicago, Ill.: University of Chicago Press, 1993.
Johnson, Harold. "The Ontological Argument and the Languages of 'Being.'" In *Sprache und Erkenntnis im Mittelalter,* edited by Jan P. Beckmann, 2:724–37. Berlin: W. de Gruyter, 1981.
Johnson, Oliver A. "God and St. Anselm." *Journal of Religion* 45 (1965): 326–34.
Katz, Steven. *Mysticism and Philosophical Analysis.* Oxford: Oxford University Press, 1978.
————. *Mysticism and Religious Traditions.* Oxford: Oxford University Press, 1983.
King, Peter. "Anselm's Intentional Argument." *History of Philosophy Quarterly* 1 (1984): 147–66.
Kiteley, M. "Existence and the Ontological Argument." *Philosophy and Phenomenological Research* 18 (1958): 533–35.
Knowles, David. *The Monastic Order in England.* Cambridge: Cambridge University Press, 1949.
Kohlenberger, Helmut. *Similitudo und Ratio.* Bonn: H. Grundmann, 1972.
————. "Zur Metaphorik des Visuellen bei Anselm von Canterbury." *Analecta Anselmiana* 1:11–37.
Kolping, A. *Anselms Proslogion-Beweis der Existenz Gottes.* Grenzfragen zwischen Theologie und Philosophie, vol. 7. Bonn: P. Hanstein, 1939.
LaCroix, Richard. *Proslogion II and III: A Third Interpretation of Anselm's Argument.* Leiden: Brill, 1972.
Leclercq, Jean. *The Love of Learning and the Desire for God.* New York: Fordham University Press, 1982.

Leftow, Brian. "Anselm on Omnipresence." *The New Scholasticism* 63 (1989): 326–57.

———. "Anselmian Polytheism." *International Journal for Philosophy of Religion* 23 (1988): 77–104.

———. "'Existence in the Understanding' in *Proslogion* II." *Anselm Studies* 2:261–71.

———. "Individual and Attribute in the Ontological Argument." *Faith and Philosophy* 7 (1990): 235–42.

Lewis, David. "Anselm and Actuality." *Nous* 4 (1970): 175–88.

Lewis, Charles. "Eternity, Time and Tenselessness." *Faith and Philosophy* 5 (1988): 72–86.

Loptson, Peter J. "Anselm and Rowe: A Reply to Davies." *International Journal for Philosophy and Religion* 15 (1984): 67–71.

———. "Anselm, Meinong, and the Ontological Argument." *International Journal for Philosophy and Religion* 11 (1980): 185–94.

Losoncy, Thomas. "Anselm's Response to Gaunilo's Dilemma—An Insight into the Notion of 'Being' Operative in the *Proslogion*." *The New Scholasticism* 56 (1982): 207–16.

———. "Language and Saint Anselm's *Proslogion* Argument." In *Acta Conventus Neo-Latini Bononiensis,* edited by R. J. Schoeck, 284–91. Bologna: Medieval & Renaissance Texts & Studies, 1985.

———. Review of Jasper Hopkins's *A New Interpretive Translation of St. Anselm's Monologion and Proslogion. Speculum* 64 (1989): 716–19.

———. "Saint Anselm's Rejection of the 'Ontological Argument'—A Review of the Occasion and Circumstances." *The American Catholic Philosophical Quarterly* 64 (1990): 373–85.

Lubac, Henri de. "'Seigneur, je cherche ton visage': Sur le chapitre XVIᵉ du Proslogion de saint Anselme." *Archives de philosophie* 39 (1976): 201–25, 407–26.

Lyotard, Jean-François. *The Postmodern Condition.* Translated by Geoff Bennington and Brian Massumi. Minneapolis: University of Minnesota Press, 1984.

Malcolm, Norman. "Anselm's Ontological Arguments." *Philosophical Review* 69 (1960): 41–62.

Mann, William E. "The Perfect Island." *Mind* 85 (1976): 417–21.

Marion, Jean-Luc. *God without Being.* Chicago, Ill.: University of Chicago Press, 1991.

———. "Is the Ontological Argument Ontological? The Argument According to Anselm and Its Metaphysical Interpretation According to Kant." *Journal of the History of Philosophy* 30 (1992): 201–18.

Matthews, G. B. "On Conceivability in Anselm and Malcolm." *Philosophical Review* 70 (1961): 110–11.

Mavrodes, George I. "Properties, Predicates, and the Ontological Argument." *Journal of Philosophy* 63 (1966): 549–50.

McGrath, Patrick. "Where Does the Ontological Argument Go Wrong?" *Philosophical Studies* 30 (1984): 144–64.

Miethe, T. L. "The Ontological Argument: A Research Bibliography." *The Modern Schoolman* 54 (1977): 148–66.

Morreal, John. "The Aseity of God in St. Anselm." *Sophia* 23 (1984): 35–44.

Morris, Thomas. *Anselmian Explorations.* Notre Dame, Ind.: University of Notre Dame Press, 1987.

Nakhnikian, George. "St. Anselm's Four Ontological Arguments." In *Art, Mind, and Religion,* edited by W. H. Capitan and D. D. Merrill, 29–36. Pittsburgh: University of Pittsburgh Press, 1965.

Nakhnikian, George, and W. Salmon. "'Exists' as a Predicate." *Philosophical Review* 66 (1957): 535–42.

Pacht, Otto. "The Illustrations of St. Anselm's Prayers and Meditations." *Journal of the Warburg and Courtauld Institutes* 19 (1956): 68–83.

Pailin, David A. "Some Comments on Hartshorne's Presentation of the Ontological Argument." *Analecta Anselmiana* 1:195–221.

Pegis, A. C. "St. Anselm and the Argument of the 'Proslogion.'" *Mediaeval Studies* 28 (1966): 228–67.

Penelhum, Terence. "On the Second Ontological Argument." *Philosophical Review* 70 (1961): 85–92.

Pike, Nelson. *Mystic Union.* Ithaca, N.Y.: Cornell University Press, 1992.

Plantinga, Alvin. "Aquinas on Anselm." In *God and the Good: Essays in Honor of Henry Strob,* edited by C. Orlebeke and L. Smedes, 122–39. Grand Rapids, Mich.: Eerdmans, 1975.

———. "Kant's Objection to the Ontological Argument." *Journal of Philosophy* 63 (1966): 537–46.

———. "A Valid Ontological Argument?" *Philosophical Review* 70 (1961): 93–101.

Plantinga, Alvin, ed. *The Ontological Argument.* New York: Doubleday, 1965.

Potter, V. G. "Karl Barth and the Ontological Argument." *Journal of Religion* 45 (1965): 309–25.

Preuss, Peter. "Ontological Vertigo." *International Journal for Philosophy of Religion* 11 (1980): 93–110.

Proudfoot, Wayne. *Religious Experience.* Berkeley and Los Angeles: University of California Press, 1985.

Purtill, Richard L. "Hartshorne's Modal Proof." *Journal of Philosophy* 63 (1966): 397–409.

Rabinowicz, Wlodzimierz. "An Alleged New Refutation of St. Anselm's Argument." *Ratio* 20 (1978): 149–50.

Read, Stephen. "Reflections on Anselm and Gaunilo." *International Philosophical Quarterly* 21 (1981): 437–38.

Rescher, Nicholas. "The Ontological Proof Revisited." *Australasian Journal of Philosophy* 37 (1959): 138–48.

Richardson, C. C. "The Strange Fascination of the Ontological Argument." *Union Seminary Quarterly Review* 18 (1962): 1–21.

Richman, Robert. "A Serious Look at the Ontological Argument." *Ratio* 18 (1976): 85–89.

Rohatyn, Dennis. "Anselm's Inconceivability Argument." *Sophia* 21 (1982): 57–63.

Ross, James. "God and 'Logical Necessity.'" *Philosophical Quarterly* 11 (1961): 22–27.

Roth, M. "A Note on Anselm's Ontological Argument." *Mind* 79 (1970): 270–71.

Rowe, William. "Comments on Professor Davies' 'Does the Ontological Argument Beg the Question?'" *International Journal for Philosophy of Religion* 7 (1976): 443–47.

Rowe, William. "The Ontological Argument." In *Philosophy of Religion.* Encino, Calif.: Dickenson, 1978.

―――. "The Ontological Argument and Question-Begging." *International Journal for Philosophy of Religion* 7 (1976): 425–32.

―――. "Response to Dicker's 'A Refutation of Rowe's Critique of Anselm's Ontological Argument.'" *Faith and Philosophy* 5 (1988): 203–5.

Ruja, H. "The Definition of God and the Ontological Argument." *Australasian Journal of Philosophy* 41 (1963): 262–63.

Russell, Bruce. "The Ontological Argument." *Sophia* 24 (1985): 38–46.

Rynin, D. "On Deriving Essence from Existence." *Inquiry* 6 (1963): 141–56.

Schmitt, F.S. "Anselm und der (Neu-) Platonismus." *Analecta Anselmiana* 1:39–71.

―――. *Ein neues unvollendetes Werk des hl. Anselm von Canterbury.* Beiträge zur Geschichte der Philosophie und Theologie des Mittelalters, vol. 33/3. Münster: Aschendorff, 1936.

―――. Introduction to *Monologion.* Stuttgart (Bad Cannstatt): Friedrich Frommann Verlag, 1964.

―――. Introduction to *Proslogion.* Stuttgart (Bad Cannstatt): Friedrich Frommann Verlag, 1962.

―――. Introduction to *Sancti Anselmi Opera omnia.* Stuttgart (Bad Cannstatt): Friedrich Frommann Verlag, 1968.

Schufreider, Gregory. "A Classical Misunderstanding of Anselm's Argument." *The American Catholic Philosophical Quarterly* 66 (1992): 489–99.

―――. "Heidegger on Community." *Man and World* 14 (1981): 25–54.

―――. "Heidegger's Contribution to a Phenomenology of Culture." *Journal of the British Society for Phenomenology* 17 (1986): 166–85.

―――. "The Identity of Anselm's Argument." *The Modern Schoolman* 54 (1977): 345–61.

―――. *An Introduction to Anselm's Argument.* Philadelphia, Pa.: Temple University Press, 1978.

―――. "The Metaphysician as Poet-Magician." *Metaphilosophy* 10 (1979): 265–88.

―――. "Overpowering the Center: Three Compositions by Mondrian." *Journal of Aesthetics and Art Criticism* 44 (1985): 13–28.

―――. "Reunderstanding Anselm's Argument." *The New Scholasticism* 57 (1983): 384–409.

―――. "What Is It for God to Exist?" *The New Scholasticism* 55 (1981): 77–94.

Sen, Sushanta. "The Ontological Argument Revisited." *Indian Philosophical Quarterly* 10 (1983): 219–42.

Sessions, W. L. "Feuer, Psychology, and the Ontological Argument." *Inquiry* 12 (1969): 431–34.

Shaffer, Jerome. "Existence, Predication, and the Ontological Argument." *Mind* 71 (1962): 307–25. (Reprinted in *The Many-Faced Argument.*)

Slattery, Michael. "Parmenides: Anselm *eminenter.*" *Anselm Studies* 2: 229–39.

Smart, H. "Anselm's Ontological Argument: Rationalistic or Apologetic?" *Review of Metaphysics* 3 (1949): 161–66.

Smith, John E. "Some Aspects of Hartshorne's Treatment of Anselm." In *Existence and Actuality,* edited by John Cobb, 103–12. Chicago, Ill.: University of Chicago Press, 1984.

Sokolowski, Robert. *The God of Faith and Reason.* Notre Dame, Ind.: University of Notre Dame Press, 1982.

Sontag, Frederick. "Anselm and the Concept of God." *Scottish Journal of Theology* 35 (1982): 213–18.

―――. "The Meaning of 'Argument' in Anselm's Ontological 'Proof.'" *Journal of Philosophy* 64 (1967): 459–86.

Southern, R. W. "Anselm at Canterbury." *Anselm Studies* 1 (1983): 7–22.

―――. *The Making of the Middle Ages.* New Haven, Conn.: Yale University Press, 1953.

―――. *Saint Anselm: A Portrait in a Landscape.* Cambridge: Cambridge University Press, 1990.

―――. *Saint Anselm and His Biographer.* Cambridge: Cambridge University Press, 1963.

Spade, Paul Vincent. "Anselm and Ambiguity." *International Journal for Philosophy of Religion* 7 (1976): 433–45.

Stearns, J. B. "Anselm and the Two-Argument Hypothesis." *Monist* 54 (1970): 221–33.

Stock, Brian. *The Implications of Literacy.* Princeton, N.J.: Princeton University Press, 1983.

Stolz, Anselm. *The Doctrine of Spiritual Perfection.* St. Louis, Mo.: Herder, 1938.

―――. "Introduction." *Anselm von Canterbury.* Munich: Kosel-Pustet, 1937.

―――. "Das *Proslogion* des hl. Anselm." *Revue benedictine* 47 (1935): 331–47.

―――. "'Vere esse' im *Proslogion* des hl. Anselm." *Scholastik* 9 (1934): 400–409.

―――. "Zur Theologie Anselms im *Proslogion.*" *Catholica* 2 (1933): 1–24. (English translation in *The Many-Faced Argument,* 183–206.)

Stone, Jim. "Anselm's Proof." *Philosophical Studies* 57 (1989): 79–94.

Strasser, Stephan. *The Phenomenology of Feeling.* Evanston, Ill.: Northwestern University Press, 1977.

Ulrich, Ferdinand. "Cur non video praesentem? Zur Implikation der 'griechischen' und 'lateinischen' Denkform bei Anselm und Scotus Erigena." *Freiburger Zeitschrift für Philosophie und Theologie* 22 (1975): 70–170.

Vitali, Theodore R. "The Ontological Argument: Model for Neoclassical Metaphysics." *The Modern Schoolman* 57 (1980): 121–35.

Vuillemin, Jules. *Le Dieu d'Anselme et les apparences de la raison.* Paris: Aubier Montaigne, 1971.

―――. "Id quo nihil cogitari potest: Über die innere Möglichkeit eines rationalen Gottesbegriffs." *Archiv für Geschichte der Philosophie* 53: 279–99.

Waldenfels, Hans. *Absolute Nothingness.* New York: Paulist Press, 1980.

Wainwright, William J. "On an Alleged Incoherence in Anselm's Argument: A Reply to Robert Richman." *Ratio* 20 (1978): 147–48.

Walton, Douglas. "The Circle in the Ontological Argument." *International Journal for Philosophy of Religion* 9 (1978): 193–218.

Warnach, Victor "Wort und Wirklichkeit bei Anselm von Canterbury." *Salzburger Jahrbuch für Philosophie* 5–6 (1961–62): 157–76.

―――. "Zum Argument in *Proslogion* Anselms von Canterbury." In *Einsicht und Glaube,* edited by Joseph Ratzinger and Heinrich Fries, 337–57. Freiburg: Herder, 1962.

Welch, A. C. *Anselm and His Work*. New York: Scribner and Sons, 1901.

Wells, Norman J. "The Language of Possibility—Another Reading of Anselm." In *Sprache und Erkenntnis im Mittelalter,* edited by Jan P. Beckmann et al., 2:847–51. Berlin: W. de Gruyter, 1981.

Wierenga, Edward. "Anselm on Omnipresence." *The New Scholasticism* 62 (1988): 30–41.

Wilmart, Andre. *Auteurs spirituels et textes dévots du moyen âge latin.* Paris: Bloud et Gay, 1932.

Yolton, John. "Professor Malcolm on St. Anselm, Belief, and Existence." *Philosophy* 36 (1961): 357–70.

Zabeeh, Farhang. "Category Mistake." *Philosophy and Phenomenological Research* 23 (1962): 277–78.

———. "Ontological Argument and How and Why Some Speak of God." *Philosophy and Phenomenological Research* 22 (1961): 206–15.

DATE DUE

			Printed in USA